FLL
8/16

FUTURE IRAQ

Geoff Simons

FUTURE IRAQ

US Policy in Reshaping
the Middle East

SAQI

British Library Cataloguing-in-Publication Data
A catalogue for this book is available from the
British Library

ISBN 0 86356 132 2

This edition first published 2003

Saqi Books
26 Westbourne Grove
London W2 5RH
www.saqibooks.com

Contents

Figures

Introduction

The future of Iraq and every other country is an imponderable, not discoverable by easy calculation but of immense importance to human beings. We may try to predict but as soon as we go beyond banality we are sure to be wrong in important particulars. In 1937, for example, a group of highly respectable American scientists produced the *Technological Trends and National Policy* report for the US National Resources Committee, predicting the course of technological development for the next thirty years. Unfortunately they missed out computers, radar, antibiotics and the jet engine (aircraft, they thought, would not travel any faster). These were important omissions and there were others. Nor is prediction any easier in the social and political fields, except in the realm of the obvious: if the world population continues to increase at a rapid rate we will put increasingly heavy demands on the life support systems of the planet.

We can look at today's events; we can identify what we take to be crucial trends; we can extend these – inflated, modified, embroidered – into an imagined tomorrow; and our optimism, pessimism, knowledge and political attitudes will paint the new world. Our awareness of trends, informed by our knowledge of historical precedent, is our only beacon to the future. Our speculations need to be cautious, though also mediated by fertile imagination since most historical thinkers have not been bold enough. Lucian never envisaged radio; and Cyrano de Bergerac would gape at a primitive internal combustion engine.

The shaping forces in the modern world are easy to identify: the economic and military power of the United States; the growing resentment in the Muslim world, confined to authoritarianism and exploitation; the tensions between religions and cultures; an expanding globalisation of trade and technology; a growing internationalism among oppressed people around the world. In this context it seems obvious that in the short-to-medium term American power will remain unassailable, though the United States has financial fragilities that have yet to be fully explored. This suggests that America's allies, whether aggressively robust like Israel or predictably supine like Britain, will continue to see advantage in their familiar acolyte role. Other states, driven by internal tensions, will make pragmatic accommodations at the domestic level where possible, and remain sensitive to the dynamics of a global scene shaped by superpower ambition.

It is inevitable that American aggression will stimulate a response, not only in the Muslim community but in the wider world also. The post-Saddam regime in Baghdad is unlikely to be based on the Western democratic model. The Shi'ite and other religionists are unlikely to tolerate the emergence of a fresh secular state. Iraq may become a loose federation, but one in which the influence of Sharia philosophy will threaten the Western concept of human rights, including the emancipation of women. In these regards the Iraqi people may see no social benefit in the fall of Saddam, particularly if a new authoritarianism, as harsh as that of the Ba'athists, emerges to protect the contours of an Islamic state. The other regimes in the area, responding to a new American colonialism, will respond in characteristic but similar ways. States with powerful Islamist dynamics – Iran and Saudi Arabia – are likely to see a resurgence of Muslim commitment. The steps towards reform in Iran will be extirpated by the mullahs, and the Saudi royals – and possibly also the Al Sabah monarchists in Kuwait – will be increasingly pressured by Islamist movements. The Saudi Kingdom, home of most of the September 11 terrorists, was already considering, before the 2003 war, the expulsion of all American forces from Saudi soil. In the post-Saddam world the pressure for such a move is likely to intensify.

The other states in the region will continue to make their own adjustments and accommodations. Turkey, despite its continued secularisation and vulnerability to domestic military influence, has become increasingly subject to the democratic will of a politicised national constituency. The army is unlikely to relinquish its power, though the influence of a Muslim electorate is likely to grow. Turkey, in circumstances of a growing Islamic consciousness, is unlikely to welcome the continued American presence across the border, even though Ankara will still see a future for Turkey in both Europe and the North Atlantic Treaty Organisation (NATO), from which the Turkish state derives most of its weaponry and much of its military training.

Israel, content with its own massive militarization, including possession of many weapons of mass destruction, will continue to cultivate its vast American protector, and will feel encouraged by the continued US occupation of parts of Iraq to expand its own illegal occupation of the Palestinian territories. In this context, as with all the other feeble apologies for a 'peace process', the so-called 'road map' to peace will produce no worthwhile results. With publication constantly delayed, the 'road map' details came to antagonise Tel Aviv which clearly never had any intention of observing the spirit of negotiation.

The small Gulf States – Oman, Bahrain, United Arab Emirates – will pause before attempting to introduce further Western-style reforms: the power of the Islamicists has been strengthened there also. Egypt and Jordan, relying on US-aided repression, will continue with their authoritarian control, relying on security advice and weaponry from the United States, and struggling to crush any attempts at a Muslim politicisation or democratic reform.

The United States will maintain its long-term neo-colonial relationship with the new Iraqi regime – to consolidate its expanded strategic advantage and to ensure that the Iraqi oil resource remains in the proper hands. The inevitable corollaries are the permanent shackling and humiliation of the United Nations, and the continued abuse of international law.

When the United States decided that the UN weapons inspectors would not return to Iraq under the framework of the original inspection regime, Washington was committing a clear violation of Security Council resolution 1441 (2002). All the American rhetoric that had been expended, only weeks before, on the obligation of Baghdad to avoid committing a 'material breach' of SCR 1441 was exposed as blatant hypocrisy. Washington itself felt free to jettison yet more legal obligations it had to UN resolutions. The Security Council had been rendered an 'irrelevance' to all the US preparations for war, and it would be allowed a role in the post-Saddam era only when the United States felt like it.

Such events have demonstrated that the United Nations will remain unable to assume its proper authority in the affairs of the Middle East and the wider world. The United States will continue to exploit the Security Council when it can, and ignore it when it cannot. International law will be what Washington decides it is. Recalcitrant states – that is, ones objecting to US foreign policy – will face abuse, economic sanctions or war. Iraq, fragmented and impotent, is no longer an effective player on the world stage, and other states – Syria, Iran, Libya, Sudan, North Korea, perhaps even Saudi Arabia – are now in America sights. There will be more US-led wars – the US military culture, the arms factories, the shareholders demand it – but precise predictions are hazardous.

The trends are clear, and they are presented in detail in the present book. Many of the general predictions are expanded, but the main purpose is to explore the historical and current developments to provide a context for understanding the future. There are no absolutes in a deterministic world shaped by an incomprehensible complex of causal factors. American power will not be eternal, and perhaps an end will come to the social divisions caused by disparate and superstitious interpretations of reality.

Humankind has always longed to know the future, but all we have are the knowledge of current trends, our imagination, and our hopes for the future. Perhaps we were not able to predict the electronic computer. Few of us predicted the collapse of the Berlin Wall or the extirpation of the Soviet Union. We cannot predict the next regime collapse or the next political assassination. But once we study the trends we shine a light into the mist of tomorrow.

In April 2003 the US-led war against Iraq drew to its chaotic close. Tens of thousands had been killed and maimed; the lives of millions had been put at risk; and massive destruction had been inflicted on a sovereign nation. The future will reveal the magnitude of the catastrophe suffered by the Iraqi people.

Iraq had been bombed for years but in the prelude to war there was a massive escalation in the number of air attacks to prepare the ground for invasion. At the same time millions of leaflets were dropped in the south, some warning the Iraqis not to repair bomb damage. When the war began on 20 March few observers doubted the outcome. The United States was spending an annual $400 billion on war and preparation for war, and Iraq was about as poor as Rwanda or Sierra Leone. In December 2002 Iraq had external debts of more than $200 billion, and had only managed to pay part of the billions of dollars the country owed as compensation for the 1990–91 Gulf crisis. Around $250 billion-worth of compensation claims against Iraq had yet to be adjudicated by the UN compensation committee.[1]

One estimate suggested that the 2003 war would cost the world economy between $300 billion and $500 billion, with the Bush administration then seeking an increase of not less than $60 billion in the Federal budget to fund the military conflict.[2] The direct cost to Britain was initially estimated at £1.75 billion, but in early March Chancellor Gordon Brown judged that the cost could be more than £3 billion. It is significant to contrast US military spending with its spending on aid. The opening blitz on Baghdad of 320 cruise missiles, at $800,000 each, cost around $256 million. The United States was then spending about $1.3 billion per year in aid to sub-Saharan Africa, almost exactly the cost of a single stealth bomber.[3]

The war, in addition to being obscenely expensive, was also illegal – a view taken by the vast majority of international lawyers who scrutinised the case (see Chapter 11). Here it is enough to quote the specialist Ed Firmage, Professor of Law, Emeritus, at the University of Utah College of Law:

> President George Bush is leading this country into a war that is at once unconstitutional, a gross violation of international law, aggresses our own civil liberties, and threatens our national security by violating norms of common sense …
>
> First, this war violates the US constitution …

Second, international law, including scores of treaties to which we are party, made part of our domestic law by the supremacy clause of the Constitution, forbids our waging aggressive war. We have not been attacked by Saddam Hussein's Iraq ...

The late Supreme Court Justice Robert Jackson, the American prosecutor of the war criminals at the Nuremburg trials following World War II, stated the American definition of international law, later made the universal law of the entire world by unanimous acceptance by the United Nations: 'Our position is that whatever grievances a nation may have, however objectionable it finds the status quo, aggressive warfare is an illegal means for settling grievances or for altering those conditions.

Mr Bush's war violates international law and constitutes a war crime.[4]

Kofi Annan, UN Secretary-General, had stated that without an authorising resolution from the Security Council military action against Iraq would be illegal. Stephen Solley QC, an international human rights lawyer, reflected the widespread legal opinion: 'no-one has made a legal case for war.' And this in turn led to the paradox that British soldiers could be arraigned before the newly constituted International Criminal Court (ICC). American soldiers would be immune since the United States had refused the sign the Rome treaty. President Bush, intending a reference to the Iraqis, had emphasised that soldiers could be liable for prosecution: 'War criminals will be punished, and it will be no defense to say I was just following orders.'

The prospect of war was already causing anxiety among children, primarily among Iraqi children (Chapter 1, Figure 3), but elsewhere also. A survey by the BBC children's *Newsround* programme found that the imminent war was causing anxiety in the playground. Childline, the young person's helpline, was already receiving calls. One girl called to say that she did not see the point of doing her homework if there was going to be a war. Some British schools were trying to help their pupils to deal with events by lighting candles for peace or discussing their concerns.

The Pentagon, already preparing for military action, was also seeking exemption from some of America's environmental laws to facilitate its activities. The aim was to give the military free rein to dump spent munitions, pollute the air, and poison endangered species at its bases without risk of liability for any damage.[5] The environmental law, argued the Pentagon, got in the way of training troops, a view contradicted by a congressional report from the General Accounting Office (GAO), which saw no negative impact from environmental statutes on military readiness. In fact the White House already had powers to grant case-by-case exemptions where national security might be at stake. The real reason for the Pentagon's proposal was finance. The 2002 Pentagon budget report estimated that the military's liability for environmental degradation was about $28 billion.

The Pentagon was concerned also that the news from the war be appropriately censored, a task which the leading broadcasting networks could be relied upon to perform. During the war on Iraq approved reporters were 'embedded' among the US infantry and marines, and made to observe specific rules and regulations. In addition, a system of 'script approval' was introduced by the major broadcasting networks. CNN, for example, required that all journalists copy be sent to anonymous officials in Atlanta to ensure that the reports were suitably sanitised. The journalist Robert Fisk quoted a CNN document, *'Reminder of Script Approval Policy'*: 'All reporters preparing package scripts must submit the scripts for approval ... A script is not approved for air unless it is properly marked approved by an authorised manager and duped (duplicated) to burcopy (bureau copy) ... When a script is updated it must be re-approved, preferably by the originating approving authority.'

There were concerns also that the Americans were interpreting unknown satellite telephones as evidence of hostile activity, which meant that the offending phones might be rocketed or bombed. The embedded journalists were regarded as relatively safe but any more objective reporting was made extremely difficult: 'American reporting of the coming war will mostly be restricted to these 'embedded' reporters, and to the correspondents who are based at military headquarters and announce the official version of everything ... Those journalists who try to operate more independently will be attacked for peddling the enemy viewpoint.'[6] In fact it was not long into the war when independent journalists were being killed by American fire in Baghdad.

The allied sensitivity about unfavourable journalistic accounts was demonstrated on many occasions, not least when Downing Street strongly criticised the BBC on 11 April 2003 for claiming that looters in Baghdad had left Iraqis more frightened that they had been under Saddam Hussein. Andrew Gilligan had reported in a despatch from the capital that Baghdad residents were living in greater fear than they had ever known. At the same time the British government was prepared to lie about an alleged execution of British soldiers and to disseminate propaganda forgeries to justify the case for war. Thus forged documents purporting to demonstrate that Iraq had tried to buy 500 tonnes of uranium from Nigeria were described by a senior UN inspector as so badly forged that his 'jaw dropped'.[7] Even when the forgeries were unambiguously exposed Dick Cheney, US vice president, continued to make the allegations and the British government refused to remove the offending documents from the internet.

Such examples indicate the difficulty in obtaining an accurate picture of the prelude to war, the war itself or the chaotic aftermath. The reliable information in the public domain indicates a post-war situation of immense suffering and devastation, but the full story has yet to be told.

It was soon apparent that virtually all humanitarian provision throughout Iraq had collapsed, leaving millions of civilians without water and electricity, forced to scavenge and to drink polluted river water in order to survive (see Chapter 1, *Chaos*). And it was also apparent that US corporations were now competing to secure huge contracts for the reconstruction of a country that thirteen years of economic sanctions and the US military had comprehensively devastated. On 3 April 2003 the US House of Representatives voted that no money at all from federal contracts in Iraq could ever pass to companies from those countries that had opposed the war in the UN Security Council: France, Germany, Russia and Syria.[8] The lead US companies were already known. Halliburton, whose former head was Dick Cheney, would soon win one of the reconstruction contracts; and Bechtel was one of the first corporations to secure a deal worth around $1 billion.

On 9 May 2003 Halliburton admitted paying millions of dollars in bribes to tax officials in Nigeria. The company conceded in its quarterly financial report that it had payed $2.4 million in exchange for illegal tax cuts. Halliburton was obliged to pay a further $5 million in taxes in

Nigeria to make up for those payments the company had evaded (*The Times*, 10 May 2003).

Fluor Corporation, a US building giant, was also in the running for contracts in Iraq, despite legal accusations that it exploited and brutalised black workers in apartheid South Africa. A $1 billion law suit, filed in California on 7 April 2003 by lawyer Ed Fagan on behalf of former black workers, argued that Fluor paid blacks less than whites and helped to repress workers during a 1987 strike in which two were killed. Fagan alleged that Fluor helped the country evade UN oil sanctions, and that black workers were 'starved, forced to go without water, beaten or tortured' (*Business Report*, 30 April 2003). John Ngcebetsha, a lawyer for former employees, commented: 'This company has a long history of human rights violations in South Africa. It cares nothing about the societies in which it works and its involvement in Iraq would be disastrous' (*The Observer*, 6 April 2003).

The United States was continuing to expand its global posture, but with scant regard for human rights. The collapse of the case involving Iraq's alleged weapons of mass destruction had forced Washington to rely on Saddam Hussein's appalling human rights accord, but the US itself was unimpressive in this regard. Arab and Afghan prisoners were being tortured, some to death, at the Bagram air base in Afghanistan; the captives at Guantanamo Bay, Cuba, were still being denied rights guaranteed under the Geneva Convention; and the Bush administration was encouraging a degree of domestic abuse that clearly violated civil rights.

Alan Dershowitz, Harvard law professor, acknowledged that US interrogators were resorting to torture and that the United States currently 'freely subcontracts its torture to Jordan, Egypt and the Philippines', some obviously 'moderate' Washington allies. In early April the US State Department released its latest global report on human rights – and was immediately accused of hypocrisy since US personnel were then carrying out many of the condemned practices, as were some of America's allies around the world.[9]

The Bush administration was also intent on developing a 'Big Brother' society where all private citizens could be comprehensively scrutinised. In late–2002 the government had introduced a Total Information Awareness System, allowing the administration to monitor every American's credit card transactions, phone calls, emails and even borrowed library books. Terrorist suspects were being arrested at 2am, scores of foreign nationals were being illegally detained, and Britain was following the US example.[10]

The United States quickly began the process of 'regime change' in post-war Iraq, but soon ran into a plethora of troubles. The civil infrastructure was in a state of collapse, there were looting and arson in the streets, and the Iraqi population seemed reluctant to support US plans to reshape the country. No-one, American or Iraqi, seemed to notice the terms of Security Council resolution 1325, adopted on 31 October 2000, urging UN Member States 'to ensure increased representation of women at all decision-making levels in national, regional and international institutions ...' The tensions within Iraq had been exacerbated by the war – an entirely predictable outcome. The minority Sunni groups, associated with the Saddam regime, were under threat; Shi'ites were fighting Shi'ites; the northern Kurds had not yet resolved their tensions with Turkey; and beneath the surface of Iraqi society the tribal leaders were struggling for control (Chapter 2).[11] In the midst of this turmoil was the American military presence, brutal and uncomprehending, indifferent to looted museums and banks, intent only on securing permanent military bases in the country and access to the oil resource, whatever the views of the local people and whatever regime might eventually emerge.

Throughout the region the tensions had been fuelled by the 2003 war. Rockets were being fired at US forces in Afghanistan; two dozen Israeli tanks swept into the Occupied Territories on 19 April, demolishing houses, killing five Palestinians and wounding around one hundred; the Arab regimes were struggling to come to terms with the eclipse of Baghdad; and the Arab 'on the street' was confused and demoralised. It was widely recognised that the aggression against Iraq was not the end. Iran and Syria were in Washington's sights, and the destruction of either would gratify Tel Aviv. But first the US arsenals would have to be replenished:[12] no-one would be surprised to learn that there would be money enough for that.

On 1 April 2003 Stephen Eagle Funk, the first American conscientious objector, believing that the war was 'immoral because of the deception involved by our leaders' gave himself up at a marine base in California. He remembered the recruits who were envious of those being sent to the Gulf; 'They would say things like: "Kill a raghead for me – I'm so jealous."' Funk, a Catholic, was told by the chaplain that 'Jesus says to carry a sword', but he was unconvinced: 'War is about destruction and violence and death. It is young men fighting old men's wars. It is not the answer. It just ravages the land of the battleground. I know it's wrong but other people in the military have been programmed to think that it is OK.'

In late-February 2003 John Kiesling, a senior career diplomat who served under four presidents in US embassies, resigned in protest at America's stance on Iraq; 'No one of my colleagues is comfortable with our policy.' His resignation letter included the words:

> The policies we are now asked to advance are incompatible not only with American values but also with American interests. Our fervent pursuit of war with Iraq is driving us to squander the international legitimacy that has been America's most potent weapon of both offence and defense since the days of Woodrow Wilson. We have begun to dismantle the largest and most effective web of international relationships the world has ever known.

It is easy to sympathise with such sentiments but they do not reveal an intimate knowledge of political events since the Second World War, Kiesling asked: 'Have we indeed become blind, as Russia is blind in Chechnya, as Israel is blind in the Occupied Territories, to our own advice, that overwhelming military power is not the answer to terrorism?' He talks as if the 2003 aggression were unique in recent American history, but we may also remember Korea, Vietnam, Cuba, Lebanon, Somalia, Libya, Panama, Grenada and Iraq itself. The modern United States has a dismal record in its many violations of international law, its gross insensitivity to the call of natural justice. This book describes the impact of the war as providing clues for possible political developments in the future. Essential background information is included, without which the future options cannot be understood. Some indication is given of the vast humanitarian disaster confronting the Iraqi people and the next Iraqi regime, whatever its character (Part I). The war's impact on the region is charted, and pointers are given to likely developments in the Middle East (Part II). Part III focuses on specific elements – the development of Iraq, the ubiquitous significance of oil, and the role of the United Nations – that have conspired to shape the present situation and that will continue to shape the future. Here particular attention is given to the role of the United States, posturing as a moral force but ultimately cynical in the scale of its global ambition.

This is above all a commentary on the hazards of power. We all know the words in the letter of Lord John Acton (*Life and Letters of Mandel Creighton*, 1904): 'Power tends to corrupt, and absolute power corrupts absolutely', but commentators less frequently quote what follows: 'Great men are also always bad men, even when they exercise influence and not authority.' In this spirit the novelist Anthony Trollope observed: 'We know that power does corrupt, and that we cannot trust kings to have loving hearts.' (In the modern age we would add to 'kings' – 'presidents' and 'prime ministers'). In 1770, a century before the Trollope words, William Pitt, Earl of Chatham, declared in the House of Lords: 'Unlimited power is apt to corrupt the minds of those who possess it.'

The unassailable military power of the United States, with no countervailing empire in the world, is the most significant factor in the shaping of the political affairs of the 21st century. This situation will change: empires, like individuals and institutions, are mortal. But for the forseeable future it is the US government that will attempt to remake the Middle East – and the wider world – in American interest.

PART ONE

IRAQ

ONE

Social Collapse

The long US-led war against Iraq, at first economic only, began early in 1990 before the Iraqi invasion of Kuwait. It continued with the draconian sanctions regime introduced in August 1990, through the massive military onslaught of 1991 and the long years of bombing and economic siege, and climaxed in the vast aggression that began in March 2003.

The 2003 invasion was launched against an impoverished nation, what many people regarded as the equivalent of a huge refugee camp. The 1991 war had begun the process. Before it began, US Secretary of State James Baker made a promise to the Iraqis: 'We will return you to the pre-industrial age.' Between 16 January and 27 February 1991 American aircraft dropped the equivalent of one Hiroshima atomic bomb a week on Iraq, a rate of destruction that had no parallels in the history of warfare.

The economic siege – what Woodrow Wilson had called 'this silent deadly remedy' – continued, with predictable results. In 1995 the UN

Food and Agriculture Organisation, reporting on the deteriorating plight of Iraqi civilians noted: 'More than one million Iraqis have died – 567,000 of them children – as a direct result of sanctions ...'[1] The International Red Cross was protesting at the 'dire effects' of sanctions on civilians, with reputable Western journalists such as Victoria Brittain reporting 'chronic hunger ... with 20,000 new cases of child malnutrition every month.'[2] In March 1996 The UN World Health Organisation (WHO) reported that the economic sanctions had caused a six-fold increase in the mortality rate of children under five with 'the vast majority of Iraqis' surviving 'on a semi-starvation diet'.[3]

In December 2001 some 15,000 Iraqi civilians died as a result of the sanctions regime, including more than 7,000 children under the age of five dying through (otherwise treatable) diseases such as diarrhoea, pneumonia and malnutrition illnesses. A month later, Baghdad informed the United Nations that '1.6 million Iraqis had died from diseases that could not be treated because of the embargo'. The total mortality figure of 1,614,303 included 667,773 children under five who had died as a result of the sanctions. At the same time a group of Americans, members of the activist group Voices in the Wilderness, sent a message to President George W. Bush after visiting the children's wards in hospitals across Iraq: 'We have indeed discovered that weapons of mass destruction exist ... hundreds of thousands of little children have died as a direct result of the sanctions the US has maintained.'

The UN Analysis

On 19 March 2003 Kofi Annan, UN Secretary-General, expressed his alarm at the prospect of imminent war:

> In the past 20 years, Iraqis have been through two major wars, internal uprisings and conflict, and more than a decade of debilitating sanctions. The country's vital infrastructure has been devastated, so that it no longer meets the most basic needs for clean water, health and education.[4]

Iraq's most vulnerable citizens – the elderly, women and children, the disabled – were already being denied basic health care. Around one million Iraqi children were suffering from chronic malnutrition, with most Iraqis heavily dependent on the food ration handed out each month to every family in the country. It was obvious that the imminent US-led war could only serve to disrupt this fragile humanitarian support structure. Kofi Annan commented:

> *In the short term, the conflict that is now clearly about to start can only make things worse – perhaps much worse.*[5]

No-one could doubt what this meant, though the implications were given little attention in the Western media. Even Kofi Annan, usually diffident to the point of invisibility, had been driven to comment that the US-led war would have serious consequences for the already appalling humanitarian situation in Iraq. No doubt he read important UN documents, especially those marked 'STRICTLY CONFIDENTIAL'. One such document judged that the devastation in Iraq 'would undoubtedly be great', with the resulting humanitarian situation being worse even than that in Afghanistan.[6]

The population in Afghanistan is predominantly rural, unlike the relatively urbanised Iraqi population where the state aimed to provide the basic needs of the people: 'As households have generally become poorer during the course of the sanctions regime, the Iraqi people have become even more reliant on the state to meet their basic needs.'[7] Some 60 per cent of the population – 16 million people – had become highly dependent on the monthly 'food basket' provided by the government as there were no other means available to meet essential survival requirements.

It seemed unlikely that the level of services being provided by the government would collapse simultaneously for the entire population, rather that an early cessation of services in some areas would quickly be followed by a collapse of services in others. The report estimated that a total of 5.4 million people would be in immediate need of humanitarian support, to which would be added a further 2 million internally displaced persons and refugees – a total caseload population of around 7.4 million.[8]

The UN report emphasised that various social groups would be particularly vulnerable 'because of the likely absence of a functioning primary health care system in a post-conflict situation'. In this context reference was made to 4.2 million children under five, about one million pregnant and lactating women, 2 million internally displaced people and unquantified numbers of the infirm, the chronically ill and the elderly. It was also judged that the outbreak of diseases such as cholera and dysentery 'in epidemic if not pandemic proportions' was 'very likely'.

A United Nations Childrens Fund (UNICEF) estimate, cited in the report, suggested that the nutritional status of some 3.03 million persons countrywide would be so dire that such individuals would require therapeutic feeding. This included 2.03 million severely and moderately malnourished children under five, approximately 5,000 persons confined to institutions (orphaned children, the severely handicapped, detained children and 21,000 elderly).[9] To these figures were added the number of patients in hospitals (the total bed capacity was estimated at 27,000) and prisoners.[10]

Hence, three months before the United States initiated its massive new aggression against Iraq, the United Nations was estimating the likely human cost for the Iraqi civilian population. The immediate humanitarian interventions required on an emergency basis are summarised in Figure 1, with substantially larger interventions 'likely to be required for a protracted period of time, certainly longer than one year'.[11]

On 27 December 2002 Ruud Lubbers, UN High Commissioner for refugees, commented in a BBC radio interview that a war on Iraq would be a 'disaster from a humanitarian perspective'. On 23 January 2003 international health experts, in an open letter published in *The Lancet* and the *British Medical Journal*, urged Prime Minister Tony Blair to consider what would be the horrific humanitarian consequences of war on Iraq. More than 550 staff, students and alumni at the London School of Hygiene and Tropical Medicine – coming together for the first time in such a way – warned that hundreds of thousands of people, mostly civilians, would be killed and injured in the war. The medical experts cited evidence from the WHO, the UN report and Medact, a British charity of health professionals, to emphasise that the aftermath of the war would include civil conflict, famine, epidemics, refugees and displaced people, and catastrophic effects on children's health and development.

Bridging, material handling and transport.

Food and necessities for some 5.4 million people.

Health supplies to treat injuries for approximately 10,000.

Health supplies to treat the highly vulnerable for 1.23 million.

Health supplies to cater for the ongoing needs of 5.4 million

Nutrition supplies for 0.54 million.

Water treatment equipment for 5.4 million.

Chemicals and consumables for 5.4 million.

Sanitation materials and chemicals.

Total range of services for 2 million internally displaced persons, some
of whom may well become refugees.

Emergency shelter for 1.4 million.

Family reunion facilities for unaccompanied minors.

Facilities for 100,000 Iraqi refugees in neighbouring countries.

Mine action activities (demining, unexploded ordnance, awareness).

Figure 1. *Immediate humanitarian interventions required in post-war
Iraq*
Source: *UNHCR, WHO, UNICEF, UN Health Sectoral Working Group in Iraq*

Suffer the Children

Jonathan Glover, director of the Centre of Medical Law and Ethics at
King's College, London, asked pungently: 'Can we justify killing the
children of Iraq?'[12] He pointed out that thousands of children would die
in a war with Saddam – 'So why aren't we agonising over this in the way
we would the possible death of a child in Britain?' Medical ethics,
considered by Glover, focus on such questions as whether to sustain the
life of a baby born with severe disabilities. But were the people of Iraq
so different to those treated in British hospitals? Some of the doomed
Iraqis would be old, and many would be babies and children:

> To think of just one five-year-old girl, who may die in this war, as
> we would think of that same girl in a medical crisis is to see the
> enormous burden of proof on those would justify killing her.

Decisions for war seem less agonising than the decision to let a girl in hospital die. But only because anonymity and distance numb the moral imagination.[13]

On 1 February 2003 the British Ministry of Defence admitted that the electricity system that powered water distribution and sanitation for the Iraqi people could be a military target, despite warnings that this would cause a humanitarian tragedy. Clare Short, secretary of state for international development, had already commented on the possible targeting of the electricity system: 'There would be the resultant danger that people would not have access to water and that sanitation facilities would be even worse than they are now … preparations need to be made against that eventuality so that the health of the people does not suffer.'

On 12 February Charles Clements, a public health physician and Vietnam veteran, reported on the health conditions of the impoverished society about to suffer massive bombing by the United States. With other public health experts, Clements had just returned from a 10-day emergency mission to Iraq 'to assess the vulnerability of the civilian population to another war'. Most families, already reduced by the US sanctions to the status of refugees, were without economic resources and were surviving on a food ration that was the minimum for human sustenance: 'Much of the population has a marginal nutritional status.'

The hospital wards were filled with severely malnourished children, many of them suffering from diseases that were controlled before pesticides were banned under sanctions. One mother had travelled 200km with her young daughter, afflicted by leschmaniais, because she had heard that a particular hospital had a supply of Pentostam that would effectively treat the disease. The paediatrician told the mother that there was none and then said to Clements in English: 'It would be kinder to shoot her here rather than let her go home and die the lingering death that awaits her.' The interpreter instinctively translated the words into Arabic and the mother's eyes overflowed with tears.

Leading British relief agencies, including Oxfam and Christian Aid, were warning that a new war on Iraq would cause immense civilian suffering, while UNICEF and the UN High Commission for Refugees (UNHCR) were judging that their resources were inadequate for the relief demands anticipated in its budget for 2002.

It was also plain that Iraqi's 12 million children, more vulnerable in

2003 than before the 1991 Gulf War, would be drastically effected by a new military onslaught. Even before the onset on hostilities in March 2003 Iraqi children were suffering degrees of trauma to which little attention was being given by Western leaders or in the Western press. In early 2003 a team of international experts, including two of the world's most foremost psychologists, conducted pre-conflict field research with Iraqi children and concluded that they were already suffering 'significant psychological harm' from the threat of a US-led war against their country.

The investigators, welcomed into the homes of more than 100 Iraqi families, found the overwhelming message to be one of fear and the thought of being killed. Thus the 13-year-old Hadeel said: 'I think every hour that something bad will happen to me'; Assem, aged five, commented: 'They have guns and bombs and the air will be cold and hot and we will burn very much'; and the 13-year-old Hind, speaking in a breaking voice, told the researchers: 'I feel fear every day that we might all die, but where shall I go if I am left alone?' The investigators were shocked to find that the majority of children were expressing such fears.[14]

An immediate consequence of the imminent war would be that the fragile support structure maintained by Baghdad would collapse, tipping an entire population of already malnourished children into starvation. The key findings of the researchers (Figure 2) showed that Iraqi children would be 'at grave risk of starvation, disease, death and psychological trauma in the event of war':

> According to the International Study Team, should war occur, Iraqi children will face a grave humanitarian disaster. While it is impossible to predict both the exact nature of any war and the number of expected deaths and injuries, casualties among children will be in the thousands, probably the tens of thousands, and possibly in the hundreds of thousands.[15]

The investigators spoke to teenagers and to nine children below seven years of age, and judged that their way of expressing themselves 'did not have the flavour of rote learned political rhetoric'. The children were not concerned with the political issues but with their own specific anxieties (Figure 3), revealing a pattern of mental sufferings and problems:

'Central to all their statements were their personal feelings of being powerless victims of deprived lives (the sanctions) and prospects of having their life and future totally destroyed by an inevitable war.' The results were headaches, tension, fear, irritability, depression, bad dreams, bouts of sleeplessness, and feelings of loneliness and that life is not worth living: 'The mental resources of Iraqi parents have been depleted over a long period of time, and in combination with other negative health effects this may have a catastrophic effect on children's mental health.'[16]

On 12 February 2003 Clare Short emphasised how difficult it had been to persuade the US military to include humanitarian protection in its planning. She also urged the need for explicit UN authorisation for military action again Iraq, and stressed that any military campaign should not damage power stations and other infrastructure assets essential to civilian welfare: 'We are making the humanitarian points very clearly and being listened to by our military. It is proving very difficult to get the US to take on the humanitarian consequences.' It was likely that the 'oil for food' programme, already grossly inadequate, would break down if there were a war and that people would starve.

On 17 February 2003 the Campaign Against Sanctions on Iraq (CASI) released a confidential UN document predicting that 30 per cent of children under five in Iraq, around 1.26 million, 'would be at risk of death from malnutrition' in the event of war. The draft document, *'Integrated Humanitarian Contingency Plan for Iraq and Neighbouring Countries'* produced on 7 January 2003 by the UN Office for the Co-ordination of Humanitarian Affairs (OCHA), suggested that the collapse of essential services in Iraq 'could lead to a humanitarian emergency of proportions well beyond the capacity of UN agencies and other aid organisations'; and that the effects of over 12 years of sanctions, preceded by war, had 'considerably increased the vulnerability of the population'.

Iraqi children are more vulnerable in early 2003 than they were in 1990, before the 1991 Gulf War.

16 million Iraqi civilians – half of them children – are 100 per cent dependent on government-distributed food rations. War would disrupt the distribution system, leading to food shortages, malnutrition and possibly starvation.

There is only estimated one month's supply of food in Iraq.

Approximately 500,000 Iraqi children are acutely malnourished or underweight. These are particularly vulnerable to disease and death in the event of war.

The health care system is only a fraction of its pre–1991 state. The UN estimates that hospitals and clinics will run out of medicine 3–4 weeks after the start of a war.

The death rate of children under five is already 2–3 times greater than it was in 1990. This greater vulnerability means greater illness and death rates among children in conflict circumstances.

Water and sanitation systems are in a bad state of repair following more than 12 years of sanctions. 500,000 metric tons of raw sewage is dumped into fresh water every day, which means that only 60 per cent of Iraqis have access to fresh water. Further disruption through war would be a disaster.

The UN estimates that the war could lead to more than 1.4 million refugees and 2 million internally displaced persons. This would include three quarters of a million refugee children and one million internally displaced children.

Iraqi children are already badly traumatised. The imminent war is causing fear, anxiety, nightmares and depression. Forty per cent surveyed do not think that life is worth living.

The UN estimates that 500,000 people could require emergency medical treatment in the event of war.

The level of emergency preparedness is currently very low. There is inadequate provision for meeting the special needs of children in the war.

A new war in Iraq would be catastrophic for Iraq's 12 million children, already highly vulnerable due to prolonged economic sanctions.

Figure 2. *Key findings of Our Common Responsibility: The Impact of a New War on Iraqi Children*
Source: *International Study Team, Toronto, 30 January 2003*

'They come from above, from the air, and will kill us and destroy us. I can explain to you that we fear this every day and every night' – Sheima (5 years old).

'I have only one thought in my head most of the time. War means death to me and my family. Of course' – Aizar (18 years old).

'There will be a lot of destruction and loss of lives. We know that. What concerns me most with the situation afterwards if I am still alive' – Isra (16 years old).

Aesar (10 years old) wished to send a message to President George W. Bush, saying: 'A lot of Iraqi children will die. You will see it on TV and then you will regret'.

'I do not expect them to kill so many. It is not acceptable. Maybe American people have some sympathy with us since we are peaceful and do not want to attack them' – Shahad (11 years old).

Figure 3. *Pre-war messages from Iraqi children, 2003*
Source: *Our Common Responsibility, op. cit.*

At the end of February there were reports that a human disaster was imminent as the aid funds dried up.[17] Daleep Mukarji, Christian Aid director, commented: 'There is a raft of evidence suggesting that preparations may turn out to be woefully inadequate' – a judgement echoed by many observers decrying aid regulations that stipulated the withholding of funding until disaster had struck. Brendan Paddy, a Save the Children spokesman, commented that while people fear chemical and biological warfare, 'the things that kill most people are disease and malnutrition'. (Experience of the war aftermath in Afghanistan provided no comfort. In early 2002 the World Bank estimated that the country needed $10.2 billion over five years. International pledges were about half that amount, and the CIA was spending some of the incoming funds paying selected warlords and militias for help in the alleged 'war on terror'. One Western observer, commenting on Afghanistan, said: 'If Americans think this is success, then outright failure must be pretty horrible.'[18] All the signs were that the Afghan experience would be repeated in Iraq. It was unlikely that Washington, prepared to spend well in excess of $100 billion on the war, would have any enthusiasm for funding the peace).

It was obvious that the Iraqi civilian population was less adequately prepared for war than in 1990–91. For nearly thirteen years the United States and Britain had systematically sabotaged the humanitarian provisions of the sanctions regime, a malicious campaign that had forced the bulk of the Iraqi people into a desperate struggle for survival.[19] Even in March 2003, with war imminent, Washington and London were working to restrict the flow of humanitarian goods to Iraq. Thus, because Iraq lacked the necessary oil-revenue funds (deliberately constrained by US-UK policies), some 2632 UN-approved humanitarian supply contracts worth some $5.1 billion were effectively blocked. The humanitarian sectors affected by the revenue shortfall were agriculture ($850 million), food handling ($808 million), housing ($666 million), electricity ($562 million), telecommunications and transportation ($454 million), water and sanitation ($491 million), education ($400 million) and health ($385 million).[20] Hence at a time when the United States and Britain were preparing to launch a massive military onslaught on Iraq they were deliberately restricting the access of the Iraqi people to food, clean water and medical supplies.

The aid agencies were continuing to warn that war would trigger a humanitarian catastrophe. Save the Children, Care International and Christian Aid were saying that the new Gulf War would create up to three million refugees who, along with military attacks on Iraqi's fragile infrastructure, would cause appalling problems of starvation and disease. Thus Mike Anderson, director-general of Save the Children, noted: 'Meeting the humanitarian needs of the Iraqi population will not be compatible with a military agenda where the priority is winning the war'; and Margaret Hassan, Iraq director of Care International, commented: 'The people of Iraq are already having to live through a terrible emergency. They simply do not have the resources to withstand an additional crisis brought about by military action.' Daleep Mukarji judged that 'political and humanitarian shockwaves' might be sent throughout the Middle East, 'especially to Israel and the Occupied Palestinian Territories'; and emphasised that Israel, not only Iraq, should observe UN resolutions.

The exodus from Baghdad was already under way. Many families who could afford it were hiring large vehicles for their families and possessions to take either the ten-hour drive across the desert to Jordan or the eight-hour drive northwest to Syria. One man, separated from his family by the crisis, said how terrified they were for the babies. Another man, returning home to Mosul commented: 'We are all going to die eventually, but no-one wants to get incinerated by a missile.' A veteran of the 1991 war, showing his serious war wound, said to the Western journalist: 'Please help me. Please tell me how to get out. We are terrified. We can't endure another war. We can't survive.'

Kathy Kelly, Voices in the Wilderness activist and a member of the Iraq Peace Team (pledged to remain in Iraq during the war), reported the attitudes of Iraqi civilians confronted with imminent war. The eight-year-old Sohab, a cancer victim in the Al Mansour Hospital, delighted in making bright pictures in a children's colouring book: 'We seemed light years away from warfare during the calm quiet morning with this radiantly beautiful child.' A Peace Team banner noted the departure of UN staff from Baghdad:

Farewell UN. Please advise: Who will protect Iraqi children?

The US military was announcing that 3,000 bombs and missiles would be launched on Iraq, more than used in the entire 1991 Gulf War, in the first 48 hours of the campaign; and the *New York Times* was quoting Pentagon officials: 'There will be no place in Baghdad that will be safe.'

War

The vast bulk of the reportage in the Western media focused on what were deemed to be the exciting aspects of the conflict. The exploits of 'our boys', the many military engagements, the final 'push' on Baghdad – all were endlessly described with the help of newspaper illustrations, computer graphics and a reliable regiment of tame political pundits. The most horrific images of the war seldom appeared in the press and never on television: the news managers were usually happy to play their propaganda part in the war effort. The Independent Qatar-based Al Jazeera broadcasting network was frequently criticised for showing what war really meant in human terms, and was still denounced after the network had run into trouble with the Iraqi authorities.

The US-UK political slogans were generally presented to Western publics without commentary or challenge:

We have no quarrel with the Iraqi people.

Using precision weapons we are only attacking military targets.

Extraordinary care is being taken to avoid civilian casualties.

But it proved impossible to disguise the character and purpose of the war. Once the war had started, the scale of the human casualties soon became obvious. At first there were dozens of dead and wounded, then hundreds, then thousands. As the war continued it was increasingly obvious that the number of human casualties – dead, wounded, traumatised, diseased, starving, bereaved – would be reckoned in the millions.

On March 20 a Jordanian taxi driver was blown to pieces in the first US missile strike on Baghdad. Two days later the International Committee of the Red Cross (ICRC) was treating about 100 civilian casualties, including about 30 women and children, at Baghdad's Yarmuk teaching hospital. At the same time the population of Basra (1.5 million people) was facing a water supply crisis and a break in its electricity supplies. The Red Cross warned of a humanitarian disaster, with the Iraqis claiming on 23 March that 77 civilians had been killed and 300 injured by US-UK bombing. In Baghdad, five-year-old Doha Suheil, one casualty among hundreds, had suffered shrapnel wounds when a cruise missile hit the Radwaniyeh residential suburb. With shrapnel in her spine she was partly paralysed. Doha was one of more than a hundred patients brought to the Al-Mustansaniya College Hospital immediately after the US started bombing the city.[21]

The facts were plain: whether or not civilians were being targeted they were certainly being killed and wounded in large numbers. The 50-year-old Amel Hassan, a peasant woman, lay in hospital with multiple shrapnel wounds in her chest. The legs of her five-year-old daughter Wahed, in another hospital bed, were still bleeding. Two boys in the next room, Sade Selim (11 years old) and his brother Omar (14) had suffered shrapnel wounds to their legs and chest. It seemed that 'multiple shrapnel wounds' was a natural disease, noted Robert Fisk, having reported so many.[22] In this early phase of the war some 320 cruise missiles, fired from USS *Kitty Hawk*, had already hit Baghdad. On 22 March Al-Jazeera claimed that about 50 Iraqi civilians had been killed by coalition bombing in Basra, with one child shown with the back of its skull blown off and blood-stained people being treated on the floor of a hospital. One woman, standing among the casualties, said: 'It's a huge mass of civilians. It was a massacre.'

The *Sunday Mirror* (London, March 2003) showed an Iraqi baby with a badly burnt face in Baghdad, and two headless Iraqi soldiers clutching a makeshift white flag. In al-Qadassiya residential district, seven houses had been destroyed and 12 badly damaged, with people still buried beneath the rubble. In the Yarmuk Hospital the three-year-old Abbas Ali, with ghastly wounds, was suffering 85 per cent burns; in the next bed a 21-year-old student, his face horribly swollen, was wrapped in yellow gauze; and nearby a badly burnt man was forced to perch on all fours.[23] At the same time many of the horrors were occurring unreported and unremarked, with the media totally excluded from certain areas.

The Red Cross was continuing to highlight the humanitarian crisis in Basra, where a large population without water was being compelled to drink from a river that carried raw sewage. Geoffrey Keene, UNICEF spokesman, commented:

> There must now be a threat of disease as tens of thousands of people in their homes, hospitals and care institutions attempt to cope and find what water they can from the river and other sources ... the children of Iraq are some of the most vulnerable people in the world ... there is the very real possibility now of child deaths, no only from the conflict, but from the additional effects of diarrhoea and dehydration. We estimate that at least 100,000 children under the age of five are at risk.

Soon the Basra catastrophe would be afflicting many towns and cities throughout Iraq, with vital services severed and millions of civilians subjected to effective siege. And everywhere the bombing continued. Zina Sabah was one of the many Iraqis who were bombed in a residential area. Her four-year-old daughter Menah, screaming in pain and terror, had suffered a deep leg wound when the bomb exploded; in the next bed lay 80-year-old Bedria Hassan; and nearby lay Walid Aziz (62), blinded by the bomb while out buying a birthday present for his daughter. Dr al-Mussaui, who treated these victims, said: 'These people are from a residential area. There is no military target even close to where this happened. Please explain this.'

UNICEF was struggling to cope in the deteriorating conditions of an expanding war. A spokesman, having visited an orphanage in the frontline city of Kabala, reported that the children wanted, above all, the bombing to stop. Carol Bellamy, UNICEF executive director, commented: 'UNICEF is deeply concerned about the deteriorating conditions for the children in the areas most impacted by military operations. The last few days have raised real concern about the welfare of civilians caught in the conflict.' UNICEF had hired commercial tankers to bring water to Basra from Kuwait but was unable to make deliveries because of the military siege ('We are not suicidal and we don't expect other people to be'). On 25 March the WHO reported that 60 per cent of the Basra civilian population was without clean water.

The pattern was plain. The civil infrastructure was being targeted in many parts of Iraq, and a growing number of Iraqi civilians were being killed and wounded by cruise missiles and bombs, including depleted uranium ordnance, cluster bombs and high explosives. Here it is enough to cite some Western newspaper headlines, a few of many:

Battle for city leads to 'massacre of children' claim.[24]

The Yank opened up. He had absolutely no regard for human life. He was a cowboy out on a jolly.[25]

Children killed and maimed in US 'cluster bomb raid.[26]

The proof: marketplace deaths were caused by a US missile.[27]

Civilians killed in bombing near hospital.[28]

Hospital struggles to cope as civilian injuries mount.[29]

Wailing children, the wounded, and the dead: victims of the day cluster bombs rained on Babylon.[30]

American troops kill seven women and children at checkpoint.[31]

Some observers have suggested that the civilian casualties were not accidental, unintentional examples of 'collateral damage'. Thus the New York-based Action Centre suggested that in the face of determined Iraqi resistance in the early phases of the war the US High Command called for open warfare against the Iraqi civilian population. On 2 April 2003 the Action Centre reported that 'hundreds of civilians have been shot down on the roadways, in their homes, on their farms'.

This shift of policy, according to the Centre, was caused by a defiant and resisting population, encouraging US troops to 'shoot first and ask questions later'. The *Washington Post* (1 April 2003) quoted a Pentagon official as saying that every Iraqi 'is now seen as a combatant until proven otherwise'. There would be acts of kindness, medical care and the like, 'but the large scale aid effort will have to wait'. The policy had ramifications that constituted gross violations of international law: for example, Article 54 of the 1977 Protocol 1 Addition to the Geneva Conventions, stipulating that '*Starvation of civilians as a method of warfare is prohibited*'. The Action Centre indicated the full horror of the emerging US policy:

> In fact the new US strategy now is deliberately preventing Iraqi civilians in Nasiriya and other towns from receiving food and water unless they co-operate with the occupation forces.
>
> US Marine Operations Commander, Lt. Colonel Paul Roche told reporters on March 31 that the US strategy towards the people of Nasiriya included the use of food and water as a weapon to terrorise and break the will of the civilian population.[32]

This US policy was euphemistically portrayed in *The Washington Post* headline: 'US troops instructed to use tougher tactics'.

On 30 March Mark Franchetti, writing for *The Sunday Times*, recorded the impact of US policy on Iraqi civilians. He witnessed some fifteen civilian vehicles riddled with bullets by American troops: 'Amid the wreckage I counted 12 dead civilians, lying in the road or in nearby ditches ... one man's body was still in flames ... down the road a little girl, no older than five and dressed in a pretty orange and gold dress, lay dead in a ditch next to the body of a man who may have been her father. Half his head was missing.' An American soldier, Lieutenant Matt Martin, commented: 'Did you see all that? Did you see that little baby girl? … It really gets to me to see children being killed like this, but we had no choice.' Corporal Ryan Dupre, surveying the scene, said: 'I am starting to hate this country. Wait till I get hold of a friggin' Iraqi. No, I won't get hold of one. I'll just kill him.'

A Reuters article ('Iraqis delirious with grief after missile attack', March 29) described a US attack on a poor section of Baghdad. Arouba Khodeir wailed hysterically and hit herself in the face and chest: 'My son had his head blown off. Why are they hitting the people? Why are they killing the children?' Shaza Shallum, 20 years old, was also killed when the explosion sent a shard of shrapnel through her neck: 'Six-month-old Fatima was found alive in her dead mother's arms and brought by neighbours to her grandmother. The wails of the mourners drowned the cries of the hungry infant.'

The course of the war dragged on from days into weeks and the toll of civilian dead and wounded mounted by the hour. Under the remorseless power of modern technology the Iraqi casualties grew into tens of thousands. As with the 1991 Gulf War the US generals and politicians refused to give any reckoning of the numbers of Iraqi dead and injured. Any explicit indication of the scale of the slaughter would not 'play well' in the world's media. And no figures were given for the hundreds of thousands of Iraqis who had succumbed to war-induced disease and starvation.

Chaos

For the most part, the Western media did not focus on the human casualties of the war. As with the 1991 conflict and the starvation effects of sanctions much of the available film footage was judged to be too gruesome to show on television. But there was plenty of information in the newspapers for those who cared to notice what was happening. One account, for example, described what happened to Iraqi villagers in Hilla, near Babylon, as a result of a ferocious American air and land assault. Unedited TV footage, seen by *The Guardian* (London), showed the tiny corpse of a baby wrapped up like a doll in a funeral shroud being carried out of a morgue to lie next to the body of a boy, who looked about 10.[33]

Villagers swarmed round the bodies of their dead relatives as they were heaped onto pick-up trucks, and followed the horrifically injured corpses as they were taken for burial. Bed after bed of injured women and children were shown in the hospital along with large pools of blood. Nazim al-Adali, an Edinburgh-trained doctor at the hospital, commented on the disaster that had overtaken the Iraqi civilians: 'All of these are due to the American bombing of the civilian homes. Hundreds of civilians have been injured, and many have been killed … There are not any army cars or tanks in the area.'[34] One woman, Aliya Mukhtaf, said that her husband and her six children had been killed in the attack, and nearby a teenage boy was shown with bandages over the stump where his right hand had been sheared off by shrapnel.

The American and British forces had brought carnage, civil collapse and mounting resentment. The Western media, desperate for politically sound footage, managed to broadcast pictures of jubilant Iraqis cheering the fall of Saddam, but little attention was given to the bleak despair of the civilian casualties, denied adequate medical care and watching their cities being torn apart:

UN and army at odds as troops encourage looting.[35]

Aid effort founders while water and food crisis spreads.[36]

'Umm Qasar gets clean water' – at a price[37] – People were stealing from the tankers meant to serve the hospital, and then selling the water to desperate civilians. One American soldier was interviewed on television saying how good it was to see the Iraqis 'behaving like capitalists'.

'Humanitarian effort dismissed as a disaster'[38] – The aid agencies reported that many Iraqis were suffering from a lack of water, food and medical supplies. Many were complaining that they were 'far worse off now than they were before the war'.

Lack of fresh water threatens hospitals swamped by casualties.[39]

Amid Allied jubilation, a child lies in agony, clothes soaked in blood.[40]

A picture of killing inflicted on a sprawling city – and it grew more unbearable by the minute.[41]

'Iraqi's children will pay ultimate price of war'[42] – The 12-year-old Ali Ismail Abbas, who was severely burnt and lost both arms (with his entire family killed), had become an international symbol of the suffering of Iraqi children. Some commentators pointed out that there were thousands more like Ali.

The Baghdad hospitals, inundated with civilian casualties and often lacking water and electricity, were running out of anaesthetics, drugs and medical equipment. Nad Doumani, a Red Cross spokeswoman, warned that 'hospitals have reached their limit' and commented on the shortage of anaesthetics. The WHO also reported a 'shortage of equipment to deal with burns, shrapnel wounds and spinal injuries' and described the situation as 'critical'. The water station near Baghdad's Medical City group of hospitals, a modern facility, had been bombed, cutting the water supply. Water treatment works and sewage pumping stations in eastern and southern Baghdad had also been bombed, crippling hospital facilities as the casualties continued to arrive. The WHO said it was impossible to provide even an estimate of the number of Iraqis killed and wounded: 'Nobody is adding up all the numbers, but it's clear they are huge.'

There were reports of babies being delivered in the dark, in filthy hospitals without access to water or electricity. Children were suffering amputations without anaesthetic, and looters were ransacking the hospitals, stealing the few remaining drugs, beds, incubators and intensive-care equipment. Then the doctors, staying at home to protect their families from looters, stopped turning up for work. Iraqi civilians with appalling wounds were left in hospitals without water, electricity, anaesthetics, medical equipment and staff. On 9 April the aid agencies suspended their operations as a result of 'lawlessness', saying that there was no point in delivering aid if it was going to be looted and demanding that the allied forces observe their legal and moral obligations to restore order. The military campaign was not over and the chaos continued:

Hospital looters stealing incubators and drugs.[43]

'A civilisation torn to pieces'[44] – Iraq's National Archaeological Museum was looted and trashed: 'The looters had gone from shelf to shelf, systematically pulling down the statues and pots and amphorae of the Assyrians and the Babylonians, the Sumerians, the Medes, the Persians and the Greeks and hurling them onto the concrete.'

Anger rises as US fails to control anarchy.[45]

Geoff Hoon, British defense secretary, declared in an interview with *The Observer* (London) that 'what we want' is 'to create as quickly as we can … an air of normality'. Having helped to create devastation, chaos, misery, mutilation, death and disease on a vast and expanding scale, Hoon and his colleagues seemed comfortably unaware that they were deeply implicated in the catastrophe of Iraq.

What would Hoon and the rest say to Ali Abbas and the thousands of other injured Iraqi children, those orphaned by allied bombs, and the parents who had witnessed the dismembered corpses of their babies? What could be said to Murtudhr Kadhum, forced to give her 11-month-old baby filthy water in Basra and then to nurse her in despair as she died from the resulting disease?

Perhaps Blair and Bush might like to consider how they might have responded to what the Nuremburg judges said, trying the Nazis:

> To initiate a war of aggression is not only an international crime. It is the supreme international crime differing only from other war crimes in that it contains within itself the accumulated evil of the whole.

Here, in explicit commentary, the Nuremberg judges rejected all attempts to provide justification for the doctrine of pre-emptive military action against a country. Ed Firmage, Emeritus Professor of Law, included in his commentary the judgement that Bush's violation of international law constituted a war crime (see *Introduction*). In the same vein Tam Dalyell, a Labour Member of Parliament and Father of the House of Commons, commented (*The Guardian*, 27 March 2003):

> I … believe that since Mr Blair is going ahead with his support for

a US attack without unambiguous UN authorisation, he should be branded as a war criminal and sent to the Hague.

It is certainly possible to argue, in the terms set out so clearly at Nuremberg, that the initiation by Bush and Blair of a war of aggression is 'the supreme international crime'. In addition, there were many acts committed by the coalition forces during the war that might be judged suitable for the prosecution of war crimes.

At the end of April 2003 Jan Fermon, a Brussels-based lawyer, was preparing a legal complaint on behalf of about ten Iraqis who claimed to be victims or eyewitnesses to atrocities committed during Operation Iraqi Freedom. The complaint would accuse allied commander General Tommy Franks and other US military officials of such war crimes as the indiscriminate killing of Iraqi civilians, the bombing of a marketplace in Baghdad, the shooting of an ambulance, and the failure to prevent the mass looting of hospitals (*The Washington Times*, 28 April 2003). The Bush administration reacted angrily to the complaint, with one official warning that there would be 'diplomatic consequences for Belgium' if the complaint were taken up in court.

Other matters related to the US gunnery sergeant Gus Covarrubias, investigated for executing an Iraqi prisoner (*The Guardian*, 2 May 2003) and who admitted: 'I went behind him and shot him in the back of the head'; claims that US military strikes against known media locations, killing three journalists, had violated the Geneva Conventions; and the continual denial of the rights of prisoners held at Guantanamo Bay, Cuba, including children (*The Guardian*, 24 April 2003). Throughout May there were no reports concerning the whereabouts of the leading Iraqis who had been captured or their treatment. The International Committee of the Red Cross (ICRC) had not been allowed to visit the captives – itself a violation of international law.

The comprehensive ravaging of Iraq and its people had various consequences for the post-Saddam American administration based in Baghdad. On 21 April 2003 retired US General Jay Garner arrived in Baghdad to begin his work (see Chapter 3, *Enter Jay Garner*). It was necessary to begin the restoration of elements of Iraq's civil infrastructure, bearing in mind the need to guarantee a congenial climate for the exploitation of Iraqi resources by US corporations. At the same time the American government was indicating that it would require a long-term relationship with the new Iraqi regime, whatever government were to emerge, guaranteeing a permanent US presence in Iraq. Four sites, including Baghdad International Airport, were identified as likely future American military bases.

A host of Western propagandists continued the task of portraying the Muslim Iraqis as joyful at their 'liberation' by Christian troops and their subjection to the whims of an Israel-friendly ex-arms dealer. But already the Iraqi people were demonstrating in their thousands against the Americans occupation.

TWO

The People

The post-Saddam administration in Iraq could not ignore the complex tribal structure of the country. It was one of the skills of Saddam, whatever his shortcomings, that he was able to use his knowledge of the tribes to achieve a measure of social stability. The Tikriti clan, of which Saddam was a member, was uniquely favoured in Iraqi society but attention was given also to the many other tribes and clans that remained in a position to exert local influence on the people. Saddam used repression to maintain his political grip on the country, but also offered a range of blandishments to tribal elders and other influential men in their communities.

Throughout the history of modern Iraq the rights of many groups – Kurds, Shi'ites, Turkomen, Assyrians, Chaldeans, Yezidies, Jews, Sabias and others – were sometimes recognised and often violated. Successive authoritarian regimes, including those supported by the British in the era of Hashemite monarchy (1921–58), added to the burdens on the tribes and increasingly limited their traditional powers. The characteristic disunity among the various tribal groups had often served to exacerbate the problems, and the geographical disposition of the tribes also helped to create ethnic tensions adding to local confrontations and instabilities. At the same time foreign powers, not least the US and Britain, have often seen much advantage in exploiting tribal tensions to facilitate access to Iraqi resources. For example, the US-led war effort in 2003 was aided in various ways by the long- standing tensions between the northern Kurds and the ruling Sunni minority.

There remained a serious potential for conflict between Iraq's diverse religious and ethnic groups. On 23 March 2003 David Pryce-Jones, author on Arab affairs, headed an article (*Sunday Telegraph*) 'For Sunnis, Shias, Kurds and Turks, when war stops, the trouble starts'. The war had set the scene for prolonged ethnic conflict in the region. The US-dominated administration was well aware of the principal national divisions (Sunni, Shi'ite, Kurd) but there were few signs that it had serious knowledge of the complex tribal character of Iraq. It is useful to glance at the tribal nature of the country to highlight aspects that should be addressed by any foreign administration striving to impose stability on Iraq.

Kurds, Turkomen, Shi'ites

Today the Kurds, perhaps the best known of the many Iraqi groups, straddle five countries – Armenia, Turkey, Iran, Syria and Iraq – with ethnic pressure for Kurdish autonomy and statehood constantly arousing alarm in the various states. The Turkomen (or Turkmen) are another group burdened with political problems caused by the geographical demarcations created by foreign powers. They speak an Oguz-Turkic language and, after the start of the Arab conquest in the 7th Century, expanded across Turkmenia into the Middle East. During the final phase of the Soviet Union about four million people lived in the Turkomen Soviet Socialist Republic (now Turkmenistan), with about two million distributed through Afghanistan, Iran, Iraq, Syria and Turkey. The Turkomen are typically rural, with many cultural attitudes (for example, hostility to female emancipation) that today are widely seen as repressive and old-fashioned.

Iraq, though heavily urbanised, still contains many characteristic features of tribal social organisation, despite modern efforts to erode traditional attitudes. This is particularly the case in the more isolated rural areas, such as the rugged tableland of the northwest and some southern regions. The marsh areas of the south were once the home of many rural tribes, but Turkish dams and Iraqi agricultural schemes have severely affected the regional ecology. Thus Azzam Alwash, a 44-year-old Iraqi exile now living in California, has considered the current state of the marsh regions: 'I remember all the green, and that wonderful smell of decaying vegetation.'[1]

The common view is that Saddam Hussein ordered the marshes drained when the wetlands became a refuge for Shi'ite rebels in the 1990s, though it is true also that the imposed schemes were remarkably similar to those proposed by English engineers in the 1920s. But converting the vast swamp into a salt-encrusted wilderness in less than a decade was a significant feat, with Western environmentalists still wondering how it was accomplished. Hassan Partow, a UN expert who has studied the destruction of the marshes, once home to a million people, has commented: 'There's virtually no water left. It's absolutely phenomenal to see the destruction of an ecosystem of that scale in just five to six years.'[2] This development has been one of the major events to have drastically affected the lives of Iraqi tribes in recent years.

Tribal Society

The traditional tribal modes evolved in the unstable social conditions that grew out of the protracted decline of the Abbasid caliphate in the 9th and 10th centuries. With the decay of urban society and the collapse of a strong central authority, society was encouraged to function in smaller units. The evolution of a more centralised urbanisation had been arrested and many communities were driven to adopt earlier traditional modes of social existence. In these circumstances the tribal sheikhs emerged as a warrior class that assumed ascendancy over the cultivator.

In the mid–19th century, under the impact of Ottoman administration, there was a gradual erosion of sheikhly power and a corresponding diminution of parochial tribal influence. Under the assumption of the British mandate – after the First World War, the final collapse of the Ottomans and the creation of the League of Nations –

the tribal sheikhs enjoyed a sudden resurgence. The British had an interest in developing a local ruling class that had enough legitimacy to maintain security in the countryside and to discourage political challenges to the British exploitation of Iraq's mineral and agricultural resources. But the British approach – like that of Saddam, using carrot and stick – often bore heavily on tribal society.

The introduction of land registration threatened the traditional patterns of cultivation and pasturage, where a framework of rights and duties had evolved between the sheikhs and tribesmen. One consequence was that in many areas the status of the tribesmen was reduced to that of labourers and sharecroppers. The British encouraged the assumption of judicial and police powers by the sheikhs, who often took over tribal lands, reducing the tribesmen to virtual serfs, always in debt to landlord and master.

The traditional role of the tribe as the main politico-military unit in Iraqi society had been severely diminished by the time the Faisal II monarchy was overthrown in 1958. In some areas (for example, in the mid-Euphrates region) the tribesmen had managed to register small pieces of land in their names, so avoiding the status of mere tenancy on a sheikh's land. Here tribal customs were preserved, leading to further problems with the increasingly centralised Baghdad government. Civil administrators were sent to the rural areas in an attempt to implement modern attitudes to education, health and agricultural development. Government officials with the important task of administering the water distribution system became leading figures in many of the tribal areas, with tribal sheikhs being expected to provide the necessary labour for such tasks as the cleaning and maintenance of canals. Such activities were combined with work on the tribal grazing and producing lands, and were seen as generally beneficial to the tribes. Officials often found it prudent not to become involved in local judicial or political disputes, leaving it to the sheikhs to apply traditional tribal solutions. In such a fashion, an intelligent leader such as Saddam Hussein was able – not only to crush serious militant threats to the regime – but also to expand the government's authority into the traditional tribal areas unaccustomed to effective central control.

The character of the residual tribal structures has been shaped in various ways, not least by foreign influences. Thus there are significant differences between the surviving tribal elements along the Tigris, historically subject to Iranian penetration, and many of the tribes of the Euphrates, with traditional links to the Arab Bedouin tribes of the desert.

At least until the time of the 1991 Gulf War, and perhaps to a lesser extent thereafter, the Iraqi tribe has represented a concentric social system with many nomadic features but heavily modified by the modern trend towards sedentary life and the more limited access to useful territory. The primary tribal unit is an acknowledged lineage several generations deep, a kinship unit that is invested with many traditional responsibilities – for example, in feuds and other conflicts, in the control of marriage customs, and in the administration of tribal land. The family unit belongs to a clan, comprising two or more lineage groups, with the clan able to switch its allegiance from an ancestral unit to a more appealing tribe. The traditional pattern, heavily stressed by modern pressures, has been for several clans to unite as a tribe (*ashira*) under a single sheikh. Socio-political patterns are also influenced by the extent to which a tribe has maintained nomadic customs. Thus authority in the Bani Isad, settled for several centuries, is much more centralised than in the Ash Shabana, sedentary since the end of the 19th century.

Saddam's Policies

Saddam Hussein, developing earlier trends, often imposed representatives of the central government to assume roles formerly fulfilled by the sheikhs, and there was obvious scope in this agreement for further tensions. In circumstances where the local people may have preferred a leader with traditional tribal lineage, they were often forced to accept an official from Baghdad with little knowledge of local customs and attitudes. The 'carrot', usually welcomed by the tribes, was for Baghdad to make available such facilities as electricity and clean water – in the days before the 1991 war devastated the Iraqi social infrastructure, and the economic sanctions preserved the destruction – to villages that under the Ottomans, the British and the Iraqi monarchy had been denied such benefits.

Saddam Hussein, born in the poor town of Tikrit, had grown up surrounded by the tribes of the region. When he took power he saw the sheikhs as useful allies with influence over large swathes of the Iraqi population. Despite the modern erosion of the tribal system many traditional attitudes had survived as folk culture, and Saddam was quick to see the tribal system as a useful adjunct to his power base. He helped to restore a tribal identity that had been ebbing in the country, under the pressure of foreign administrations, for generations. This meant that, despite the problems, the tribes became a prime source of Saddam's power outside Baghdad, 'a combination of mercenary army, local government and loyalty club, paid and patronised for maintaining order and fealty'.[3] The imposition of economic sanctions, devastating for the country as a whole, served to increase Saddam's power over the tribes since scarce resources could be disbursed to favour selected groups, so advertising Saddam's seeming beneficence. Thus Faleh Abdul Jabar, a London-based sociologist, commented: 'The only way to get a job for many Iraqis today is by returning to the tribe. Sanctions created a vacuum, and the tribes filled it.'

One typical urban sheikh, happy to be loyal to Saddam, was Bassem Abd al-Shammari, living in a ranch house in Mosul with about 30 members of his extended family. He was paid regularly, drove a car and was given $2,000 a month to distribute among the Shammar tribe's 500 families – a small amount but one that under sanctions seemed to demonstrate Saddam's goodwill. In May 2000 the tribe was given a new truck from Baghdad, at a time when Washington was struggling to keep the sanctions regime as punitive as possible. Shammari also acted as mayor, judge and social worker. However, the tribes, with their deep-rooted power, were also able to pose a threat to the Saddam regime.

While Saddam saw advantage in building up the tribes, he was fully aware that they could turn against him. Thus Ghanim Jawad, a director at the London-based al-Khoei Foundation, an Islamic research institution, commented: 'Saddam knows it is the tribes who can destroy him.'[4] This has meant that Saddam had been keen to placate key tribal figures. In one tribal dispute Saddam judged whom to support. Machann al-Jaburi was on the fringes of a power struggle after his father, a sheikh, was killed by members of another tribe. Saddam summoned Jaburi to Baghdad and, to guarantee the young man's future tribal loyalty, gave him a watch, $10,000, a car, a villa and a well-paid job in Baghdad. This calculated move had the immediate effect of ending the tribal power struggle, and ensuring Jaburi loyalty to the Baghdad regime – at least for a time.

In 1980, at the start of the Iran-Iraq War, Jaburi was keen to help Saddam: 'I went to my hometown with 50 buses, and came back with 50,000 men.' But years later, when Saddam judged that the Jaburi tribe was growing too powerful, he cut off its patronage, excluded the tribe from his first post-war government, and later purged all Jaburi tribal members from the military. These developments forced Machann Jaburi to choose his tribe over Saddam and to become involved in *coup* attempts against the Baghdad regime. The principal plotters were arrested and executed, at a time when Jaburi was in Paris. He then moved to Damascus and, though losing authority in his own tribe, managed to build up his connections with other recalcitrant clans inside Iraq: Jaburi was then one of the many tribal leaders working to topple Saddam: 'We are trying to make small incidents into large ones. But it won't happen overnight.'[5]

By the mid–1990s, under mounting economic and other pressures, the Saddam regime was coming under increasing threat from the tribal factions. A Jaburi *coup* plotter was discovered among other dissident members of the elite Republican Guard, and in March 2000 members of the Bani Hasan tribe clashed with regular Iraqi forces in the southern marshes. This latter followed another military confrontation between regular troops and members of the al-Dulaimi tribe in north-western Iraq. It seemed that Saddam was losing control over some of the tribal groups. Thus Sami al-Zara al-Hajam, a London-based dissident sheikh of the 8000-strong Bani Hajam tribe, declared that 'the tribes can rise up overnight if the sheikhs give the word' – 'The British know us, because they understand how the tribes work. But not the Americans.'[6]

In 2000 there were signs that the United States was beginning to take more notice of the tribal outbreaks, with some State Department officials making efforts to communicate with dissident tribal groups. But the monarchist Sharif Ali bin Hussein, in contact with US officials, observed that American officials did not feel easy trying to make contact with the tribes: 'When I talk about the tribes, they give me blank stares' – though Sharif Ali himself believed that the tribes were worth cultivating: 'They can take any town, but they can't hold it. For that, they need outside support.' It appeared that Washington could address cultural, ethnic and religious differences but was unable to contemplate family structures, the ties that bind the tribes and pose the greatest threat to a central authority when they unravel.

It is estimated that at least three-quarters of the Iraqi people belong to the country's 150 tribes, where membership involves powerful loyalties and commitments that *in extremis* can threaten the stability of an authoritarian regime. And the *hierarchy* of tribes has traditionally posed various problems for centralised administrators. Since Saddam was from Tikrit, for example, it was always well-known that anyone in dispute with a Tikriti would be at a severe disadvantage, particularly if specific tribal factors could be identified. An individual had always been able to seek protection from his tribe, but tribal leaders were naturally reluctant to exceed their authority in conflict with the Baghdad regime. Again, it may be emphasised that Saddam strove to exploit the tribal structures, in ways that have been largely incomprehensible in the West, to retain power in a potentially very unstable environment. Thus the researcher Judith Yaphe comments:

> Baghdad through the 1990s encouraged the reconstruction of clans and tribal extended families where they existed. In other areas, the government allowed the manufacture of new 'tribal' groups based on economic ties or greed. Where the initiative was weak, Baghdad apparently encouraged prominent citizens to take the initiative or permitted non-leading families to manufacture an entity in order to gain power and wealth ... This has created a new symbiosis ... the state advances the favoured tribes and the favoured tribes protect the state. The state benefits from the absorption of the tribes and the tribes use the state to enrich themselves.[7]

It is easy to see that the 'symbiosis' came under increasing threat in the early 21st century, with the mounting pressure of American plans for another military aggression against the Iraqi people.

Ethnic/Political Opposition

Western observers seldom realise the linguistic and ethnic diversity of Iraq, a country that is unfortunately conflated with Saddam Hussein and treated as one political, cultural and geographical entity. In one listing (Figure 4) no less than 23 languages spoken in Iraq are identified, with

Adyche – 19,000 speakers in Iraq (1993); 280,000 in Middle East and elsewhere

Arabic (Gulf) – 40,000 in Iraq; 2,400,000 elsewhere

Arabic (Judeo-Iraqi) – 100–150 in Iraq, all elderly (1992); up to 125,000 in all countries

Arabic (Mesopotamian) – 11,500,000 in Iraq; 15,100,000 in all countries

Arabic (Najdi) – 900,000 in Iraq; 9,700,000 in all countries; different dialects spoken by various Bedouin groups and elsewhere

Arabic (North Mesopotamian) – 5,400,000 in Iraq; 6,300,000 in all countries

Arabic (Standard) – throughout the region; used for education and official purposes

Armenian – 60,000 in Iraq; 6,836,000 in all countries

Assyrian Neo-Aramaic – 30,000 in Iraq (1994); 200,000 in all countries, including the United States, Australia, Canada, Russia

Azerbaijani (South) – up to 900,000 in Iraq (1982); 13,865,000 or more in all countries

Bajelan – 20,000 in Iraq (1976)

Behdini – spoken in Iraq (estimate needed)

Chaldean Neo-Aramaic – up to 120,000 in Iraq (1994); 200,000 in all countries

Domari – 50,000 in Iraq; 500,000 in all countries

Farsi (Western) – 227 in Iraq; 26,523,000 in all countries

Hawrami – spoken in Iraq (estimate needed); spoken elsewhere

Herki – spoken in Iraq (estimate needed); spoken elsewhere

Koi-Sanjaq Sooret – up to 1,000 in Iraq (1995); spoken elsewhere

Kurdi – 2,785,500 in Iraq; 6,036,000 in all countries

Kurmanji – spoken in Iraq (estimate needed); up to 8,000,000 in all countries

Luri – spoken in Iraq (estimate needed); spoken elsewhere

Shikaki – spoken in Iraq (estimate needed); spoken elsewhere

Surchi – spoken in Iraq (estimate needed); spoken elsewhere

Figure 4. *Languages spoken in Iraq*
Source: *The Assyrian Society of Canada*

acknowledgement that in addition there are many dialects not yet explored by foreign researchers.

Iraq's ethnic and political diversity is indicated also by any comprehensive list of opposition groups that have struggled over the years to secure political and other human rights for oppressed minorities.[8] Here we need only mention the following (not an exhaustive list but indicative):

The Assyrian Democratic Movement;

The Assyrian National Congress (includes the Bet-Nahrain Party and is run from California);

Iraqi Turkomen Front;

Islamic Da'wa Party (Shi'ite);

Kurdistan Democratic Party;

Patriotic Union of Kurdistan;

Turkomen People's Party;

Supreme Council for Islamic Revolution in Iraq (Shi'ite).

In the United States there were Assyrian-Americans lobbying in Washington at both the grassroots and political organisational level, as the uncertainties over the Middle East grew through the 2002–3 period. On 25 April 2003 Congressman Henry Hyde, chairman of the Committee on International Relations, released a letter addressed to Secretary William Burne, assistant secretary of state for Near Eastern Affairs. The letter formally declared the chairman's concerns over the future of the Assyrians, including Chaldeans and Syriacs, in any American plans for the reshaping of Iraq.

Here Henry Hyde drew attention to the 'treatment of the Assyrian community under the current Iraqi regime as it relates to the reported repression of their cultural and religious traditions.' He wondered whether the fact that the Iraqi Assyrians were Christians would 'detrimentally effect their well-being' and whether 'they are required to use Islamic names and forbidden to use traditional or cultural or religious names'. 'What protections', Hyde asked, 'are the Assyrian people enjoying under Operation Northern Watch?' [the US-UK patrolling of the 'no fly' zone). Hyde said: 'I remain a steadfast supporter of President Bush's policy of promoting regime change in

Iraq. I hope that as the administration proceeds to implement this policy, it will be mindful of the unique concerns of the Assyrian community.'

The official reply (Paul Kelly, assistant secretary for legislative affairs) noted that the 'Iraqis of Assyrian, Turkomen and Kurdish ethnicity suffer additional abuses due to the ongoing Arabisation campaign of ethnic cleansing', and observed that 'in northern Iraq Assyrian schools teach using the Assyrian language', that Assyrian parties are allowed to print newspapers and broadcast in Assyrian, that Assyrian villages and churches destroyed by the Iraqis have been rebuilt, and that Assyrian parties participate in regional administration. Kelly did not mention that the Kurdish Democratic Party (KDP) discriminates against Assyrian secondary schools, leaving them unfunded in contradistinction to secondary schools using the Kurdish language.

The Baghdad regime was continuing to oppress tribal factions considered a threat to the regime, though at the same time accommodations were being made with many loyal tribal groups. According to reports in *Kurdistani Nuwe* (23 January 2002) the Baghdad government was continuing with its plans to resettle Arab tribes in the traditionally Kurdish and Turkomen areas of the Shamamik region of the Arbil plains. The Arab tribes (Hadidi, Lahayb, al-Shammawi and al-Jabur) had been armed by the Iraqi government, and supplied with construction materials to help them build their own homes in the villages of Mira, Sadawah, Awenah and Binmarabaz. The Sulaymaniyah newspaper *Hawlati* (21 January 2002) reported that the re-settlement plan had met with fierce local resistance: 'The forces and authorities of the regional government and the political parties in that region have shown indifference and kept quiet regarding these aggressions of the regime.'

Enter the United States

The United States, following Saddam's customary practice, was then trying to buy the allegiance of the Iraqi tribes. Dozens of teams of US troops and intelligence specialists were sent into Iraq with millions of dollars to induce local tribal leaders to turn against Saddam Hussein.[9] This 'cash-squad' campaign, used extensively in Afghanistan, was seen as a critical part of the US-UK military and political strategy being developed to topple the Saddam regime. In the conflict with the Taliban, CIA operatives had carried briefcases full of cash to buy off the local war lords, who responded by withdrawing support from the Afghan regime and identifying factions, sometimes innocent, whom the US military should target. The focus in Iraq was on the Sunni leaders; the Shi'ites, remembering well America's broken promises in 1991 were perceived as less likely to succumb to another phase of US bribery.

The American operatives probably knew that the Sunni Arabs, including Saddam Hussein and most Arabs in the US-backed opposition, accounted for only about 16 per cent of the Iraqi population. The Sunnis, as Saddam's principal supporters, were seen as particularly important in any attempt to wean the Iraqis away from their leader and to undermine the Baghdad regime. Substantial sectors of the Shi'ite population were already hostile to Saddam: if the Sunnis could be bribed over to the West the ideological battle would be largely won and Saddam's position would be terminally insecure.

Among the opposition groups the Iraqi National Accord (INA) tended to be supported by the US State Department, while the Iraqi National Congress (INC) was supported by the Defense Department. Both these groups are dominated by Sunni Arabs (though Ahmad Chalabi, INC head, is a secular Shi'ite), which means – in US reasoning – that a union between such groups and the Sunni tribes within Iraq would make a powerful and effective anti-Saddam coalition.

The Shi'ites had always posed problems for the Baghdad regime.[10] But there were suggestions that they would pose various difficulties for supposed American attempts to remake Iraq as a democratic society. The Shi'ite majority would, in any truly democratic system, quickly acquire all the levers of power in Iraqi society. This in turn would lead to closer ties between a newly-Shi'ite Baghdad regime and its co-religionist Iran, a fully accredited member of the Bush-designated 'axis of evil'. An even worse possibility – from the US perspective – would be that a Shi'ite Iraq would evolve into an Islamic state, in contrast to the evident secularism of Saddam Hussein. Did the United States really prefer the prospect of a new Islamic state that would be predictably hostile to Israel? At least the secular Saddam Hussein had remained deeply hostile to Muslim fundamentalism. And there were other problems to consider.

A Shi'ite Baghdad might encourage militancy among the Shi'ite majority in the Gulf state of Bahrain; and encourage the Kurds in northern Iraq, largely Sunni and fearful of Shi'ite oppression, to demand their own secure independence – a prospect guaranteed to alarm Turkey and Syria with their own resentful and impatient Kurdish populations.[11]

On 25 March 2003, days before the outbreak of war, Saddam Hussein addressed the tribal chiefs in a television broadcast: 'The day has come for you to assume your responsibilities – fight them [the US invaders] with your clans and tribes.' For months, after the Ba'athist regime had stripped the chiefs of most of their powers, Saddam had been courting the tribes with money and arms. When, in the early days of the war, a US Army Apache helicopter was shot down, allegedly by Ali Obeid with his antique bolt-action rifle, the elderly farmer was shown on Iraqi television wearing traditional robes and an Arab headdress – yet another attempt to enlist the country's tribal loyalties.[12]

Even while Baghdad was under daily bomb attack by aircraft and cruise missiles, Saddam managed to hold a meeting with 300 tribal leaders in the capital to win support in the war. The sheikhs wore traditional gold-trimmed robes and carried pistols tucked into their belts. A leader from the al-Boamer tribe in Kabala claimed that 2,000 men under his command were already fighting the advancing US forces. The sheikhs made defiant statements and renewed their pledges to the Ba'athist regime – for which they were rewarded with cash and fresh stocks of weapons.

In 1991, Saddam had convened the first tribal meeting and five years later created a high council of tribal chiefs, rewarding them richly for the oaths of loyalty. The chiefs were given arms, land, extra-judicial powers, foreign cars and even privileges such as exemption from serving in the army. One tribal group remained central – Saddam's own Albu-Nasir tribe based around Tikrit, comprising 50,000 adult men who held all the important military, intelligence and political posts in the regime.[13]

Saddam Hussein recognised the importance of Iraq's tribes, encompassing about three quarters of the Iraqi population. It remained to be seen whether the US-led administration in Baghdad would do the same. Without such a recognition it would prove even more difficult to achieve the required degree of stability in a devastated land.

THREE

Regime Change

The scale of the war and the human cost had quickly become apparent to anyone who cared to notice. Over a period of less than three weeks American tanks had entered Baghdad, the coalition launched around 800 Tomahawk cruise missiles, flown nearly 20,000 sorties, dropped more than 50 cluster bombs and discharged 12,000 precision-guided munitions. Use had been made of a number of air-fuel bombs, each with the explosive power of tactical nuclear weapons. The Iraqi casualties from direct military action were numbered in the tens of thousands, against 88 Allied dead, of whom 34 had been killed by 'friendly fire' incidents or battlefield accidents.

In the early weeks of the war it was impossible to quantify the scale of the civilian casualties: information and estimates available to the Allies were not being released to the public domain. What was known was that after two weeks of war 1,500,000 people in southern Iraq had no access to clean water, 200,000 children in that region alone were at risk of death from diarrhoea, and 17,000,000 Iraqis would soon become totally reliant on food aid which had been stopped by the military action.

Weapons of mass destruction were being used by the Allied forces on a frequent basis. No Iraqi weapons of mass destruction were used or found.

The outcome of the war had always been largely predictable. There was no way that a crippled country of 22 million people could withstand a military onslaught from a superpower of nearly 300 million people currently spending an annual $400,000,000,000 on its war-making capacity. The Iraqi armed forces, subject to punitive sanctions for more than a decade, were quickly overcome. The Iraqi guerrilla resistance would continue but there was no way that the Iraqi people could prevent yet another foreign occupation of their country.

Before and during the war there was much debate in the United States and Britain about what would follow the inevitable military victory. As was predicted, the security structures that had supported the regime were destroyed and the key elements of the regime leadership were crushed. Much of the civil infrastructure had been seriously damaged and there was a massive humanitarian crisis. Unexploded ordnance and radioactive depleted-uranium debris littered the country. Who was to administer the devastated land and address the vital needs of a suffering people? How would a new government for Iraq be constructed in the post-Saddam era? The arguments about such matters were set to continue after the war.

Here it is useful to profile such aspects as the possible UN role, the likelihood of a US military occupation, the exiled contenders, the claims of monarchy and where the trends were leading.

A UN Role?

Even before the end of the war it had been plain that serious differences existed between Washington and Europe on the scale and character of the preferred United Nations involvement in post-war Iraq. In early April 2003 Colin Powell, US secretary of state, emphasised that he would be talking to Kofi Annan about the appointment of a special representative to supervise humanitarian aid, but stressed that the UN's political role was uncertain: 'We all understand the UN must play a role, but the nature remains to be seen.' America and its coalition partners would 'play the leading role to determine the way forward'.

The United Nations, before the war, had speculated on possible scenarios following the military conflict. The 'oil for food' programme, interrupted by war, would be restarted. Perhaps the UN would be asked to take responsibility for much of the civil institution-building required in the wake of war. A mechanism for addressing grievances against the old regime would have to be established, possibly through a 'truth and reconciliation' mechanism or a suitable tribunal. A long-term mechanism for weapons monitoring would need to be established and also some means of monitoring the implementation of human rights throughout the country.

The post-Saddam Iraq would need a new constitution, judicial reform and the creation of security and policing mechanisms. Would the UN have a role in such matters? Here the United Nations considered that it might adopt a role similar to that it had adopted in Eastern Slavonia and East Timor, but that it could not act unless requested to do so:

> The UN role is likely to be determined according to the request of either the new authority or the foreign forces that will provoke a regime change through war. Hence, the UN role may be confined to assisting the new authority in its quest for establishing a new governance structure.

In this context, explored in a UN document 'Portrait of Iraq' (7 January 2003) marked 'STRICTLY CONFIDENTIAL', tasks were specified for 'the first 100 days' and as a 'Road Map for Reform' (two to three years of operations). Thus the United Nations suggested 'some of the major tasks' that would need to be carried out during the first hundred days after the war:

– Devise and implement a transitional justice policy addressing past violations in conformity with UN human rights standards.

– Clarify the applicable legal framework to ensure consistency with international human rights law.

– Carry out a review of existing laws and judicial structures, and a survey of the justice system.

– Launch a national mechanism for rebuilding the justice system.

- Establish a national human rights institution.

- Vet and reconfigure existing law enforcement and corrections institutions.

- Establish a strategy for rebuilding an appropriately-sized security sector under civilian control and protective of human rights.

- Identify training needs and implement a training programme for justice personnel.

The longer-term 'Road Map for Reform' would address such matters as constitutional reform, the electoral system, a programme for strengthening the rule of law, a national system for promoting and protecting human rights, civil service reform, the promotion of a policy dialogue between the government and civil society, and the establishment of such oversight mechanisms as Auditor General, an Ombudsman Office and an independent Human Rights Commission.

The debate about the possible character of UN involvement in the peace continued throughout the period of the war and after – partly to disguise the increasingly transparent nature of the American ambitions. The journalist Ahmed Rashid, writing in *The Daily Telegraph* (28 March 2003), summarised a common perception: 'A bunch of Iraqi exiles run by the CIA are waiting in the wings to take over in Baghdad – and will presumably work alongside an American general who will be the *de facto* ruler of the country.' Washington remained deeply divided about the post-Saddam scenario but it seemed clear that the United Nations would only be allowed to operate in Iraq with American permission.

The Blair regime had views on UN involvement until told by the United States to alter them. For a time Tony Blair himself backed a Kosovo-UN model to introduce a degree of 'internationalisation' to the post-Saddam era but then, under US pressure, agreed to an unqualified American occupation of Iraq. In March it was reported that the United Nations had developed its own contingency plans for a post-Saddam administration but there were no signs that Washington would accede to the United Nations programme. The British Government, before the onset of war, tried to win US support for two new UN resolutions on humanitarian aid and reconstruction of Iraq but was frustrated by the posture of rightwing elements of the American government. On 26 March Blair played down the UN role in Iraq: then he judged it 'premature' to consider the UN role in the country immediately after the conflict. Again the Blair regime had lined up behind the United States, setting the scene for further tensions between Washington and Europe.

On 4 April 2003 France joined Russia and Germany in calling for a rapid end to hostilities in Iraq and for a leading UN role in the administration of the country after the war. The three countries express their alarm at the humanitarian crisis that had been created by the US-led invasion and urged a swift end to hostilities. Dominique de Villepin, French foreign minister, declared: 'The priority now is on the humanitarian side. We are all aware that there is an open crisis in Iraq. There is a humanitarian emergency.' At the same time it was acknowledged that the United States and its allies would inevitably have physical control over Iraq after the conflict was over, but that the United Nations should be given a significant role as soon as possible. De Villepin commented: 'It is absolutely natural ... that in the security phase, the forces present on the ground have a specific responsibility', but when it came to the UN role, 'nobody can hope to build peace alone'.

The US Colony

At one level the American policy, however criminally derelict (Chapter 11), was straightforward. There had been no effective way that Iraq could repel a United States military onslaught, so the war in Iraq had not been basically problematic. 'The problem will be the peace.'[1] Would a federal system be created, to give the local regions of Iraq a degree of autonomy? Would the Kurds insist on developing their own quasi-state in north Iraq? Who would write the new Iraqi constitution? Would the leaders of the former regime be arraigned before a war crimes tribunal? Would such a tribunal require a vote, without a French or Russian veto in the UN Security Council? Who would find and staff the new administration? And who would control the Iraqi oil resource?

There had been much talk of establishing a unified and democratic state, even if the traditional tribal and religious difference meant that elements of power had to be devolved to the regions. What sort of democracy was envisaged? Would all the traditional Iraqi parties be allowed to campaign for power? The Iraqi Communist Party? The

Ba'athist Party? Islamic fundamentalist parties? It was obvious that much would depend on the speed and scale of the American victory, and on the response of the Iraqi population to a foreign military occupation. The persistence of disruptive guerrilla activity would give the US administrators a good excuse to prolong the occupation, to maintain an expanded strategic presence in the region. The historical lessons are illuminating.

When the British were administering the League of Nations mandate over Iraq in the early 1920s it became necessary to establish some sort of national government over the country. Thus at the Cairo Conference of 1921 the British established a political structure that was set to last for a few decades. The imposed laws, institutions and political limitations would remain in effect – and preserve Iraq as a British client state – until the bloody revolution of 1958, which in turn led to the rise of Saddam Hussein. What is interesting is how the British came to establish the new political order after the collapse of the Ottoman authority.

The idea was to inject a Hashemite royal, Faisal, as monarch of Iraq. This was not a locally popular move since the Kurds, Turkomen, Shi'ites, Sunnis, Christians, Jews and others remained fiercely independent, with clear ideas about the status of imposed rulers. The British, indifferent to such details, tried to quell any dissent by manipulating a one-question plebiscite for the Iraqi people: 'Do you agree to Faisal as King and Leader of Iraq?' No other question was allowed, the voting register was uncertain, and the British were the only people in a position to administer the voting procedure. (Was it Stalin who said: 'The key question is not who has the vote, but who counts it'?) The result of the plebiscite was unsurprising. A remarkable 96 per cent of the voters – for reasons that remained mysterious and undeclared – decided to approve Faisal as the new king of Iraq. The British, somewhat puzzled by the evident success they had contrived, concluded that the plan had worked and the country was secure – and they could not have been more wrong. A period of turmoil ensured and the country remained divided and insecure until the time of the Bakr *coup* in 1968 when Saddam Hussein was set firmly on the route to ultimate power.

Such considerations suggest that the task of establishing order in Iraq would not be a straightforward task, and that the United States had done little to think through the massive problems that would be involved in creating a stable state that served Western interests.

Several options *were* discussed in the 2002–3 period, but with little obvious attention to the necessary detail. Perhaps the Iraqi army, without Saddam at its head, would agree to become a pliant servant of Washington. Perhaps a provisional government, acceptable to the United States and drawing on disparate nationalist factions, could be knitted together to form an effective administration. Perhaps a new Faisal could be conjured out of the likely chaos and planted in Baghdad. *Or perhaps the US armed forces would have to maintain a permanent presence until the political dimensions of the new situation became clearer.*

What *was* clear was that a post-Saddam Iraq would be chaotic and that a massive administration burden would descend on the conquering US forces – unless, having achieved a sort of victory, Washington decided to walk away from the business of trying to create a stable political system in the country. Some observers, from a safe distance, suggested that the war against Iraq might destabilise the Middle East, 'but that is precisely what the region needs'.[2] Here it could be argued that the American conquest would be a 'liberation', as if bombing a civilian population is one effective way of removing the political yoke from their shoulders.

The possibility of a US military occupation of a post-Saddam Iraq was being discussed at length, and precedents were being scrutinised to illuminate this option. The United States had imposed a military occupation on Japan and parts of Germany at the end of the Second World War. Perhaps similar arrangements would work in Iraq. Already Saddam and Iraq were being compared to Hitler and Nazi Germany – essentially for rhetorical and propaganda purposes – so perhaps the military occupations imposed in 1945 could provide clues for the proper administration of post-Saddam Iraq.

In August 1990, after Iraqi troops had invaded Kuwait, President Bush, knowing the protocols in such circumstances, quickly branded Saddam Hussein 'Hitler revisited' and 'the new Hitler'. In other depictions Saddam was 'another Hitler', who should not be 'appeased', as had happened with Adolf in the 1930s. One writer, comparing Hitler and Saddam, opined: 'And yes, the one is as bad as the other. There's not a dinar's worth of different between them.' And two US senators, Ted Stevens and John Warner, writing under a *Washington Times* heading: 'Hitler's Disciple in Baghdad', commented: 'As two ... Senators who served in World War II, we see the next Hitler in Saddam Hussein.'

Pundits as widely separated as Noam Chomsky and Patrick Buchanan addressed the question, 'Is Saddam another Hitler?' – and for the most part decided he was not (Buchanan: 'No, this is not the Fuehrer and the Republican Guard is not the Wehrmacht').

A letter in *The Independent* (London) equated the overthrow of Saddam with the 'liberation of the German people from their Nazi slave state in 1945'. Other writers refer to Iraqi soldiers as 'stormtroopers', a manifestly Germanic and Nazi appellation.[3] A speech-writer for President George W. Bush, coining the 'axis of evil' label that supposedly included Iraq, Iran and North Korea, probably knew that the 'Axis powers' in the Second World War at first comprised Nazi Germany and Italy. And it was not long before the image of Winston Churchill was invoked to combat the baleful character of 'Hitler' Saddam.

On 28 August 2002 Donald Rumsfeld, speaking to marines in California, reminded his audience that scepticism had faced Churchill but he had been proved right. In *The Guardian* (London) political editor Michael White discussed why Winston Churchill had been dragged on stage,[4] and celebrated writers and academics were commenting on the bizarre image of 'Churchill' Bush. And much of the commentary focused on the issue of 'appeasement':

If Churchill were alive today, he would strike at Saddam.[5]

Appeasement won't stop Saddam, any more than Hitler.[6]

On 11 October 2002 American officials were commenting that US troops would occupy Iraq as part of a post-war coalition force to stabilise the country until a new government was formed. One option was the creation of a US-run military government in Baghdad. Thus Ari Fleischer, a Bush spokesman, said: 'The administration is determined that, if this becomes a matter of military action, we will not let Iraq fall apart.' He declared further that Washington was working through options to ensure stability, including 'civil affairs units' of the military, playing a role in the governing of Iraq: 'In the process, we want to make certain that stability is achieved so the Iraqi people can have water, food, heat, electricity.' British defense sources acknowledged that only the United States and Britain would be able to mastermind the necessary peacekeeping force of tens of thousands of troops.[7]

The American plan, revealed in *The New York Times*,[8] involved a senior American general becoming the *de facto* governor of Iraq, overseeing the destruction of the (alleged) weapons of mass destruction, and securing the US control of the oilfields. It was suggested that the scheme, modelled on the post-WW2 occupation of Japan, would avoid the hazards of a provisional government run exclusively by civilian nationals. Discipline and order would be imposed by military force, and the Iraqi opposition groups would be left out of the picture for months, if not years. One US official commented: 'We're just not sure what influence groups on the outside would have on the inside. There would also be differences among Iraqis and we don't want chaos and anarchy in the early process.'

In the early phase Iraq would be governed by a US military commander – possibly General Tommy Franks, the commander of the US forces in the Gulf and the man who supervised the Afghan campaign. The imperialist implications of such a scheme were obvious, and leading US opinion formers, including military commanders and John Shalikashvili, former chairman of the Joint Chiefs of Staff, had expressed concern over the feasibility of a long occupation, the likely impact on the Arab world and the possibility of stimulating the flow of recruits into al-Qa'ida ranks. Henry Kissinger commented that he was 'viscerally opposed' to a prolonged occupation of 'a Muslim country at the heart of the Muslim world.[9] Robert Fisk speculated on the possibility that Tommy Franks would have to combine the role of emperor and colonial governor since, unlike the Japan precedent, there would be no surviving emperor to hold the country together.[10] And there were other questions that any putative US governor needed to think about: 'What if the mosques defy the American occupation? What if the Shi'ites in the south and the Kurds in the north set up their own secret administrations? Will the US arrest all the imams who preach against America's hegemony?'[11]

The Pentagon was reportedly enthusiastic about the occupation plan – unsurprisingly, since it would give a US general extensive powers over a country with massive oil reserves. The US State Department had expressed concerns that the occupation would cause an inevitable breach between America and its traditional Muslim allies in the region, sowing the seeds for discord and instability. There would also be a host of associated problems. Would the defeated Iraqi leadership be arraigned before war crimes tribunals? Would there be a process akin to the post-WW2 phase of 'denazification' to purge and purify the society under occupation? Would it be possible, as one senior defense analyst had asked, to determine who were 'the good bureaucrats and who were the Ba'athists'? The experience in Afghanistan was not encouraging. The United States had pledged 'not to walk away from the problem', but in 2003 much of Afghanistan remained chaotic, with local warlords still retaining power and sustaining an oppressive culture little different to that of the Taliban era.

It seemed that many US strategists were nervous about a long occupation but that a short period of American military control might be tolerated. Germany had been administered under foreign military control for four years after 1945, while Japan had been occupied for more than six. No-one in the Bush administration claimed to support an occupation of Iraq for several years, though some pundits were saying that a years-long occupation would be unavoidable. Thus John Chipman, director of the International Institute of Strategic Studies (IISS), commented on 17 October 2002:

> It will certainly be necessary for the US and others to remain present in Iraq ... to incubate the new, necessarily weak government that would in time come to office after regime change. It would be next to impossible to develop a government in exile that could safely be imported. After any war against Iraq, the US and any of its allies would not only have to engage in nation-building, they would also have to do 'region-building' in the Middle East.[12]

On 2 January 2003 *The New York Times* reported that the Bush administration was planning an American military occupation of Iraq that would last for at least eighteen months after the fall of Saddam Hussein. The plan, already in its final stages, called for the prosecution of only Saddam's 'key' lieutenants before war crimes tribunals while 'much of the rest of the Government will be reformed and kept'. Any Iraqi officials who had assisted in toppling Saddam would be offered leniency. And the plan also specified two key objectives: 'to preserve Iraq as a unitary state, with its territorial integrity intact' and 'to prevent unhelpful outside interference, military or non-military' – this last supposedly a warning to neighbouring countries, particularly Iran.

The plan, already presented in detail to President Bush, recognised the significance of the huge Iraqi oil reserves and the matter of creating a transitional government. Bush reportedly did not wish to stay in the country 'a day longer' than was necessary to create a stable situation. In the new scheme the possibility of a civilian administrator was proposed, to deflect criticism of the imperialist implications of a military government. Even the Europeans had expressed alarm at the idea of a US general running a post-war Iraq,[13] and Iraq's neighbours were predictably hostile to the idea. On 24 October 2002 Kamal Kharazzi, Iran's foreign minister, condemned the US plans to install an American general to run Iraq. This 'unwarranted neocolonialism' would never be accepted by Iran, and such administration could lead to future bloodshed and instability.[14]

The Washington strategists continued to speculate on the possibility of a military administration for post-war Iraq, but not all the US planners were keen to support arrangements like those of General Douglas MacArthur in the post-WW2 Japan. On 6 January 2003 one White House official commented to *The New York Times*: 'The last thing we need is someone walking around with a corncob pipe, telling Iraqis how to form a government' – though we may judge MacArthur's smoking habits to be irrelevant. Perhaps the subsequent idea – of a civilian administrator, appointed if necessary by the United Nations – would be preferable; or even a mixed military-civilian administration, though it was easy to predict that the Pentagon would not be keen to tolerate UN (or even civilian) involvement. In any event it seemed plain that some sort of continued US military presence would be essential. The country would be in ruins, the population traumatised and disorganised, and little of the normal infrastructure would be working. In this context it seemed plausible to argue that the US occupation experiences in Japan, Korea and parts of Germany in the aftermath of the Second World War would be highly relevant.

The 1945 occupation of Japan was intended to be an Allied, rather than a solely US, enterprise but the circumstances of the Cold War quickly brought Japan into the American sphere of influence. It is easy to see a similar situation developing in a post-war Iraq. Already it was clear that any military action against Saddam Hussein would be under

US command, and a peacetime administration would obviously be run from Washington. As early as July 2002 senior British defence officials were suggesting that British troops would have to remain in Iraq for five years after the fall of the Saddam regime, though with no suggestion that America would relinquish its primary authority in the region.

In December 2002 US Secretary of State Colin Powell was speculating on America's occupation plans for Iraq: 'Should it come to that, and the president hopes it does not come to that, but should it come to that we would have an obligation to put in place a better regime. We are obviously doing contingency planning, and there are lots of different models from history that one could look at: Japan, Germany.' There are illuminating aspects of the Japanese precedent.

General MacArthur dismantled aspects of the fascist bureaucracy, but also took pains to dislocate the capacity of the socialists to rebuild their political bases. The *zaibatsu* corporations, many with wartime links to the military, were allowed to function as before, but life was made difficult for trade unions that tried to protect workers' rights. MacArthur's basic theory for the occupation was simple and manifestly racist: 'Measured by the standards of modern civilisation, the Japanese would be like a boy of twelve as compared with our development of 45 years'; but the US Army would be able to implant 'basic concepts', such as respect for authority and for institutional power.

One key element in the reform of Japanese institutions was the provision of a new constitution and its supporting legislation. The Japanese authorities seemed reluctant or unwilling to draft a new constitution, so in February 1946 MacArthur ordered his own staff to produce one. This document, with only minor changes, was then adopted by the Japanese government as an imperial amendment to the 1889 constitution and became effective on 3 May 1947. The new constitution invested supreme political power in the Diet, and replaced the House of Peers by an elected House of Councillors. An attempt was made to establish an independent judicial system, and a newly created supreme court was assigned powers to review the constitutionality of new laws. The role of the emperor was reduced to merely symbolic status.

Other reforms focused on female emancipation, an extension of compulsory education, land reform and labour policy. MacArthur was determined to keep the labour unions free of communists, but the post-

WW2 situation of Japan encouraged a fresh labour militancy. When the unions threatened a general strike on 1 February 1947, MacArthur warned that he would take whatever action was necessary to crush such a militant challenge to the new order. It proved impossible to disband the great *zaibatsu* families – Mitsui, Mitsubishi, Yasuda, Sumitomo and others – and, though some changes were made, most continued to behave as in the pre-war days.[15]

The experiences of the US administration in South Korea may also be taken as relevant to what may be expected in a post-war Iraqi environment. Thus the nature of the American occupation was soon made clear to the Koreans and others who had assumed that the defeat of Japan would have brought Korean independence. On 7 September 1945 General MacArthur issued his Proclamation No.1:

> By virtue of the authority vested in me as Commander in Chief, United States Army Forces, Pacific, I hereby establish military control over Korea south of 38 degrees north latitude and the inhabitants thereof ...

> All powers of government ... will be for the present exercised under my authority. Persons will obey my orders and orders issued under my authority. Acts of resistance to the occupying forces or any acts which may disturb public peace and safety will be punished severely.

> For all purposes during the military control, English will be the official language ...

The US military authorities then seemed more hostile to the Koreans than to the Japanese – a surprising situation in view of the declared US aim of liberating subject peoples. Thus Lieutenant-General John R. Hodge, the American commander of US troops in Korea, dubbed Korea an 'enemy country of the United States', duty bound therefore to 'abide by the terms of capitulation'. In the same spirit, Major-General Archibald V. Arnold, the first of Hodge's three military governors, noted the serious problem of finding Koreans to work for the military government who had the 'American version' of integrity and efficiency to handle matters.

He added that Koreans would be given their country when they were fit to run it: 'I have told them that it might be one year, ten years, or fifteen years.'[16] Until that time the American occupation forces would not only continue to employ Japanese officials and pro-Japanese Korean officials but would also preserve the laws enacted under Japanese imperial rule. Thus on 2 November 1945, through 'Military Government Ordinance No. 21', it was announced that 'all laws which were in force, regulations, orders and notices of other documents issued by any former government of Korea having the force of law' would continue in full force and effect. The Korean people, having suffered decades of oppression, were now being forced to endure a new military occupation.

What lessons are there here for the character of a post-war US occupation of Iraq? The main lesson is that political patterns that accord with American interests will be imposed through force. Talk of *liberation* and *democratisation* is no more than sloganising in the context of US global ambitions. This means that the political and economic structures of a post-war Iraq will be structured to conform with the demands of such bodies as the World Trade Organisation (WTO) and its offshoot, the General Agreement on Trade in Services (GATS). A principal aim of GATS is to give private capital unimpeded access to public services throughout the world, which means that in many cases public investment will be made illegal and public services will be run for private profit rather than to meet the needs of people in society. The transnational corporations, in whose interests GATS was created, have not been satisfied with the extent of global privatisation, but are today determined to own and deregulate those surviving public services that are still nominally regulated and funded by national governments.

The consequences of such considerations for a post-war Iraq, being reshaped in the interests of US capital, are that all state-funded enterprises will be given to US-friendly corporations, that the Iraqi people will no longer have a stake in their own oil revenues, and that global penetration by American corporations – motivated solely by private profit – will be massively increased. Such an outcome would do nothing for Iraqi democracy, human rights or the social welfare of the Iraqi people.

In Japan the MacArthur administration made little effort to curb the power of the *zaibatsu*, while suppressing leftist trade unions. In Korea no effort was made to acknowledge the mass political feeling in the South, while Washington continued to support a procession of right-wing dictators.[17] There can be no assumption that a US-orchestrated administration in a post-war Iraq will have any interest in human rights or democracy, and every assumption that the country will be structured for the US command of Middle East oil and the enhanced profits of American corporations.

In the 30 September 2002 edition of the Israeli newspaper *Ha'aretz* American congressman Tom Lantos was quoted as saying to a visiting Israeli: 'Don't worry, you won't have any problem with Saddam. In his place we'll install a pro-Western dictator who will be good for us and you.' Lantos later denied the quotation but *Ha'aretz* refused to publish a retraction. And even if the United States does use its military occupation to 'plant the seeds of democracy', what will be the reaction of the ordinary Iraqi to the foreign invader? James Pinkerton, writing in *Newsday*, asked: 'If America invades Iraq, some 1.2 billion Muslims will still influence the politics of countries from Morocco to Malaysia. So it's an open question. Will Iraqis model themselves after the Americans astride their country, or will they seek aid and comfort from their fellow Muslims around the world?'[18]

It has also been emphasised that the MacArthur analogy is flawed in many crucial particulars. In 1945 the United States enjoyed moral legitimacy. In 2003 few countries were willing to recognise the moral legitimacy of the projected American invasion of Iraq. In 1945 Emperor Hirohito, however much discredited in the wider world, was willing to support the American presence and aid the US plans for reform. Japan surrendered unconditionally, whereas no such convenient outcome could be expected from Baghdad where armed resistance was likely to continue. Any US military occupation, whether disguised by a civilian administrator or not, would be likely to face a fractured and recalcitrant country. In the same sceptical vein an editorial in the *Los Angeles Times* pointed out that, if the Japan model were truly relevant to the Iraq situations, it would be necessary 'to keep Saddam in place and to work through him.'[19]

It seemed that whatever Washington intended with its military presence in Iraq, the Japan precedent could not serve as a model: the American strategists would gain little guidance from the post-WW2 situation in Asia. They would have to begin from scratch, devising appropriate means to benefit US corporations – their main concern. The Iraqi people – already having been punished remorselessly – would have to suffer the consequences.

In January 2003 President Bush's national security team was assembling plans for a post-Saddam Iraq. It was reported that the most senior Iraqi leaders would be tried for war crimes, the country's oilfields would be used to pay for reconstruction, and an American occupation would be maintained for at least 18 months.[20] A civilian administrator, approved by Washington, would run the Iraqi economy, rebuild the schools, develop new political institutions and run the aid programmes. There was no timetable for the handover of responsibility from the military administration to an international civilian administration and eventually to an Iraqi-run government.

There were no signs that the bulk of the Iraqi people, whatever their attitudes to Saddam, would welcome a US-led occupation of their country, a humiliating return to the semi-colonial era before 1958, when treaties were imposed on Iraq to protect British influence in the region:

> Britain maintained military bases and an 'advisor' in every ministry and landowning families like [today's] Ahmad Chalabi of the INC (Iraqi National Congress) were a law unto themselves. There were also 10,000 political prisoners, parties were banned, the press censored and torture commonplace. As President Bush would say, it looks like the re-run of a bad movie.[21]

It seemed obvious that the intended recolonisation of Iraq could not be sold as 'liberation'.[22]

In February 2003 contingency plans were being drawn up by the British Ministry of Defence for up to 20,000 troops to remain in Iraq for three years to prevent the disintegration of the country after the collapse of the Saddam regime.[23] It was judged that such a force, supporting the American 'stabilisation' troops, would be necessary to aid the humanitarian efforts and to prevent the country's fragmentation into a collection of Kurdish, Sunni Muslim and Shi'ite Muslim successor states. Kate Hudson, vice-chairwoman of the Committee for Nuclear Disarmament (CND), commented that the British government should come clean about its long-term interests in Iraq and stop pretending that the war would be about disarmament: 'The British public has a right to know why its money is going to be spent on the illegal occupation of another country when our own public services are crumbling through lack of investment.'

By early February the inner circle of the Bush administration had supposedly thrashed out a scheme for the post-war administration of Iraq. At first there would be a period of US military rule; then a transitional phase with an American military governor ruling alongside a US-appointed civilian leader; and finally a handover to an Iraqi regime sympathetic to Washington. In short, there would be a US colonisation followed by the planting of a puppet government.

After the first phase of military occupation, lasting from six to eighteen months, the military presence would diminish in favour of a US-appointed civil administration. Argument still raged about who would be the civilian governor (or 'High Representative') to rule alongside the US military during the second phase. The veteran peace-broker George Mitchell, with his experience in Ireland and the Middle East, was a possible candidate; Norman Schwarzkopf, military leader in the 1991 Gulf War and popular with the Bush administration, was another.

The third phase of reconstruction remained controversial and vague, with the Bush administration deeply divided about which Iraqis to allow a measure of power in the new Iraq. Dick Cheney, US vice-president, and the Pentagon had long been pushing for a robust role for the Iraqi National Congress (INC) (see *Iraq for Iraqis?*, below); but the CIA and State Department distrusted the INC, regarding it as self-serving and lacking credibility among the Iraqis. There was uncertainty also about how the Ba'athist Party was to be treated in the post-war environment. Were all the Ba'athists tainted by association with Saddam or should some party members be retained to facilitate the basic administration of the country after the war? Many Nazis were left in post in Germany after the Second World War, and many were given lucrative jobs in the United States.[24] The process of denazification had limited scope in the post-war years. What lessons were there in this for the coming 'de-Ba'athisation' of Iraq?

Enter Jay Garner

By mid-February 2003 it was obvious that ex-General Jay Garner would become the effective governor of Iraq after the fall of Saddam. The 64-year-old Garner, who had led Operation Provide Comfort to help the fleeing Kurds at the end of the 1991 Gulf War, was already heading a virtual government-in-waiting created by the Pentagon.

In theory the retired US Army general would quickly make way for a new civilian administrator, perhaps a former state governor or ambassador, who would supervise the transition to an Iraqi government. On 25 February General Eric Shinseki, US Army chief of staff, told the senate armed services committee that Iraq was 'a piece of geography that's fairly significant', and that 'a US military occupation comprising several hundred thousand troops would be necessary'. Assistance from friends and allies 'would be helpful'.

On 26 February President Bush told the American Enterprise Institute, Washington, that a new regime in Iraq would serve as a 'dramatic and inspiring example of freedom' to other nations in the region: 'The world has a clear interest in the spread of democratic values because stable and free nations do not breed the ideologies of murder. They encourage the peaceful pursuit of a better life ... We will remain in Iraq as long as necessary, and not a day more.' At the same time Tony Blair was expressing his support for the American plans, implying that the United Nations would be ignored: 'This argument about the UN is premature. We are not at the stage of determining the details.'[25] At Prime Minister's Questions in the House of Commons Blair had told MPs he believed that the countries whose troops had risked their lives in Iraq were entitled to take the leading role in deciding what was to happen next.

The idea was that Tommy Franks would provide the military security while Garner would operate as 'co-ordinator of civilian administration', providing humanitarian support and administering the lucrative business of reconstruction. Garner was known to be closely linked with a group of Washington Hawks centred on US Defense Secretary Donald Rumsfeld, his deputy Paul Wolfowitz and vice-president Dick Cheney – an American faction that remained keen to exclude the United Nations after the collapse of the Saddam regime.

Some UN officials expressed doubts about the appointment of

Garner to run Iraq. Said one: 'Powell [pro-UN] has already lost the battle. It is clear that Rumsfeld, Cheney and the rest have the ascendancy and they think, having gone it alone in the war, they should get the benefit of being seen as liberators. Garner is their man. He is a true believer.' As president of SY Coleman, a missile system contractor, Garner was involved in the supply of advice and support for the Patriot and Arrow missile systems, used to protect Israel among others. In 1999 the firm won a Star Wars contract worth $365 million to provide US forces with advice on space and missile defense. In 2002 SY Coleman was bought by L–3 Communications and awarded $1.5 billion in March 2003 to provide logistics services to US special operations forces. Garner's attitude to Israel has often been made plain. In 2000 he put his name to a statement declaring that 'Israel had exercised remarkable restraint in the face of lethal violence orchestrated by the leadership of a Palestinian Authority'.[26]

Jay Garner, as a supporter of Star Wars, had helped to undermine the 1972 anti-ballistic missile treaty, and became a strong supporter of unilateral US action in the alleged war against terrorism. Keen to support the development of a strong Israel, he was well prepared to arrange Iraqi recognition of Israel after the fall of the Saddam regime. Many observers, including some in the Bush administration, doubted that the arms-dealing, pro-Israel Garner was likely to bring harmony and stability to a post-Saddam Muslim Iraq.

The controversial nature of Garner's appointment also led to tensions in the Bush administration, fuelled further by disagreements about which individuals would be invited to support Garner in his administrative role. On 1 April the Pentagon vetoed a list of senior officials proposed by the State Department to help run Iraq after the war. Donald Rumsfeld had reportedly objected to the group as 'too bureaucratic' and recommended James Woolsey, a former CIA director and a robust supporter of the war against Iraq. The Pentagon was also keen to offer a job to Ahmad Chalabi, unpopular with the State Department. *The Washington Post* (1 April 2003) reported that the nominated group had been due to leave Washington for Kuwait but had been told to 'stand down' after Pentagon objections.[27]

The disagreements in Washington were widely regarded as unhelpful attempts to create a stable post-Saddam Iraq. Thus Rend Rahim Francke, executive director of the Iraq Foundation, a group promoting democracy and human rights, commented: 'Quarrelling between the US government agencies is terribly detrimental to Iraq. The best way of bringing the Iraqi opposition groups together is to end the divisions inside the US government. There should be one Iraq policy, not five or six.' In early April, with the war well under way, there were still many uncertainties about the composition of the administrative team that would work for Jay Garner.[28] The British government, obviously marginalised, was proposing that a special conference, an Iraqi equivalent of the Afghan *loya jirga*, should be held to determine the composition of the interim administration to be set up after the war.

Garner, brought out of retirement in Florida, announced that he intended to stay no more than 90 days, overseeing the basics of government, distributing aid and starting the process of de-Ba'athisation. While biding his time in a sunny beach villa in Kuwait he declared: 'We're here to do the job of liberating them and providing them with a government that represents a freely elected will of the people. We'll do this as fast as we can. And once it's done, we'll turn everything over to them.' He did not speculate in public about who would write the new constitution for Iraq, or whether Ba'athists, communists and Islamic fundamentalists would be allowed to stand in elections that would represent the Iraqi people's 'freely elected will'.

It was plain that Jay Garner, darling of the American Right, would be influential in the disbursement of contracts to US corporations keen to rebuild an Iraq devastated by the US-led aggression. It was *not* known, when Garner first arrived in Baghdad, that he would soon be exposed as not up to the job and would be sacked after three weeks in post (see Chapter 13).

To the Victor the Spoils

There had long been speculation about the real causes of the war since it quite obviously had nothing to do with 'liberation' or alleged weapons of mass destruction. The US determination to control Iraqi oil resources was an important cause (see Chapter 10) but it was not the only reason for the war. Strategic domination of the region was clearly important to the Washington planners, as were such factors as protection of Israel, support for the US arms industry and the use of intimidation to strengthen America's global posture. And, in addition to the key matter of oil, there were abundant profits to be made in other ways – largely by favoured American companies.

In early April 2003, with the war still raging, American construction companies were being lined up for multi-million-dollar contracts to rebuild Iraq after the war. Talks between the US government and American corporations had been running for months. In early March the US Agency for International Development (USAID) had invited six contractors – Fluor Daniel; Kellogg, Brown & Root (KBR); Perini International; Parsons; Louis Berger; and Bechtel – to tender for a $900 million contract to manage reconstruction work in Iraq. The US Army Corps of Engineers (USACE), responsible for extinguishing the oil-well fires and civil reconstruction in Kuwait after the 1991 Gulf War, had also contacted US firms to discuss post-war work in Iraq. One senior British engineer, commenting to the *Middle East Economic Digest*, remembered what had happened after the 1991 war: 'You only have to look at Kuwait after it was liberated to see what might happen' – British contractors would be squeezed out of the reconstruction bonanza.

USAID was carrying out restricted briefings for selected bidders, and USACE was declining to reveal its post-war plans. When, before the war, British companies approached Trade Partners UK (an arm of the Department of Trade and Industry) for information they were told that war was not inevitable but that the government was in touch with international organisations that would co-ordinate post-war work in Iraq. This did little to reassure British companies keen to exploit the opportunities offered by the prospect of a war-devastated country. Colin Adams, Chief Executive of the British Consultants and Construction Bureau, representing export firms, commented: 'Our own view is, given what the UK is doing in terms of supporting the US, it would not be unreasonable if the UN were to enable UK companies to bid for work. The UK has a lot of experience of working in Iraq.' There were no signs that the US government would heed such commentary.

It was significant that one of the favoured US contractors – Kellogg, Brown & Root – was a subsidiary of Halliburton, the oil-services corporation once headed by Dick Cheney. Halliburton was refusing to give details of the contracts secured for reconstruction in Iraq but confirmed that it was working on relevant plans for the post-war situation in the country (see also Chapter 12). It was also of interest that

Halliburton, determined to develop its interests in a post-Saddam Iraq, was still making annual payments of around $1million to Cheney, well placed as President Bush's deputy to influence the placing of contracts.[29] In fact, having secured a preliminary contract, Kellogg, Brown & Root was already in a strong position to bid for further post-war work.[30]

Wendy Hall, a Halliburton spokeswoman, addressed the question of whether the continuing payments to Vice-President Dick Cheney represented a conflict of interest: 'We have been working as a government contractor since the 1940s. Since this time, KBR has become the premier provider of logistics and support services to all branches of the military.' At the time Cheney resigned as chief executive Halliburton business with the US government amounted to $2.3 billion, and the company was making political contributions of $1.2 million, overwhelmingly to Republican candidates. It was (and remains) a neat system: Halliburton helps to secure election of Republican candidates whereupon they work to expand the company's business with the US government. It is clearly helpful if a leading Halliburton crony happens to be US vice-president.

Before the start of the war, American agencies were planning to establish in Iraq all the institutions of a Western capitalist economy – including a central bank, a finance ministry, commercial banks and financial markets. USAID documents showed that America was very advanced in its commitment to the creation of an Iraqi economy that would be favourable to US corporations. It was suggested – ironically in the light of future events (see Chapter 13) – that troops would prevent the 'looting of bank vaults and government documents', and that technical teams would be ready to move into Iraq 'to assist a vetted Iraqi financial leadership team'. A small 'business lending facility' would be made available, and after six months the central bank and ministry of finance would be operational. Private banks would be offered a 'permissive environment', and if necessary a new currency would 'be ready for issuance'. Then the many state-owned companies would be privatised.

It still seemed clear that all the significant contracts would be offered to US corporations. On 21 March Clare Short returned from the United States, having lobbied fruitlessly for United Nations involvement in post-war reconstruction – an arrangement that might have provided increase flexibility in the placing of reconstruction projects. *The Wall Street*

Journal had already reported that USAID had invited US corporations to bid for work, including running the Iraqi health and education services, with Whitehall lawyers suggesting that there was no legal mandate for that sort of work: 'It's all quite bizarre.' The option was suggested that some UK firms might be invited to act as subcontractors for American companies, just as UN agencies might be expected to take orders from the US occupying power. Justin Forsyth, policy head at Oxfam, said: 'We are worried that the US believes and acts like it can replace the UN in delivery of humanitarian aid and reconstruction. We don't believe they have the skills or the legitimacy.' Then it emerged that Patricia Hewitt, trade and industry secretary, had been lobbying directly with Washington on behalf of British companies, but seemingly to little effect. Andrew Natsios, USAID Administrator, reassured Hewitt that British firms would be given work though no details were made public.

In summary, it seemed highly likely that US corporations would be given all the major opportunities to profit from the war against Iraq:

- At the end of April USAID sent a 12-page synopsis, *Vision for Post Conflict Iraq*, setting out ten priorities, to selected American contractors. The emphasis was on restoring basic services such as water and sanitation, and on establishing democratic government in Iraq. Eight framework contracts were also identified: seaport administration, airport administration, capital construction, logistical support, education, personnel support, public health, and local government.

- USACE was most concerned with the immediate repair of damage caused through war. For example, it was focusing on the restoration of the oil infrastructure, including the extinguishing of well fires. KBR was seen as the key contractor for the oil restoration job; and Halliburton had in turn awarded two fire-fighting contracts to the US specialists Boots & Coots and Wild Wells Control. Other contracts, covering civil reconstruction work and worth a total of about $400 million, were awarded to contractors from a list of mainly US bidders.[31]

On 1 April, a fortnight into the war, it was reported that USAID had selected Stevedoring Services, a Seattle-based company, to manage the captured port of Umm Qasr. The British government was said to be 'deeply unhappy' about the American plan to hand over Iraq's only port to an American corporation. But by now the plan was clear: every element of the Iraqi social infrastructure and economy was to be donated to American companies.

Iraq for Iraqis?

The United States had no doubt that a period of military occupation would follow the war but there was great uncertainty about how the intended transition to a post-Saddam Iraqi regime would be managed. How would a pro-US Iraqi regime be constructed after the fall of Saddam? Would the new political leaders of Iraq be appointed – and by whom? Or would the new leaders be elected – and under what constitution? Would the Iraqis who had lived in exile, some for decades, have a role? How would it be determined? And what would happen if the post-Saddam regime proposed policies that were hostile to American ambitions?

It seemed that the plethora of exiled factions would have made the concept of an alternative regime easy to contemplate: such wide-ranging disparity would seem to suit the idea of a pluralistic democracy – if indeed Washington had the slightest interest in a genuine Iraqi democracy. At the same time the factions were *so* disparate that the idea of a harmonious polity, in which many different views would peacefully strive for power, seemed an increasingly unlikely option. Condoleezza Rice, Bush's advisor, had proclaimed that this time around the United States would be 'completely devoted' to the reconstruction of Iraq as a unified democratic state. A post-Saddam chaos seemed more likely. Rice had stated that the values of freedom, democracy and free enterprise did not 'stop at the edge of Islam', and emphasised the US interest in 'democratisation and the march of freedom in the Muslim world'. But how Iraq's forthcoming new 'democracy', subject to the United States military, was expected to work, remained a metaphysical enigma.

The strategists had long known that in the immediate aftermath of the war there would be appalling conditions of chaos and turmoil. Many Iraqis would be injured, starving, traumatised. The social infrastructure would be totally dislocated, and the human casualties would be numbered in the millions. William Nash, a retired two-star general, stated: 'You are going to start right out with a humanitarian crisis. In the drive to Baghdad you are going to do a lot of damage. Either you will destroy a great deal of infrastructure by trying to isolate the battlefield or they will destroy it, trying to delay your advance. Right away you need food, water and shelter – these people have to survive. Because you started the war, you have accepted a moral responsibility for them.' The sheer scale of the task, to be inherited by the new Iraqi regime after the US military occupation, would clearly require a committed government led by competent people. Where were they?

It seemed clear that Iraq had no obvious sources of new and competent leadership. Some groups – for example, the Kurds – seemed to have little interest in trying to run a post-Saddam Baghdad, preferring to focus on their age-old dream of Kurdish autonomy in northern Iraq and the surrounding states. Some people were suggesting that the leading exile group, the Iraqi National Congress (INC), would be able to provide the basis for an interim provisional government pending democratic reform. But the INC, sustained by America funds and lacking support inside Iraq, seemed an unlikely route to a stable post-war country. So what would the American occupiers decide to do? Run the place themselves? Conjure a useful puppet out of thin air? Or hand over power to a disunited, inexperienced and unpopular exile group? One observer suggested that the Americans would have to begin a process of *'loya-jirgasation'*. In such a fashion a leadership might be elected or selected to supervise the progress to a transitional government.[32]

The Washington strategists took heart at the series of failed *coup* attempts, some supported by the CIA, against the Saddam regime. At least there were dissident groups prepared to be active in the anti-Saddam struggle. Washington began its support for the Iraqi National Congress in the hope that the dissident organisation might eventually emerge as an alternative Iraqi government. Whether or not the INC had any democratic credentials was irrelevant: the important consideration was that the organisation was bitterly opposed to Saddam and prepared to posture as an alternative government.

The Iraqi National Congress was formed when the two main Kurdish factions – the Kurdistan Democratic Party (KDP) headed by Massoud Barzani, and the Patriotic Union of Kurdistan (PUK) headed by Jalal

Talabani – decided to attend a 1992 meeting in Vienna comprising nearly 200 delegates from dozens of opposition groups. The Kurds were prepared to participate in a conference that might advance a range of ethnic and other ambitions. In October 1992, four months after the convention, the major Shi'ite groups joined the coalition, whereupon the INC held a pivotal meeting in northern Iraq. A three-man leadership Council and a 26-member Executive Council were chosen, suggesting that the many dissident Iraqi groups were adequately represented. Even at that time the United States was working to influence the composition of the INC leadership. One of the three Council leaders was Bahr al-Ulum, a relatively unrepresentative Shi'ite cleric who was acceptable to the United States. Ahmad Chalabi, a Shi'ite who had previously worked as chairman of the Petra Bank in Jordan, was selected to chair the Executive Council. Washington was content that Chalabi, later perceived as largely ineffectual, would present no political challenge to American interests in the region.

The INC was the first major attempt made by Saddam's opponents to unite around a common platform – one that conveniently matched US values. The main US interest, as always, was the consolidation and extension of capitalist enterprise: but, as always, this naked obeisance to pure greed had to be cloaked in attractive garb. The INC programme included the establishment of 'human rights and rule of law' within a constitutional, democratic and pluralistic Iraq; the country's territorial integrity would be preserved, and there would be full compliance with international law. The INC, condemning the Iraqi invasion of Kuwait, proclaimed its commitment to the emirate's sovereignty. In its early days the INC refrained from declaring itself a provisional government, but the course was set. The organisation began seeking international support as a viable and democratic alternative to the Saddam regime. In due course, despite ceaseless internal bickering and ideological differences, the INC responded to American encouragement – rarely consistent – and claimed the status of an alternative Iraqi government.

The internal political differences soon emasculated the INC as a viable challenge to Saddam Hussein. In May 1994 the two main Kurdish parties began fighting each other over territorial claims in northern Iraq, while seeking outside support for their respective positions. The INC struggled to adjudicate between the disparate claims, and in the process found itself diverted from the main task of fighting the Saddam regime.

One consequence was that dissidents began looking to alternative organisations that might provide a more realistic opposition in the harsh world of Iraqi politics.

One group, the Iraqi National Accord (INA), headed by Iyad Alawi, comprised mainly military and security officers who had defected from Iraq and who claimed residual influence over the various military and security élites that surrounded Saddam. But it soon seemed obvious that the INA would be no more successful than the INC in tackling the Iraqi regime. In the mid–1990s King Hussein of Jordan gave permission for the INA to operate in his country, but the organisation was soon penetrated by the Iraqi intelligence services. In June 1996 Baghdad arrested 100 military officers with links to the INA and thirty others were executed. Alawa, struggling to keep the INA ambitions alive, continued to claim that sympathisers were continuing to operate throughout Iraq – though clearly to little effect.

In late-August 1996 Saddam's forces launched an attack on an INC base in Salahuddin, a city near Arbil in northern Iraq, and at the same time routed the few pockets of remaining INA operatives in the region. Some 2,000 oppositionists were arrested and about 200 were executed. About 650 activists, mainly INC, were hurriedly evacuated to the United States under the parole authority of the US Attorney General. The dissident groups have never fully recovered from such catastrophic reverses, and the INC has continued to be plagued by internal dissent, vacillating American support and unremitting pressure from the Iraqi intelligence services.

Ahmad Chalabi, despite the problems of the INC, remained one of the prominent oppositionists favoured by various influential US pundits and politicians. Then he was one of the six members of the leadership Council and operated as the INC's chief strategist and head of intelligence. He appears unconcerned about threats to, and attempts on, his life by the Mukhabarat, Saddam's intelligence service: 'I don't like to talk about attempts on my life. The details are sordid – thallium, rockets, car bombs, snipers. Many of our people have been killed by thallium. There have been many deaths in northern Iraq – that's what matters.' But it seemed that Chalabi, despite retaining well-placed support in the United States, no longer had the confidence of the US government.

Then the CIA, headed by George Tenet, had little contact with

Chalabi who had contacts in the Pentagon and the Defense Intelligence Agency. Bob Baer, a former CIA officer oblivious to his own unconscious racism, applauded Chalabi: 'He knows how to make himself clear and knows what they want to hear. He doesn't go round in circles like every Arab you ever sat down with in the Middle East.' Chalabi had always claimed that he had no ambitions to stand for office in a post-Saddam Iraq: 'This is about creating a civil society, liberating Arab history from despotism. The thing about a civil society is that there are common ideas about how it should be run – what people think of taxation, health and education services. That is what binds them now.' Such remarks, uttered in a comfortable part of central London, seemed far removed from the US determination to launch a fresh and overwhelming attack on the Iraqi nation. (After the fall of Saddam, Chalabi returned to Iraq with a small private army but still maintained that he was not seeking office.)

Chalabi's seemingly modest attitudes to power did not prevent comments about his being 'the man who could be Saddam Hussein's successor'.[33] In April 2002 he visited the United States to encourage the Bush administration to press ahead with its plans to topple the Iraqi regime: 'We are always in a hurry because every day that passes, we want to get him out. But great powers move at glacial speed. We want to move them faster.' Chalabi was interested also in securing American help with the training of INC personnel to fight the Iraqi forces. He complained that though training was being given 'we're not getting any lethal training'; and yet again Saddam was likened to Hitler: 'Saddam is a hybrid of Stalin, Hitler and Genghis Khan. He has medieval clan loyalties and ways of thinking combined with modern propaganda and the use of media with a militaristic approach which is Hitler-like.'[34]

The United States still seemed reluctant to embrace the INC wholeheartedly, even though Chalabi had struggled for support over the years. At the same time Washington was retaining its contacts with various INC members, such as the various Kurdish factions. Thus in May 2002 it was reported that US officials had met secretly in Germany with Massoud Barzani and Jalal Talabani, to explore ways in which the Kurdish groups could assist the United States in toppling Saddam Hussein. At the same time, according to *The Washington Post*, the Bush administration remained deeply divided about which opposition groups to support. A measure of support for the INC would continue – on 11 June 2002 the US State Department gave the INC $5 million to cover the year's operating expenses – but links were also being built up with other Iraqi groups such as the Group of Four, constituent parts of the INC independent of Chalabi. Richard Boucher, State Department spokesman, said that discussions with the various groups were continuing, and that a conference of the groups would be held later in 2002 to consider how to govern Iraq after the collapse of the Saddam regime.

The lukewarm US support for the INC was attributed to the State Department's wariness of the organisation's pro-democracy agenda. Again there were clues that the Washington strategists had no enthusiasm for a democratic restructuring of Iraq during the turbulence of a post-Saddam era. At the same time there were tensions between the Pentagon, a recipient of INC intelligence, and the CIA, not normally provided with INC data from Iraq. It seemed that a Washington turf war was sending confusing messages to the Iraqi opposition groups, with journalists commenting that Washington's 'confused double-think' was unhelpful to Iraqi attempts to overthrow the Saddam regime.

In July 2002 a two-day meeting in Vienna between Kofi Annan, UN secretary-general, and Naji Sabri, Iraqi foreign minister, on the return of UN weapons inspectors to Iraq was followed, a week later, by a large gathering in London of about 90 former Iraqi military officers planning the overthrow of Saddam Hussein. Major-General Tawfiq Yassiri, hosting the gathering in Kensington Town Hall, commented on the scale of support: 'The response has been amazing. People are coming from all over the world to take part. We welcome any Iraqi who wants to contribute.'[35] It was then possible to identify most of the leading oppositionists, some of whom were present at the Kensington Conference:

Major General Tawfiq Yassiri, former army commander wounded in the uprising against the Iraqi forces in 1991; leader of the Iraqi National Coalition and organiser of the London meeting;

General Nizar Khazraji, former chief of staff of the Iraqi military; defected in 1995 and then living in Denmark; dubbed 'Iraq's Hamid Karzai'; accused by critics of using chemical weapons against Kurdish civilians and Iranian troops;

Major-General Wafiq al-Samarrai, former head of Iraqi military intelligence; lived in London; favoured covert action to overthrow Saddam Hussein;

Major-General Najib al-Salhi, commander of an armoured division of the Republican Guard in the 1991 Gulf War; defected in 1995 and headed Iraqi Free Officers Movement; received most votes in a leadership election held by Iraqi exiles on the internet;

General Fawzi Shamari, commanded nine divisions in the Iran-Iraq War; defected in 1986; headed Iraqi Officers Movement in United States;

Ahmad Chalabi, Massoud Barzani, Jalal Talabani and Iyad Alawi;

Sharif Ali bin Hussein, cousin of Iraq's former King Faisal II who was assassinated in 1958, London-based banker; headed the Constitutional Monarchy Movement;

Ayatollah Muhammad Baqer al-Hakim, head of the Supreme Council for the Islamic Revolution in Iraq; formerly based in Tehran and backed by Iran; represented interests of Iraq's majority Shi'ite Muslims.

The organisers of the Kensington meeting, well aware of the varying ambitions of the participants, were keen to secure an agreed commitment that the overthrow of the Saddam regime would not lead to the replacement of one dictatorship by another. The declared aim was to establish a democracy, possibly structured on federal lines, that would reflect Iraq's three dominant groups (Shi'ite, Sunni and Kurd), with the military excluded from a political role and confined to defensive duties. But the tensions between the participants were already evident. Some of the exiles in the United States and London wanted a strong leader to replace Saddam: it would plainly be necessary to impose authority as quickly as possible after Saddam's fall, to avoid social chaos and to prevent an ethnic civil war.

On 13 July Brigadier-General Saad Alobaidy, speaking for the conference, called on the British government to help to overthrow Saddam Hussein and to install a democratic government in Iraq. The opposition, he emphasised, needed such help from Britain and the United States to end thirty years of rule by the Iraqi dictator: 'I would like to thank the British government for allowing us to hold our meeting in London. Now we need Britain and America to help us persuade the people of Iraq that the time has come for Saddam to go.' Alobaidy acknowledged that it would be difficult to topple the regime because Saddam 'remains very strong'.

Critics of the conference suggested that the participants were out of touch with real events in Iraq, that assumptions about the likelihood of an army uprising were misplaced, that the conference had shown too many internal disagreements, and that in any case the whole exercise had been nothing more than a transparent move by London and Washington to garner support for an anti-Saddam campaign. Even the Iraqi Communist Party had been welcomed in Washington in an attempt to gain more information about events in Iraq. One observer suggested that the US lack of knowledge about the Iraq issues was 'unlikely to be rectified by the London conference'. Many of the exiled officers had not visited Iraq for years, and the Kensington gathering was widely perceived as little more than a talking shop that would have little practical effect on the ground. A working group had been established to open contacts with senior officers in Iraq and encourage them to revolt. Such pious aspirations seemed to have little connection with reality.

The conference participants emphasised that they would welcome 'any foreign help' to depose Saddam, and urged Iraqi soldiers inside the country to assist in ending the Saddam regime. The question of federalism was raised, and left unresolved. The Turkomen representative and some others urged that the decision on the system of government in a post-Saddam Iraq should be left to a popular referendum, but the Kurds declared that an early post-war referendum would only inflame ethnic and sectarian rivalries. And there was constant reference to the character of an army collapse in the event of a US-led invasion of the country: 'Morale is at a disastrous level and the troops are sick of continuous war. Saddam will find himself surrounded by a few hundred soldiers.' Major-General Najib al-Salhi, voicing this judgement, commented also that concern about Saddam's chemical and biological weapons was misplaced: he did not have the means to deliver such weapons. The US, he asserted, should make it clear that it was only opposed to Saddam and not the army, otherwise army defections could not be relied upon: 'This cannot be two armies facing each other. The United States must make it clear that it is only after Saddam's head.'

The conference had passed off without incident. A council had been elected and various pious aspirations proclaimed. British and American observers had maintained a discreet presence, and doubtless a few Saddam spies had monitored the proceedings with interest. The deep divisions among the representatives had been largely kept under wraps, but these were due to surface later.

On 25 July 2002 the INC issued invitations to a press conference in Kensington to announce 'plans for a provisional government to be established on Iraqi soil'. The INC was supposed to be joined by another group, the US-based Iraqi National Movement (INM) lead by the exiled general, Hassan al-Naquib. The monarchist Sharif Ali bin Hussein had already declared: 'Saddam's regime is about to fall. We must move from being exiled opposition into preparing a broadbase provisional government representing all Iraqis.' But hours before the press conference was due to be held, the INC announced it had been indefinitely postponed 'to enable further discussion among Iraqi opposition groups'. Dilshad Miran, the London representative of the Kurdistan Democratic Party (KDP), commented: 'A provisional government is not something to be taken lightly. It dents the credibility of the opposition and reinforces the impression that it is disunited. We are not happy with what is going on. The INC is not functioning.' Journalists judged that the Iraqi opposition groups had fallen into 'open disarray'.[36] Other commentary also noted the significance of the fiasco:

> Saad Saleh Jabr, head of the London-based Free Iraqi Council, said that to announce a provisional government was stupid: 'It's too early, too premature. The guys who are not in will be all against it.'

> Brigadier Tawfiq Tassiri, who had hosted the Kensington Conference, commented: 'A provisional government is usually the last card for an opposition in exile to play. If you play it now you burn it prematurely and you create a new target for the enemy to attack and possibly destroy.'

> Officials from the British Foreign Office also described the announcement of a provisional government as 'premature'.

It seemed plain that the hundreds of exiled Iraqi representatives and the dozens of groups they espoused were hopelessly disunited. It had proved impossible to create a stable base of unity and purpose, and it was easy to see why Washington and London were contemplating options other than an imported provisional government for a post-Saddam Iraq.

On 9 August 2002 the Bush administration, still prepared to maintain contact with the Iraqi opposition groups, met what journalists chose to call 'six rivals to Saddam's seat'[37] – Sharif Ali, Chalabi, al-Hakim, Barzani, Talabani and Alawi. It was regarded as a significant diplomatic achievement that: 'the notoriously divided opposition and the increasingly split [Bush] Administration were able to sit down together'.[38]

Francis Brooke, the INC's advisor in Washington, also indicated the divisions in the Bush camp. Vice President Dick Cheney had agreed to join the talks via a video link, and Donald Rumsfeld had agreed to speak to the opposition leaders, but Brooke perceived that the situation was unclear: 'This is more about the divisions within the Bush administration than about divisions among the opposition.' The Iraqi opposition, Brooke insisted, was unanimous. It seemed significant that neither Bush nor Cheney had been prepared to appear alongside the opposition leaders at a joint press conference, though INC spokesmen continued to praise the level of American commitment to toppling the Saddam regime. Thus Sharif Ali bin Hussein declared:

> It was absolutely clear to us that the United States is completely serious, committed and determined to bring about a regime change in Iraq. We were very heartened by what we heard and we will be passing on the message to the Iraqi people that their liberation is, God willing, going to happen soon. They support a democratic regime in Iraq. They would not support replacing one dictator with another. Their vision for Iraq was for a free Iraq that was democratic and liberalised.

However, it was clear that, despite large areas of agreement, a consensus had failed to emerge. What exactly would be the role of the exiles? How could such a role be combined with that of the traditionally strong institutions such as the military, the tribes and the government bureaucracy. One participant suggested that the trick was to devise a scheme whereby the exiles would be given a role but where they do not control the transition to the new system of government. Other meetings had already been held on such topics as possible legal systems, the financing of the transition and the role of the media. It was intended that future meetings would focus on health and 'outreach' efforts to convince the world that the Iraqi people actually supported the efforts to oust the Saddam regime.[39]

The problems facing the United States in trying to devise a post-Saddam scenario seemed obvious. There would be a post-war chaos and no opposition leader equipped to replace Saddam Hussein. In the words of one journalist: 'If Saddam Hussein is America's frying-pan, these men [the opposition leaders] are the fire into which President Bush may be jumping.' In this view the US would need its own strongman to put in Saddam's place – and none was available. And there was a veritable 'cacophony of proclamations from new movements, councils and parties that purport to represent the voice of the authentic Iraqi individual.'[40] The various contending bodies included:

- national organisations created inside Iraq before 1990;

- groups representing sectarian or ethnic interests;

- new groups, often formed under US auspices after 1990.

It was of little comfort to the Washington strategies that some of the most widely supported organisations included the Iraqi Communist Party and the al-Da'wa al-Islamiyya (Islamic Call), the latter with close ties to the Islamic radicals in Iran. Many of the groups, though large, were of little use to the US strategic plans since they were unsympathetic to American global ambitions and in any case were often deeply divided within their own ranks.

Ahmad Chalabi remained on the fringes and was quite prepared to applaud any American suggestion – even the notion of a military governorship for Iraq – if he thought it would increase his influence in the Bush administration. Many of the US schemes continued to sideline the Iraqi exiles, if only because no pro-American Iraqi strongman could be discerned in the exile community. There was no Arab Karzai on the horizon who might be expected to impose a nationalistic order on post-war Iraq in ways that would conveniently accord with Washington's ambitions for oil and strategic advantage.[41] By 2003 it seemed clear that the United States would have to be deciding on the form of the post-Saddam government in Iraq, and perhaps this would involve the choice of a Saddam successor.[42]

The Bush administration was reportedly training scores of civil servants to administer the transformation of the Iraqi economy in the aftermath of military strikes – and the effort was said to have cost hundreds of thousands of dollars. The State Department had contracted a private firm, the Virginia-based ICF Consulting Company, to train Iraqi exiles in economics, accountancy and finance *in preparation for restructuring the country's state-controlled into a Western, market-driven economy*. Entifadh Qanbar, director of the Washington office of the INC, said that he was aware of the training being provided by ICF, believing that up to one hundred Iraqis had been involved in the programme. Faisal Qaragholi, the London-based INC operations officer, commented: 'It will be important for Iraqis in the West to help bring up standards, to try and develop different ways of looking at things.'

Further opposition meetings were held, though consensus was as illusive as ever; and a blow was struck against the exile factions when unwelcome publicity attached to the war-crimes reputation of General Nizar Khazraji, a likely member of any pro-US provisional government. On 19 November 2002 Danish police arrested the general and charged him with war crimes, violating the Geneva Conventions and other human-rights abuses. An opposition spokesman said: 'His arrest is a major setback for us. He is a man with credibility back home. His arrest will make it that much harder to encourage other officers to defect if they fear that they will be charged too.' It was now plain that the Iraqi opposition was not only incompetent and divided, but also tainted with many of the crimes being levelled at Saddam Hussein and his circle. Washington and London continued to explore their plans for a post-Saddam Iraq but their task was not made easy by the quality of the Iraqi opposition leaders. There was not much in this to encourage optimism about a smooth transition to any form of democratic government in the country.

On 13 December 2002 some 300 opposition delegates representing around fifty ethnic, religious and political groups converged on a London hotel to develop their plans for regime change in Iraq and what would follow. Again, councils were elected, fine sentiments expressed, disagreements aired and a few practical conclusions reached. There was nothing here resembling a provisional government, and Washington had still failed to find a convincing leader to hold together the dislocated and devastated Iraq that the United States was determined to create.[43] A power struggle was then discernible among the opposition groups, Washington continued to develop its war plans, and work was under way on collecting evidence for a war-crimes tribunal – not for General Khazraji but for Saddam Hussein and the men close to him. Now there was speculation that Saddam might 'go the same way as Milosevic' – a fate that seemingly befitted all the 'new Hitlers' that Washington could label and apprehend, unless of course they had an interest in serving the United States and advancing the cause of American corporations around the world.

In early February 2003 it was announced that America intended to install Ahmad Chalabi as the interim president of Iraq once Saddam Hussein had been overthrown. Thus a Bush administration official told *The Daily Telegraph* (London): 'It's pretty clear it's going to be Chalabi, barring some dramatic development during the war.' But, the official added, it would be a mistake to reach any firm conclusions until the war was over. Chalabi remained popular with the Pentagon's civilian leadership and Dick Cheney, but senior figures in the State Department were still arguing against him: 'One school of thought was that people in Iraq would resent someone from outside.' Chalabi himself had always been keen to promote the political rights of the exile community:

> It is necessary to begin planning for the transition to democracy immediately, and the democratic Iraqi opposition should form the nucleus of a transitional administration. That should immediately expand to include those Iraqis currently living under Saddam's control as soon as it is safe ...
>
> The idea that Iraq's different ethnic or religious communities will propel the country into chaos is a myth. It is a convenient preconception that fits the Western image of unruly and warring tribes but it is untrue. In Iraq there is no primary violence between communities. Communal violence in Iraq is a political phenomenon.[44]

In this context there was no record of a Shi'ite village attacking a Sunni village or of an Arab quarter attacking a Kurdish quarter. Violence was fomented by political forces for their own benefit: 'From the isolation of an outlaw nation, we yearn to participate openly in the social, commercial and political life of the golden age.'[45]

The Bush administration, having favoured Chalabi, then moved to marginalise him – to the point that a leading INC member even raised the possibility of an Iraqi revolt against the American occupation troops after the war was over. Chalabi said, of the US approach: 'Their vision is of US military officers three deep in every ministry. It isn't workable.'[46] There was now an obvious rift between the Washington and the exile groups, though Zalmay Khalilzad, the Bush administration's special envoy to Iraq, was trying to repair the damage: the Iraqi people, he declared, should be allowed to run their affairs 'as soon as possible'.

A meeting of exiles in Iraqi Kurdistan at the end of February was overshadowed by the presence of heavily armed Americans. Again the tensions between Washington and the opposition exiles was plain, with Chalabi writing in *The Wall Street Journal*: 'American help is essential and is welcome in winning the fight against Saddam. But the liberation of our country and its reintegration into the world community is ultimately a task that we Iraqis must shoulder.'[47] In Washington the battle over the reshaping of post-war Iraq continued, with the State Department fighting to prevent the Pentagon from installing Chalabi as the interim leader of Iraq.

A principal reason for the Pentagon shift was that Rumsfeld, Wolfowitz and others had finally realised that Chalabi's intelligence was worthless. Despite what he had long declared, the Iraqi army and civilian regime were not about to crack and fall apart. Chalabi appeared to have no insight into the mood in Iraq – a simple fact that would be patently obvious when the war began.

A Monarchy Restored?

The pretensions of the US and Britain to democracy have never been allowed to deter their enthusiasm for pliant monarchies around the world to protect Western economic and strategic interests. This obvious fact has been particularly evident in the Middle East where monarchies, emirates and sheikhdoms have not only been buttressed by the West over the decades but planted by the West in the first place. Thus Britain connived at the secession of Kuwait, once part of the Ottoman vilayet of Basra, under the upstart Sheikh Mubarak; aided the acquisition of most of the Arabian peninsula by the Saud family; and was influential in the creation of the smaller Gulf emirates that in consequence were reliably pro-British. We should also remember that Britain planted monarchies in Jordan, Iraq and (in concert with other powers) Libya – a process that had nothing to do with democracy or the protection of human rights.

Washington has enthusiastically supported such historical British achievements as likely to be sympathetic to Western economic penetration and strategic advantage, and been distressed when pro-West monarchies have been overthrown. Thus the United States and Britain were anguished when King Farouk was forced to abdicate from the Egyptian throne in 1952, when the Hashemite monarchy was crushed in Iraq in 1958, and when the young Muammar Gaddafi overthrew the Idris monarchy in Libya in 1969. There was much Western concern when the Iranian Pahlevi dynasty was toppled by the ayatollahs in 1979, an event that buttressed the power of Saddam Hussein and fed all the associated turmoil that was to follow.

The British and American enthusiasm for monarchies – and, where appropriate, dictatorships – has suggested to some observers that the West may welcome the restoration of a monarchy in a post-war Iraq. As the war drew to its bloody close in April 2003, having brought chaos and misery to the bulk of the Iraqi people, the possibility of a restored monarchy seemed unlikely. The United States then had other plans. But the royal option, as implemented in history and advocated by monarchists today, remains instructive. The creation of the Libyan monarchy by Britain and other states in the immediate aftermath of the Second World War was significant in this regard.

Libya had been liberated from an Italian colonial occupation but was then forced to tolerate a British, French and American presence. The Western powers had no interest in bringing democracy to Libya and were concerned only with economic opportunities and strategic advantage in the circumstances of the Cold War. On 7 October 1951, under the nominal auspices of the United Nations, a Libyan constitution was introduced creating a monarchy that could be relied upon to safeguard Western investments, Western military bases and Western control of much of the territory of a supposedly independent Libya.

The 1951 Constitution of the United Kingdom of Libya was shaped by both domestic pressures and external influences. The Libyans themselves, with little experience of detailed legal drafting and national constitutional autonomy, had been heavily reliant on substantial input from the UN Commissioner, the pro-West Adrian Pelt, and other foreigners with their own perceptions of how Libya should fit into the post-WW2 world. The constitution, congenial to the Western powers, enshrined an Islamic monarchy enjoying authoritarian powers over a two-chamber parliament. The preamble to the constitution began and ended with religious affirmation, and – with Articles 44 to 77 – affirmed the role of the King. Here there was no doubt about the extensive powers of the monarchy. The sovereignty of the United Kingdom of Libya was entrusted 'to King Mohamad Idris Al Senussi and after him to his male heirs', with 'the order of succession to the Throne ... determined by Royal Decree promulgated by King Idris I ... The Royal Decree ... shall have the same force as an article of this Constitution.'

The King, according to the constitution, was above the law (though pledged to observe the laws of the country) since he was 'inviolable' and 'exempt from all responsibility'. He 'sanctions and promulgates the laws' and 'in exceptional circumstances' could issue decrees that had 'the force of law' (though they had to be approved by parliament). The King could also adjourn parliament for thirty days (though only once during the same session), and he could declare war, conclude peace, enter into treaties (with the approval of parliament), and proclaim martial law and states of emergency (also with the approval of parliament). Parliamentary acquiescence could generally be guaranteed since the King appointed ministers:

> The King shall appoint the Prime Minister, he may remove him from office or accept his resignation; he shall appoint the Ministers, remove them from office, or accept their resignation ... the King shall appoint diplomatic representatives and remove them from office ... The King shall establish the public services and appoint senior officials and appoint them ... the Council of Ministers shall consist of the Prime Minister and of the Ministers whom the King deems fit to appoint ... the King may appoint Ministers without portfolio in case of necessity.

Hence the authority of the King was made explicit throughout the constitution, with Article 197 guaranteeing the permanence of the monarchy: 'No provision may be made to review the provisions relating to the monarchal form of government, the order of succession to the Throne ...' The Western powers had succeeded in installing Sayyid Idris as their instrument for continued hegemony in the region. If Libyan independence could no longer be blocked or delayed, then the West was determined to prevent – via the mechanism of an authoritarian monarchy – the emergence of a genuine democracy in North Africa.

The Iraq case, predating the planting of Idris in Libya, was familiar. In March 1921 Winston Churchill, then British colonial secretary, convened a conference in Cairo to consider how his government's responsibilities should be implemented in the Middle East. One consequence was that the 1916 Arab Bureau was superseded by the newly created British Colonial Office Middle East Department. Under the terms of the Cairo scheme Mesopotamia was renamed Iraq and the Hashemite royal, Faisal bin Hussain, son of Hussain bin Ali of Mecca, was installed as king. The cynical deal, a betrayal of Arab aspirations to independence, secured continued Royal Air Force (RAF) bases in Iraq and arrangements for the administration of Faisal's Iraq by Anglo-Persian Oil Company officials. When the US State Department protested on behalf of American Standard Oil Lord Curzon, British foreign secretary, felt confident enough to declare on 21 April 1921 that no concessions would be given to American companies wanting access to the oil resources of the British Middle East.[48]

King Faisal, the first of the Hashemite family to rule Iraq (1921–33), considered that the army was an essential 'protective force' to guarantee his reign. He well appreciated the possibility of an uprising against a monarchy seen to be installed by unpopular foreign powers, and the need in such circumstances to have a means of suppressing the people. The corollary, as in many other states, was that if the army – by bribery and foreign inducement – could be kept loyal, the monarch would be seen to have legitimacy and authority. But there was no suggestion that Faisal's armed forces would be allowed to serve as a route to Iraqi independence. When the Ministry of Defense under Jafar al-Askari was created in 1921, the Iraqi armed forces comprised three elements:

– some 33 battalions of the British imperial troops;

- a detachment of the RAF;

- about 4,000 Iraqi Levies, mainly Assyrians.

The 1921 Cairo conference had ensured that all elements of the Iraqi armed forces would be under the control of the British. The funding was provided from London and Iraqi defense policy was determined solely by the British government, though efforts were made to suggest a joint British-Iraqi approach. Britain provided training and equipment for the subsequent expansion of the army following a 1922 decision in the British Cabinet. In 1927 al-Askari introduced a conscription bill that was blocked by London, but in 1934 King Faisal issued the Decree of Civil Defense requiring every Iraqi to serve time in the army. Britain maintained control over the Iraqi armed forces, supplying all the necessary support and sending Iraqi graduates to Britain in an effort to supervise their progress and to guarantee the necessary ideological loyalty to their colonial masters.

The pattern was clear. The pro-West Faisal had been planted in Iraq; and the area of Transjordan (later Jordan) – once dubbed the 'vacant lot' between Palestine, Syria and Iraq – had been donated to Faisal's brother Abdullah, another reliably pro-West Hashemite. But Iraq, unlike Jordan, proved unable to withstand the pressures of the growing Arab nationalism in the region. It was said that Faisal himself never abandoned a developing commitment to pan-Arabism, though his early turbulent experiences 'made him more cautious and explicitly gradualist'.[49] He never escaped from the orbit of British influence, and died soon after Iraq had achieved its nominal independence as a sovereign state.

After his death on 8 September 1933, King Faisal was succeeded by his son Ghazi I (1933–39) seen as competent but unpopular. When, after a brief reign, Ghazi was killed in a car crash many Iraqis blamed the British for his death.[50] Faisal II (1939–58), four years old, inherited the throne and reigned with Abd al-Ilah, Ghazi's cousin, as regent. Abd al-Ilah was incompetent, unpopular and staunchly pro-British: the British government could feel that Iraq was safe in his hands. But there then began a period of immense instability, exacerbated by the turbulence of the Second World War. The Iraqi monarchy survived for more than a decade in the post-war world, but on 14 July 1958 the army staged a *coup d'état* and Iraq became a republic.

The young King Faisal II, poorly equipped to withstand the tide of history, had been shot dead, along with many of his supporters, and a new phase in the brutal theatre of Iraqi politics had begun. Today there are Iraqis and others prepared to argue that the only salvation for a post-Saddam Iraq is the return of the monarchy, a traditional institution that will unite the country. This is the ambition of The Constitutional Monarchy Movement headed by Sharif Ali bin Hussein who was born in Baghdad in 1956, attended a Lebanese high school and read for a British MA in economics. If the West wanted a new Iraqi monarch he would seem to fit the bill.

The Constitutional Monarchy Movement has produced a National Covenant (Figure 5) to emphasise the importance of such considerations as sovereign independence, religious tolerance, human rights, the free market and national reconciliation 'based on forgiveness and absolution far from a desire for revenge and retribution with due consideration for the rule of law and justice'. It is claimed that such a monarchy would be 'constitutional' – which is unhelpful until the character of the agreed constitution is known. The (written) constitution of the United Kingdom of Libya was authoritarian to the point of dictatorship, rendering the various affirmations of human rights largely meaningless. The (unwritten) constitution of Britain, while nominally granting political power to elected representatives, does in fact grant the monarch considerable powers that are rarely discussed or publicised.[51] There are political hazards in the concept of hereditary monarchy that advocates seldom address.

The proponents of a restoration of an Iraqi monarchy pointed out that successive political regimes in Iraq have shown little concern for the welfare of the people. This has meant in turn that force has been necessary to maintain such regimes in power. (Does this apply equally to the Iraqi monarchies imposed by Britain?) In addition, it was argued, Iraq comprises a multitude of diverse ethnic, religious and social groups, all beset by the traditional rivalries between tribes and the perpetual conflict between urban and rural areas. Hence there was a complex amalgam of elements that comprised modern Iraq, a society that had become 'incapable of co-operating or forgiving, let alone creating harmony and speaking with one voice'. This state of affairs was exemplified by the state of the Iraqi opposition, where conferences and discussions were invariable characterised by fractious argument and the failure to reach consensus on important issues.

The Constitutional Monarchy hereby solemnly pledges:

1. To uphold the unity of the Iraqi nation and to maintain its sovereign independence.
2. To affirm the Islamic identity of Iraq while respecting all religions …
3. To implement a … referendum to decide the nature of government …
4. To draft a permanent Constitution to be confirmed by the people …
5. That the nature of the Monarchy will be hereditary …
6. The establishment of a pluralistic democratic state …
7. The affirmation of the sanctity of the judiciary and its independence from any group of person in the state.
8. To completely uphold the principles of Basic Human Rights as laid down by religion, the United Nations and international institutions.
9. That the armed forces belong to the people … and are prohibited from any political activity.
10. To institute a free economy … while maintaining a balance between the rights of ownership and the fee market and the rights of people to social justice …
11. To implement a comprehensive national reconciliation …
12. To amend the legacy left by the dark era on the basis of just laws with foremost consideration for ethnic and secular issues, the nationality of law, voluntary and forced emigration and on the foundation of equal rights and responsibilities of all citizens …

Figure 5. *Covenant of The Constitutional Monarchy Movement – Extract*

The Constitutional Monarchy Movement attempted to address this situation in various ways. It believed in the need for 'fair competition' among competing political forces, and supported parliamentary elections 'conducted in an atmosphere of stability and continuity'. The Head of State should keep out of the fray but function as a guarantor of the constitution, defending the rights of the people and their representatives in a democratically elected assembly.

It is difficult to make much sense of this. If the monarchy has no political powers then it is impotent to impose unity or order in a situation of political turmoil. But if it does possess political powers, how can these ever be legitimised while upholding the essence of democracy and the will of parliament? Either the monarchy is a useless complication or it relies on the presumption of an hereditary authoritarianism.

The Movement acknowledged that monarchy cannot be imposed on the people but if, as Article 5 of the Covenant claimed, it was to be a hereditary system then what would happen when the people wanted to remove it? It is one thing to establish a monarchy by referendum, quite another to remain sensitive to the popular will over subsequent years and decades. It is hard to see, as the Movement claimed, that only a constitutional monarchy 'could rescue Iraq from the factional conflicts between the various groups'. The monarchy would become yet another factional group in a complex constitution that would inevitably undermine the popular will. Iraq did not experience a 'golden era … under her monarchy', as the movement claimed. It is useful in this context to remember the sort of society that the Iraqi monarchy found congenial.

Local notables, sympathetic to the British, were able to acquire vast semi-feudal estates and to reduce local tribesmen to the status of debt-bonded serfs. Rural areas became divorced from the rest of the national economy, which tended to generate 'severe distortions' in the country's economic and political systems'.[52] The position of the absentee landlords was strengthened under British administration during the period of the monarchy, with much of the population left in poverty; in 1957, when the monarchy had reigned for more than a third of a century, the bulk of the rural population of 3.8 million was landless. The impoverished peasants struggled to rebel, but the real powers in the country, sustained by the armed forces, were 'the monarchy and its entourage, the great landowners, the Iraq Petroleum Company, and the British economic and military dominations.'[53]

A mere two per cent of the landowners owned more than two-thirds of all the useful land, with the sharecropper peasants massively exploited, forced to provide up to two-thirds of their produce to the landlords. In 1952 unrest grew among the peasants when they heard about the land reforms in Egypt, and soon thousands were fleeing to the cities to escape rural destitution. Throughout the 1950s massive slums spread around Baghdad, with the hovel inhabitants frequently swamped by muddy overflows from the Tigris. One keen observer described the prevailing conditions: 'There is much trachoma and dysentery, but no bilharzia or malaria because the water is too polluted for snails and mosquitoes. The infant mortality is 250 per thousand. A woman has a 50:50 chance of raising a child to the age of ten. There are no social services of any kind ... On the adjacent dumps dogs with rabies dig in the sewage, and the slum-dwellers pack it for resale as garden manure.'[54]

This was the 'golden age' advertised by The Constitutional Monarchy Movement, apparently oblivious to the lives of ordinary Iraqis under the British-imposed monarchy. At the same time the Movement continued to claim that 98 per cent of the Iraqi people wanted a return to the royal system because monarchy was the only system able to solve the crisis created by the era of republican government. And the Western press, untroubled by the ambitions of Sharif Ali bin Hussein, remained content to provide occasional supportive publicity.

On 1 April 2001, interviewed in a 'heavily draped Kensington apartment', Sharif Ali acknowledged the problems that stood in the way of a royal restoration in Iraq. He had abandoned his ambitions as a 'pinstriped investment banker' and was resolved to advance the monarchist cause: 'The appeal of the monarchy is that it is not dependent upon one single constituency.'[55] He seemed unaware that without any constituency there was no obvious route to power.

There were other complications that seemed unhelpful to Sharif Ali: in 2002–3 it seemed that he was not the only candidate for King. On 12 July 2002 the Iraqi exiled officers and opposition groups attending the London conference were surprised to witness the sudden arrival of Jordan's Prince Hassan, brother of the late King Hussein and heir to the throne of Jordan until the terminally-ill King removed him from the succession and replaced him with his son, the present King Abdullah. Why had Hassan decided to attend the Kensington meeting? Was he manoeuvring for regal power in a post-Saddam Iraq? Ahmad Chalabi had already declared that King Abdullah had become too close to Saddam: 'It is unfortunate that Abdullah has hitched his throne to Saddam's wagon. He is under pressure from Saddam to do something about Hassan's decision to show solidarity with the Iraqi people by visiting the conference ...' In fact Hassan's unexpected appearance at the conference had been laden with symbolism, for Hassan would clearly be a prime candidate for any restoration of the monarachy in Iraq. The Hashemites would again be in nominal control of two of the key states of the Middle East, as indeed they would be if Sharif Ali bin Hussein were to become King.

The impact of Hassan's appearance at the conference was out of all proportion to any contribution he made to the proceedings. He took a seat at the front next to Sharif Ali, so perhaps signalling his support for The Constitutional Monarchy Movement, and then left after 45 minutes to give a press conference. He declared, perhaps disingenuously, that he had not intended to attract so much media attention. Some Arab journalists suggested that Hussan would have been unlikely to visit the conference without first seeking the approval of King Abdullah – or perhaps there were tensions in the Jordanian Royal Family, with Hassan resenting his exclusion from the succession.

Some observers noticed that Hassan had entered the conference hall arm-in-arm with Chalabi – a further complication since Chalabi, a former financier, had been sentenced *in absentia* by a Jordanian court to 22 years hard labour for embezzling money belonging to the Jordanian people when he headed Petra Bank in the 1980s (*The Times*, 11 April 2003). And more speculation was invited when the Jordanian government denied in a statement any prior knowledge of Hassan's participation in Iraqi opposition activities. The Prince, according to the official Amman response, was acting as an ordinary Jordanian citizen representing only himself. In summary, there appeared to be four possible interpretations of Prince Hassan's visit to the London conference:

- King Abdullah had mandated him to attend;

- Prince Hassan had taken a personal decision on the matter, keen to impress the Americans and others with his political independence (Washington was already said to prefer Hassan to Abdullah);

- Prince Hassan was keen to become the crowned King of Iraq if the United States decided to restore the monarchy, since he stood no chance of becoming the Jordanian King, and Iraq was the next best option;

- Prince Hassan had behaved in such a fashion since he had a psychological craving for publicity, having been the focus of Jordanian media attention for 34 years. Feeling isolated, perhaps he had relished the thought of a dramatic appearance in Kensington.

Journalists were keen to emphasise that Hassan was an intelligent and competent operator, unlikely to act without careful thought. He chaired the Club of Rome, a reputable think-tank and centre of innovation and initiative, and was acting head of the Arab Thought Forum. He had sat on the boards of universities and scientific forums, chaired intellectual seminars and written books on politics. But Hassan himself made no effort to explain his motives.[56] He spoke of 'assuming his ancestral responsibilities' in the region, which may have hinted at his regal ambitions, but said little else. Some reports suggested that the King and the Prince of Jordan 'do not get along'.[57] Perhaps Hassan speculated that an unduly pro-Saddam Abdullah might be toppled in the turmoil that would follow the anticipated collapse of the Saddam regime. Perhaps Hassan, favoured by Washington, would then regain a right to the Jordanian throne.

However, for the moment King Abdullah seemed more secure than Saddam Hussein. The most promising regal option had to be Iraq. There was said to be support in the Pentagon and among conservative thinkers in the United States for planting Hassan in Iraq as a new monarch.[58] Perhaps, as Sharif Ali argued, only a monarch could transcend the traditional factionalism that plagued the Iraqi nation. Thus Michael Rubin, of the Washington-based American Enterprise Institute, commented: 'Prince Hassan is perhaps the only person who can transcend the ethnic and political complexities.' Perhaps Iraq's new royal *golden age* would surpass the previous one:

> Hassan's experience and lineage – Hashemites claim direct descent from the Prophet Mohammed – give him the unique ability to usher a post-Saddam Iraq back into the family of nations, with him chairing a future constitutional convention and overseeing the reconciliation process. With Saddam's days numbered, Hassan's appearance in London may signal that Iraqis will have a future far brighter than their past.[59]

At the same time King Abdullah, perhaps not speaking for Hassan, declared in a television interview on 11 October 2002 that there were no Hashemite ambitions to rule Iraq: 'I am the head of this family and I frankly say that the Hashemite family has no ambitions to return back to ruling Iraq, and there should not be anyone in this family that thinks the opposite.' Any family member who thought differently 'would only represent himself' – an obvious reference to Prince Hassan?

Sharif Ali bin Hussein and Prince Hassan have not been the only contenders for the Iraqi throne. Many of the Iraqi exiles would have been happy to create a ruling dynasty, with or without real or imagined blood links to The Prophet. And some players on the Iraqi scene have been branded metaphorically as 'pretenders to Saddam's throne'. Thus the previously exiled Ayatollah Mohammed Baqer al-Hakim, a key anti-Saddam ally of the West, has been labelled such a 'pretender' and has expressed confidence that he would be at least a major player in the post-Saddam Iraq.[60]

Perhaps the arguments about monarchy have been rehearsed more in Britain than in the United States, and it is not difficult to find an English academic prepared to argue for a restoration of the monarchy in a post-war Iraq:

> In Iraq I did not find a yearning for democracy, but a nostalgia for the past. On display at the book auction market in Baghdad were books with pictures of the old kings ... One man said there was a special sympathy for the young murdered King [Faisal II] ... Other said that if there were a free vote now, '90 per cent would opt for the monarchy'. This yearning for some sort of traditional rule may sound quixotic, but in Iraq it could just work.[61]

A parliamentary system like that of Jordan, answerable to the Hashemite monarchy, could be introduced, and the Kurds and Shi'ites could be ruled with a 'lighter hand'. The state would still be 'authoritarian' – 'but neither a naked military dictatorship nor a mere puppet state'.[62]

Democracy or What?

There was much talk of introducing *democracy* to Iraq in the post-Saddam era but little public discussion about what form it would take in the new context. In American parlance 'democracy' is no more than a synonym for 'free-enterprise capitalism' – a detail which, when grasped, brings clarity to many otherwise obscure considerations (see also Chapter 13). Money buys political power in the United States, including the power to wage business-friendly wars at regular intervals. (We cannot have the arms factories grinding to a halt because the arms warehouses are full.) Some commentators, seduced equally by the vision of vast wealth and the pleasant aura that surrounds the word 'democracy', have suggested that the United States is a 'pluto-democracy'. The Iraqis will get their democracy, which basically means that their national assets will be donated by American administrators to US corporations.

Some people are still prepared to query the democracy that will be generously donated, gift-wrapped in corporate logos, to the Iraqi people. Peter Preston, writing in *The Guardian* (London), knew before the war what was at stake in Iraq:

> This is a big country, 23 million strong, divided by race, religion and bloody history and about to overdose on cruise missiles. This is a country of separatism, feuds, poverty and infinite corruption ...
> What acceptably Islamic electoral system for this 'liberated' Iraq? First General past the post, like Pakistan? First son of former dictator past the post, as in Syria? The two-round system they use in Iraq and Egypt (and France)? The block vote system of Kuwait with as many votes in multi-member districts as there are candidates (and no women in sight)? Jordan's way with the single non-transferable vote (and monarch)? Israel's renowned list PR system, Sharon-plus?[63]

Neal Ascherson, pundit and author, wrote in the same vein, though less pungently: 'Incredibly, with American tanks half way to Baghdad, there is still no agreement on how to run a military occupation regime, let alone on a programme to reconstruct an Iraqi state.'[64] If the United

States were forced to fund reconstruction, then Washington might choose to write off such 'odious' debts to guarantee lucrative pickings for American companies.

The journalist Simon Carr was one of a number who rightly perceived the obvious absurdities of facile Western talk of democracy in the new Iraq. The country would be restored to its own people 'as long as they don't democratically vote for religious fundamentalists, Arab nationalist or gun-crazy strongmen'.[65] Carr and his ilk probably agreed that a British leader who basked in the 'royal prerogative' and an American leader who came to power through ballot-rigging were not the best people to supervise the introduction of democracy to Iraq or anywhere else. Perhaps there was comfort in the fact that Bush and Blair disagreed about how Iraq should be ruled in the post-Saddam era – a disagreement that was obvious from Blair's troubled trips to Camp David, at the Northern Ireland summit on 5 April 2003, and thereafter.[66] Perhaps it was good also that there were tensions in the Bush administration itself about where it was all leading.[67]

In early April the United States was reportedly finalising the team that would take charge of Iraqi ministries in the post-Saddam Iraq. One of the appointees was the 54-year-old Michael Mobbs, a Pentagon lawyer who had previously sought to have US citizens imprisoned indefinitely without charge as part of the war against terrorism. Other appointees were James Woolsey, a former CIA director with Israeli connections, and Zalmay Khalilzad, the Bush envoy, who was once an enthusiastic supporter of the Taliban. One of the latter's tasks was to organise a conference of 250 prominent Iraqis, the equivalent of the *loya jirga* in Afghanistan. In 1997 Khalilzad wrote an article in the conservative *Weekly Standard* urging the overthrow of the Saddam regime.

On 9 April Dick Cheney declared that the United States was inviting groups likely to become part of the future government of Iraq to a meeting that would be held in Nasiriyah: 'We will bring together representatives of the group from all over Iraq to begin to sit down and talk about planning for the future of this Iraqi Interim Authority (IIA).' The Pentagon hawks were insisting that the United States take the lead in the IIA, consigning the United Nations to a subsidiary role: 'To the victor the spoils, and in this case the spoils are choosing who governs.' Britain, preferring a multilateral solution, was recommending that the

UN play a more prominent role. At this time the plan specified a four-pillar IIA, involving the US and British military, leading Iraqi figures, the UN and the Pentagon-run Office for Reconstruction and Development. It was suggested that the Iraqi body would be 'representative' but without necessarily involving elections. One Western diplomat commented: 'There has never been universal adult suffrage in Iraq. You don't need an election to have a degree of representation.'

The meeting in Nasiriyah was advertised as a major step forward in the search for a new Iraqi leadership, but the major Shi'ite opposition group and Ahmad Chalabi were boycotting the talks. The United States claimed that dozens of representatives from ethnic, tribal and opposition groups were invited, although no official list was published. *The New York Times* quoted Jay Garner as saying that his mission to rebuild Iraq's political structures would be messy and contentious.

A demonstration at the conference, organised by the Shi'ite opposition and numbering about 20,000 people, graphically illustrated the fractious divisions in the post-Saddam situation. In the centre of Nasiriyah the crowd chanted:

YES TO FREEDOM ... YES TO ISLAM ... NO TO AMERICA ... NO TO SADDAM

The Shi'ites were a majority in Iraq. Would Jay Garner really be forced to witness – in the name of democracy – the creation of an Iraqi Islamic state?

Members of the Shi'ite faithful had arrived at the al-Nasiriyah hospital, formerly Saddam General Hospital, and at first protected it from looters, but over the course of a few days they took over the place. Some of the doctors were searched and women patients told to cover their hair with scarves. When a senior doctor remonstrated with the Shi'ite interlopers, they broke his nose. Another physician commented:

This is a time for freedom, but those religious men interfere with everything. They want to run everything, and they want to be seen to help, because they want power. I don't like these religious people. If I compare them with Saddam, Saddam is better.[68]

The Nasiriyah talks, hosted by Jay Garner, yielded a 13-point plan that gave every indication of being a US-drafted wish list that would play well in the Western media:

- Iraq must be democratic;

- Government must not be based on communal identity;

- Government should be democratic federal system after country-wide consultation;

- Rule of law must be paramount;

- Iraq must be built on respect for diversity, including respect for women;

- The meeting discussed the role of religion in state and society;

- The meeting discussed the principle that Iraqis must choose leaders and not have them imposed from outside;

- Political violence must be rejected and Iraqis must organise rebuilding at local and national levels;

- Iraqis and the coalition must restore security and basic services;

- The Ba'ath Party will be dissolved;

- There should be an open dialogue with all national political groups;

- The meeting condemned looting;

- There should be another meeting in a location to be determined with additional Iraqi participants to discuss developing an Iraqi interim authority.

Nothing had been resolved, no rudiments in the IIA established. In one statement the Iraqis and the coalition 'must restore security', and in another 'looting' was condemned. Women were mentioned as an afterthought, an evident acknowledgement that female suffrage might be a problem in a state with strong Islamic instincts. And, even though the Ba'athists were to be banned, there were no hints as to what political groups would be allowed as legitimate contenders for the Iraqi Interim Authority. What of the Iraqi Communist Party? What of the Islamic groups, Shi'ites and others? Saddam would still have residual followers, not necessarily Ba'athist. What of them? Moreover, in a plan that spoke of democracy why did the word 'election' not appear? Because elections were for later? And who would write the new Iraqi constitution?

The American objectives had long been obvious – oil and strategic advantage. US troops were already guarding the oilfields, but not the museums or hospitals, and now it was time to focus on the option of a long-term occupation. On 21 April 2003 it was announced that the Bush administration was planning to maintain a long-term military presence in at least four key bases in Iraq after the transfer of power to a new government in Baghdad.[69] Washington intended to negotiate a 'military basing relationship' with the Iraqi government, a move that would confirm Arab suspicions that the United States was determined to maintain a permanent occupation. The bases, already determined by the Washington strategists, would be sited at the international airport outside Baghdad; at Talil, near Nasiriyah in the south; at an airstrip called HI in the Western desert near Jordan; and at the Bashur airfield in the Kurdish-held north. Such a strategic presence in Iraq was designed in part to allow Washington to run down its forces in Saudia Arabia, an increasingly fragile military presence, and to maintain a military occupation at the heart of the Arab world.

The priorities were plain. Washington had no interest in the shape and character of a new Iraqi regime in Baghdad, providing it recognised the strategic interests of the United States. In the 13-point plan that emerged at Nasiriyah there was nothing significant about human rights, and already Baghdad's Christians were worried.[70] There was 'little optimism for the future' on Easter Sunday in Baghdad:

> Christian girls wearing bright lipstick and no headscarves voiced fears that such freedoms would come to a rapid end if hardline clerics among Iraq's Shia majority impose Sharia, Islamic law, and turn the once-secular state into an Islamic republic ... elders shrugged at the end of the Ba'athist era, pointing out that, for all the evils of Saddam Hussein, persecution of Christians was not one.[71]

Samir Ahad, 57, Secretary of the National Evangelical Protestant Church in Baghdad, said of Saddam: 'He could be a very, very bad man in many ways, but he donated an organ to our church ... especially during Saddam's time, we have been treated well.' How would a Shi'ite government treat Iraq's 700,000 Christians, a population that included Protestants, Roman Catholics, Chaldeans, Orthodox adherents and others? There was no sign that this was a matter of concern to the US occupiers of the country.

On 21 April 2003 Hatem George Hatem, a UNICEF spokesman interviewed on television, deplored the plight of Iraqi children, plunged into conditions of appalling privation by the US-led aggression. Apart from the dead, the fatally wounded, the amputees, the diseased and the traumatised, millions of Iraqi children had been variously orphaned, deprived of drinkable water and an adequate diet, and denied any hope of medical attention, schooling or other social support. The United States had accomplished social collapse as well as regime collapse but 'regime change', implying a properly functioning replacement government, had yet to be achieved.

PART TWO

The Region

FOUR

The Kurds

In recent history the United States found the Kurds a useful propaganda device; their suffering, to which Washington has always been indifferent, helpfully advertised the criminal excesses of the Saddam regime. This has always been part of the cynical world of *realpolitik*. There was never any real prospect that the United States would try to advance the long-standing cause of Kurdish statehood and in consequence upset a primary NATO ally in the region – Turkey. When one US official was asked in the mid–1990s about the predicament of the Kurds, he replied: 'We have bigger fish to fry and the Kurds are not very big fish.'[1] Washington found the Kurds useful in the 2003 war, not only as a helpful propaganda tool but also in practical terms. A future Kurdish state, with all the sovereignty of an independent political entity, was not on the agenda.

Towards Kurdistan

The Kurds have always been one of those strange anomalies in the modern world – a nation without a state, like the Palestinians. Ethnically distinct from the Arabs, the Turks and other neighbouring groups, the Kurds have historically struggled to achieve statehood in the teeth of their political manipulation by foreigners over the centuries.

Many ethnic groups have moved through the region, some to settle, and today the Kurds, of ancient origin, occupy parts of various countries. Historically they were a pastoral nomadic people who – despite frequent historical and modern references to *Kurdistan* – have never been an internationally recognised nation or even united under a single government. The Kurds have claimed kinship with the ancient Medes, one of the founding races of the Persian empire; their language, with many dialects, is related to Persian. The Turks, keen to suppress Kurdish aspirations to statehood, have claimed that the Kurds are 'mountain Turks' with ethnic roots in Turkey. There is no structural relationship between the Kurdish and the Arabic languages or between Kurdish and Turkish, which helps to confirm that the Kurds are a well-defined group with distinct ethnic and linguistic origins. The Kurds are one of the largest ethnic groups never to have achieved statehood. In one reckoning there are around 17 million Kurds spread around various countries.[2] David McDowall, author of the Minority Rights Group report,[3] suggests a total of 16 million Kurds and other similar estimates have been given.

This all highlights the dilemma of the Kurds in a post-Saddam world. It has been obvious since the 1990s that, despite persistent factionalism and frequent bouts of violence, a coherent 'Kurdistan' has been firmly established in northern Iraq, much to the disquiet of Turkey and other neighbouring states. How should the Kurds respond to the creation of a US-led regime in Baghdad? At one level many Kurds, not all, welcome the end of the Saddam regime, but to what extent would Kurdish political gains be safeguarded by a new pro-West government in Iraq? In early 2003 it was plain that there would be no consensual Kurdish attitude to a final US-led onslaught on Baghdad. In a post-Saddam world should the Kurds seek to protect their existing autonomy in a federal Iraq, or should they struggle to realise the age-old dream of statehood? And if they pressed hard for international recognition would

Washington order an authoritarian suppression of the Kurds in the attempt to impose regional stability?

At the end of the First World War Kurdish nationalists throughout the Kurdistan region, encouraged by Woodrow Wilson's famous Fourteen Points (8 January 1918),[4] seized the opportunity to press their claims. However, Britain's main interest lay in the creation of a pliant Iraqi state, a goal that was assisted in no small measure by manifest divisions among the Kurds themselves – a condition that has often damaged Kurdish ambitions over the decades. In the summer of 1920 the Treaty of Sèvres, to which Britain and Turkey were both signatories, recognised the 'independent states' of Armenia and Kurdistan, but this formal recognition was not destined to yield an international recognised Kurdistan. The Sèvres terms, according to which the Kurds would have achieved nationhood, were nullified by the Treaty of Lausanne (24 July 1933), which again cast the Kurds into limbo.

Contact with the West

Throughout this period the Kurds made frequent attempts to assert their national independence, though repeatedly repressed by the Turks and the British. Squadrons of the Royal Air Force were active in policing Iraq and Kurdistan before the Arab rebellion in 1920. Thus Lieutenant-General Aylmer Haldane had praised the 'admirable work of … the RAF under extremely arduous conditions' after British aircraft had bombed the Kurds in 1919–20. RAF planes were also used to protect the British line of communication between Baghdad and Mosul, and to bomb and strafe the Sufran tribe in the Diwaniyah area. In 1993 there were still Iraqis and Kurds who remembered being bombed and machine-gunned by the RAF in the 1920s.[5] A Kurd from the Korak mountains of Kurdistan commented, seventy years after the event: 'They were bombing here in the Kaniya Khoran … sometimes they raided three times a day.' Wing Commander Lewis, then of 30 Squadron (RAF), Iraq, recalled how quite often 'one would get a signal that a certain Kurdish village had to be bombed … with the RAF pilots being ordered to machine-gun any Kurds who looked hostile.' In the same vein the former Squadron-Leader Kendal of 30 Squadron recalled that if the tribespeople 'were doing something that they ought not to be doing then you shot them'.[6] Similarly, Wing-Commander Gale, also of 30 Squadron, commented:

> If the Kurds hadn't learned by our example to behave themselves in a civilised way then we had to spank their bottoms. This was done by bombs and guns.[7]

Wing-Commander Arthur Harris (later 'Bomber Harris', head of wartime Bomber Command and responsible for incinerating tens of thousands of German civilians in World War II) was happy to emphasise that 'The Arab and Kurd now know what real bombing means in casualties and damage. Within forty-five minutes a full-size village can be practically wiped out and a third of its inhabitants killed or injured …'. It was an easy matter to bomb and machine-gun the tribespeople because they had no means of defense or retaliation.'

Iraq and Kurdistan were also useful laboratories for new weapons – just as more recently the United States has been keen to test various 'weapons of mass destruction' on the people of Afghanistan and Iraq. In the 1920s the British Air Ministry developed devices specifically for use against tribal villages, some of these the forerunners of modern incendiaries and air-to-ground missiles: 'Phosphorus bombs, war rockets, metal crows feet to maim livestock, shrapnel, liquid fire, and delay-action bombs.' Many of these devices were first used in Kurdistan. There was no doubt that in the circumstances British technology, exploited in the full wisdom of British politics, was highly effective for colonial control. In the political climate of the day – as with Washington's current attitude to Iraq – the British government could not tolerate a situation in which Kurdish and Iraqi tribes refused to acquiesce in British rule.

Winston Churchill, as colonial secretary, was sensitive to the costs of policing the British empire; and was in consequence keen to exploit the potential of modern technology to best advantage. This approach had particular relevance to military operations against the Arab and Kurdish tribes in Iraq. On 19 February 1920, before the start of the Arab uprising, Churchill (then secretary of state for war and air) wrote to Sir Hugh Trenchard, a pioneer of air warfare, to ask whether he could take control of Iraq. This would entail 'the provision of some kind of asphyxiating bombs … for use in preliminary operations again turbulent tribes.'[8] Churchill emphasised that this was a proper approach in the circumstances: 'I do not understand this squeamishness about the use of gas. I am strongly in favour of using poisoned gas against uncivilised tribes.' He was keen to argue that gas, fired from ground-based artillery or dropped from aircraft, would cause only 'discomfort or illness but not death' to dissident tribes people but this view of gas was mistaken. It was highly likely that the suggested gas would permanently damage eyesight, as when mustard gas was used in World War I, and would 'kill children and sickly persons, more especially as the people against whom we intend to use it have no medical knowledge with which to supply antidotes.'

Churchill remained unimpressed by such considerations, arguing that the use of gas, a 'scientific expedient', should not be prevented 'by the prejudices of those who do not think clearly'. In the event, gas was used against the Arab and Kurdish rebels in 1920 with 'excellent moral effect'.[9] Gas shells were not dropped from aircraft because of practical difficulties but ground-based guns proved adequate to the task.

Towards Autonomy

It must be judged highly likely that such events, still recollected in the region and allied to the 1991 US betrayal of the anti-Saddam Kurdish rebellion,[10] would help to condition Kurdish perceptions of a new pro-West government in Baghdad. In the past, different Kurdish factions have variously conspired with the CIA, negotiated with Saddam Hussein, sought local autonomy, and kept alive the vision of a truly independent Kurdistan, with a seat at the United Nations. In 1922 the British mandatory authorities in Iraq conceded that the Kurds should be granted a degree of autonomy in the north, a key part of their traditional homeland; but Sheikh Mahmud Barzinji, whom the British had wanted to install as a suitable client ruler, was reluctant to accept any element of Iraqi suzerainty over the Kurdish territory. The British responded by deciding to put him down by force. In July 1924 Sulaymaniyah was occupied by British troops, and in December the RAF was ordered to bomb parts of the town. Once the necessary stability had been restored the British decided to make various prudent gestures towards the recalcitrant Kurdish population.

It was determined in 1926 that civil servants in the Kurdish area should be Kurds, that Kurdish children should be educated in the Kurdish language, and that Kurdish should have the same status as Arabic in the region. These were seen as significant concessions, though cynically devised to take the steam out of the Kurdish activism for a truly independent homeland. Under the Iraqi monarchy it became the practice to include one or two token Kurds in the government, and to allow the Kurds a measure of ethnic recognition. But such moves, far from quelling Kurdish aspirations, served only to stimulate the ambition for a national homeland. In 1929, on the brink of independence, Kurdish deputies at the Iraqi parliament sent a memorandum to the prime minister, demanding that earlier promises of movement towards Kurdish independence be implemented more effectively. Nothing was done, and it soon emerged that the Anglo-Iraqi treaty of 1930, allowing Iraq an independent status with continued British influence, contained no safeguards for the many ethnic minorities in the country. An independent pro-West Iraq would be established with no protection for the Kurds.

In September 1930 rioting again broke out in Sulaymaniyah, and Sheikh Mahmud, nominally exiled from Iraq, resolved to go on the offensive. He was comprehensively defeated but his efforts stimulated the development of another opposition group in the tribal lands. Mustafa Barzani, the younger brother of the Barzani religious and tribal leader, Sheikh Ahmad, emerged as one of the main Kurdish political leaders, but was destined to die in exile in 1979.

In 1936 the Barzani brothers were captured and forced to live under house arrest in Sulaymaniyah, where they came into contact with sympathetic political writers, some of whom co-operated to form the covert Hewa (Hope) Party in the late 1930s. But the party was split. Should it be looking to a socialist solution? Was revolt the only way forward? Should there be accommodations with the British? Would it be possible to enlist international support for Kurdish independence? The Iraqi Communist Party, later to be ruthlessly suppressed by various authoritarian regimes, was agitating in favour of Kurdish rights, with communist groups set up in Arbil and other Kurdish towns in the early 1940s. The first Kurdish political journal, *Azadi*, was edited by communists, with an editorial in the first issue (1944) declaring:

We urge the politically conscious among the sons of our people and every sincere Kurd who loves his people and his homeland, not to leave his people unorganised an unprepared ... we urge him to struggle for democratic parties and associations to organise the Kurdish people, to prepare them and enable them to achieve self-determination so that their unity with the Arabs in Iraq would be a voluntary union based on equality of rights.[11]

The Iraqi Communist Party was the first political party 'to develop a coherent policy on the Kurdish question, which generally amounted to a plan for autonomy based on Kurdish self-determination'.[12] So how is the United States, committed to reshaping of a post-Saddam Iraq into a pro-West mould, likely to respond to Kurdish demands for autonomy that were first propagated by communist activists?

In July 1943 Mustafa Barzani escaped from Sulaymaniyah and began organising a further revolt against the British forces. During November and December he made various appeals to the British to support Kurdish claims for autonomy; and then, following correspondence with Sir Kinahan Cornwallis, the British ambassador, made the remarkable promise to obey him, 'whatever your orders may be'. By now the Iraqi government was increasingly worried that any move towards autonomy for the Kurds might simply herald political separatism. In October 1945 Barzani was forced to flee to Iran when the government sent 14,000 troops against his poorly equipped forces. The Kurdish nationalists were now compelled to lay low, awaiting the collapse of the monarchy. The Kurdistan Democratic Party (KDP) had been created in 1946, and already the Iraqi Kurds had won some concessions not granted to the Kurds of Iran, Syria and Turkey. The hope was that a Kurdish victory in Iraq would bring significant progress towards a Kurdistan with genuine independence.

In 1942 about a dozen citizens of Mahabad in Western Azerbaijan met secretly to form the *Komala*, a nationalist association that later developed links with Hewa. Almost four years later the Iranian Kurds attempted to establish an autonomous republic in Mahabad, but in mid-March the Iranian army launched a major offensive against the Kurds which lasted for about five weeks. On 31 March Qadhi Mohammad, the Kurdish leader, was hanged in public, along with two close relatives and various political allies. Some months later, four Kurdish ex-officers of the Iraqi army, who had accompanied Barzani to Mahabad, were also hanged, even though they had given themselves up to the Iraqi authorities. Barzani and some of his closest followers now decided that it was no longer safe for them to remain in Iraq, and in June 1947 they fled across Turkey and Iran, covering more than two hundred miles over the mountains, to seek refuge in the Soviet Union. There they remained until 1958.

The Kurdish cause, in Iraq and elsewhere, seemed to be making little progress. There was further conflict between the Kurds and the post-monarchy Kassem regime, and tribal disputes occurred between various Kurdish groups. What had at times appeared to be a route to Kurdish unity and independence had rapidly degenerated into factional conflict and state harassment. Through much of the 1960s and early 1970s the Kurds and the central Iraqi government were in virtual state of war. The persecution of the Kurdish nation did not begin with Saddam Hussein.

At times, when the military capacity was available, Iraqi aircraft bombed scores of Kurdish villages in northern Iraq indiscriminately (much as the British had done in the 1920s). Barzani's Kurdish army, the *peshmerga* ('those who walk before death'), numbered around 50,000 men in the late–1960s; and at the peak of their power the Kurds controlled all the mountains in northern Iraq. At that time the Kurdish people were even receiving international aid from such countries as Iran, Israel, the Soviet Union and the United States. Again this was all a matter of *realpolitik* calculation. If the Kurds could be either bribed or bolstered in northern Iraq they may create fewer problems elsewhere, and some states saw a strong Kurdistan as a counterweight to their own traditional enemies. Despite this, the Kurds were still taking heavy casualties: between 1960 and 1970 around 9,000 military dead and 100,000 civilian dead (though some lower estimates have also been given). The Kurds had struggled for more than a decade, at great cost, and it was not clear that much had been accomplished. In March 1970 the Iraqi government, perhaps weary of the conflict, offered autonomy to the Kurds, and a new phase in Iraqi-Kurdish relations had begun. But again the reality fell far short of the promise.

On 11 March 1970, following three months of talks between Barzani and the Iraqi government, a joint Manifesto was published that recognised 'the legitimacy of the Kurdish nationality', promising Kurdish language rights, Kurdish representation in government, Kurdish administration in the northern Kurdish region, and a new Kurdish province based on Dohuk. But the Iraqi Ba'ath Party soon perceived what it took to be the disadvantages of the Manifesto. Iraqi authority in the north would be eroded, and so perhaps the Manifesto could be redrafted. Then the Iraqi government went further, evicting Kurdish families from their homes in some areas, particularly around Kirkuk, where the Ba'ath authorities wanted to alter the ethnic balance in favour of the Arabs. Thus in September 1971, for example, some 40,000 Kurds were expelled from the border region near Khaniqin, and forced to settle in Iran, on the grounds that they were not really Iraqis. Iran could not have welcomed such a development: it had its own Kurdish problem. In the same month the Iraqi authorities tried to assassinate Barzani, and more assassination attempts were made in subsequent years.

In fact the attempt at ethnic cleansing was stimulated by a clause in the March Manifesto: 'necessary steps shall be taken ... to unify the governorates and administrative units populated by a Kurdish majority as shown by the official census to be carried out ...'. This meant that the Iraqi government had an interest in reducing the Kurdish population in areas over which the government wanted to retain control. Barzani later claimed to have recognised the Manifesto as an Iraqi delaying manoeuvre ('I said this was a ruse. I knew it even before I signed the agreement'), but Barzani had negotiated from a position of weakness: there had been no opportunity to change the document or to control the pace of its implementation.

While the terms of the Manifesto were being discussed, two explosions rocked the room: two clerics were killed and, when Barzani's bodyguard opened fire, five sheikhs were killed. It later transpired that the two clerics had been innocent couriers of the bombs, which had detonated when tape-recorders were operated. Barzani said: 'Iraq is a police state run by Saddam Hussein who is a power-obsessed megalomaniac'. And Barzani then moved to develop relations with Israel and the shah of Iran, giving the Iraqi regime further cause to be hostile to Kurdish aspirations. The United States also found that its relations with the Kurds were improving, a development that Washington welcomed. In May 1972 President Richard Nixon approved a CIA scheme to give Barzani $16 million over a three-year period, at a time when Saddam was seeking agreements with the Soviet Union. The reason for the American interest was not hard to find.

Barzani, happy to accept CIA funding, declared to *The Washington Post* in the summer of 1973 that once the Kirkuk oilfields had been returned to their 'rightful owners', he was prepared to hand over the oil resources to the Americans: 'We are ready to do what goes with American policy in this area if America will protect us from the wolves. If support were strong enough, we could control the Kirkuk field and give it to an American company to operate.'[13] If Saddam wanted evidence that the Kurds intended to donate Iraqi assets to the imperialist United States, here it was. Barzani, it appeared, was willing to dismember Iraq as a prelude to rewarding his American paymasters. Saddam responded by saying that Iraq would 'remain as it is within its present geographic boundaries forever'.[14]

Civil War

The turmoil continued in subsequent years – both in the confrontation between Barzani's KDP and the Baghdad regime, and in the frequent bouts of conflict between the KDP and the Patriotic Union of Kurdistan (PUK), a competing opposition group headed by Jalal Talabani. The fall of the Persian shah, a supplier of Israeli and US arms to the Kurds, did nothing to advance the Kurdish cause. The new theocrats in Tehran had no interest in Iraqi minority rights. It is significant that the Iraqi Ba'athists had tended to support the Iranian KDP as a useful dissident faction threatening a traditional enemy, whereas for analogous reasons Tehran had supported the KDP-Provisional Command in Iraq.

Such developments served to consolidate the fratricidal divisions in the Kurdish movement: even to the point that in 1978 the KDP fought several pitched battles with the PUK. In these circumstances Baghdad could play one Kurdish faction off against another, just as Washington has used the Kurds to further its own interests in the region. The various foreign powers have always seen the Kurdish factions as useful tools that can aid national policy. And Saddam, as the horrific *Anfal* campaign of genocide indicated, felt free to persecute the Kurdish minority as he wished.[15] Any post-Saddam regime would be free of at least one of the elements that caused immense Kurdish suffering over the years.

On 31 August 1996 Saddam Hussein ordered forces to advance on the north in an anti-Kurd offensive that looked likely to cause another confrontation with the US-led alliance. American forces were put on full alert as Western pundits began assessing the relative Iraqi and allied military capacities in the area.

About 60 Iraqi tanks had pushed into Arbil after an artillery barrage before dawn. Civilians were reported fleeing in panic as the relatively weak Kurdish defenders were routed by the Iraqi onslaught. Baghdad was now insisting that it was giving support to Barzani's KDP to force the rival PUK out of Arbil, and Tariq Aziz, Iraq's foreign minister, warned the United States not to interfere: 'We decided to launch a limited military operation in defense of our sovereignty, our people and their properties'. The US, British and French forces attacking northern Iraq had brought the Kurds 'nothing but death, destruction, anarchy and the loss of opportunities for development and decent living'.[16] A Baghdad government spokesman announced that in accordance with the plan for supporting Barzani the Iraqi forces would return to their former positions 'in a very short period of time'.

The US Role

Washington was quick to emphasise the 'seriousness' of the situation. Plenty of US fighter aircraft were in the region, and the carriers USS *Enterprise* in the Mediterranean and USS *Carl Vinson* in the Gulf were 'on short tether', able to move into action at short notice. Talabani, head of the PUK, was saying that he had warned the United States of the attack and had been promised 'lethal' American retaliation, but Washington had 'failed to act decisively'.[17] Now, according to the Western media itself, the West was 'floundering', Saddam was 'taunting the West again' and 'US credibility was at stake'. President Bill Clinton was under pressure to act: Iran and Turkey were periodically invading parts of Iraq, but Iraq was not allowed access to parts of its own country. What was to be done?

On 1 September western aircraft and cruise missiles were being prepared for use against Iraq amid reports that Saddam Hussein was already ordering his forces to withdraw from Iraqi Kurdistan. The Iraqi flag had been hoisted over the parliamentary building in Arbil, and Iraqi intelligence units were said to be hunting down opposition figures. Iraqi aircraft were reportedly bombing Bustaneh and Kifri. And again

Baghdad was warning Washington not to interfere, with the official newspaper *al-Jumhouriya* declaring: 'The Iraqi people, in the forefront Iraqi Kurds, are ready to provide an example that will inevitably remind the Americans of the Vietnam complex.' On 2 September 1996 the Iraqi troops withdrew from Arbil, leaving their Kurdish allies in control and reportedly carrying out mass killings of rival Kurds in the streets.

At 4:15am (GMT) on 3 September the United States fired 27 cruise missiles from B–52 bombers and two warships in the Gulf at military targets in Southern Iraq. Clinton announced: 'Our objectives are limited but clear – to make Saddam pay a price for the latest act of brutality, reducing his ability to threaten his neighbours and America's interests', while Defense Secretary William Perry declared that Iraq posed a 'clear and present danger' to the neighbouring countries. Britain, instructed by Washington, then drafted a Security Council resolution which was angrily vetoed by Russia. France and China, the other Permanent Members of the Security Council, remained cool over the whole issue. It seemed that the movement of Iraqi forces *within their own country* was not an adequate ground for a consensus of international outrage. But the current phase of bombing strikes was not yet over.

At about midnight (GMT) on 4 September a second wave of 17 cruise missiles was launched at Iraq, creating widespread destruction and an unknown number of human casualties. No doubt the Clinton administration was pleased to observe that the bombing had helped the president in the opinion polls. Britain had abandoned its Security Council resolution after Russia had refused to withdraw its veto; France's President Jacques Chirac pointed out to Clinton that Iraq had broken no United Nations resolutions; and the anti-Saddam Kurds were again complaining that they had been abandoned by the United States.

Saddam Hussein predictably reacted to the missile attacks with defiance and bombast: 'Once again the humiliated and lowly Americans have come to perpetrate their ... cowardly act by hiding behind technological development.' Moreover –

> The aggressors have come again with their cowardly and humiliating raid ... But the raid will be full of sublime meaning for the noble Iraqis and their courageous stands and great steadfastness. The missile aggression started at 9 am of the morning of September 3, 1996. It will be a glorious day that the

Iraqi people will write down, in the name of the Almighty, in their chronicle of great honour. For the aggressors it will be a day of cursing in history as well as on the level of the globe, following the curse that has befallen them from God.

Tariq Aziz, speaking in more measured tones to CNN, explained that Iraq had acted to counter 'the adventurism of Iran', and declared that the US missile attack had been a violation of international law. Washington had succeeded in wrecking what was left of the 1991 coalition. The Security Council was irrevocably split, and there was mounting dissent throughout the Arab world. For example, *al-Ahram*, the most prestigious Egyptian newspaper, asked why the United States did not intervene when Turkey invaded the Kurdish 'safe haven' or when Iran sent its artillery into Iraqi Kurdistan. One Qatari newspaper suggested that the United States found it useful to 'field test' its modern weapons against the Arabs; and even Syria, still hating Saddam, denounced Washington for violating international law.

Now the PUK's Talabani, defeated in the fight for Arbil, was saying that if the West refused to support his struggle he would be forced to call in Islamic forces from Iran, possibly the Iranian-trained 'Badr Brigade' of fugitive Iraqi Shi'ite Muslims camped across the frontier. In either case Washington's 'dual containment' policy for Iraq and Iran would be in tatters: the regional situation was graphically illustrating the contradictions in US foreign policy. Launching a batch of cruise missiles against the Iraqis who supported the KDP opposed to Iran was inevitably serving to strengthen Talabani's Iranian connection. It was hard for Washington to keep both Saddam Hussein and the Iranian mullahs in their respective boxes at the same time.

It was then emerging that the movement of Iraqi forces into Kurdistan had succeeded in demolishing a long-standing CIA covert operation designed to topple the Baghdad government. More than one hundred Iraqis associated with the operation had been arrested and executed, and the headquarters of the Iraqi National Congress (INC) in Arbil had been destroyed. The INC had been in decline, partly because of the Kurdish feuds, but it had continued to spread propaganda and to collect useful morsels of intelligence. Now all this was in ruins. Some American CIA officers, covertly stationed in Arbil, had escaped by fleeting to southern Turkey. Some INC members complained that the

United States had washed its hands of them as soon as the Iraqi assault began.

On 8 September the KDP allies of Saddam Hussein were managing to take key towns in the region, and PUK rebels were pleading for American help after their defenses had crumbled. Baghdad was then denying Iraqi help in the KDP successes, but many refugees from the region spoke of heavy Iraqi shelling, armoured vehicles on the road and even the use of chemical weapons. General John Shalikashvili, chairman of the US Joint Chiefs of Staff, seemed keen to play down such reports, saying he did not know the extent of Iraqi involvement: 'What you're seeing is Kurdish fighting. The United States, rather than siding with one Kurdish faction … has always put its effort on trying to get the two sides together to resolve their differences.' If Washington had been unwilling to defend the Kurds from the 1991 Iraqi onslaught it was unlikely to help them now.

On 9 September the KDP and Iraqi forces captured Sulaymaniyah, striking a massive blow against US policy in the area. Barzani was now claiming that the KDP was in control of all the three Kurdish provinces, the whole of northern Iraq. Observers suggested that this represented a significant strategic gain for Saddam Hussein. The INC's Ahmad Chalabi commented: 'This is a victory for Saddam. He has won a battle but not the war. This means that Saddam is back in effective control of the whole area … The stage is set for political deal between the KDP and Saddam.' But the victory was short-lived. On 13 October PUK managed to retake its former headquarters in Sulaymaniyah, and quickly replaced the KDP's yellow colours with the PUK's green flags. Saddam Hussein was then forced to rethink his links with Barzani's KDP, urging the Kurdish factions 'to keep away from the foreign powers and not to deal with them' and to resume talk under Baghdad's auspices: 'The leadership is ready to extend an invitation to all parties regardless of their background and our opinion or evaluation of this faction or the other, for dialogue in Baghdad, under the sponsorship of the state.'

The PUK continued its conquest of lost ground, taking more towns for the KDP forces. There were no plans to retake Arbil since it was surrounded by Iraqi tanks, but that task could be 'left to the people' of the town. Sami Abdul-Rahman, a KDP leader, said: 'More than 15,000 Iranian Revolutionary Guards have taken part in the latest attacks, with heavy weapons, Katyusha rockets and cannons.' Iran and the PUK issued strong denials, but Iraq warned Iran not to 'play with fire' by meddling in the Kurdish border region. KDP officials, going via Turkey to America, said that they would urge the United States to respond to 'Iranian aggression'.

On 17 October 1996 Massoud Barzani threatened to bring Saddam Hussein's troops back into the war unless the West persuaded Iran to stop backing his rival Kurdish faction: 'If Iran has the right to support the PUK, why shouldn't we have the right to demand support from Iraq?' On 23 October the KDP and the PUK agreed to observe a ceasefire, and a week later they signed a peace agreement pledging to maintain stability in northern Iraq.

The rivalries, tensions and periodic skirmishes were set to continue, exacerbated by the Saddam regime, American pressures and frequent Turkish attacks. But it seemed likely that the KDP and the PUK would be able to achieve a measure of real consensus in the interest of the broader Kurdish cause. In the aftermath of the 2003 war the durability of a pragmatic Kurdish unity seemed uncertain.

The Turkish Threat

The Kurds were aware that a US-led war against Iraq might work to the disadvantage of the fragile Kurdish autonomy already achieved. In early February, when war seemed increasingly inevitable, Professor Sa'ad Jawad at Baghdad University commented to the journalist Jon Snow: 'It won't be the bombs, but the internecine bloodletting that follows any bombs that will wreck this country. The Kurds will suffer worst. The Americans will deny them a state, the Turks will deny them a state, and I can tell you, at the end of all this, they won't even have the autonomy they enjoy now.'[18]

There was growing Kurdish alarm at what were perceived to be American intentions for the regime after the fall of Saddam. Thus Sami Abdul-Rahman, disparaging the US posture, commented: 'Conquerors always call themselves liberators.' And in the same vein Hoshyar Zebari, a veteran Kurdish leader, declared that if the United States wanted to impose its own government, regardless of the religious and ethnic composition of Iraq, 'there is going to be a backlash'. Already Turkey was demanding that its troops be allowed to take over a swathe of territory alongside the border inside Iraq, a permanent consolidation of land that Turkey had often invaded in the past (Chapter 5). Would Washington agree to Turkish military facilities? And would this mean in turn that Turkey would move to end the *de facto* autonomy enjoyed by the Iraqi Kurds for more than a decade? It seemed clear that if the Turks entered northern Iraq it would lead to further fighting with the Kurdish factions.[19] Thus in early March 2003 the Kurdish Commander Kemal Musa Faqi said that his men would sooner fight and die rather than come under Turkish orders:

> If the Turks are coming here there will be war here. I myself will take my gun and shoot every Turk I see. Everybody here, the men, women and children, will fight the Turks ... Saddam's forces are better than the Turkish; both are dictators but he is Iraqi and we are Iraqi also.

He added that in 1917 the British army had helped the Kurds drive the Ottoman Turks out of the area: 'We had some problems with them [the British] after that but they helped us then. We would like them to help us now.'

The scale of the Turkish conflict with the Kurds (mainly the PKK Marxists) in northern Iraq and Turkey itself is rarely advertised in the Western media. The United States and Britain are not keen to dwell on the fact that Turkish forces have caused tens of thousands of Kurdish casualties, destroyed 4,000 Kurdish villages and displaced more than two million Kurds from their homes. In early March 2003 Osman Ocalan, the fugitive younger brother of the captured PKK leader Abdullah, declared: 'If the Turks come it means they are here to destroy the freedom of the Kurds. We will launch a new guerrilla war. We will take military actions throughout Turkey, in the countryside and in the cities. We will attack Turkey's economy, its military and its bureaucracy.' The 10,000-strong PKK force was judged to be far tougher than the PUK and KDP militias, which meant that the Washington strategists could ignore the possibility of serious conflict between the Kurdish guerrillas and the US-supplied Turkish army. On 20 March the Ankara parliament approved a government motion authorising Turkish troops to enter Kurdish areas on its borders.

War and Aftermath

On 19 March the Iraqi Kurds, mainly the PUK and the KDP, agreed that their 100,000 soldiers would co-operate with the US-led forces in the war against the Saddam regime. For months American special forces had been working with the Kurdish *peshmerga* in preparation of the conflict, but the Kurds had refused to accept direct US command. Kurdish leaders had also been talking in Ankara to prevent a Turkish invasion of northern Iraq – at a time when Turkey was turning down an American request to use Turkey for a land invasion of Iraq in the coming war. Turkey was also supporting the rights of the Turkomen minority expelled from Kirkuk by Saddam Hussein. It seemed unlikely that the competing interests of Kurds, Turks, Turkomen and the United States could be resolved without rancour and military conflict.

The war, driven bloodily to its predictable conclusion at great human cost, had various consequences for the Kurdish factions. Territorial gains were made, with American assistance, though there were significant Kurdish losses, on one occasion through 'friendly fire'. On 6 April 2003 two American F–15 bombers mistakenly attacked a frontline position, killing 18 American soldiers and *peshmerga* fighters and wounding 45 others. Wajeeh Barzani, a senior Kurdish Commander and brother of KDP leader Massoud Barzani, was critically wounded and taken on a US military aircraft for treatment in Germany. Abdul Rahman Kawrini, another *peshmerga* commander, recalled the incident: 'I didn't even see the bombs. I saw oceans of fire. People were screaming terrible screams. There were pieces of flesh and blood everywhere. Some of those left alive didn't know what had happened. They were in total shock.' John Simpson, veteran BBC correspondent, was slightly injured.

A concerted American and Kurdish offensive had opened up in northern Iraq. Action at Dibagah, about 20 miles south of Arbil, the Kurdish capital, was intended to cut off Mosul from Kirkuk and to capture territory that overlooked the Kirkuk oilfields. The anxiety remained that an all-out offensive by the Kurds could provoke a Turkish invasion of northern Iraq. Already the Iraqi army in the north, pounded by US bombing, was beginning to disintegrate, quickly retreating from contested land. The Kurds, by contrast, were highly motivated to advance as far as the United States would let them. Now there was a great incentive for the Kurds to penetrate former Kurdish territory that had been ethnically cleansed by the Saddam regime over 30 years. Many Kurds were returning to land where their families had lived but which the modern generation of exiles had never seen.

The town of Shehan, the first northern populated town to be taken by Kurdish and US forces, fell on 8 April 2003. Jasem Abdi, aged 40, expressed a widespread view: 'We can finally breathe again.' In some places the KDP militia raised its yellow flag on buildings to proclaim itself the new local authority, while pick-up trucks cruised the streets blaring patriotic Kurdish folk songs through loudspeakers. In the Arab quarter of the town the feeling was different. Unis Saleh (38) referred to what he called the US 'invasion' of his country and declared that the Iraqis would resist until the last man. Many Arabs had already fled the town, some to escape the remorseless American bombing and others because of their close association with the Saddam regime in its dying days. One Arab pointed out that Iraqis have never welcomed 'colonisers', adding: 'We judge Americans by the destruction of their bombs, not by their words. Look at what they have done in this town. You call this liberation?' A Baghdad dentist in Shehan said the bombing was bad, 'but nothing like Baghdad'. Issa Matou, a 53-year-old father of five said: 'I want the war to finish. We want to live in peace.' In Kirkuk, the northern equivalent of the south's Basra, human rights groups feared the onset of a wave of ethnic violence. Saddam's regime had expelled an estimated 120,000 Kurds, Turkomen and Assyrians and replaced them with Arab families as part of the notorious 'Arabisation' program. It seemed likely that after the fall of Saddam it would be the Arab families that would be targeted in Kirkuk and elsewhere.

The fate of the Kurds in the post-Saddam era seemed uncertain, not least because Washington had not decided how to reconcile Kurdish aspirations for autonomy and statehood with the Turkish insistence on a secure northern frontier with Iraq; and how to secure a united federal Iraq that would respect the element of Kurdish independence that had been won at such high cost. According to pundit Timothy Garton Ash, writing in *The Guardian* (London) on 27 March 2003, 'we don't have an answer' about 'what is to be done for the Kurds?' But the Kurdish question 'is the largest unexploded bomb in all Iraq'. Surely, if the Kurds are to be judged as having contributed significantly to the US victory on the northern front, while Turkey refused to give the expected help, they would not be deserted as they had been in 1991. It all depended on whether the United States 'had bigger fish to fry'.

It seemed likely that the rivalries, tensions and periodic skirmishes among the Kurdish factions would continue in the post-Saddam era, but perhaps the KDP and the PUK would adopt a new pragmatism in the interest of the broad Kurdish cause. The Kurdish PKK, as a Marxist group, would never be countenanced by Washington and for the most part had been marginalised.

The Kurdish dilemma in the post-Saddam world was straightforward – to secure a degree of autonomy in a federal state or to press for a fully independent Kurdistan. Most Kurdish spokesmen, fearing a loss of autonomy, seemed prepared to settle for the status quo, perhaps with an enlarged territorial base and with guarantees that no further Turkish invasions of northern Iraq would occur. It seemed too much to hope that Kirkuk and its oilfields would become secure Kurdish territory.

The Kurds had experienced repression, genocide and ethnic cleansing at the hands of Saddam Hussein, but the Iraqi leaders had sometimes made pragmatic accommodations. And the Kurds had also experienced bombing, economic sanctions and cruel betrayals by the United States, not to mention the genocidal impact of frequent Turkish invasions facilitated by US-supplied arms and US diplomatic cover. When it became clear what the United States intended to do with the post-Saddam Iraq, the various Kurdish factions – beset over the years by sectarianism, military conflict and repression – would have new decisions to take. As 'small fish' their scope for manoeuvre would be limited but they were living in a rapidly changing environment that would offer fresh opportunities for political development.

FIVE

Turkey

The position of Turkey has been one of the crucial factors in the conflict over Iraq. As NATO's only Muslim member and a neighbour of Iraq, Ankara enjoys a regional status that cannot be ignored by Washington. The election of a new Muslim parliament in the prelude to the 2003 war meant that Turkish support for the American aggression was limited, much less than the US strategists planning a northern front would have wanted. And there were post-war complications involving the long-standing Turkish conflict with the Kurds. Both Turkey and the northern Kurds had an interest in Kirkuk and its oilfields – a sure recipe for further regional instability exacerbated by the war.

The Turkish political situation in some ways resembled that of Saddam's Iraq and that of Israel. Like the erstwhile Baghdad government the Turkish regime suppresses its own Kurdish population. Like Israel, Turkey is totally immune to the strictures and demands of international law. The Turkish authorities have tortured and murdered their own people, and have frequently ordered massive invasions of northern Iraq

– facts that have never troubled Washington as it works to cultivate a strategically important NATO member. Turkey has slaughtered tens of thousands of Kurds which, when Saddam did the same, was a reason in the United States for ostracism, moral outrage, economic sanctions, endless bombing, war and regime change. Turkey has frequently sent troops, tanks and warplanes in aggression against a neighbour – illegal acts ignored by the US strategists.

Turkish Repression

The US indifference to Turkish domestic and international crimes is shown in many ways. The United States supplies Turkey with its weapons, encourages the development of Turkish-Israeli relations, and provides Ankara with all necessary diplomatic and political support at the United Nations and elsewhere. It is significant that the US is even willing to rewrite history in the interest of its Turkish ally. We need to remember the American response to certain events that occurred during the First World War.

In a sustained genocide that began on 24 April 1915 the Turkish army began a systematic massacre of hundreds of thousands of Armenian Turks; men, women and children. When Adolf Hitler was planning his 'final solution' to the Jewish question he asked: 'Who remembers the Armenians now?' The United States does not. When in 1990 Senator Robert Dole moved a resolution in Congress for US recognition of the 1915 massacre Senator Robert Byrd urged caution: 'I say we ought to stop, look and listen before we take a fateful step here to offend a friend, to offend an ally.' The resolution was defeated by 51 votes to 48. Washington had decided that the Armenian massacre, committed by Turkish forces and cynically consigned to oblivion by Adolf Hitler, had never happened.

Hence any attempt to consider the likely Turkish response to the fall of Saddam Hussein must take into account Turkey's historical status as an imperial power, its appalling human rights record, its long persecution of its Kurdish minority, and its firm position as a NATO ally of the United States.

Suppressing the Kurds

The Turks have long been intent on repressing the ethnic Kurds within Turkey, at times granting the Turkish Kurds fewer rights than their Iraqi counterparts. One consequence of the 1991 Gulf War was to give the Turks a freer hand in attacking Kurdish culture, destroying Kurdish villages and waging war, often across the border into northern Iraq, against the organised Kurdish resistance. The United States and Britain frequently conspired with these Turkish acts of aggression; for example, by suspending overflights in the northern 'no fly' zone to allow Turkish aircraft to bomb the Kurds.

In March 1991, following the end of the Gulf War, the Turkish army was firing on Kurdish nationalists in southern Turkey: two people were shot dead and twenty wounded by the Turkish security forces. Turkey – in the interest of dismembering a recalcitrant Iraq – had shown some support for Kurdish independence in Iraq, but conservative Turkish factions reckoned that such a move would strengthen the dissident Kurds within Turkey. There was already conservative hostility to the efforts of the Turkish president, Turgut Ozal, to lift a Turkish law banning the Kurdish language. There were already signs that the Turkish Kurds were being emboldened by the political struggle of their brothers across the border in Iraq – in turn provoking the inevitable Turkish backlash. In April Turkish soldiers were reportedly stealing blankets, sheets and food from terrified Kurdish refugees in southern Turkey.

Turkish Aggressions

On 5 August 1991 Turkish F–4 and F–104 fighter-bombers flew ninety-two sorties into northern Iraq to bomb Turkish Kurdish rebels, alleged members of the Kurdish Workers Party (PKK) struggling – along with some of the Iraqi Kurds – for an independent homeland. The Turkish air strikes were accompanied by a land invasion that penetrated eleven miles into Iraqi territory. One US spokesman at the Incirlik air base in Turkey commented that any Turkish action against the PKK was solely the business of the Turkish government. This meant that Washington was unconcerned that the US-equipped armed forces of Turkey were frequently invading the sovereign territory of a fellow member of the

United Nations, with no reference to the allied forces supposedly protecting the Kurds of northern Iraq and with no reference to what should have been the proper role of the UN Security Council.

It may also be argued that both Washington and Ankara, as NATO members, should have been more sensitive to the North Atlantic Treaty. Thus Article 1 declares that the Parties undertake 'to settle any international dispute in which they may be involved by peaceful means ...'; while Article 2 specifies the domestic obligations of the signatories:

> The Parties will contribute towards the further development of peaceful and friendly international relations by strengthening their free institutions, by bringing about a better understanding of the principles upon which these institutions are founded, and by promoting conditions of stability and well-being ...

Elsewhere in the treaty there are references to the primary responsibility of the UN Security Council for the maintenance of international peace and security, suggesting that the frequent Turkish invasions of northern Iraq should be a proper concern of the United Nations.

After the 1991 Gulf War Turkey was induced to act as a host country for the 'rapid reaction' forces intended to protect the Kurds in Iraq, but Turkey itself reserved the right to attack selected Kurdish targets over the border whenever it chose to do so. The August action by the Turkish armed forces had been predictably applauded by the Turkish general staff: 'New targets discovered during the operation have also been bombed. It should never be forgotten that the Turkish army is ready to punish severely and decisively those responsible for all kinds of actions and treachery against our country.'

At the same time Turkey had decided to establish a permanent 3-mile deep 'buffer zone' in northern Iraq to prevent Kurdish guerrillas infiltrating its territory. Thus the Turkish prime minister, Mesut Yilmaz, announced: 'We are declaring a 5km region along the border a buffer zone. Everyone who steps into that area [without permission] will be fired upon.'[1]

It was claimed that the military operations had been successful. A regiment of troops back by warplanes and artillery had attacked likely rebel bases in northern Iraq and won control of hills overlooking the region where a 'cleaning-up' operation had been carried out. Kurdish reports conveyed a different image of what had transpired. A spokesman for the Kurdish Democratic Party (KDP) claimed that the Turkish aircraft had bombed a Kurdish refugee village in northern Iraq, killing eleven refugees and wounding thirteen at the Kherazook settlement in Shirwan district. Bombing strikes by Turkish planes against another refugee settlement, in Khakork, had killed 18 people, including women and children: 'We call upon the Turkish government to end these atrocities and attacks on innocent Iraqi Kurdish refugees and we call upon the allied forces to intercede to prevent such attacks from reoccurring.'

Washington had no interest in such matters, apart from choosing to deny what no-one was asserting. Thus US Army Major Michel McKinny declared at Incirlik that US forces had not been involved in the Turkish operation. He declined to comment on the fact that the US had provided the Turkish armed forces with military training, a prodigious range of armaments and political cover.

The Turkish troops were then withdrawn from northern Iraq, apart from those well entrenched in the buffer zone and pending the next invasion of sovereign Iraqi territory. On one occasion in August 1991 American F–16 fighters almost attacked Turkish aircraft by mistake. The American jets had taken off from Incirlik to investigate the incursion by the Turkish F–104 Starfighters into Iraqi air space, after which the US aircraft returned to base. In one account the American plans had come within three minutes of firing at the Turkish aircraft. One problem was that the US forces had been given no prior warning of the Turkish invasion: 'We found out about the Turkish operation as it happened. But there was no confrontation between Coalition forces and Turkish planes' (McKinny). The Turkish government was claiming that the main part of the attempt to obliterate the PKK was over, but it was widely know that Turkish forces were still engaged on reconnaissance and other missions inside Iraq.

Over the subsequent months there were further Turkish raids on the Kurds in Iraq, some on the 'safe haven' set up for their protection.[2] In one account around 3,000 Turkish troops invaded Iraq in an attempt to root out PKK guerrillas, with estimates suggesting that more than one hundred Iraqis had been killed by Turkish artillery fire.

Massoud Barzani's Iraqi Kurds were aiding the Turkish forces, so generating a Kurd-against-Kurd conflict involving around 6,000 fighters. Barzani, with a primary interest in toppling Saddam Hussein, was bitterly resentful of the PKK posture: 'Under cover of being Kurds and revolutionaries, they want to make us lose the historic chance of our people.' In this brief phase of the conflict up to 30 Iraqi Kurds and 50 alleged PKK members had been killed. Fouad Masoum, prime minister of the Kurdish administration in northern Iraq, declared that the aim was 'not to annihilate or crush' the PKK fighters but to make them leave the area.

On 23 October 1992 some 5,000 Turkish troops drove six miles into Iraq in pursuit of Kurdish rebels regarded in Ankara as nothing more than terrorists and bandits. Turkey's state television showed Cobra helicopters firing rockets while jet-fighters bombed targets as the Turkish troops advanced. One Turkish soldier who had stepped on a mine and lost a leg was shown being carried away in a blanket. Suleyman Demirel, Turkish prime minister, saw no immediate end to the military action: 'The operations will continue until the annihilation of separatist militants taking refuge in northern Iraq.' He estimated that there were between 7,500 and 10,000 PKK militants in northern Iraq and 2,500 in Turkey. The air and land incursions into Iraq 'constituted the legitimate self-defense of Turkey to prevent rebels from infiltrating ... and that they would continue until the swamp was dry'. Some unconfirmed reports claimed that up to 2,000 Iraqis had been killed in the recent raids. But the Kurdish resistance was still able to mount offensives against the regular Turkish forces.

On 25 October as many as 500 PKK guerrillas mounted an attack on Turkish troops across the border, whereupon Turkey immediately retaliated with F–104 strikes and helicopter-borne troops attacking Kurdish positions. The Kurds had planned their raid to coincide with the aftermath of Turkey's parliamentary elections, narrowly won by the conservative Demirel. The new government was considering a war against the Kurdish minority, and the conflict was threatening to involve the other states in the region. Turkey's ambassador in Damascus had already informed the Syrians that Turkey might feel forced to attack the camp run by PKK leader Abdullah Ocalan in the Syrian-controlled Bekaa Valley in Lebanon, and that if Turkey did not receive Syria's co-operation, it 'would seek help from Israel'.

There were also reports of Turkish brutality against Kurdish civilians, with mass executions and bodies flung into mass graves.[3] On 5 May 1992 a British delegation, led by Lord Avebury, chairman of the Parliamentary Human Rights Group, called on the British government to impose economic sanctions on Turkey in response to its torture and massacre of Kurdish civilians. The government did not respond and, a week later, Kurdish civilians were again being bombed by Turkish planes. Clashes continued throughout 1992, with some 82 combatants killed on 29 September in the worst single engagement of the war. Now some of the Iraqi Kurds, fearing for their own survival, were again co-operating with the regular Turkish forces to defeat the radical PKK. President Ozal met an Iraqi opposition coalition that Kurdish leaders hoped to establish as a US-back provisional government in northern Iraq. By now it was abundantly clear to independent observers that the West, so exercised about Saddam's persecution of his Kurdish minority, had no interest in Turkey's repression of its own Kurds.[4] A bloody battle at the end of September left some 200 dead, mostly PKK, as it became increasingly clear that military force alone would be unlikely to quell the rebellion.

On 29 October an official Turkish statement reported that regular troops had penetrated ten miles into northern Iraq on a 20-mile front, and again the option of a permanent Turkish presence in Iraq was being considered. Dogan Gures, the Turkish armed forces chief of staff, hoped that the Turkish forces would be able to withdraw before the winter but did not rule out the creation of a Turkish security zone in the mountains of Iraqi Kurdistan: 'Our security comes first. Can the *peshmerga* do this [alone]? We said, let's clear this marsh out.'

The Turkish army now claimed to control 62 square miles of Iraq on two main fronts: at Haftanin, north east of the Iraqi town of Zakho; and at the Hakurk valley, close to the Iranian border. The army was claiming also that the current PKK death toll might rise to around 400, compared to eleven Turkish soldiers killed in action. Some observers suggested that Turkey might be interested in pursuing the old Ottoman ambitions to gain control over the oil reserves of northern Iraq. This indication of post-Saddam claims for control of Kirkuk and Mosul was a further sign of Turkish ambitions for the region.

By early November 1992 the Turkish army claimed to be in control of 150 square miles of Iraqi territory (Figure 6). Bombing raids and troop movements across the border were happening on a daily basis, with reports that a thousand Kurdish PKK had been killed when Turkish

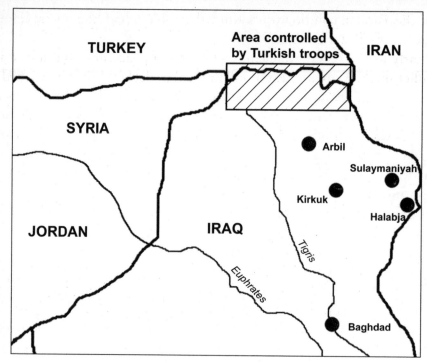

Figure 6. *Turkish occupation of Iraq (November 1992)*

forces overran a bas at Haftanin. The US was continuing to monitor the situation but seemingly had little interest in the escalation of cross-border raids in a region supposedly protected under the terms of Operation Provide Comfort. Washington was forced to remember that its air umbrella over northern Iraq relied upon US aircraft based in Turkey and that the mandate for the American operation ('Poised Hammer') was to be discussed before the Turkish parliament in December. But now the anti-PKK Kurds in northern Iraq were resentful of the massive Turkish incursions into Iraqi territory. Ahmad Birmani, PUK, commented: 'The Turkish military leaders are now behaving just like Menachim Begin and Yitzhak Shamir did towards the Palestinians. They fear the growth of moderation. They want terrorists for enemies.' Ankara knew that if the non-PKK Kurds in Iraq were to achieve federation in a post-Saddam Iraq, it would set a disturbing example for the oppressed Kurdish minority in Turkey.

The 'international community', remorselessly moralising about the Iraqi invasion of Kuwait, had nothing to say about the Turkish occupation of Iraq. The world 'looked the other way' while it seemed that the Turkish solution to its Kurdish problem had 'the unconditional backing of Western states'.[5]

Early in 1993 there were some signs that a peaceful resolution of the conflict might be possible. Abdullah Ocalan declared that he wished to negotiate and would mount no PKK attacks during the celebrations for the Turkish New Year of Nowrug on 21 March. Now it seemed that both the war-weary PKK and their Syrian backers had an interest in a truce. But Ocalan declared that if the Turkish government continued to say to the Kurds 'you don't exist', there would be a return to 'continuous war'. Within weeks the conflict had resumed.

On 23 December 1994 there were fresh reports of fighting between the main Kurdish factions, the KDP and the PUK in northern Iraq – in part as a battle for control of the profits made from smuggled oil and cigarettes. Every day more than a thousand lorries from Turkey poured across the border carrying goods for Iraq, and later – in their enormous spare fuel tanks – brought cheap Iraqi petrol back to Turkey to be sold at an enormous profit. This obvious breaking of the sanctions regime was well known by Washington, but ignored to keep Ankara happy. The Kurds levied $150 on each lorry, generating revenue that was plainly attractive to the various competing factions. However, a factional war was of little help to Western strategists struggling to maintain an 'autonomous' Iraqi Kurdistan inside a 'sovereign' Iraq. At the end of January 1995 Britain warned the Kurds that unless they stopped fighting among themselves they would lose Western protection.

On 20 March 1995 the Turkish armed forces began Operation Twilight whereby some 35,000 troops again invaded the 'safe haven' of northern Iraq – the largest use of Turkish troops over its borders since Ankara launched the invasion of Cyprus in 1974. The troops were supported by tanks, artillery and aircraft in what Turkey's prime minister, Tansu Ciller, described as a 'hot pursuit of operation'. She explained: 'We are not against innocent civilians', but added that 'we will be there as long as necessary'.[6]

Colonel Ihsan Ongun then announced at a press briefing that the Turkish forces planned to push 25 miles into Iraq on a 150-mile front. Turkish television reported that 76 bombs had been dropped on ten alleged PKK positions, and Turkish troops were said to have arrested hundreds of suspects. On the second day of the invasion Turkish aircraft were pounding Kurdish targets on what had expanded to a 185-mile front inside northern Iraq. One Turkish officer declared that the aim was 'to cause as much destruction as possible', while a Turkish commander claimed that his men had secured a swathe of territory some 20 miles deep. A British military analyst noted that the Turkish forces were not always careful to distinguish between PKK fighters and refugees: 'The actual rebels may have just melted away. They certainly had time.' The United Nations was investigating reports that Turkish troops had rounded up Kurds in the town of Zakho and were forcibly taking them back into Turkey.

The West had been shocked at the sheer scale of the Turkish invasion. At the same time there was no suggestion that Washington would exert pressure to curb Turkish policy. Sadako Ogata, UN high commissioner for refugees, announced she was 'making representations to the Turkish authorities to signal that there should be no action against refugees'; and in the same vein Amnesty International expressed its concern about the safety of prisoners taken in Iraqi Kurdistan, given the Turkish government's disregard for human rights. The British Foreign Office announced with unconscious risibility that it had received assurances from Turkey that the principle of Iraq's territorial integrity would be upheld. On 22 March various European Union (EU) countries criticised the Turkish action, but with no effect. Ciller said in Ankara: 'We are determined in this final operation the job will definitely be done.'

On 25 March Rupert Colville, a spokesman for the UNHCR, announced that a convoy of 50 vehicles had been assembled for the evacuation of 2,000 Kurdish villagers out of the battle zone, but there were few signs that the Turkish forces were planning for an early withdrawal from Iraqi territory. For the first time the United States was expressing concern that the Turkish army was planning a longer stay than it had promised, while an army spokesman said that Turkish soldiers were still combing the area for Kurdish guerrillas 'cave by cave and valley by valley'. One Turkish commentator declared: 'The sense of national pride is higher than at any time since the invasion of Cyprus in 1974.'

After several weeks the bulk of the troops withdrew from Iraq, but the prospect of further invasions remained and Ankara was suggesting that the Turkish-Iraqi border should be redrawn to Turkey's advantage. Thus President Demirel commented: 'The line here is wrong. The border should skirt the mountains on the Iraqi side … to block the passage of terrorists ... Now let us correct this border ... lower it from the mountains to the planes.' Hoshyar Zebari, a KDP spokesman, suggested that the problem was compounded by the millions of mines that had been put down by the Turkish forces – 'and still it is impossible to seal the border completely'. On 5 July 1995 two Turkish brigades – about 6,000 troops – pushed ten miles into Iraq and 'indiscriminately' shelled villages. The United States, continuing the flow of arms to Turkey, hoped that civilians would not be hurt and that the operation would not last long.

The pattern had been established – frequent Turkish invasions of Iraq, repeated talk of 'buffer zones' and 'security cordons', a residual Turkish army presence in Iraq, the destruction of villages, the persecution of civilians, and the usual indifference of Washington and London, keen to advertise their moral superiority over the likes of Saddam Hussein. In 1996–7 there were further Turkish invasions, and in March 1997 the Turkish forces were reportedly using Kurdish prisoners as mine detectors.[7] The Turks continued their efforts to suppress Kurdish culture, and there were reports that Saddam Hussein was offering sanctuary to Kurdish refugees from Turkey. In 1998 Ankara claimed an important victory after forcing Syria to drop its support for Kurdish rebels in a new deal that required Damascus to cut off assistance to the PKK, which had been using Syria to launch attacks on Turkey. Now there were suggestions that the PKK was intending to move to a more political phase in an effort to project a more moderate international image.

On 13 November 1998 Abdullah Ocalan, the PKK leader, was arrested at Rome's Fiumicino Airport after flying from Moscow on a false passport. After an extradition battle involving Italy, Germany and Turkey, Ocalan disappeared from Rome, only to be captured later in Kenya and taken to Turkey. There it seemed likely that Ocalan, facing Turkey's 'trial of the century', would eventually be executed for his long 'terrorist' war against Ankara. In the event Ocalan begged for his life, promised to urge his followers to adopt a peaceful posture, was first condemned to die by hanging, and then exploited the Turkish objective of EU membership by taking his appeal to the European Court of Human Rights.

In April 2000 – 'in what has become an annual event that marks the arrival of spring' – thousands of Turkish troops invaded northern Iraq in search of Kurdish guerrillas, despite PKK assurances that they would respond to Ocalan's appeal for peace.[8] Little had changed. The United States continued to supply Ankara with a substantial range of military hardware, the PKK factions saw little hope in the peaceful route to emancipation, and the Iraqi authorities remained powerless to stop the frequent Turkish incursions into Iraqi territory. The Turkish military had declared that it would continue to pursue the war until the last PKK fighter was dead or had surrendered. Turkish troops remained camped in northern Iraq and there seemed no prospect that Ankara would be forced to observe the demands of international law: 'It is this power vacuum in the region, Turkish analysts say, which has forced Ankara to act. That in turn is another reminder of the failings of Western policy in effecting change in Iraq.'[9]

The Turkish troops were guided by 'village guards', local mercenaries recruited and armed by the Turkish army, with support from the Ankara-backed KDP. Over the previous five years, thousands of Kurdish villages in northern Iraq had been destroyed by Turkish troops using US-supplied tanks, Super Cobra helicopters, F–16 warplanes and the rest. Just prior to the new Turkish onslaught William Cohen, the US defense secretary, praised Turkey as a key NATO ally and a bridge between East and West, and urged closer ties between Washington and Ankara.

Human Rights Abuses

It remained obvious that Ankara, despite pressure from Europe, was doing little to improve its human-rights record. Ocalan, originally condemned to death, was languishing on a prison island, but torture and extrajudicial killings remained commonplace. One investigator recounts the experiences of a Kurdish prisoner:

> I cannot write his name here. He told me how he was arrested on his way from Istanbul to visit relatives in Kurdistan. He was beaten, sprayed with hot and cold water, and given electric shocks to his genitals. When I asked him if he wanted revenge on his torturers, he said he just wanted never to see them again.[10]

On 4 May 2000 Turkish MPs reported that torture was widespread in police stations, where sanitation and treatment fell far below international standards. The report described how suspects, living in filthy jails, were beaten, sprayed with water canon and given electric shocks: 'The commission reached the opinion that maltreatment and torture are a widespread practice in police stations and identified some methods and equipment used in this practice.' It was noted that police staff had obstructed a full inspection of their stations.

In December troops moved to end a mass protest in Turkish prisons about appalling conditions, torture and other forms of abuse. After three days of raids on more than 20 prisons, some 400 inmates remained barricaded in Istanbul's Umraniye prison, with the death toll rising elsewhere: 19 inmates and two soldiers had been killed. Many people had protested in the streets in support of the prisoners but the right-wing media were urging strong government action. In January 2001 Amnesty International accused Turkey of torturing prisoners:

> These sources consistently indicate that prisoners were beaten and some tortured before, during and after the transfers to the new prisons. It is alleged that prisoners were stripped and subjected to rape with a truncheon on arrival at Kandira F-type prison near Izmit. The claims could not be corroborated because lawyers' requests for forensic examinations to be carried out receive no response.

Some 30,000 common criminals had been pardoned as part of a prison 'reform' plan, but all political prisoners remained behind bars. Around 400 prisoners were continuing a death fast that had begun two months before. On 20 September Abdul Bahri Yusufoglu died on the 137th day of his protest, bringing the death toll in the hunger strikes to 36, a number that would increase in the weeks to come.

It was also being reported that rape victims were being put in the dock. Fatima Polattas, one example among many, was raped while in the custody of the Turkish police. She filed charges whereupon her four alleged tormentors were put on trial – and so was she. Polattas faced up to six years in jail for insulting Turkey's security forces and the moral integrity of her country by speaking publicly about her ordeal. She was one of 11 women put on trial for appearing at a conference to describe sexual torture.[11] Some faced jail terms of up to 30 years.

A New Parliament

In November 2002 the Justice and Development Party (AKP), a moderate Islamic party, won parliamentary elections with little more than a third of the popular vote. Prime Minister Bulent Ecevit handed in his resignation, whereupon the AKP moved quickly to assure Washington that Turkey would remain a NATO member and continue to allow the United States to use Turkish air bases. But it was not certain that the new Turkish government would allow Washington to move thousands of troops to Turkey to facilitate the planned northern invasion of Iraq. In January 2003 the government, unaware of the political obstacles ahead, announced that it would seek support in parliament for the American military plans. The Turkish war on the indigenous Kurds – in which 30,000 people had been killed and millions uprooted – had eased, and it seemed likely that the Turkish government, intent on cultivating US goodwill, would work to overcome the public hostility to Americans intentions.[12]

On 31 January 2003 Turkey's military and political leaders approved the idea of basing foreign troops in the country, a decision that signalled a willingness to allow US troops to open a second front in northern Iraq. Turkey's powerful national security council, whose 'recommendations' were generally followed, issued a firm declaration urging parliament to authorise the basing of foreign troops on Turkish soil and the stationing of Turkish troops abroad – this latter an obvious reference to Kurdish Iraq. Murat Yetkin, the Ankara bureau chief of the *Radikal* newspaper, commented: 'The decision-makers in Ankara are no longer discussing whether or not to support an American intervention. What is really being discussed is the most suitable timing for the decision.'[13] Some 10,000 Turkish troops had already been sent to the border region. It seemed likely that US troops would be allowed into Turkey and that Turkish troops, perhaps acting with their American allies, would invade northern Iraq. But the Washington strategists had underestimated the hostility of the Ankara parliament to the US plans.

American Pressure

The US tactics in seeking to gain acquiescence were characteristic: the familiar mix of threat and bribery. Inducements in the form of billions of dollars of aid, military support and political help in Europe were expected to persuade the Turkish parliament to support the planned influx of American troops. One American official said: 'Ultimately, they have as much interest in getting rid of Saddam as the rest of us. It is hard to see them disagreeing with a direct request from President Bush for help.'

Already the Turkish forces were building up their military presence in preparation for the anticipated invasion of northern Iraq while the army's general staff issued a statement: 'It is necessary to increase readiness of our units to prepare them ahead of possible security developments in the region. As of today, units under the Second Army Command will be reinforced with equipment and materiel.' Some estimates suggested that some 20,000 troops equipped with tanks and heavy artillery were massing on the border, but Turkey's political position remained ambiguous. It was still not clear whether the US troops would be allowed into Turkey or whether the Turkish army would take action in the event of war, while the Kurds were struggling to reassure the Turkish government. Thus Hoshyar Zebari, KDP head of international relations, speaking at an international conference, said that the Kurdish enclave would not seek independence in the event of war. Kurdish anxieties were plain: 'One danger we face is the possibility of military intervention by our neighbours, particularly Turkey and Iran, in our internal affairs ... any such military intervention would be resisted by the people of the region and cause severe complications. It would invite further intervention by other countries. Such a prospect would not be in anyone's interest.' But Turkey was concerned not only by the possibility of Kurdish claims for statehood: any Kurdish advance on Kirkuk and Mosul and the surrounding oilfields would be certain to alarm Ankara.

The United States was now suggesting that Turkish troops might be allowed to patrol parts of the Iraq in peacekeeping operation after the fall of Saddam, but this suggestion, sure to disturb the Kurds, was not sufficient to placate the Ankara parliament. Then Washington emphasised that $6 billion was available in grants and up to $20 billion in loan guarantees in return for Turkish military assistance. Even these blandishments were insufficient to win Turkish support for the American strategy. Yasar Yakis, Turkish foreign minister, commented after a meeting with President Bush that the US offer was not enough and that Turkey would not respond to US deadlines for a decision: 'The reasons why it was difficult for us to present the request to parliament … remain … when conditions are fulfilled we are prepared to present it in the shortest possible time.'

On 25 February it seemed that Washington's attempts at bribery, a typical US tactic, were bringing results. The Turkish government expressed agreement with the American proposals and announced that a recommendation would be sent to the country's parliament for approval. The White House was making every effort to achieve a 'coalition of the willing' by constructing a 'coalition of the bought' to launch an illegal invasion of a sovereign member of the United Nations. On 27 February the Ankara parliament was expected to approve the US plans.[14]

America Rebuffed

The idea was that the United States would be allowed to base 60,000 American troops in Turkey, ready for the planned invasion of Iraq from the north, and that 40,000 Turkish soldiers would occupy parts of northern Iraq. The Americans, Turkish officials claimed, had agreed to disarm hostile Kurdish factions in order to prevent any expansion of Kurdish autonomy in the region. It seemed that Washington was again prepared to alienate the Kurds, this time to win Ankara's support for its military plans.

After further delays the Turkish parliament finally voted on the US strategy, backed by the Turkish government. The vote was 264 to 250 in favour, but some 16 members of parliament abstained and the total was just short of the necessary majority. The American plans and the government recommendations had been defeated. Tayyip Erdogan, AKP chairman, announced: 'The government is working on alternatives that will serve Turkey's best interests and this may come at a certain price. Our decision will emerge in line with developments.' In short, the government had suffered a serious setback and was uncertain how to proceed. A source close to Erdogan noted the resentment that Washington had caused by its clumsy attempts at bribery and its setting of ultimatums for Turkish decisions: 'The US has behaved in a seriously irresponsible way. It would have been a lot easier if they had acted properly.'

Nesrin Aloglu, a Turkish bank clerk, voiced the popular view about American behaviour: 'Serves them right. Now they can apologise ... for the way in which the United States so rudely took Turkey for granted and issued threats, insults and ultimatums when it did not get what it wanted.' Zafer Dorttas, a 27-year-old customs official, commented that the parliamentary vote had dispelled the image abroad that Turkey can be bought. The American press had not been helpful: some newspapers depicted Turkey as a money-grabbing belly dancer or a prostitute haggling over the price of her favours. Ayse Akin, a student, responded bluntly to such depictions of his country: 'I can't tell you how awful I felt when I saw the cartoons. They were so deeply insulting, America can stick its money and its troops up its backside.'

The Turkish rejection of the US demands had immediate consequences for the Turkish economy. The financial markets plunged and Ankara was forced to introduce austerity measures including tax rises, a reduction in worker benefits and limits on hiring labour. Analysts predicted that Turkey would face a weaker lira, costlier borrowing and a substantial slide in stock values. Washington was reportedly reeling from the Turkish rejection of US plans for troop deployment, while US officials were 'discussing implications'. Perhaps they took heart at their continued support among the Turkish military. On 5 March General Hilmi Ozkok, chief of the general staff, expressed the support of the Turkish armed forces for the Washington plans, increasing the chances that a second recommendation would be presented to the Turkish parliament.

Kurdish Concerns

On 6 March 2003 Sami Abdul-Rahman, regional deputy premier of 'Kurdistan', warned that the Iraqi Kurds were committed to fighting any Turkish troops that entered their self-governing area: 'Whichever way the Turks come, our people will resist them with all means at our disposal. Believe me, if we are faced with death or military occupation, the first would be lighter ... It would be worse if they came with the

Americans. We don't want to be seen fighting part of the coalition. So what are they coming for? To repress Kurds.' Already some analysts were predicting that when the US-led war began the Kurdish forces would try to take Kirkuk, the main centre of northern Iraq's oil industry and historically a Kurdish city. This would then encourage a Turkish invasion of the region.

On 13 March Turkey's highest court banned the largest pro-Kurdish political party, declaring that it was acting as a front for separatist rebels. At the same time Turkish troops were reportedly moving into northern Iraq, with more soldiers massing on the border, to discourage Kurdish expansion and claims to statehood. Hasip Kaplan, a senior official of the banned Hadep Party, commented: 'Today's developments show that there has been absolutely no change in Turkey's policy towards the Kurds. They are bent on blocking all democratic channels through which the Kurds can articulate their demands freely and openly.'[15]

War and Aftermath

The Turkish government continued the search for a way to placate the Bush administration. The regime, urged on by the military, hinted at the possibility of a new parliamentary vote and moved as far as it could without full parliamentary acquiescence. On 19 March the government announced that it would allow American warplanes to use its airspace, an urgent demand made by Donald Rumsfeld in a meeting with Vecdi Gonul, Turkish defense minister and negotiated by Colin Powell and Abdullah Gul, foreign minister. It was a small concession but useful to a White House bent on war.

On 20 March fears were heightened that Turkey would move troops into the Kurdish areas on its borders, while again there were hints that the Ankara parliament might vote again on permission for US troops to use Turkish territory. On the following day there were reports that 1,500 Turkish troops had moved into northern Iraq as a forerunner to a larger deployment as the US-led war developed. Abdullah Gul had already predicted that his country's forces would move into the region to prevent an 'influx' of refugees and to prevent 'terrorist activity'. Donald Rumsfeld commented that Mr Gul's remarks were 'notably unhelpful'. The Kurds feared a Turkish land grab in their autonomous area.

Iraq's neighbours were now concerned that the war would lead to a break-up of the country. On 8 April Syria, Turkey and Iran were reportedly working together to prevent a collapse of Iraq's territorial integrity, a development that would cause problems for the region. Bussaina Shaaban, head of the Syrian information office, said at a press conference: 'The three countries want to preserve the unity of Iraq ... and to put an end to the horrible suffering of the Iraqi people.' Both Ankara and Tehran were now worried that American troops might help the Kurds to seize Kirkuk – which in turn would boost Kurdish claims for an enhanced autonomy, so threatening the stability of Turkey and Iran. On 10 April such fears were shown to be well grounded: a force of US and Kurdish troops occupied Kirkuk, and the Ankara regime declared that a permanent Kurdish presence in the region would not be acceptable. Washington had found the Kurdish *peshmerga* a useful ally in northern Iraq but it seemed unlikely that the US would risk a permanent rupture with Turkey by agreeing a permanent Kurdish occupation of Kirkuk and the surrounding territory.

The failure of the Ankara parliament to agree the American plans for a northern front in the war had created tensions that were still manifest – an obvious reason why the United States had tolerated a Kurdish expansion that Washington knew would alarm the Turks. How would Ankara be expected to respond to the US-orchestrated administration in Baghdad and the American occupation in Iraq? In summary, three broad factors should be considered in assessing the likely Turkish response to the collapse of the Saddam regime and the imposition of an American neo-colonial presence:

- Under the Ottomans Iraq had once been a Turkish colony. It could not be assumed that Turkish awareness of its imperial past, which lasted well into the 20th century, would not swell its ambitions in the new post-war situation. Turkey had a permanent geographical status in the region, where Washington was claiming that the US occupation would only be a temporary phenomenon.

- The Kurdish problem had a deep-seated historical dimension and would persist. This circumstance alone would be likely to tempt Ankara into considering an expanded and permanent Turkish presence in the north of Iraq. Allied to the burgeoning Turkish interest in Kirkuk and Mosul and the surrounding oilfields, Kurdish expansion into these areas, aided by the United States, was a powerful incentive for the Turks to organise its own permanent military occupation of the region.

– Turkey was fortunate in that, as with Israel, the US perceived it as strategically important – allowing Ankara a substantial but reduced political leverage in the region. Ankara was also a friend of Israel, which was highly congenial to the US policy planners. Turkey's human rights abuses would be ignored by Washington, just as the United States sanctions Israel's daily ethical and legal derelictions. Ankara seemed well placed to exploit its alliance with the United States in the post-Saddam Iraq but Ankara's lukewarm support for the war had not helped the relationship. Moreover, Turkey's strategic importance to the United States was diminished in the post-Saddam era: it could be assumed that a US-friendly Turkey would not be necessary to 'contain' the new regime in Baghdad.

From the American perspective Turkey had not had a good war. Ankara had resisted US bribery and threat but allowed its airspace to be used by American warplanes. There was heightened tension between Kurds and Turks but little to worry the Washington strategists. It was likely that Turkey would maintain a permanent presence in northern Iraq – another post-Saddam occupation; and likely also that the northern Kurds would maintain a degree of autonomy far short of statehood. The US-led war had exacerbated the tensions in the region. The Kurds and Turks both posed problems for the US planners in the post-war world but the political contours of the region had not changed dramatically. There would be bitter recriminations and military conflict over Kirkuk and Mosul, but Washington would work to guarantee its own control of the oil resources. The United States faced bigger problems elsewhere in the Middle East.

SIX

Iran

Iran watched the 2003 American aggression with mounting alarm and resentment. The United States had already branded Iran a 'terrorist' state and refused to acknowledge the reformist trends in the country's national politics. Iran feared that it would be next on Washington's target list.

The historical background to Iran was also relevant to how it regarded the 2003 war. People who talk about the US-led campaign as being Gulf War II do not only forget the Iran-Iraq War (1980–88) but also the many historical wars between Persia (Iran) and Mesopotamia (Iraq). There have been dozens of Gulf wars, many of them long before Christ. Iran, like Turkey, has a rich imperial past that inevitably influences national perceptions of events in the modern world. Where the Arabs reflect on the Abbasids and the Muslim contribution to world science and art the Iranians also can consider with pride an ancient Persian past of which the modern imperialists from America have little knowledge or understanding.

Such matters help to explain why the United States is so widely regarded as an arrogant interloper in the Middle East, ignorant of other cultures and insensitive to any manifestations of national pride that do not accord with American ambitions. And such considerations also throw light on the modern tensions between Iran and Iraq, often historical enemies and today unable to find common cause under the banner of Islam, despite the massive onslaught on the region by a brutal foreign power. It is useful to glance at the history of conflict between Iran and Iraq, if only to remind ourselves of Iran's imperial ambitions and the traditional pride that is sure to resent foreign attempts at intimidation.

Historical Roots

After the death of Nebuchadnezzar in 562 BC, the army of Babylonia (ancient Iraq) rapidly fell into disorder. The traders were interested only in profiteering, and the parasitical priestly class did no more than accumulate treasure at the expense of the people, a beckoning finger to envious forces beyond the gates. When Cyrus, at the head of a disciplined Persian army, stood outside Babylon in 538 BC, the gates were opened to him, and for two centuries Babylonia was ruled as part of the Persian empire. Herodotus described some aspects of the Persian campaign against Babylon.[1]

Cyrus, like many conquerors wanting to be perceived as a liberator, took the title of 'King Babylon, King of the Land', and returned to their rightful temples all the statues of the Gods that Nabodinus, the last monarch of Babylon, had brought to the capital. At the next New Year festival, Cyrus followed the tradition of the Babylonian kings by taking the hand of the god Bel and so legitimised a new Babylonian destiny. He also issued a decree for the emancipation of the Jews, whereupon they hailed Cyrus as a liberator, sang songs of joy, and dubbed the new Babylonian ruler 'the anointed of the Lord'.

After Cyrus the Persian empire, including Babylonia, was ruled by Cambyses II (529–522 BC), who had killed his brother Smerdis to gain the throne. Thereafter the dynasty continued up to the time of Darius III (336–330 BC). An inscription on a high cliff between Kermanshan and Hamadan – in Old Persian, Babylonian and Elamite – declares that

Darius was the ninth Achaemenian King, a number that includes two branches of the dynasty. In his first two years as king he is said to have defeated nine rulers in nineteen battles – and then he encountered Alexander from Macedonia.

The conflicts between Persia and Macedonia were set to continue over the centuries to follow. In 247 BC Arsaces founded the Parthian empire, which at its peak in the first century AD embraced parts of Persia and extended from the Euphrates to the Indus. Its decline began with defeats by the Romans in 39–38 BC. Parthia was taken over in 226 AD by Ardashir I, founder of the Sassanid empire, and it took the Parthians over a century to recover substantial parts of Persia and to consolidate their western frontiers on the Euphrates (these western regions were to remain in the Persian orbit until the Arab conquest in the 7th century. It was not until the 16th century that the Persians were able to regain substantial parts of Mesopotamia).

A Persian national revival was accomplished by the Safavids, a dynasty (1501–1736) founded by Ismail I who conquered most of Persia and added much of Iraq to his empire. In 1508 he took Baghdad and then Mosul, and added the bulk of the country to his other Persian conquests. Soon, however, the Safavids were forced to confront the expanding Ottoman empire, a Turkish challenge that was set to dominate Iraq and much of the surrounding region for centuries. For a time the Safavids retained Basra and Baghdad, and attempted to establish the Shi'ite heresy in place of the orthodox Islam in the region that had once been the very heartland of the Abbasid caliphate. In 1534 Sultan Suleiman, at the height of his powers, decided to attack the Safavids, so beginning a Turkish Ottoman occupation of the region that would continue, with one brief interruption (1624–38) until modern times.

This history is significant because it reminds us that over the centuries both Turkey and Persia (Iran) have had imperial ambitions with regard to Iraq. Sometimes the ambitions were put into practical effect, and sometimes they lay dormant over time. In this context we may speculate that both Turkey and Iran, not insensitive to past imperial attitudes, would respond with opportunistic enthusiasm to a dislocated and helpless Iraq in the regional chaos of the post-Saddam era. The religious dimension also deserves attention.

The emergence of a Safavid Iraq in 1501 gave a significant boost to the Shi'ite wing of Islam against the Sunni commitments of the Ottoman Turks. In these circumstances, Iraq became a battleground not only for competing imperialisms but for the respective branches of Islam that have divided the Muslim community since the time of The Prophet. During the Ottoman-Safavid conflict of the 16th and 17th centuries both the Ottoman Sultan and the Safavid Shah referred to themselves as the sovereign of Islam. The conflict was regarded as substantially a religious matter, so greatly exacerbating the Shi'ite-Sunni strife that had characterised Islam from the earliest times. The schism has persisted and remains a source of conflict in Iraq and elsewhere in the Muslim world.[2]

Iran-Iraq War (1980–88)

It certainly can be argued that historical attitudes, indelibly marking a nation's collective consciousness, can continue to shape personal beliefs and political policies. Thus the circumstances that led to the outbreak of the Iran-Iraq War in 1980 have been partly interpreted in this fashion. The Levant correspondent for *The Economist* commented:

> This is one of the world's oldest conflicts across a primarily racial divide … The origins of the present hostilities between Iraq and Iran can be traced all the way back to the battle of Qadisiya in southern Iraq in 637 AD, when an army of Muslim Arabs put paid to a bigger army of Zoroastrian Persians and to the decadent Sassanian empire.[3]

In the same vein Geoffrey Godsell, writing in *The Christian Science Monitor*, called the Arab-Persian frontier 'one of the great ethnic and cultural divides on the earth's surface'; and *The New York Times* referred to the Iran-Iraq War as an 'ancient struggle' and a continuation of the Arab attempt to subdue the Persians in 637. When, as part of the war, Iranian forces invaded Iraq three years later, *The Economist* judged that this was the Iranian Shi'ites 'chance at revenge' for the massacre at Karbala in 680.[4]

Iran's relations with Baghdad had been poor since before the 1979 Iranian revolution. The shah had acted as a conduit for Israeli and American arms to the northern Kurds, but the fall of the Pahlevi dynasty did nothing to improve Iran-Iraq relations. The agents of Ayatollah Khomeini helped to finance Da'wa, a Shi'ite organisation in Iraq bitterly opposed to the Sunni domination of Iraqi politics under Saddam Hussein. Tehran radio was urging the Iraqi Shi'ites to resist the government, if necessary by violent means. The Baghdad authorities were convinced that Iranian operators in Iraq's main Shi'ite cities (Basra, Najaf, Karbala and Kufa) were behind massive Shi'ite demonstrations displaying huge pictures of Khomeini and their own Shi'ite religious leaders. A serious of violent attacks on Ba'ath officials in Iraq were also ascribed to Iranian agitation. In April 1980 an Iranian threw a hand grenade, wounding Tariq Aziz, a high official in the Saddam administration, and also two students; a few days later a second bomb exploded.

On 4 July 1937 Iran and Iraq had signed a frontier treaty agreeing to the demarcation of their borders, with the Shatt al-Arab waterway a shared conduit for commerce and other traffic. In 1969 the pro-West shah of Iran pressed for a change in the frontier arrangements, while a Kurdish rebellion in northern Iraq encouraged the Iranian regime to press its claims. In effect, the Tehran regime had unilaterally abrogated the 1937 treaty and was using the Shatt al-Arab waterway as if it were Iranian territorial waters. At the same time Iran was providing material support to the Kurdish rebels. These were not circumstances guaranteed to produce equanimity in the Saddam administration.

Baghdad was nursing a host of other grievances, many of them having deep historical roots. The dispute over the contested region of Khurzistan/Arabistan had persisted since Ottoman times, and there seemed to be no peaceful way to resolve the dispute. When the Lesser Tunb Island, Iraqi territory, was suddenly occupied by Iran on 30 November 1971 there was a further deterioration in relations between the two states. On 6 April 1980 the Iraqi government cabled Kurt Waldheim, UN Secretary-General, to demand that Iran pull back from the occupied Iraqi territory, whereupon Iran responded by putting its troops on full alert.[5] Iraq's effort to involve the United Nations had come to nothing.

Ayatollah Khomeini was then urging the Iraqi people to rise up and overthrow the Saddam regime: 'Wake up and topple this corrupt regime in your Islamic country before it is too late'; and he advised the Iraqi army 'not to obey the orders of the foes of the Koran and Islam, but join the people'. Saddam responded with the comment that 'anyone who tries to put his hand on Iraq will have his hand cut off without hesitation', whereupon Khomeini expressed the hope that the Iraqi regime would be 'dispatched to the refuse bin of history'.

The scene was set for a war that would take a huge toll in human casualties, and Khomeini must be judged a principal instigator. Soon after taking power he had said to a Tehran newspaper: 'The Ummayad rule [661–750] was based on Arabism, the principle of promoting Arabs over all other peoples, which was an aim fundamentally opposed to Islam and its desire to abolish nationality and unite all mankind in a single community, under the aegis of a state indifferent to the matter of race and colour.' The Ummayads, Khomeini claimed, were aiming to distort Islam completely 'by reviving the Arabism of the pre-Islamic age of ignorance, and the same aim is still pursued by the leaders of certain Arab countries who declare openly their desire to revive the Arabism of the Ummayads'.[6] There is no doubt that by 'leaders of certain Arab countries' Khomeini had Saddam in mind. In a Paris interview in late–1978 Khomeini gave as his enemies: 'First, the Shah; then the American Satan; then Saddam Hussein and his infidel Ba'ath Party.'[7]

This theological offensive was not without effect on Saddam Hussein. He declared that the Islamic Revolution 'must be a friend of the Arab revolution', and he began praying more frequently, at both Sunni and Shi'ite shrines; he made Imam Ali's birthday a national holiday; he encouraged the use of Islamic symbols; and he resolved to 'fight injustice with the swords of the Imams', calling at the same time for 'a revival of heavenly values'. But there was no way of preventing a deepening of tension between the Iranian ayatollahs and the Iraqi Ba'athists, following the Khomeini revolution. Differences between the Iraqi Sunnis and Shi'ites were exacerbated and, immediately after Khomeini had taken power, the new regime in Tehran committed itself to unyielding opposition to the Saddam regime.

Saddam, after consolidating the seizure of the presidency from Ahmad Bakr, expelled between 15,000 and 20,000 Shi'ites from Iraq; hundreds more were arrested, tortured and executed. In March 1980 the Iraqi authorities executed 97 civilians and military men, half of them members of Da'wa, now a banned organisation. Da'wa activists then began attacking police stations, Ba'ath Party offices, and Popular Army recruiting centres. The repression of the Shi'ites continued and then news leaked out concerning the secret hanging of Ayatollah al-Sadr and his sister Bint al-Huda on 8 April 1980. An incensed Khomeini, hearing of the death of one of his principal supporters, declared: 'The war that the Iraqi Ba'ath wants to ignite is a war against Islam ... The people and army of Iraq must turn their backs on the Ba'ath regime and overthrow it ... because this regime is attacking Iran, attacking Islam and the Koran ... Iran today is the land of God's messenger; and its revolution, government and laws are Islamic.'

Border skirmishes between Iran and Iraq were now happening at the rate of ten a month, and leading Iranian dissidents were being given radio stations in Iraq to beam anti-Khomeini propaganda into Iran. A pro-shah *coup* attempt on 24–25 May was routed by Khomeini loyalists; and a further attempt, staged by Shahpour Bakhtiar, the last premier under the shah, was easily repulsed. A fortnight later, on 27 July 1980, the last shah of Iran, the last occupier of the Peacock Throne, died of cancer in Cairo. It was obvious to Saddam that he could not rely on Iranian monarchist generals or the imperialist United States to topple the troublesome Khomeini regime – and in any case such options would be scarcely more likely to yield a government that was sympathetic to the grievances of the Iraqi government.

It seemed a propitious time for Saddam to intervene. There were constant reports of friction between the Iranian religious leaders and the then President Hassan Bani-Sadr. The Iranian army, following massive purges, was in disarray; arms had stopped flowing to Iran; and the country was diplomatically isolated. The 'great Satan' was incensed at the overthrow of its long-nurtured client and at the Iranian seizing of American hostages; and Tehran's Moscow links had collapsed following the Soviet invasion of Muslim Afghanistan. A friendless and chaotic Iran, starved of supplies and military expertise, seemed an easy target.

On 2 September 1980 Iraqi and Iranian troops clashed near Qasr-e-Shirin, and soon afterwards Iranian artillery began shelling the Iraqi towns of Khanaqin and Mandali. Four days later, Iraq threatened to seize vast swathes of Iranian land in the Zain al Qaws region, supposedly granted to Iraq in a 1975 accord, if it was not ceded within a week. Iran responded with increased artillery fire, and Iraqi troops moved to capture a number of border posts. On 17 September, in a televised speech to the Iraqi National Assembly, Saddam then claimed full control of the Shatt al-Arab, and heavy fighting broke out along the waterway. Two days later, Saddam's armies mounted a general offensive, and what some observers were later to call the 'first Gulf war' had begun. It was set to last for nearly a decade.

In due course the United Nations became involved and after several abortive attempts to limit arms supplies to the region and to arrange a ceasefire adopted Resolution 598 (20 July 1987). Khomeini bitterly accepted the terms of the Security Council decision while Iraq continued to wage war, though claiming to support SCR 598. One observer commented that the 'biggest danger to peace' was not the Iranians or the Iraqis, but 'the gathering of dozens of warships from seven outside nations, all of them steaming up and down the Gulf with limited co-ordination and even less sense of purpose'. Iran's deputy foreign minister commented that 'the USA needs the intensification of tension ... as an excuse for keeping its fleet in the region'. The Iraqis continued to launch military offensives.

A UN peacekeeping force was quickly established and despatched to the Gulf. Now Saddam's forces were succeeding in driving the Iranians out of parts of Kurdistan and in penetrating Iran at several points on the central front. The question of sovereignty over the Shatt al-Arab had not been settled, and the Kurds who had received assistance from the Iranians were still giving Saddam problems in northern Iraq. There was an ample reservoir of hatred between Baghdad and Tehran and the ground seemed prepared for further conflict.

At last the war drew to a close, with Saddam Hussein absurdly claiming a great victory. Some Western estimates put the number of war dead at 367,000 (262,000 Iranians and 105,000 Iraqis), with 700,000 injured (many badly). Iran officially stated that they had suffered 123,220 fatalities, with another 60,711 missing in action. Baghdad said that some 800,000 Iranians had been killed in the war. Figures based on estimates in NATO capitals put the number of Iranian dead at between 420,000 and 580,000 with 300,000 Iraqi fatalities.

To this horrendous toll of human life was added the financial cost of the war – around $1,000,000,000,000. Nothing had been accomplished except to prepare the way for the 1991 Gulf War, a genocidal sanctions regime imposed on Iraq for thirteen years, and the massive 2003 US aggression against Iraq.

The US Role

The number of casualties in the Iran-Iraq war (1980–88) has often been cited as one reason why the 2003 war against Iraq was necessary. It is useful to remember that the United States was an ally of Iraq in an anti-Iran coalition that included Britain, Kuwait, Saudi Arabia and other states.

In 1982, in order to support Saddam Hussein, the US State Department removed Iraq from its list of states sponsoring international terrorism. The White House and the State Department pressured the Export-Import Bank to provide Iraq with finance, to enhance Saddam Hussein's credit rating, and to enable him to obtain loans from other international financial institutions. The US Agricultural Department offered Saddam taxpayer-guaranteed loans for purchases of American commodities, to the manifest satisfaction of US grain exporters. Since March 1982, pursuant to Ronald Reagan's National Security Study Memorandum (NSSM 4–82), the United States had been providing Saddam with intelligence and military support (secretly and contrary to America's official neutrality). In 1984 Washington restored formal relations with Baghdad.

By 1983 it was known that Iraq had been using chemical weapons for some time. The United States had intelligence supporting Iran's accusations and confirmed Iraq's 'almost daily' use of chemical weapons (Joyce Battle provides sources in *Shaking Hands with Saddam Hussein; the US Tilts Towards Iraq, 1980–1984*, National Security Electronic Briefing Book No.82, 25 February 2003). The State Department responded by saying that it would limit its efforts against Iraq's chemical weapons programme 'because of our strict neutrality in the Gulf war, the sensitivity of sources, and the low probability of achieving desired results'. The department acknowledged Iraq's use of such weapons and recommended that the National Security Council discuss the matter.

In December 1983 Donald Rumsfeld, head of the multinational pharmaceutical company G. D. Searle & Company, was despatched to the Middle East as a presidential envoy. He met Saddam Hussein in Baghdad, discussed their shared enmity towards Iran and how Iraqi oil exports could be facilitated in the difficult war conditions. According to detailed notes on the meeting (source cited in Joyce Battle), no reference was made to chemical weapons. Rumsfeld also met with Iraqi Foreign

Minister Tariq Aziz and affirmed the willingness of the Reagan administration 'to do more' to help Iraq in the war. Later Rumsfeld was assured by the US interests section that Iraq's leadership had been 'extremely pleased' with the visit, and that 'Tariq Aziz had gone out of his way to praise Rumsfeld as a person'.

In late-March 1984, after Washington had condemned Iraq's use of chemical weapons, Rumsfeld returned to Baghdad to express the Reagan administration's hope that it could obtain further Export-Import Bank credits for Iraq, facilitate Iraq's export of oil, and make vigorous efforts to block arms exports to Iran. Howard Teicher, a former NSC member who accompanied Rumsfeld, recorded in an affidavit that Rumsfeld also conveyed to Iraq an offer from Israel to provide military assistance, which was rejected. The United States had already been supplying Iraq with military equipment for some time. In March 1983 a congressional aide asked whether heavy trucks sold to Iraq were intended for military purposes, whereupon a State Department official replied: 'We presumed that this was Iraq's intention, and had not asked.' In April 1984 the Iraqi Ministry of Defence was buying Bell Textron helicopters, which were not to be 'in any way configured for military use'.

During the spring of 1984 the Reagan administration studied the possibility of providing equipment for Iraq's nuclear programme and decided that the preliminary results of the study 'favour expanding such trade to include Iraqi nuclear entities'. After a further US denunciation of chemical weapons in March 1984, a State Department spokesman was asked at a press briefing whether Iraq's use of chemical weapons would have 'any effect on US recent initiatives to expand relations' with Iraq. The spokesman replied: 'No. I'm not aware of any change in our position. We're interested in being involved in a closer dialogue with Iraq.'

At this time Iran had submitted a draft resolution to the United Nations condemning Iraq's use of chemical weapons. Jeane Kirkpatrick, US ambassador to the UN, was instructed to lobby friendly delegations in order to obtain a general motion of 'no decision' on the resolution. If this was not achievable the United States, with Britain and France, would abstain on the Security Council vote. Iran took this US posture as encouragement to develop its own chemical weapons.

On 5 April 1984 Ronald Reagan issued a presidential directive (NSDD 139) stressing the US determination 'to avert an Iraqi collapse'.

Reagan declared that US policy required an 'unambiguous' condemnation of chemical weapons (without naming Iraq) while emphasising 'the urgent need to dissuade Iran from continuing the ruthless and inhumane tactics which have characterised recent offensives'. The condemnation of chemical warfare required no change in the US support for the Iraqi military campaign. On 26 November 1984 Tariq Aziz met US Secretary of State George Shultz in Washington and was pleased to declare that 'the US analysis of the war's threat to regional stability is "in agreement in principle" with Iraq's'. Aziz also expressed thanks for US efforts to cut off international arms sales to Iran (see also Chapter 9).

The US behaviour during the period of the Iran-Iraq War inevitably helped to shape Tehran's perceptions of American agendas in the 2003 war against Iraq. The Iranian experience of the war with Saddam Hussein left a legacy of bitterness and suspicion, not only with regard to the Iraqi dictator but also regarding the *realpolitik* duplicity of the United States. The Iranian position in the post-Saddam world can only be understood in this context.

Political Reform

Iran had been convulsed by the war with Iraq. Over the subsequent decade the hardline ayatollahs were seen to be losing power, the political scene was increasingly fragmented and despite predictable American hostility there appeared to be signs of liberal reform. By May 2001 the Iranian people were prepared to vote for a shift in political focus but the mullahs were determined to retain their control over Iranian society. Four years before, Mohammad Khatami had routed his conservative opponents by winning 70 per cent of the popular vote, but this had not yielded a victory for reform but a massive clamp-down by the mullahs. Khatami associates and student supporters were arrested and imprisoned, some forty pro-reform publications were closed down, and the main opposition party, the Freedom Movement, was suppressed.

The United States was typically unhelpful, maintaining a punitive sanctions regime that only served to exacerbate domestic tensions, vilifying Iran as a 'rogue state', and considering indictments against senior government figures allegedly involved in a 1996 terrorist attack in Saudi Arabia.

In early June 2001 it seemed likely that the reformist Khatami would secure an overwhelming victory in a one-sided election. Support for rival candidates was thin, as his supporters flocked to mosques and polling stations to give the president a resounding mandate for reform of the theocracy. Now it seemed that, unlike the situation in 1997, the religious conservatives would allow the elections to take place in a free and fair atmosphere. Despite a few violent incidents the Islamist militia had held back from the physical aggression favoured during Khatami's first term. Was the cultural ground really shifting or was this the lull before yet another repressive storm sponsored by the mullahs?

On 9 June Khatami achieved his landslide victory and immediately promised to 'realise the rights of the people'. But how much would Khatami be able to achieve against entrenched religious prejudice? And how would such developments affect relations with a secular Iraq and other states in the region? The political powers of Ayatollah Ali Khamenei, successor to the revolutionary Khomeini and now Iran's Supreme Leader, still dwarfed those of the elected Khatami; and Khamenei had traditionally allied himself with the conservatives. Moreover, the political stability in Iran was being affected by external developments: for example, the US-led war on Afghanistan, which Iranian hard-liners were claiming was completing the final stage in the US military encirclement of their country. In addition to the massive American arsenal in the Gulf, the United States then had thousands of troops close to Iran's eastern border with Pakistan and to the north in Tajikistan. And Western talk of bringing back Zahir Shah, the exiled King of Afghanistan, was arousing fears of a similar plot to restore the monarchy in Iran. Already the Iranian opposition in Los Angeles was beaming satellite television channels into Iran in an effort to stimulate nostalgia for the Pahlevi dynasty.

But there appeared to be movement in the cultural fabric of Iranian society. While women were still barred from attending football games, in November 2002 some forty Irish women were allowed to attend a World Cup game held in the imposing Azadi Stadium. With 120,000 men in the stadium the women were watched constantly for any sign of aberrant behaviour:

One woman let her veil fall momentarily, another unbuttoned her long coat. Both acts provoked an extraordinary tantrum by an Iranian Football Association official who complained bitterly to an Irish FA observer. The donning of veils by some Irishmen in solidarity drew more Iranian scowls – and a few female giggles … rebellious fans taunted some women by making obscene gestures, acts which could result in imprisonment or a lashing. An experienced Irish female photographer started sobbing as the abuse became more hysterical.[8]

In 2002 women were being allowed to occupy the front desks in Iranian hotels and to walk hand-in-hand with their boyfriends in the streets, activities that would have been denounced a short time before. Few observers could doubt that there were mounting liberal pressures in Iranian society, and that these would have consequences for Iran's domestic and international political gestures.

Axis of Evil?

Washington seemed oblivious to such liberal pressures and rested with the Bush denunciation of Iran as an 'axis of evil' member.[9] There were even suggestions that Iran would become a US target after Iraq – a course of action favoured by Israel.[10] By contrast, Iran's relations with Iraq seemed to be warming, a circumstance that would be unlikely to affect Iran's political posture in the post-Saddam world. On 17 February 2002 Iran and Iraq exchanged the remains of 134 soldiers killed during the 1980–88 war, following months of negotiation. The exchanges took place at the border police station of al-Faka in Meisan province under the supervision of the Iraqi-Iranian committee responsible for searching for the remains of troops killed in the war. The ceremonies, involving the exchange of bodies of 59 Iraqi troops and 75 Iranian soldiers, were attended by representatives of party and people's organisations, and the Iraqi Red Crescent Society. Naji Sabri, Iraq's foreign minister, had already returned from a 'positive and satisfying' trip to Iran, saying that Tehran wanted to resolve outstanding issues between the two former enemies. A main aim of the Sabri visit had been to resolve differences over such issues as refugees and prisoners of war, issues that had long impeded the normalisation of relations. Tehran had repeatedly denied Baghdad's claim that it was still holding 29,000 Iraqi prisoners; and claimed, for its part, that Iraq was still keeping some 3,200 Iranian soldiers in prison. Baghdad admitted to holding about 60 Iranians, involved in the Shi'ite uprising after the end of the 1991 war. Both sides were claiming good faith in their approach to talks.

The 'axis of evil' speech had done little to aid the Iranian reformers, giving the old guard an excuse to block reforms and to derail President Khatami's policy of *détente* abroad. Now the reformers were struggling to address the Bush posture by urging the authorities to investigate whether Iran had tried to smuggle arms to the Palestinians and to give refuge to al-Qa'ida fugitives. No fewer than 172 reformist deputies declared in a statement that if such things were true, those responsible should be punished. What more could Washington want? Now it had Iranian reformers, with a huge popular mandate, urging a Muslim regime to withdraw support from the Palestinians. Why did the Washington strategists not rush to embrace Khatami? Did the United States perhaps want an excuse for a further aggression in the region?

Anticipating War

It was now being assumed that the US-led war on Iraq would cause thousands of new refugees throughout the area, and the United Nations was beginning to respond to the likelihood of military conflict. In March 2002 Pierre Lavanchy, head of the Tehran office of the UNHCR, was overseeing the movement of tens of thousands of tents and blankets to western Iran in readiness for a huge wave of Iraqi refugees in the event of war: 'We've started to prepare for a possible influx. We are in discussions with Iranian officials. We are taking stocks which were in place in south-eastern Iran for refugees from Afghanistan and moving them across the country to be near the border with Iraq.' Already tents, blankets, kitchen utensils, pots, plastic sheeting and jerry cans for water were being transported.

Lavanchy commented that enough supplies were being moved for 40,000 people ('It's better to have at least a minimum in place'). Some diplomats believed that there could be as many as 150,000 refugees when the bombing started, though Saddam Hussein might be expected to close the borders, as he had done in previous conflicts. During the US bombing of Afghanistan both Iran and Pakistan mounted extra guards on their borders to keep the refugees out. It seemed likely that Iran would agree to accept Iraqi refugees but that, with blocked borders, there would be tens of thousands of starving and displaced people inside Iraq.

In Iran little progress was being made to erode the power of the mullahs. The public morality police, the *Komiteh*, was engaged in a crackdown on 'spiritual pollutants', including the Barbie doll. One shop owner in Tehran reported: 'They came and took away every one of my Barbies – around $11,000 of goods. I was taken to a police station and detained there for three days.' A subsequent trial was expected but shopkeeper Medhi did not know what the charge would be: 'I thought the atmosphere was more relaxed, which is why I opened this shop.' At the same time Iran's Guardian Council was rejecting a Bill passed by parliament to ban the use of torture to gain information from detainees. The conservative constitutional watchdog judged that five articles of the Bill were against Islamic law, two were against the Constitution and two needed clarification. But the rapprochement with Iraq was continuing. Fresh talks were scheduled for arranging more exchanges of soldiers' remains, and arrangements had been completed for opening a third border centre between the two countries.

The Iranian people were continuing to protest at the Bush posture regarding their country. On 19 July 2002 tens of thousands of demonstrators paraded in Tehran to denounce the United States. Amid cries of 'Death to America, Death to George Bush', Ali Akhbar Hashemi Rafsanjani, the former Iranian president, declared of the US: 'We are facing a cruel and powerful government and we have to be cautious and awake. The most important thing is the presence of people', noting that American spy satellites 'should take pictures of today's rally to judge the loyalty of the Iranian people … We tell the Americans to put aside their arrogant behaviour, then this nation could start dialogue with you and talk to you.' It seemed plain that the US policy on Iran was only serving to encourage the Iran-Iraq rapprochement.[11]

Bush was disparaging the Iranian reformists and backing the dissidents committed to the violent overthrow of the Iranian regime, but many observers were suggesting that the US abandonment of the moderate President Khatami would be counter productive, stimulating a conservative renewal and fuelling hostility to the US. Russia, determined to supply a nuclear reactor to Tehran, seemed oblivious to American fears, and Iran itself remained committed to pursuing an independent policy on the development of nuclear power. President Khatami visited Afghanistan on 13 August 2002 to show his commitment to the struggle against al-Qa'ida, but in Tehran the Iranian Supreme Leader was comparing Bush to Hitler(!): '*The President of a country which claims to support human rights and freedom speaks the same language* to *the people of the world as Hitler used.*' Arrogance, according to Khomenei, 'has drawn the bullying West into disgrace'.

Human Rights Abuses

In early October 2002 the Iranian police arrested 120 party-goers and charged them with mingling with the opposite sex and dancing. The young detainees were fined and signed pledges that they would not repeat such behaviour. On 13 October the reformist newspaper *Etemad* reported a conservative Iranian prayer leader who had denounced the 'moral depravity' of dog ownership: 'I demand the judiciary arrest all dogs with long, medium or short legs together with their long-legged owners. Otherwise I will arrest them.' At the same time Iran was increasing the number of floggings and executions as the West turned a blind eye to human rights, hoping to gain Iranian support for the planned US military aggression against Iraq. In 2002 there were about 300 executions, most of the victims hanged from cranes in public places. Ahmed Ibrahim, from the Foreign Affairs Committee of the National Council of Resistance in Iran (NCRI), commented: 'In Iran they are stoning large numbers, never mind gouging out their eyes, cutting of their hands and hanging people and no-one says anything.'

Jack Straw, British foreign secretary, visited Iran in early October and evinced no interest in human rights. Rather than condemn the regime for its gross abuses, he reassured Kamal Kharazi, his counterpart, that Britain would help Iran get taken off America's list of pariah states in return for its support against Saddam. This offer was made a few days after five young men, alleged rapists, had been hanged in a bus station in Tehran; and at a time when Khatami was protesting at the death sentence imposed on a liberal academic for criticising the Islamic faith.[12]

Then thousands of people were demonstrating in favour of liberal reforms, partly in support of students urging the freeing of political prisoners.

Post-war Ambitions

In May 2002 Mohsen Mirdamadi, Iran's Foreign Affairs Committee chairman, admitted that secret talks had taken place with the US government, contrary to what the foreign ministry had formerly declared. The subject of the 'negotiations' was not revealed though it was clear that Tehran was considering its opportunities in the light of the planned US-led war. In late–2002 Tehran was making it clear that it wanted a say in a post-Saddam Iraq. Already Iran had moved to allow several Iraqi opposition leaders to visit the country for consultations with Iran-based Iraqi Shi'ite groups. Ahmad Chalabi, Massoud Barzani and Ayatollah Mohammed Baqar al-Hakim (head of the Supreme Council for the Islamic Revolution in Iraq, SCIRI) had met in Tehran to discuss the shape of a post-Saddam Iraq. SCIRI worked as an umbrella organisation for a number of Shi'ite groups, including some that had in the past co-ordinated activities with Iran's intelligence services.

Tehran judged that the United States was determined to introduce a new government into Iraq following a war to overthrow the Saddam regime, and that Iran – with its links to Shi'ite groups in southern Iraq – had a natural interest in the outcome. It seemed likely that this view, fashioned by a candid assessment of political realities would prevail over conservative dogma that the United States would always remain the 'Great Satan'.

In September 2002, while the United States was preparing for its planned war against Iraq, Washington was also depicting Iran as a serious threat to regional security. At the same time some circles in Israel were asserting that the real threat to the region was Tehran and not Baghdad. Many observers were wondering whether Iran would be the next state to be targeted for a US military onslaught.

Iran had tried to appease Washington in various ways. Tehran was quick to condemn the terrorist outrages of 11 September 2001, had offered to assist downed American pilots in the Afghanistan war, and was reportedly conducting clandestine diplomatic meetings with US officials. But the pro-Israeli elements in the Bush administration had no interest in developing better relations with Tehran, citing Iran's long-range missile programme and its development of weapons of mass destruction. Iran, it was alleged, could have a nuclear bomb by 2005. Iran was known to support such 'terrorist' groups as Hamas and Hezbollah, showing that the US and Israel had common interests. In August the Bush administration was accusing Iran of harbouring key members of al-Qa'ida, and Zalmay Khalilzad, Bush's special envoy, was emphasising the risk posed by Iran's chemical weapons and its support for terrorism.

It seemed that a US-led regime change was on the American agenda. Khalilzad was insisting that US policy 'is not to impose change on Iran', but there was no doubt about the US attitude: 'Our policy is not about … reform or hardline. It is about those who want freedom, human rights, democracy, and economic and educational opportunity for themselves and their fellow countrymen.' Such commentary suggested an American hidden agenda, where the fall of Saddam would be followed by military attacks on other states. The Iranians feared and hated Saddam Hussein but remained hostile to any American ambitions for greater US influence in the region. Hashemi Rafsanjani saw little virtue in an alliance with the United States: 'How can we turn to a python to repel the menace of a scorpion?' In December 2002 three Iranian opinion pollsters were sent for trial after releasing a survey showing that most Iranians supported dialogue with the United States.[13]

Iran was again pressing for influence in a post-Saddam Iraq. Perhaps, the Iranian leaders reasoned, they could at least cultivate good relations with the leaders of a post-Saddam Iran. It seemed that Tehran was taking the pragmatic decision to back, or at least to tolerate, what was almost certain to be the winning side. Hence Kamal Kharazi, Iranian foreign minister, had accepted Blair's offer of talks in February, despite the continuing US conviction that Iran was part of the 'axis of evil'. The British policy of 'constructive engagement' was the best chance available to Tehran for staying out of the coming conflict. Iran certainly had no intention of aiding a brother Muslim regime in what would be a desperate fight for survival.[14]

Targeting Iran

Iran certainly had no grounds to be complacent. It was being accused by America and Israel of supporting terrorism, of possessing chemical weapons, and of having a growing nuclear weapons programme. On 13 December 2002 the White House expressed 'great concerns' over two secret Iranian nuclear plants which it charged could be used to produce parts of nuclear weapons. Ari Fleischer, White House spokesman, declared that Iran was building a plant that could be used to produce highly enriched uranium, and a heavy water plant that could support a reactor to produce weapons-grade plutonium:

> Such facilities are simply not justified by the needs that Iran has for their civilian nuclear programme. Our assessment when we look at Iran is that there is no economic gain for a country rich in oil and gas like Iran to build costly indigenous nuclear fuel cycle facilities. Iran flares off more gas every year than the equivalent power that it hopes to produce with these reactors.

On the same day Iran asserted that the suspect construction sites were for 'peaceful purposes', and were fully open to United Nations nuclear experts. Mohamed El-Baradei, head of the International Atomic Energy Agency (IAEA), said that the sites were not yet operational, but criticised Iran for withholding details of the projects. A planned inspection by El-Baradei was postponed because Iranian officials 'needed some time to prepare for the visit'.

On 10 February 2003 Gholamreza Aqazadeh, head of Iran's Atomic Energy Organisation, announced that a uranium ore processing plant should come on line soon in the central city of Isfahan and that preliminary work had begun on a uranium enrichment plant. Iran's first operational reactor, being built with Russian help, was due to come on-stream by early 2004. Gary Samore, a non-proliferation expert at London's International Institute for Strategic Studies (IISS) commented that his suspicion centred on the development of another facility at the central town of Natanz, a gas centrifuge enrichment plant 'clearly intended to develop an infrastructure for a nuclear weapons capability'. US officials had already charged that sites at Natanz and Arak, seen in commercial satellite photographs, were suitable for the building of nuclear weapons.

In a televised speech President Khatami insisted that Iran had no plans to build such weapons: 'Iran has discovered reserves and extracted uranium ... we are determined to use nuclear technology for civilian purposes.' In the London talks with Kamal Kharrazi, prime minister Blair urged Tehran to sign up to more extensive inspections; for example, to an additional protocol allowing for more intrusive inspections of its nuclear programme. Russia had been criticised by Washington for helping Iran with its nuclear programme but gave assurances that all spent fuel from the reactor would be returned to Russia, ensuring that it would not be used to develop nuclear weapons. One European diplomat commented that Iran seemed 'to be making a creeping announcement of what their capabilities are'.

On 21 February 2003 Iran opened its nuclear sites at Natanz and Arak for inspection by Mohamed El-Baradei and other IAEA personnel, but it seemed unlikely that Washington would be satisfied by the Agency's findings. The United States was again charging that Iran was harbouring al-Qa'ida terrorists in defiance of the will of the international community. Thus George Tenet, CIA director, said to the US Senate intelligence committee: 'We see disturbing signs that al-Qa'ida has established a presence in both Iran and Iraq.' Already, with war against Iraq imminent, the two states were being bracketed together. In early March a group of US senators introduced an anti-Iran resolution to Congress – 'a cliché devised for the American internal use', according to Hamid-Reza Asefi, Iran's foreign ministry spokesman. Asefi also recalled the decision by President Bush to extend sanctions against Iran for another year. Iran, declared, Asefi, was opposed to war in the region.

Iran, from the American perspective, was supporting terrorism, had ambitions to develop nuclear weapons, already possessed a chemical weapons arsenal and was an enduring threat to Israel. It was inevitable in the post-war environment that the Tehran regime, despite the discernible pressures for reform, felt insecure in the new regional environment. Some Iranian interests coincided with those of the United States. For example, both Tehran and Washington were keen to restrict Kurdish ambitions and so could have co-operated over this issue. But the

United States did not need Iran's assistance: the Kurds, prepared to fight Turks but not US troops, would do as they were told.

On 28 March 2003 hundreds of Iranian demonstrators laid siege to the British embassy in Tehran, smashing windows, burning British flags and demanding an end to the US-led war across the border. The demonstrations in Tehran and other Iranian cities coincided with anti-war protests across the Arab world.[15] On 9 April a rocket, almost certainly American, killed an Iranian man as it exploded on a road near the south-western border city of Abadan in the district of Khosrowabad.[16] The US forces, preparing to consolidate their occupation of Iraq, were not far from Tehran. The Iranian regime, branded by President Bush's speechwriter as part of the 'axis of evil', had little reason to feel comfortable about the future.

SEVEN

The Arab World

The Arab world awaited the planned US aggression with a mixture of anxiety and resignation. All the regimes in the area were concerned primarily with their own survival, and the American action was putting their security under threat as never before. Most of the Arab states had been effectively bribed or intimidated by Washington, and in consequence had little freedom of movement. Small Gulf states such as Qatar and Bahrain were in no position to resist US-UK coercion and so reluctantly agreed to host massive 'coalition' forces. Thereafter such states were listed in Western propaganda as favouring the war option, whereas in reality they had been powerless to withstand the American version of megapower diplomacy. Even tiny Kuwait – granting half of its land area to US military activities – was uncertain about the war option. Government spokesmen could easily be found to applaud the US posture but there were hints also that peace was preferable to war and that the American presence was seen as akin to a colonial occupation.

In October 2002 Jack Straw, British foreign secretary, was assuring

Arab states that a destabilising carve-up of Iraq was not envisaged – as
if the West had the right to determine the geographical composition of
nations. Straw's words carried little weight in the region. 'Regime
change' in Iraq had long remained the basic US objective, and if such a
goal were feasible for Iraq it could be contemplated also for other
recalcitrant states in the Middle East and elsewhere. Most of the Arab
states, despite succumbing to Western pressure for assistance, had not
wanted the war but believed it to be inevitable. Straw noted how much
of the talks on his Middle East tour focused on 'post-Saddam
scenarios'.[1]

Iraq had struggled to rally Arab opinion against Washington plans
for a fresh military aggression. On 17 January 2003 General Ali Hassan
al-Majid, Saddam Hussein's first cousin and a key figure in the Baghdad
regime, arrived in Syria to demand Arab support. This followed a defiant
speech from Saddam in which he said that 'Baghdad, its people and
leadership, is determined to force the Mongols of our age to commit
suicide at its gates'.[2] A primary task of General al-Majid was to deny
reports that Saddam was considering fleeing the city: 'This is an
absurdity. If you ask an infant in Iraq he wouldn't believe such reports.'
Majid planned to visit Lebanon, Egypt and Jordan to plead Iraq's case,
at the same time denouncing stories of Saddam's likely exodus as 'a
psychological war technique'.[3]

In March 2001 the leaders of the Arab states met in Amman to
discuss the growing crisis over Iraq. The result was a unanimous
resolution that reaffirmed:

> the independence and sovereignty of Iraq, its territorial integrity
> and its regional security and non-interference in its internal affairs
> and demanding an end to all that it is being subjected to in terms
> of actions and measures that are touching upon its sovereignty
> and threatening its security especially those taken outside the
> framework of ... UN Security Council resolutions, especially the
> military strikes

and called for 'the lifting of the sanctions imposed on Iraq'. A year later,
at the Arab League Summit in Beirut, Iraq pledged it would never again
invade Kuwait, and in a close session Izzat Ibrahim, the Iraqi delegate,
shook hands with Sheikh Ahmed Al Sabah, Kuwait's deputy prime

minister. This show of solidarity suggested that the Arab states would never again conspire with Washington in a war against the Iraqi nation. Only months later, many Arab states – Saudi Arabia, Kuwait, Jordan, Bahrain, Oman and others were again providing practical support for the US war effort.

The Bush administration clearly intended the 2003 war to have a dramatic impact on the region. Iraq's oil would flow freely and the dominoes would begin to fall. The authoritarian regimes in Iran, Saudi Arabia, Syria and Egypt would come under mounting popular pressure, and democracy would break out everywhere. Bush aides were insisting that, with Saddam's influence removed, the deadlock between Israel and the Palestinians would swiftly be broken, and not even Ariel Sharon would be able to resist a future US-sponsored agreement on a new Palestinian state. Colin Powell commented: 'We reject the condescending notion that freedom will not grow in the Middle East.' Other observers were arguing that the new war would trigger a wave of regional anger, encouraging worldwide terrorist attacks. The Islamic world was unimpressed with American rhetoric and would be likely to respond with decades of hatred and enmity. Peter Singer, security analyst with the Brookings Institution said: 'There will be a lot of instability in the short term. But we simply can't know how things are going to shake out.'

On 28 February 2003, three weeks before the outbreak of war, Arab leaders met on the shores of the Red Sea to proclaim their support for peace. Saddam Hussein had no doubt that the 'pusillanimous' Arab leaders gathering at Sharm al-Sheikh would forsake him: 'The Iraqi people are capable of countering any American regression. The Iraqi people do not only defend Iraq, but also the Arab nation, its security and independence.' One Gulf source assessed what would be likely to happen at the Arab summit:

> The Arabs will wash their hands of Saddam Hussein. They will say they are opposed to war, but tell Saddam it is up to him to avert conflict by respecting his disarmament obligations. It will be the Arabs' way of telling the Americans 'we are with you, but please do not expose us'.

The Arab press was now expressing anger at the 'impotence' of the leaders who were meeting in Egypt. Thus a cartoon character in the Kuwaiti daily *al-Rai al-Am* said: 'I'm not going to bad-mouth the Arab League because it is wrong to speak ill of the dead.' A Jordanian cartoonist showed an Arab struggling up a steep hill to the summit carrying a white flag, and the Lebanese *Daily Star* said the Arab League had set a new standard for failure, adding that it was disgraceful that the 22 leaders in the region 'are unable to formulate and implement a common foreign policy.' The United Arab Emirates daily *al-Bayan* expressed the widespread view: 'As the crisis has intensified, the Arabs have looked more impotent and more farcical.'

Salah al-Din Hafiz, senior editor on the Cairo daily *al-Ahram*, conceded that there was nothing the Arabs could to do stop the war, and he acknowledged that the Arab leaders were trapped between the wrath of the Americans and the anger of the Arab people. The dilemma was clear and the Arab League was doing nothing to resolve it. Tariq Musarawa, writing in the Jordanian daily *al-Rai*, asked a question that applied to several Arab states: 'How are we supposed to take action to stop the war when we are hosting the American and British forces on our territory?'

Colin Powell was urging the conference to produce a strong resolution urging Iraqi compliance with UN resolutions, and had even suggested that Saddam Hussein should seek exile in order to avoid a war. Most Arab spokesmen declared that it was no business of the United States to decide who should rule Arab countries. The Arabs agreed that war on Iraq would affect the entire world, and that the states of the Middle East would pay the highest price. Amr Moussa, Arab League Secretary-General, warned that war would 'open up the gates of hell', and President Mubarak of Egypt said that it would light a 'gigantic fire' of violence and terror.

On 19 March 2003, with war imminent, Sheikh Hamad bin Isa al-Khalifa, King of Bahrain, offered Saddam Hussein exile in a desperate effort to avoid the coming military onslaught. Mubarak, receiving $2 billion a year from the United States, was blaming Saddam for the coming catastrophe, while *al-Ahram* was accusing Washington of planning a 'colonial war'. The opposition paper *al-Wafd* went further: 'Bush, the most stupid leader in the world, with his herd of the US administration's hawks, have become experts and decision-makers deciding our destiny for the coming generations. This is a setback, which will be remembered in the history of our region for a long time.' The press in Qatar declared that the United States wanted to control Iraq's oil and to reshape the political map in the region 'to serve the American and Israeli interests'. Jordan's King Abdullah, having allowed US troops into his country, was walking the familiar political tightrope, caught between American intimidation and massive public opposition to the war. A writer in *al-Rai* commented: 'It is guaranteed that Iraq will become an American and Zionist base to control the entire region. It opens doors for Israel to control the Arab oil.'

The start of the war provoked a huge response throughout the Middle East, given wholly inadequate attention by the Western media. In Sanaa, Yemen's capital, some 30,000 demonstrators shouting 'Death to America' marched on the US embassy. An 11-year-old boy and a policeman were killed in an exchange of fire with marchers, and dozens were injured. Protesters set tyres and rubbish bins alight, shouting 'No to US hegemony and hypocrisy!' In Cairo the police used water cannons and tear-gas to quell demonstrators hurling rocks and furniture from the rooftops. Journalists were attacked at the Nile Hilton Hotel and by nightfall the entire central area of the city was barricaded. Demonstrators shouted: 'With our soul, with our blood, we will defend you Baghdad!' In Jordan the protesters clashed with security police in Amman and in Maan, an Islamist stronghold. The Jordanian authorities stationed armoured troop carriers close to the Palestinian refugee camps, and King Abdullah made a television appeal for calm. In Bahrain, headquarters of the US Navy 5th Fleet, the police used rubber bullets, tear-gas and truncheons against 2,000 stone-throwing demonstrators marching on the US embassy.

Some 30,000 Palestinians, some urging Saddam to bomb Tel Aviv, took to the streets in the West Bank and Gaza Strip. In Gaza, 15,000 people protested in the refugee camps of Jabalya, Rafah and Khan Younis, while an imam in Gaza City called for the 'opening of borders' for Arab volunteers to go and fight alongside the Iraqi army. In the West Bank city of Nablus some 5,000 people marched through the streets, chanting slogans such as 'America, the mother of terrorism!' Palestinians also staged protests in the refugee camps of Ain Al Hilweh in southern Lebanon, Yarmouk near Damascus, and Wihdat in Amman. In Ain Al Hilweh around 2,000 protesters burned US, British and Israeli flags. In Beirut police used water cannons against 1,000 students to stop them marching on the US embassy. At the Qatari and Kuwaiti embassies demonstrators shouted 'Death to America! Death to Bush!' In Khartoum, Sudan's capital, the security forces closed roads to prevent thousands of demonstrators marching on the US embassy.

The Arab regimes were desperately hoping for a quick war, not a protracted Vietnam-style quagmire that would only serve to fuel the anger of their populations. One Iraqi, speaking on al-Arabiya satellite television against a background of explosions over Baghdad, asked why President Mubarak allowed American ships used for bombarding Iraq to pass through the Suez Canal. A leading Jordanian commentator said that small Arab states had been helpless to resist US pressure, but that other Arab leaders had taken bribes to support the American war effort. Cairo's *al-Ahram* noted the tragedy that Iraq was facing, while the Qatari *al-Rai* accused Saudi Arabia of hypocrisy in allowing American cruise missiles to pass through Saudi airspace. In the Egyptian port of Alexandria demonstrators carried a coffin bearing the legend: 'The conscience of the Arab leaders', and increasing support was being shown for Saddam. An Arab banker caught the general mood: 'We are so desperate for an Arab hero after all our defeats on the battlefield and 50 years of humiliation that we will even turn that old criminal Saddam into a legend.'

In this context television broadcasts showing the collapse of the Saddam regime were creating a sense of rage, despair and humiliation throughout the Arab world. Arabic television stations were showing scenes of US armoured vehicles trundling through Baghdad, American soldiers wandering into Saddam's palaces, and members of the Iraqi Fedayin discarding their black uniforms and fleeing from the advancing US forces. The Arab News Network showed Egyptian protesters screaming: 'Where are you, Arabs? We are with Saddam Hussein.' Al-Jazeera broadcast a CNN item showing American troops storming a house in Baghdad and ordering a terrified family out of their home at gunpoint. Yusra Amine, 23 years old, was watching developments on television in Beirut: 'Where are the Iraqi soldiers? Why aren't they fighting? This is embarrassing.'

Some Arabs spoke of coalition propaganda and hoped for the unexpected. In Muscat, the capital of Oman, Faisal bin Muhammad a 30-year-old government employee, said: 'I have a feeling that something will happen and it will surprise everyone.' Arab pride was at stake and there was anxiety about the future. Thus Sateh Noureddine, writing in the Lebanese daily *al-Safir*, commented: 'All Arabs feel that Iraq is our country, that the Iraqis are our people and we share the suffering of the Iraqi people, and we are afraid of what might come after the Americans have removed Saddam Hussein.'

The Arab world was dismayed at the onset of what one Palestinian called 'a new colonialism' – 'There is a big distinction between the people and the regimes who control them with tyranny. The Iraqis understand that the Americans did not come as liberators but to take control of their oil.' There was fear also that the US conquest of Iraq was not an end to American ambitions. On 9 April, with Saddam's forces virtually routed, John Bolton, US under-secretary of state, declared: 'We are hopeful that a number of regimes will draw the appropriate lesson from Iraq, that the pursuit of weapons of mass destruction is not in their interest. I think Syria is a good case where I hope they will conclude that the chemical weapons programme and the biological weapons programme they have been pursuing are things they should give up.'

One Arabic daily compared the collapse of Iraqi resistance to the 'catastrophe' (*al-Nakba*) of the creation of Israel in 1948, while other newspapers blamed the Iraqi dictator for the calamity that had befallen the Arab world. Kuwait's English-language *Arab Times* carried a headline 'Our liberation complete', and Talal Salman, editor of the Lebanese *al-Safir*, commented: 'After his long night of tyranny, Saddam Hussein has imposed on the people of Iraq the night of American and British occupation.' The Egyptian *al-Wafd* struggled to depict the Iraqi forces as holding out against American troops, while another Egyptian newspaper, *al-Jumhouriya*, acknowledged the dismal truth: 'Saddam deceived the Iraqis and the Arabs, and Baghdad fell in seconds.' The Saudi *al-Yawm* reflected on the destiny of all despots: 'This will be the fate of any dictator who kills his own people, oppresses them and steals their wealth. Had the people been with Saddam Hussein, no power … would have been able to occupy Iraq.'

The 2003 war had succeeded in humiliating the Arab world. The regional leaders now viewed the future with uncertainty and dread, some fearing the likelihood of increased turmoil in their own countries and others wondering if they would be targeted next by an emboldened superpower. Few observers judged that Iraq was the end of the matter:

the Bush administration clearly had ambitions to reshape the Middle East in ways that would benefit the United States and Israel. It remained to be seen whether Washington's most supine allies – Britain, Australia, Kuwait – would have the stomach for further aggressions.

Kuwait

The al-Sabah regime in Kuwait City gave massive help to the American military campaign, handing over their territorial waters, air space and half their land to US forces. In this they were more supportive than the Saudi monarchy, increasingly anxious about domestic pressures and unwilling to host the vast American forces that had used Saudi territory in the 1991 Gulf War. Times had changed.

Kuwait, despite all the grievances stemming from the 1990 invasion, was itself initially divided on how much help should be given to the American forces in 2003. Official spokesmen had been prepared to declare Kuwaiti opposition to war, and recent events had fuelled the domestic stresses that underlay Kuwaiti society. In May 1995 a parliamentary inquiry concluded that the Kuwaiti government had been profoundly negligent during the 1990 Iraqi invasion, and urged the emir to dismiss all the officials who had so badly misjudged the situation. A report, not made public by the Kuwaiti authorities but obtained by the *al-Hayat* newspaper, charged that the ruling al-Sabah family had ignored warnings of invasion and then deserted the country. Sheik Saad al-Abdullah al-Sabah, then crown prince, was accused of ignoring intelligence reports. The emir and his family fled the country, leaving behind no political leadership and a disorganised army.

It seems likely that such criticisms would have concentrated the al-Sabah minds in the run-up to the 2003 war. There was no prospect of a second royal flight from the country since, despite all the propaganda about Iraq's alleged hidden missiles, the emirate was under no substantial threat. There was no way that the Iraqi forces could attack the massed US troops in Kuwait, much less repeat the 1990 invasion. The outcome was that the emirate, despite its unease and Kuwaiti pledges to oppose war, decided to host a vast American invasion force. There would be no repeat of the 1990 fiasco but the war, as had happened in 1991, did put Kuwait under pressures of a different sort.

After the 1991 Gulf War the emirate had been urged to 'democratise' – to extend the franchise to women, to allow a measure of the US version of 'free speech'. It seemed unlikely that the al-Sabah dynasty would be keen to relinquish its feudal habits. On 4 May 1999 Sheikh Jabar al-Sabah, the Kuwaiti emir, had dissolved parliament after MPs threatened to oust Ahmad al-Kulaib, Islamic affairs minister, for mistakes printed in 120,000 copies of the Koran. Fresh elections were scheduled for 3 July. Now it seemed that at last women would be given the vote although the al-Sabah family would retain its undemocratic grip on the parliamentary system.

On 17 May 1999 the Kuwaiti government, following orders from the emir, approved a draft law giving women the right to vote and to stand for public office in elections. The new law was intended to become operative in 2003. It remained to be seen what impact the 2003 war would have on female emancipation. Massouma al-Mubarak, female activist and political science professor at Kuwait University, had commented in 1999: 'Finally! It is a great feeling to get something that you have been deprived of for so long.' Ahmed Baqer, a member of the disbanded parliament, had expressed the common male view that 'when a man votes he represents his whole family'. Such tensions persisted in Kuwaiti society and the likely effects of the 2003 war on female emancipation were uncertain.

The all-male Kuwaiti parliament had thrown out the draft law that would have allowed women to vote from 2003. The vote, 32–30 against, showed that some men who had formerly supported female emancipation had changed sides. The author Laila al-Othman took comfort from the closeness of the vote: 'I'm sure our supporters in parliament will try to introduce another draft law soon.' Commentary in the liberal Western media was predictable: 'Kuwait perpetuates the indefensible.'[4] The approach of the 2003 war had so far done nothing to encourage political reform in Kuwaiti society.

In December 2002 defense lawyers for al-Qa'ida suspects claimed in a Kuwaiti court that their clients had been tortured; the media remained firmly under government control; and official efforts were being made to demonise Baghdad by releasing a video showing a chemical attack on Kuwait by Scud missiles. In this climate the Kuwaiti people were anticipating war and preparing themselves for the inevitable. Hundreds of millions of dollars were being withdrawn from America and invested at home: in early 2003 the Kuwaiti stock market soared more than 30 per cent. With more than $90 million withdrawn from American banks in a few weeks, one investor observed: 'People in Kuwait are looking at what happened to America on September 11, and all the threats of further terrorism, and have reached the decision that it's safer to keep the money at home.'

As the thousands of American troops poured into Kuwait in anticipation of war, the country's fishermen were being driven out of their jobs by US fears of suicide boat attacks. Recalling the al- Qa'ida attack on the USS *Cole* off Aden in 2000, all Kuwait's coastal waters had been declared a no-go area for fishermen, forcing most of the 750-strong fleet of traditional dhows to remain in harbour. Abu Suleiman who had fished for the past 40 years, commented that the talk of war had been 'a general disaster for us and our families'. His younger brother, Abdul Karim, reflected the general view among the fishermen: 'To begin with I supported the idea of America getting rid of Saddam. That was before I knew I'd be out of a job. Now I can't even afford to buy fish at the local market.'

Fish, at expense, were being flown in from Pakistan and India, and thousands of poor Indians and Egyptians, formerly dependent on the fishing industry, had been forced to return home. It was feared that war would force many of Kuwait's million and a half expatriates to flee the country. An American official commented: 'We realise the disruption that is being caused and we would like to thank people in Kuwait for the sacrifices they are making.'

The country had been sliced in half, with the American influx resulting in a 10 per cent increase in the Kuwaiti population of 2.3 million. Half of Kuwait had been placed off-limits to its own people, and there was simmering resentment below the surface of Kuwaiti society. A few Americans were shot by Arab 'terrorists', the strongly religious minority was objecting to the US military presence, and there was widespread hostility to US policy on Palestine. Thousands of Kuwaiti sheep and camel herders had been evicted from their land to make way for the US forces, and resentment was widespread. Confined to a squalid area south of Kuwait City, Abu Abdullah, an evicted herder, commented: 'We always used to graze in the north, because the area is clean and open. Here it is dirty, and the grass is different, and it's not healthy. Our sheep are getting sick.'

The herders and thousands of other displaced Kuwaiti families were already victims of the war, and the land would take years to recover from the weight of army traffic. The scale of resentment among ordinary Kuwaitis was largely disguised by the Kuwaiti and American authorities, but the seeds of discord and instability were being sown. Abdul Razzak al-Shayji, a teacher in sharia law at Kuwait University, represented Kuwait's sizeable devout minority. The United States, he said, had not made a convincing case for war: 'Their goal is to change the map. They want to help Israel, to protect the oil, to chase down Islamist groups, and change the Islamic world as a whole.' The laws in most Arab countries 'are not so different from those operated by Saddam Hussein', and George Bush was talking about introducing democracy to Iraq: 'Iraq's been like this for 30 years.'

Kuwait, for the purposes of the 2003 war, was more than a client state: it was reduced to the status of a colony. The occupation of Kuwait, little remarked by the Western media, preceded the occupation of Iraq. Kuwait remains an obedient ally of the United States but the growing resentments among ordinary Kuwaitis, fuelled by the punishment and humiliation of a brother Arab state, are sure to have consequences in the future.

Saudi Arabia

Saudia Arabia, fearful of its own domestic militants, refused to offer unlimited support for the US land invasion of Iraq – which paradoxically increased the American commitment to military action. The Washington strategists reasoned that if the Saudis could not be relied upon then one crucial supply of Middle East oil might be in jeopardy, which in turn made the acquisition of the Iraqi oilfields even more attractive. Saudi Arabia remained opposed to the war, though less so than such states as Syria and Libya. Most of the Arab world felt powerless to affect the course of events. The dictatorship in Egypt occasionally expressed pan-Arab views but – to safeguard his annual $2 billion – President Muburak took pains not to upset the Washington war planners. There was never a hint that Egypt would restrict the access of US war ships to the Suez Canal in order to prosecute a military aggression against another Arab state more effectively.

Saudi Arabia, disturbed and highly ambivalent about the circumstances of the 2003 war, was facing unprecedented tensions. Bomb explosions, terrorist incidents, US impatience, American attempts to implicate Saudi finance in terrorism, the role of the Saudi Osama bin Laden, the Saudi involvement in 11 September, the scale of Osama's Saudi constituency – all were conspiring to shake the confidence of the Saudi dynasty, formerly a robust and reliable US ally. It had long been judged that any serious threat to the House of Saud could disrupt the essential flow of oil to the West. What if the Saudi oil resource were to fall into the hands of the fundamentalists?

The Saudi royal family had long recognised that its survival depended on the goodwill of the United States, but through 2002 and early 2003 US-Saudi relations were strained. The House of Saud depended not only on the oil revenues from Western purchases, but on US training of its security personnel, US technological expertise for surveillance, US diplomatic and political protection in the wider world. Saudi Arabia has an appalling human rights record, in many ways as bad as that of Saddam Hussein. It was well within the gift of America to arraign the Saudi royals before international courts on charges of crimes against humanity. What if US goodwill were to evaporate? What if Washington were to target the House of Saud as a serious impediment to the secure flow of oil to the West?

Through 2002–3 there was much speculation that the United States was invading Iraq to secure not only the Iraqi oil resource but also that of Saudi Arabia – and such a plan might involve the dismemberment of the Saudi kingdom and the collapse of the House of Saud. George Galloway, Labour MP and tireless peace campaigner, speculated on the likely US agenda:

> I regard the Crown Prince of Saudi Arabia as a very big step forward from what went before. I think he is a person of some dignity, but I also believe that other members of his family are corrupt and are slaves of the West. The big question in Saudi Arabia is whether Crown Prince Abdullah will be able to establish full control of the country. If he does, I think you'll see a different policy from Saudi Arabia towards the Iraq issue, the Palestine issue and the question of whether the oil wealth of the Arabs is for the Arabs or the West.[5]

Galloway declared also that there were people in London 'who are now openly discussing the dismemberment of Saudi Arabia, openly discussing its partition – a new Sykes-Picot in Saudi Arabia.[6] MPs, Ministers and ex-Ministers have all spoken to me in the past few months.'[7] It was as if people had just realised that Saudi Arabia is *an artificial state*, 'and may not always be one state'.

Perhaps the Saudis were realising that the US strategists were eyeing the Saudi oil resource.[8] In any event, as the time for war approached, they were struggling to placate the United States. Washington itself, still working remorselessly to force Saudi compliance with the planned US aggression, was making soothing noises – and managed in fact to achieve a measure of Saudi support. Perhaps American troops would not be welcome on Saud soil; perhaps there would be no rerun of the 1990–91 level of compliance. But what about the air bases?

Under ceaseless US diplomatic pressure the Saudis agreed to allow Washington to use the massive air bases in Saudi Arabia to strike Iraqi targets. This concession helped to steady the oil price but caused the pound to fall. Like Kuwait, Saudi Arabia faced no real military threat from Iraq in the 2003 war, but the fresh onslaught on a Muslim society was bound to exacerbate the domestic tensions in Saudi Arabia, threatening the security of the Saudi oil resource and encouraging the Washington strategists to consider further invasions in the interest of the United States.

For the sake of the planned war the Bush administration had been keen to enlist as much Saudi support as possible, but the Washington strategists were deeply divided on how to handle the issue. Of the nineteen September 11 suicide hijackers, fifteen were Saudi citizens and there was concern about Riyadh's reluctance to act against the financiers of al-Qa'ida. In February 2003 the White House and the Saudi authorities struck a deal to allow allied air operations against Iraq to be launched from Saudi territory. In return, the House of Saud would be allowed to insist on the withdrawal of US troops when the war was over. No publicity was given to the fact that the withdrawal of American forces from Saudi Arabia was one of the principal demands of Osama bin Laden: the Saudis had conceded a central objective of the al-Qa'ida terrorists.

In early March a witness reported that hundreds of American troops had taken control of a civilian Saudi airport, raising the prospect of a surprise US land attack on Baghdad across the desert. The town of Ar'ar, which the airport usually served, was only 255 miles from Baghdad, allowing a swift and relatively trouble-free route to the capital through unpopulated territory. *The Guardian* (London) saw a copy of an official Saudi order closing the airport to the normal traffic. At the same time the Saudi authorities were refusing to confirm that the airport had been turned over to American forces. In addition the Movement for Islamic Reform in Arabia, based in London, was claiming that between 2,000 and 5,000 US troops had landed in Tabuk, a northern garrison town.

It was obvious that Saudi Arabia had been cajoled, bribed or threatened into assisting the US war effort in various ways – hosting troops, allowing the use of Saudi airbases, and stockpiling 15 million barrels of oil as a hedge against the effects of the imminent military conflict. One anonymous official said that Saudi Arabia, Kuwait and the United Arab Emirates had agreed to provide Jordan with some 120,000 barrels of oil a day indefinitely, after pressure from the Bush administration.

Saudi Arabia had been forced to provide a substantial measure of support to the American military campaign. Riyadh, judged Washington, was now part of the 'coalition of the willing', but there would be a price to pay. Islamist factions in the kingdom, custodian of the Holy Sites (Mecca and Medina) and the original home of Osama bin Laden, were already enraged at the prospect of war. Crown Prince Abdullah was already contemplating moderate reforms, but these would only serve to anger the fundamentalists. When the course of war and its aftermath became plain, not only to the Saudis but throughout the Arab world, there were widespread feelings of humiliation, frustration and despair. Much of the Saudi population, like Arabs elsewhere, were also enraged that their leaders had conspired with Christian troops to wage a massive aggression against a sovereign Muslim state. The 2003 war could only add to the insecurities of the House of al-Saud.

Syria

Syria, of all Arab states outside Iraq the most bitterly opposed to the 2003 war, remained steadfast throughout the conflict. On 31 October

2002 President Bashar Assad, speaking at a joint press conference in Damascus, criticised Prime Minister Tony Blair for his aggressive posture:

> We cannot accept what we see every day on our television screens – the killing of innocent civilians [in Afghanistan]. There are hundreds dying every day … We should differentiate between combating terrorism and war. We are always against war. We, and I personally, differentiate between resistance and terrorism. Resistance is a social, religious and legal right that is safeguarded by UN resolutions … [likening the Palestinian groups to the French resistance].

This was a clear response to the US-UK efforts to brand the Palestinian militants as terrorists:

> Can anyone accuse De Gaulle of being a terrorist? No way. Israel is proving every day that it is against peace, and the desire for peace cannot co-exist with a desire for killing. The list of assassinations cannot be an expression of a desire to bring peace and stability in the region. Israel is practising state terrorism every day.

On 12 December, days before visiting London, President Assad defended the Palestinian suicide bombings and warned that a US-led war against Iraq would have catastrophic consequences, creating 'fertile soil for terrorism' right across the Middle East. The arguments were familiar but had stimulated few responses from Western pundits and politicians. The Syrian views were commonplace throughout the region but, because of American pressure, seldom rehearsed by Arab leaders in public.

It was not long before Washington, receptive to Israeli pressure, began criticising Syria for its alleged support for the Saddam regime. On 3 April 2003, with the war in progress, Donald Rumsfeld denounced Syria for ignoring American warnings and supplying military equipment to Iraq. Rumsfeld declared that the United States would hold the Syrian government responsible for alleged shipments of material, including night vision goggles, to Iraq. Such behaviour, declared Rumsfeld, constituted hostile acts. Already Colin Powell had increased the pressure on Syria and Iran, saying that if they did not mend their ways they would face a response from the United States after the war with Iraq had been won. Damascus, said Powell, faced a 'critical choice'. It could either 'continue direct support for terrorist groups and the dying regime of Saddam Hussein' or it could chose 'a more hopeful course'. Syria and Libya, he asserted, could be grouped 'in the same category' as Iran, echoing John Bolton, under-secretary of state, who had implied that the two states were junior members of President Bush's 'axis of evil'. Colin Powell added: 'We haven't taken any of our options off the table.'

Donald Rumsfeld was developing the theme, issuing fresh warnings against Syria and Iran – a posture condemned by British diplomats as likely to inflame Arab opinion and be counter-productive throughout the region. Prime Minister Blair said that Britain had 'absolutely no plans' for military action against Syria or Iran, and Jack Straw, foreign secretary, said that 'there would be no case whatever for taking any kind of action'. Britain, declared Straw, was working to improve relations with Syria but Syria must not allow its territory to be used as a conduit for military supplies to Iraq. He was not worried that the impression was being created that, once Iraq had been crushed, Syria and Iran would be next: 'It would worry me if it were true. It is not true, and we would have nothing whatever to do with an approach like that.' Before long, the Straw position had shifted: on 14 April, asked the same question on BBC radio, he replied: 'I'm not going to get into "what if" hypotheses.'

Syria was continuing to oppose the war, then well under way. A statement from the Syrian foreign ministry accused Washington of 'seeking a good report' from Israel: 'Syria has chosen to be with international legality represented by the United Nations Security Council. Syria has also chosen to stand by the Iraqi people, who are facing illegitimate and unjustified invasion.' Farouk al-Sharaa, Syria's foreign minister, declared that Syria 'has a national interest in the expulsion of the invaders from Iraq', and in an interview with the Lebanese daily *al-Safir* President Assad urged Arab countries to activate their dormant mutual defence agreement.

In early April it emerged that Britain had been exporting acid to Syria that could be used to manufacture chemical weapons, and supplied military equipment that could enable troops to fight at night. Thus Department of Trade and Industry reports revealed that, between 1999 and 2001, British Ministers granted export licences for £1.5 million worth of equipment that could be used by Syria for war purposes. A 2001 DTI report stated that exports included 'toxic chemical precursors', 'equipment for the use of military infrared/thermal imaging equipment' and 'military flying helmets'. Trade Secretary Patricia Hewitt had given an 'open licence' for the export of 'equipment for the use of submachine guns, assault rifles and sniper rifles'. The DTI believed that the toxic chemical precursors would be used as 'stain removers', but admitted it could not ensure that such chemicals would not be used for military purposes. Dr Julian Robinson, an expert on chemical weapons, commented that the precursors could be used for chemical weapons such as nerve gas and mustard gas. Such revelations were embarrassing to a Blair administration keen to appease the United States.

It was now obvious that Washington was developing its case against Syria. It was not only a matter of terrorism and night goggles. American officials were asserting that President Assad had actively collaborated with the Iraqi dictator to take weapons, including Scud missiles, from Iraq so that they would not be discovered by the UN inspectors: 'Significant equipment, assets and perhaps even expertise were transferred, the first signs of which appeared in August or September 2002. It is quite possible that Iraqi nuclear scientists went to Syria and that Saddam's regime may retain part of its army there.'

Donald Rumsfeld was also accusing Syria of permitting hundreds of Arab volunteers to cross into Iraq, and 'unconfirmed reports' were suggesting that Syria had helped to channel Russian Kornet anti-tank missiles to Saddam's forces. Paul Wolfowitz, Rumsfeld's deputy, declared that 'there has got to be change in Syria', then the only country in the world with a Ba'athist regime. And there were signs that the United States was already taking military action against Syria: a few days into the war, a Syrian bus inside Iraq was struck by an American missile and US planes were bombing along the Iraq-Syrian border. The Kuwaiti *al-Rai* newspaper reported that American aircraft had bombed the oil pipeline running between Kirkuk and the Syrian port of Banias, stopping the supply of 200,000 barrels of Iraqi oil a day to Syria. Farouk al-Sharaa remained defiant: 'The Americans want Syria to deploy its armed forces on the border to prevent Arab volunteers from entering Iraq. This contradicts Syria's national and nationalistic policies.'

On 12 April Mohammed al-Douri, Iraq's ambassador to the United Nations, left the United States for the Middle East, intending to search for his family; his destination was Damascus: 'I hope the US army will leave Iraq soon and that we will have free elections for a free government for a free future for Iraq and the people of Iraq. This is my message to the people of the United States.'

There were growing signs that Syria would be the next target for US attention. On 11 April President Bush stepped up the pressure by demanding that Syria hand over any Iraqi Ba'ath Party members or relatives of Saddam who might seek refuge. President Assad, said Bush, 'needs to know that we expect full co-operation'. At the same time the conviction was growing in US circles that Syria's support for Hamas, Hezbollah and other radical Islamic groups remained one of the principal obstacles to a Middle East peace plan, and that this support for terrorism would have to end. Walter Lang, former Defense Intelligence Agency specialist, commented: 'It is clear that the Pentagon's policy group is intent on eliminating the Syrian government as a factor in the Arab-Israeli dispute.' Sources in the Bush administration told *The Observer* (13 April 2003) that Washington had promised Israel that it would take 'all effective action' to cut off Syria's support for Hezbollah – implying military action if necessary. Richard Armitage, US deputy secretary of state, was already arguing that moving against Syria would be a way of cutting off aid to Hezbollah, which he dubbed 'the A team' of world terrorism.

At the same time President Bush was against asserting that Syria possessed chemical weapons, and repeated warnings issued earlier in the day (13 April) by Rumsfeld and Powell that Damascus must not harbour members of Saddam Hussein's regime: 'We believe there are chemical weapons in Syria. First things first. We're here in Iraq now and the ... thing about Syria is we expect co-operation and I'm hopeful we will receive co-operation.' He warned Syria (and Iran and North Korea) that the example of Iraq showed 'we're serious about stopping weapons of mass destruction'.

Jack Straw, ever sensitive to Washington's political posture, began adjusting his public statements. Where, only days before, action against Syria was seen by the Blair administration as unwarranted, now the British echo of the latest Bush utterance could be clearly heard. On the 14 April 2003 Jack Straw, interviewed on BBC radio, emphasised that

Syria would be expected to 'co-operate' with the United States and Britain.

The British attitude to the case of Syria was alarmingly similar to its changing view of the Iraq problem. Blair, Straw and Hoon went on public record as *not* being in favour of 'regime change' in Iraq – and then they meekly and shamelessly U-turned under instruction from Washington. Already, in April 2003, the Blair administration was practising its White House echo on Syria. Damascus would be expected to 'co-operate'. Syria was already in America's sights, but the new anticipated apocalypse would be delayed. The orders were being placed for a fresh stock of cruise missiles and smart bombs, but it would take some time to rebuild the US arsenals.

Jordan

Jordan, prepared to host American forces for the 2003 war, on occasions denied it was doing so but acknowledged the weight of US power. Before the war commenced, King Abdullah signalled that he did not want to make the mistake his father, King Hussein, had made by supporting Baghdad during the 1991 Gulf War: 'We paid a heavy price. This time we want to pursue a policy where Jordan comes first. We are not going to allow ourselves to be martyrs for either Baghdad or Ramallah' (this latter a reference to the Palestinian West Bank city ravaged by Israeli forces). It soon emerged that Abdullah was prepared to discreetly assist the US-led war in return for economic and security guarantees. Much of the Jordanian economy had formerly depended on cheap Iraqi oil and trade with Baghdad.

Jordan too, like other states in the region, was being racked by division and dissent. The 1994 treaty with Israel, under US prompting, had brought a billion dollars in debt forgiveness – but at the uncomfortable cost of planting Jordan insecurely in the Western camp. The Palestinian majority, inevitably opposed to the Bush-Blair-Sharon axis, were bound to be incensed by the new American invasion of Iraq, the one Arab country that could be relied upon to give practical aid to the struggling Palestinians of Gaza and the West Bank. Thus King Abdullah, keen to straddle both the Arab and Western worlds, was bound to feel threatened by his own people. The answer, as elsewhere in the Middle East, was to seek further American support in the interest of national security. The CIA could be relied upon to tackle the militants, and perhaps Washington would honour its pledges to help Jordan overcome the losses sustained through the collapse of Iraqi-Jordanian trade.

King Abdullah, eager to demonstrate his sensitivity to US-Israeli concerns, was also trying to clamp down on Palestinian militant groups, despite his nominal commitment to the Palestinian cause and the size of his own Palestinian population. On 21 November 1999 he exiled four top Hamas leaders to Qatar while at the same time pardoning others. It was reported that Hamas offices in Jordan would be closed and members of Hamas would be barred from political activity. Abdur-Rauf Rawabdeh, Jordan's prime minister, said: 'The case of Hamas is now considered closed after His Majesty the King decided to pardon all of the group's activists' – with no mention made of the expelled leaders. Later he added that four members had been expelled and the matter of their later return was open to discussion. One of the deportees commented: 'We were handcuffed and blindfolded and we were surprised to see ourselves at the steps of the plane.' Another said that he considered the move to be 'a forced exile'.

As the US-led war against Iraq came ever closer King Abdullah was confronted by the almost impossible task of heeding the demands of Washington, a close ally, and remaining sensitive to the pro-Iraq feelings of most of the Jordanian population. Again, as with other Arab states, Jordan stability was being seriously compromised by the Western military action. Abdel Salaam Saudi, working from a money-changer's booth, said: 'It depends on how long it takes the Americans to do the job and if they persuade some country to supply us with oil instead of Iraq. If they don't, we eat dirt.' Already Abdullah had declared that war on Iraq would unleash a 'Pandora's box' of woes on the Middle East – but the Americans had been in no mood to listen.

King Abdullah had already given permission to allow a significant American military presence in the country. By September 2002 there were already more than 4,000 US troops carrying out regular exercises in the southern desert. There were also 200 British troops and 50 vehicles, exercising for the future anticipated conflict. Jordanian officials were insisting that the military forces would leave the country the following month, but observers suggested that an enlargement of the US-UK presence was more likely. Said Mustafa Hamarneh, director of the Centre for Strategic Studies in Amman: 'If the Iraqi army puts up a good fight against the Americans, I think that Saddam will become the holiest man in the region.'

In November Jordanian forces were fighting dissident factions in the desert town of Maan – a detail that was setting alarm bells ringing in Washington. Was there an implicit threat here to the stability of the Abdullah regime? Could the Jordanians be relied upon to buttress US interests in the region? Daif Abu Darwish, a Maan shopkeeper, commented: 'The people here feel that the government treats them in an unjust way. They started to make a revolution against that injustice.' Abu Sayyef, an Islamic extremist from the Takfir wal-Hijra group, had fled to the area after being wounded in a gun battle with police and the local Bedouin chiefs refused to hand him over.

The Jordanian authorities responded by sending thousands of soldiers and armed police, supported by tanks and helicopter gunships, into the area – but they failed to find Sayyef. The scale of the problem was signalled when the Amman government announced that it would not tolerate a rival 'state within a state'. Is there really such a threat to the Abdullah regime? In any event the Jordanian forces, as befits such security elements, appear to have acted with brutality. One man reported what had happened when the police broke into his cousin's house: 'Four times we shouted "there is no-one here", but they fired into every room.'

Before the 2003 war began, the deteriorating security situation in Jordan was already plain. On 24 November 2002 the US peace corps suspended its operations in Jordan and withdrew its 60 volunteers because of the raised security risk to US personnel. An official said: 'The safety and security of our volunteers is the highest priority of the peace corps.' Independent observers had often noted that the peace corps, an 'independent' US federal agency, was often used as a cover for spying operations as it ran rural development operations across Jordan. This followed the killing on 28 October of diplomat Laurence Foley by unknown assailants. The US State Department noted the worsening security situation in Jordan by advising US citizens to 'carefully consider the risks of travel to Jordan.' The 2003 war was not expected to improve security in the country.[9]

On 4 April Jordan's prime minister, Ali Abul Ragheb, summoned Edward Gnehm, US ambassador, to condemn the deaths of Iraqi civilians in the war: 'Jordan condemns the killings and destruction caused by the invasion of Iraq, and holds the United States, Britain and any other country taking part in the war in Iraq responsible for protecting innocent civilians in line with the Geneva Convention.' The Jordan News Agency, Petra, quote Ragheb as asking for an immediate end to all military operations, and relaying the 'anger' of the leadership, government and people for the civilian casualties. He also branded as 'inadequate' the current level of humanitarian efforts exercised in Iraq, demanding that the US and Britain 'facilitate relief operations and the distribution of humanitarian assistance' (*The Jordan Times*, 4–5 April 2003). Gnehm pledged to convey Jordan's 'strong concerns' to his government and said that 'all possible means' were being used to minimise the loss of civilian life.

It was a charade. In hosting US forces the Jordanian government was complicit in the destruction and carnage being perpetrated in Iraq. Ragheb knew this and so did Gnehm. The protests and pledges were for public consumption only, and did nothing to restrict the American exploitation of Jordanian territory for military purposes.

The charade continued when King Abdullah visited the foreign ministry a few days later to monitor the diplomatic activities being conducted by the Amman authorities in connection with the US-led war. Marwan Muasher, foreign minister, later announced that the King wanted to take a personal interest in the ministry's efforts to address the Iraq crisis. On 8 April Abdullah, via a Royal Court statement, affirmed that efforts would continue to stop the war and to deliver humanitarian aid to the Iraqi people as soon as possible.

Jordan and other Middle East economies had been pushed to the brink of recession by the impact of the war. Tourism had collapsed, oil prices had shot up, trade with Iraq had halted, and direct foreign investment had plummeted. Jordan, Egypt, Morocco and Tunisia were the worst casualties. Mustafa Nabli, World Bank chief economist for the region, commented: 'Jordan is the most impacted because it is closest to the theatre of the activities of war. It had significant trade with Iraq, the tourism industry was hurt, subsidised oil imports from Iraq had halted, and foreign direct investment took a hit.'

The capture of Baghdad allowed King Abdullah to breathe a sigh of relief that the destabilising conflict was almost over, but many questions remained. What would happen now? How would the Americans manage the post-Saddam situation? And to what extent would an increasingly radicalised Jordanian population threaten the stability of the regime? One cabinet minister declared:

> It was never a question of standing on the winning or losing side, as much as it was taking a pragmatic position that allows Jordan to sail through this storm and emerge with the least damage, while protecting its strategic interests with the US and maintaining domestic stability. So far, we have managed through this crisis without any significant internal confrontation.

There *had* been domestic confrontations but these had been constrainable, though the long-term impact of the war had yet to become clear. Jordan had lost about $1.5 billion since the start of the military conflict, and there was widespread dissent among Jordan's Palestinian refugees and Islamic fundamentalists. The US had pledged to give the country around $1 billion to offset the cost of the war but it was not obvious that the pledge would be honoured.

Qatar

The increasing US involvement in Qatar was deeply symbolic. If Saudi Arabia was proving to be unreliable then the United States would go elsewhere – which in turn would add to the monarchy's diplomatic isolation and threaten the House of al-Saud. In early September 2002 it became clear that the US command headquarters was preparing to move key staff to a new airbase complex in Qatar. Reports suggested that staff and equipment would soon be moved from Tampa, Florida – a sign of growing American preparations of war. The immediate aim was for 600 personnel and equipment to be readied for an exercise in November, with some of the staff set to remain permanently in Qatar.

On 11 August David Hobson, US congressman, had visited the massive Al-Udeid base twenty miles from Doha, the Qatari capital. He had visited the site in his capacity as chairman of the House of Representatives military construction committee. The US had poured resources into expanding the $1 billion airbase, scheduled for completion by 2003. American spokesmen chose to ignore the paradox that while the Qatari government was publicly condemning the prospect of an American war on Iraq the US military was building one of the largest airbases in the region of Qatari soil – all in readiness for an invasion of a neighbouring Arab state. In addition a British military team was going to Qatar to work with the Americans.

It seemed that the Al-Udeid base, a 'restricted area' deep in the desert, did not welcome visitors. A newly-built two-lane road, lined with overhead lights, led to the base entrance, where dozens of aircraft were lined up beside a hangar made of hardened concrete. Qatar, population 700,000, may have had little choice in playing host to the world's only superpower. Said one Qatari official: 'The Gulf is not a very safe place and we are a very small country.'

The Al-Udeid could house up to forty aircraft within the estimated area of 7,000 square metres.[10] In September 2002 about 2,000 people were living at the base, but over the following months the base was equipped to accommodate up to 10,000 troops.

Qatar, unlike Saudi Arabia, had placed no operating restrictions on the American military, so encouraging the transport of further US resources from the Prince Sultan airbase in Saudi. Hasan al-Ansai, the head of the Gulf Studies Centre at Qatar University, commented that the Qatari authorities had encouraged Washington to adopt a more even-handed approach to the Israeli-Palestinian problem, but said also: 'Every country has to follow its own interests.' Perhaps there were limits on how much Qatar could dispute US policy.

One Qatari political analyst observed that Iran was a country with '80 million people sitting on top of us', but 'the Iranians won't bother us while we have American bases on our soil'. The Al-Udeid base was insurance, a partial American occupation being preferable to the hazards of Iranian ambition.

In December 2002 the United States was planning an unprecedented military exercise in Qatar to test the US command structure – a thinly veiled rehearsal for war. The operation, Internal Look, was a clear sign of US war planning. *The New York Times* (1 December 2002) commented: 'The command and control procedures practised would be the same used for a war with Iraq.'

Bahrain, Oman

Bahrain and Oman were also hosting US-UK military forces, but at the same time witnessing significant levels of internal dissent. Bahrain, a close ally of Britain, was frequently embarrassed in the 1990s by Shi'ite and other protests, and the influx of Western forces throughout 2002–3 had further fuelled dissent. In October 2002 Bahrain became the first Gulf state to hold democratic parliamentary elections in which women were allowed to vote and to contest national posts. It remained to be seen whether Bahrain's efforts to modernise would be able to sustain a secure pro-British regime or whether the burgeoning democracy would come to represent the popular Arab feeling in the region.

Thousands of British troops were deployed in Oman, another traditional Western ally. US-UK diplomacy – the familiar mix of bribery and coercion – had succeeded in securing sufficient support for the US-led aggression against Iraq, but the large measure of co-operation had involved cost. The war had nicely illuminated the familiar divisions throughout the Arab world, graphically exposing the pragmatic indifference of feudal and authoritarian pro-West regimes to the natural will and scrutiny of the people.

Most of the regimes in the Middle East have been sustained through terror and force, with the United States constantly reinforcing the repressive instincts of unrepresentative monarchies and dictatorships. Some regional states (Iraq, Syria, Libya, Yemen), unwilling to underwrite Washington's global plans, have been seen as 'rogues' and 'pariahs', 'states of concern'. Here the issue is not about human rights: in this regard it is difficult to judge between Mubarak's Egypt, Assad's Syria, Abdullah's Jordan, Saud's Saudi Arabia, the Sabah's Kuwait and Saddam's Iraq. The basic issue is about the shifting loyalties in a *realpolitik* world of foreign strategy, financial profits and hegemonic ambitions – and about who has power to impose their will.

Egypt

Egypt, a 'moderate' (that is, pro-US) state, relies on police suppression and torture to sustain the regime. Hosni Mubarak, the only candidate in presidential elections and constrained by peace deals with Israel, had no wish to threaten the security of the country by seriously questioning the US determination to wage war on Iraq. Egypt too had attended the Arab summits and signed up to the anti-war rhetoric, but there was no prospect that Egypt jeopardise its annual $2 billion worth of US bribes and aid designed to preserve Mubarak's loyalty to the United States. Egypt could be relied upon not to disturb American strategic plans – and to torture foreign and domestic prisoners in its jails.[11]

All Islamist political groups are banned in Egypt, which leads to frequent arrests and other police actions. On 9 September 2002 some fifty-one Muslim militants were arrested for various alleged crimes. A sentence of 15 years with hard labour was imposed on three men, one a Russian national, and other defendants were given shorter terms.

Human rights groups have charged that Egypt uses military justice, requiring a lesser burden of proof because it is not confident of securing guilty verdicts in civilian courts. Convicts cannot appeal their sentences but can petition President Mubarak, usually a waste of time. Few observers doubted that Egypt was exploiting the US 'war on terror' to stifle political dissent, a common phenomenon around the world. And the US determination to wage a fresh war was having a similar effect: a Washington keen to secure the acquiescence of Arab states was indifferent to the scale of domestic human rights abuses.

Again, as with other Arab states, the regime could not be assumed to be speaking for the people. On 15 November 2002 more than 100,000 Egyptians filed through the streets of Cairo holding banners and copies of the Koran aloft to mourn the dead leader of a banned movement. Thousands of people trying to reach the funeral of Mustafa Mashhour, a leader of the Muslim brotherhood, were prevented from reaching Cairo. One angry supporter said: 'We had to take dirt roads to get past the roadblocks. They didn't want people to come so they didn't broadcast it, but this is a grassroots group and people tell each other.'[12] The 81-year-old Mashhour drew up a vision in 1928 of Islamic states ruled by Sharia law: Islam 'as creed and state, book and sword, and a way of life'. A spokesman for Mashhour urged the need for free and fair elections in Egypt.

On 25 March Mubarak, in a televised address to the people, demonstrated his loyalty to the American cause:

I hope that the Iraqi government recognises the dangerous

situation it has put itself and us in ... The first and most important mistake was the Iraqi invasion of Kuwait in 1990, which created many security fears for many of the states of the region ... The second of these mistakes is the absence of any true Iraqi effort to deal with the crisis of confidence which came about as a result of this aggression ... Iraq could have done more over the past 12 years to regain the trust of its Arab neighbours as well as the international community.

A week later, to placate his domestic constituency, he warned that the war against Iraq would create '100 bin Ladens' as hundreds of Arab volunteers streamed to Baghdad to become martyrs for Saddam. On 8 April the 89-year-old Hassan Ali Radwan, a citizen of Cairo, pounded a table with his fist and resolved to go to fight US troops in Iraq: 'We cannot sleep because of what is happening in Iraq. Women and children don't stop crying over what is going on there. We must go to fight the Americans in Iraq, or else we will have to fight them here.' Thousands of young and middle-aged Egyptians had been flocking to the Lawyers' Union in Cairo to sign up to fight. Over a five-day period some 13,000 Egyptians from all over the country had pledged to fight the Americans in Iraq. Radwan having spent 12 years in Iraq, remembered the kindness of the people: 'We should stand by them in their hour of need.'

The Mubarak regime, embarrassed by this response, was placing obstacles in the way of volunteers. Police officers were preventing people obtaining exit visas, and volunteers were being turned away from government offices empty-handed. Some said that the Egyptian authorities had closed the exit points to Jordan and Libya. One volunteer, stopped with others at the Red Sea port of Nuweitha, complained: 'They beat us up and made us board a bus back to Cairo.'

The 2003 war radicalised many sections of Egyptian society, exacerbating the tensions that were already manifest. Here, as elsewhere throughout the Arab world, the fires of future instability were being fanned.

Lebanon

A senior official from the UN forces in Lebanon warned on 21 March that the war could lead to an escalation of tension on the Lebanon-Israel border. Thus Timour Goskel, a political advisor to the UN Interim Forces in Lebanon (UNIFIL) stated: 'If the situation there gets worse, if there are heavy civilian casualties and if the war takes another direction, then we might see emotional outbursts in Lebanon. We can't guess how things will turn.'

In Lebanon, as elsewhere in the region, there was a widespread anxiety that Ariel Sharon would use the cover of the US war to expand his activities in the West Bank and Gaza (see Chapter 8). The Lebanese authorities were determined to keep the country calm but there were worries that events might run out of control. Few observers imagined that the American aggression in Iraq would make for easier relations with Israel or improve the situation of the occupied Palestinian lands. The Lebanese, and perhaps especially the large population of refugee Palestinians, watched the developing situation with dread, despair and humiliation. Again the war seemed likely to fuel tensions in the region.

The 2003 war had traumatised the Arab world, exacerbating local tensions, creating a vast humanitarian catastrophe, destabilising the regimes in the area, and recruiting tens of thousands into the anti-West terrorist campaign. In the short term it was likely that the nation states would survive but Iraq had been converted into an American colony, the quasi-colonial status of Kuwait had been newly advertised, and the impotence of other regional states – Jordan, Qatar, Bahrain – to resist American ambitions had been made obvious. Syria and Saudi Arabia were variously hostile or unhelpful to the American war effort – and so were targeted for US attention. By mid-April there was widespread talk of sanctions against Syria and the possibility of military action. Paul Wolfowitz, US deputy defense secretary, declared that Syria was 'behaving badly', and implied that Damascus could draw its own conclusions about the likely American response.[13]

The Times (London) provided its own estimate of the likely course of change in the Middle East after the collapse of the Saddam regime:

 - *Syria* – 10 per cent chance of the Ba'ath Party regime surviving in present form, maintaining control over Lebanon, continuing support for 'terrorist' groups, and pursuing weapons of mass destruction;

- *Turkey* – 20 per cent chance of patching up relations with America, keeping military in check, propping up the economy, and stopping Kurdish nationalist inspirations in the south;

- *Iran* – 30 per cent chance of hardline clerics retaining military and political power in the face of popular pressure for democratic reform;

- *Saudi Arabia* – 60 per cent change of monarchy securing withdrawal of US forces from Saudi territory, introducing political reforms, curbing the influence of the militant clergy, and surviving intact;

- *Jordan* – 70 per cent chance of King Abdullah keeping the lid on popular unrest, stabilising the economy, securing foreign aid, and maintaining strong ties with America and Britain;

- *Gulf States (Kuwait, Bahrain, Qatar, UAE, Oman)* – 70 per cent chance of further political reform, economic development, and a continued US military presence;

- *Israel/Palestine* – 15 per cent chance of reaching a peace deal between Ariel Sharon and Yasser Arafat according to principles and timetable set out in the 'road map' plan.[14]

These estimates suggested the mixed political situation in the new post-Saddam environment, inevitably beset by the pivotal role of the megapower United States. It was clear that Washington's relations with Turkey, Iran and Saudi Arabia had been damaged and Syria was now in the firing line.

An emboldened White House hurried to exploit the predictable military success in Iraq by dictating the terms of an expanded American hegemony in the region. While Western politicians rehearsed the platitude of 'a new Iraq being ruled by Iraqis' – provided they were not Ba'athists, communists, fundamentalists, anti-US nationalists, etc. – Washington contemplated the vicarious thrill of new wars and further expansions of the American empire. And it seemed that Syria was not the only candidate for early attention: with all the media focus on the Middle East many commentators seemed to have forgotten about North Korea.[15] There were plenty of target states left in the world. Washington strategists, however industrious, would not work themselves out of a job.

EIGHT

Israel/Palestine

There were intimate links between the Israel-Palestine conflict and the 2003 war, with many observers seeing Zionist influence behind both the decision to topple the Saddam regime and the subsequent targeting of Syria. No-one doubted that the end of Ba'athism in Iraq and Syria would strengthen the hand of Israel in any later peace process.

It was equally obvious that American policy on the Middle East was being driven by individuals who were intensely supportive of Israel. The conservative think-tanks in the United States and the powerful Jewish lobby are linked by the Washington-based Jewish Institute for National Security Affairs (JINSA) which co-opts defense experts and sends them on trips to Israel. The retired General Jay Garner, selected to run post-Saddam Iraq, was sent to Israel in this fashion and in October 2000 co-signed a JINSA statement supporting Israel and attacking the Palestinian Authority (see p. 79). (see p. 79) He lost no time in demonstrating a crass insensitivity to the delicate task of administrating a conquered Iraq.

Paul Wolfowitz, Rumsfeld's deputy, and Douglas Feith, the Pentagon's No. 3, both have close ties to the Jewish-American Israeli lobby. Wolfowitz, who has relatives in Israel, has liaised for the Bush administration with the American Israel Public Affairs Committee. Feith, cited as a 'pro-Israel activist', was given an award by the Zionist organisation of America. During the Clinton years he collaborated with Richard Perle to produce a policy paper for the Likud party advising the Israeli government to end the Oslo peace process, reoccupy the Palestinian territories and crush the Arafat administration. Wolfowitz has signed public letters calling for the occupation of Iraq, the bombing of 'terrorist' bases in Lebanon, and military action against such states as Syria and Iran (Michael Lind, *New Statesman*, 7 April 2003). Any suggestion that such policies are designed to make the Middle East safe for Israel is denounced as vicious anti-semitism.

There are peace activists in Israel, compassionate men and women who sympathise with the plight of the Palestinians in the Occupied Territories, and courageous young people who refuse – on pain of imprisonment – to join the Israeli armed forces routinely humiliating and torturing Arabs in their own homes and streets. This important caveat apart, Israel rejoiced in the 2003 war against Iraq, just as the Israeli authorities had seen new opportunities provided by 11 September outrage. Following the terrorist attacks on Washington and New York – Israeli policies would no longer be constrained by empty talk of a 'peace process'. In the changed atmosphere of Bush paranoia and ambition, Israel too would be allowed to act solely in its own best interest, irrespective of human-rights abuses and the demands of natural justice. From 1948 Israeli policies had always been characterised by such derelictions, but from September 2001 to the early months of 2003 the Israeli state, in its treatment of the Palestinians, appeared to have abandoned any lingering vestiges of respect for morality and law.

Sacred Roots

Any attempt to understand the Israeli response to 2003 must take into account the historical claims of Zionism and the policies that these inspired. A principal theme in Zionism is that God gave Palestine to the Jews and that the 20th century provided the Israelis with the divinely-sanctioned opportunity to regain their ancient birthright. This belief is supposedly justified by the Old Testament Book of Numbers, especially Chapters 33 and 34, a vital part of the Pentateuch in the Judaic Talmud:

And the Lord spake unto Moses ...

Speak unto the children of Israel, and say unto them. When ye are passed over Jordan into the land of Canaan;'

Then ye shall drive out all inhabitants of the land from before you ... and destroy all their molten images, and quite pluck down all their high places;'

And ye shall dispossess the inhabitants of the land, and dwell therein: for I have given you the land to possess it ...

But if you will not drive out the inhabitants of the land ... it shall come to pass that those which you let remain ... shall be pricks in your eyes, and thorns in your sides, and shall vex you in the land wherein ye dwell.[1]

Evicting the Arabs

The policy of driving out the inhabitants of conquered land to facilitate a Jewish invasion and occupation was enshrined in many of the historical Zionist writings. For example, leading figures such as Israel Zangwill, a close associate of Theodor Herzl (the founder of political Zionism), worked hard to spread the idea that Palestine was 'a land without a people for a people without a land'. In 1914 Chaim Weizmann, later president of the World Zionist Congress and the first president of the state of Israel, commented:

In its initial stage, Zionism was conceived by its pioneers as a movement wholly depending on mechanical factors: there is a country that happens to be called Palestine, a country without a people, and on the other hand, there exists the Jewish people, and it has no country. What else is necessary, then, than to fit the gem into the ring, to unite this people with this country.[2]

Similarly, Weizmann once told an anecdote to Arthur Puppin, head of
the colonisation department of the Jewish agency. When Puppin asked
Weizmann what he though about the indigenous Palestinians Weizmann
replied: 'The British told us that there are some hundred thousand
negroes ['kushim'] and for those there is no value.' In the same vein
James McDonald, US ambassador to Israel, recalled in his book *My
Mission to Israel, 1948–1951* a conversation during which Weizmann
described the expulsion of the Palestinians in 1948 as a 'miraculous
simplification of Israel's tasks'. And this was a common theme in
Zionist writing. David Ben-Gurion, Israel's first prime minister, spoke in
a diary entry of 12 July 1937 of the 'compulsory transfer of Arabs from
the valleys of the proposed Jewish state', and later declared that 'we
must prepare ourselves to carry out' such a transfer. In a letter (5
October 1937) to his son Amos, Ben-Gurion wrote:

> We must expel Arabs and take their places ... and if we have to use
> force ... then we have force at our disposal.[3]

In early February 1948 Ben-Gurion told Yosef Weitz: 'The War will give
us the land. The concept of "ours" and "not ours" are peace concepts,
only, and in war they lose their whole meaning.'
    Almost all the founding fathers of Israel – including Herzl, Motzkin,
Syrkin, Ussishkin, Weizmann, Ben-Gurion, Tabenkin, Granovsky,
Zangwill, Ben-Tzvi, Rutenberg, Aaronson, Jabotinsky and Katznelson –
advocated the expulsion of the Palestinian Arabs in one way or another.
'Transfer' committees were established, enshrining the principle
advocated by Yosef Weitz, director of the Settlement Department of the
Jewish National Fund (JNF) and head of the Israeli government's
official Transfer Committee of 1948: 'The complete evacuation of the
country from its [Arab] inhabitants is the answer.' In April 1948 Weitz
recorded: 'I made a summary of the list of Arab villages which in my
opinion must be cleared out in order to complete Jewish regions. I also
made a summary of the places that have land disputes and must be
settled by military means.'[4]
    The Zionist policy of removing Palestinian Arabs from their homes
and land, a policy that continues today (2003), has been carried out by
terror and massacre.[5] Where the Palestinians could not be easily evicted
or killed the Israeli government set about creating an apartheid state,

sustained by racist assumptions and American financial, political and military support.[6] The result was a seemingly endless conflict between two unmatched sides – Israel, enjoying more or less continuous US support over the years, and the Palestinians, supported sporadically and ineffectually by some of the Arab states. A procession of UN Security Council resolutions condemning Israeli aggression, illegal settlement building, violations of the Fourth Geneva Convention (protection of civilians), etc., has been routinely ignored by every Israeli administration.[7]

In such circumstances, it is obvious that Israel ignores world opinion and all inconvenient elements of international law. Attention is given to the opinions of the United States, not always heeded, but Israel has rarely been troubled by US stricture or criticism. The post-September 2001 scene – and in particular the 2003 war – served to remove any minimal US constraint on Israeli policy. It was clear to any independent observer that Israel was determined to accelerate the acquisition of Arab land and the associated eviction of Arab families who had lived there for generations – a wholly illegal policy but one, in Zionist perceptions, sanctioned by an alleged almighty god.

Human Casualties

The Palestinians have responded with the use of hand-guns and pathetically inadequate home-made devices against Israel's US-supplied tanks, helicopters, gunships, fighter-bomber aircraft and missiles; and with suicide bombings, themselves illegal and aiding Israeli propaganda that denounces 'terrorism' while ignoring the state terrorism perpetrated by Israel every day. The result has been a growing toll of injury and death, with very many more casualties in every category on the Arab side than on the Israeli. In one estimate, for the period 24 September 2000 to 24 July 2002, there were 613 Israeli deaths and 1,449 Palestinian fatalities.[8]

On 31 July 2002 a Palestinian bombing killed at least seven people and wounded more than 18 in a crowded university cafeteria in Jerusalem – a revenge attack for an Israeli air strike in Gaza that killed 15 Palestinians, including nine children. It was not obvious that the explosion in Jerusalem had been caused by a suicide bomber. As usual the Israeli government blamed Yasser Arafat, president of the Palestinian Authority, and pledged that action would be taken in response. At the same time President Bush was reaffirming his commitment to the overthrow of Saddam Hussein and saying that Arafat should also be replaced.

President Bush was particularly incensed to learn that five US citizens had died in the Jerusalem bombing: 'I'm just as angry as Israel is right now. I'm furious about innocent life lost. However, through my fury, even though I am mad, I still believe peace is possible.' He was happy to note that the war on terrorism was being fought on many fronts – in Afghanistan, the Philippines and elsewhere: 'We're responding by working with our Arab friends and Israel, of course, to track these people down.'

Israel then responded by imposing a total ban on Palestinian travel in most of the West Bank, and used tanks to seal off much of the Gaza Strip. On 5 August a Palestinian gunman shot at the car of a Jewish settler family, killing the parents and wounding their children, aged three years and six months; while the Israeli forces shot dead two more Palestinians in the West Bank village of Burqa. Binyamin Ben-Eliezer, Israel's defense minister declared: 'We are in a situation of total closure in the West Bank. No-one goes in or out. We will continue with a series of measures whose aims are to implement a much wider closure than we are doing now.' At this time, as usual, the Israeli authorities were giving no attention to the impact of such a policy of the condition of the Palestinian people. Thus Nabil Abu Rdainah, a senior Arafat aide, condemned the Israeli tactics: 'Palestinian suffering demands an immediate international intervention because of the humanitarian catastrophe of the people.'

Humanitarian Disaster

The United States Agency for International Development (USAID) was then reporting the 'humanitarian disaster' in the West Bank and Gaza Strip caused by Israeli policies of closure. The report, released jointly by USAID and the charity Care International, claimed that 13.2 per cent of Palestinian under five were suffering chronic, or medium to long-term malnutrition, while 9.3 per cent were suffering acute malnutrition, caused very recently. *Israel was quite literally starving tens of thousands of Palestinian children.* Moreover, the Israeli policies were succeeding in eroding all powers of the Palestinian Authority – by destroying the Palestinian infrastructure and its capacity to operate, in some areas forcing an Arab return to traditional tribal law.

A few Israelis, concerned at the abuse of Palestinians by the Israeli forces, formed Checkpoint Watch, set up by the Israeli organisation Women for Human Rights. In groups of three or four the women visited checkpoints to monitor the treatment of Palestinians by soldiers and border police: 'They almost always behave better when we are around.' Graffiti was spotted on the side of one booth where police ask drivers to show their papers: 'A good Arab is a dead Arab.' Mrs Elkana, a Checkpoint Watch member, complained about the slogan, and later commented that Sharon had no interest in a peace agreement 'because that would mean removing the settlements'.

On 14 August 2002 Marwan Barghouthi, a former head of Arafat's Fatah movement in the West Bank, went on trial for orchestrating the killing of dozens of Israelis. As journalists packed a Tel Aviv courtroom Barghouthi shouted in Hebrew: 'The intifada will win!' His lawyers claimed in court that the interrogation of the Palestinian leader had involved sleep deprivation and other illegal pressure tactics, and denied that Barghouthi had acknowledged his responsibility for the attacks against Israeli targets. Again, as he was led away, Barghouthi raised his cuffed hands and declaimed in Hebrew, Arabic and English: 'The intifada will be victorious!' Many observers suspected that the treatment of Barghouthi was no more than a show trial, an attempt by the Israeli authorities to show that senior Palestinian leaders were involved in terrorist acts; and that the trial might backfire on the Israeli government, boosting Barghouthi's popularity by exposing the human-rights abuses being perpetrated daily by the Israelis.[9]

On the day the trial began, Israeli forces fired rockets into a house in the West Bank, killing a disabled Hamas leader and another Palestinian. The soldiers, advancing into the village of Tubas near Nablus, then used bulldozers to complete the demolition of the house. On 15 August the prominent Israeli human rights group, B'tselem, declared that a Palestinian youth killed in an army attempt to capture an Islamic militant had been dragooned as a 'human shield'. There was mounting evidence that this was a frequent tactic of the Israeli armed forces.

Palestinian witnesses reported that the 19-year-old Nidal Aby M'Khisan had died in a hail of gunfire after he was forced to knock on the door of a house. A senior Israeli military source said that someone had been sent because he knew Nasr Jarrar, the inhabitant of the house and a terrorist suspect: 'We assumed that a Palestinian speaking the language, a next-door-neighbour, would not be shot at.' Yael Stein, the B'tselem director, disputed the army's account, saying that their action was 'immoral and illegal'.

Palestinian Victims

Human rights groups had already accused the Israeli army of ordering Palestinian civilians to enter buildings to check if they are booby-trapped, remove suspicious objects from roads, and serve as 'gun rests' for Israeli solders firing over their shoulders. Some Palestinians had been ordered to walk in front of soldiers to shield them from gunfire. On 18 August 2002 the five-year-old Ayman Fares, waiting eagerly to begin school, was shot dead by Israeli soldiers firing into the refugee camp where he lived. He was shot in the back of the head. Said Nadid Fares, the child's grandfather, who had been shot while trying to take the boy to hospital: 'There was no mistake. The soldiers knew where they directed their weapons. Israeli tanks open fire daily against our houses and fields.' On 20 August Israeli troops shot dead the 15-year-old Ayman Zuarab at the Khan Yhounis refugee camp in Gaza.

The Israeli forces, still maintaining their clampdown on Gaza and the West Bank, were arresting a growing number of Palestinians in a sweep to capture alleged militants. This in turn was fuelling the bitterness and hatred – to the point when Jonathan Sacks, Britain's chief rabbi, declared that Israel was adopting a stance 'incompatible' with the deepest ideals of Judaism; and that the current conflict with the Palestinians was 'corrupting' Israeli culture. In an exclusive interview with *The Guardian* (27 August 2002) Sacks commented:

> I regard the current situation as nothing less than tragic. It is forcing Israel into postures that are incompatible in the long run with our deepest ideals ... There is no question that this kind of prolonged conflict, together with the absence of hope, generates

hatreds and insensitivities that in the long run are corrupting to a culture.

In 1967 he was convinced that Israel had to give back all the newly-conquered land for the sake of peace – and Sacks was not prepared to renounce that view in 2002.[10] But Israel, Sacks believed, had often tried to make peace though, in his view, the Palestinians had not made the same 'cognitive leap' towards compromise. He declared that he would be prepared to meet with Sheikh Abu Hamza, the fundamentalist north-London cleric who claimed to share the views of Osama bin Laden. Such a meeting, said Sacks would be 'a thought worth pursuing ... I absolutely don't rule it out'. The immediate critics of Dr Sacks were quick to accuse him of 'moral blindness', and declared that his statements would do no more than fuel violence against the Israeli state.

However, one Israeli government minister did decide to support the Sacks comments. Michael Melchior, deputy foreign minister and former chief rabbi of Norway, criticised those – especially from the Israel right – who ignored the moral dilemmas posed for Israel each day by the conflict: 'If the Palestine situation continues, then this is something that will be tragic for all the peoples here.' A straw poll conducted by *Ha'aretz*, the Israeli daily, found almost overwhelming support for Sacks among British Rabbis then living in Israel. Thus Rabbi Marmur, dean of the Hebrew Union College in Jerusalem, said:

> I agree wholeheartedly with Dr Sack's opinions as expressed in the article. Occupation and terror are brutalising us. It behoves him to say what he thinks in a responsible way. His criticism is appropriate and if we can't bear to hear it, the problem is ours.

On 29 August 2002 four fruit-pickers from the same Palestinian family were killed when the Israeli army fired tiny metal darts, 'flechettes', into the orchard where they were sleeping. Some of the darts bore deep into the fig-tree wood, only their fins protruding from the bark. The Israelis had fired the hail of darts – 3,000 are contained in one shell that bursts in the air – that killed Ruwaida Hajeen (aged 55), her son, Ashraf (23) and Nihad (17), and a cousin, Mohammed (20). Two other family members were critically wounded. One of the survivors, the 16-year-old Saleh, was expected to live, even though the Israelis stopped ambulances reaching him for an hour. Benyamin Ben-Eliezer, Israeli defense minister, said he regretted the deaths of innocent people. In apparent agreement, Abdel-Razak Yihya, Arafat's security chief, was then demanding an end to the Palestinian suicide bombings. However, such commentary was contributing little to reducing the fatality rates among both Israelis and Palestinians, especially children.

Suffer the Children

Since the beginning of the second intifada, the Palestinian uprising in September 2000, Israeli and Palestinian children had been targeted by both sides in an unprecedented fashion. From 29 September 2000 to the end of August 2002, some 1,700 Palestinians, including more than 250 children, were killed, and more than 580 Israelis, most of them civilians and including 72 children.[11] Thus for every Israeli child death more than three Palestinian children perished.

The Israeli children had been killed in 'direct and indiscriminate attacks', including suicide bombing and shootings both inside Israel and in the Occupied Territories, but many of the much higher number of Palestinian child deaths had been caused by sophisticated US-supplied weaponry:

> The overwhelming majority of Palestinian children have been killed in the Occupied Territories when members of the Israeli Defense Forces (IDF) responded to demonstrations and stone-throwing incidents with excessive and disproportionate use of force, and as a result of the IDF's reckless shooting shelling and aerial bombardments of residential areas. Palestinian children have also been killed as bystanders during Israel's extrajudicial execution of targeted activists, or were killed when their homes were demolished [often by tanks or bulldozers]. Others died because they were denied access to medical care by the IDF. At least three Palestinian children have been killed by armed Israeli settlers in the Occupied Territories.[12]

Amnesty International referred to the 'alarming pattern of killing Palestinian children by the IDF', as a pattern 'established at the outset of the intifida and ... continued.' Here it is pointed out that through 2002 some 48 per cent of the Palestinian children killed were 12 years old or younger:

> Most of the children were killed when there was no exchange of fire and in circumstances in which the lives of the [Israeli] soldiers were not at risk.[13]

In the overwhelming majority of cases the Israeli authorities have made no effort to investigate the killing of Palestinian children. In the very few cases where convictions have been secured the sentences have been derisory. For example, in January 2001 the Jerusalem District Court sentenced a 37-year-old Israeli man to six months community service for killing an 11-year-old Palestinian child. At the same time an 18-year-old Palestinian woman was sentenced to six and a half years imprisonment for wounding an Israeli settler, an offence she had committed when she was 15 years old.

On 31 August 2002 Israeli helicopter gunships fired three missiles into a car near Jenin, killing five people. The car had been targeted as containing a suspected militant, but two children, both aged nine, standing nearby had also been killed. On 1 September Moshe Katsav, Israeli President, felt driven to ask whether the Israeli army had become 'trigger happy' after soldiers killed 11 Palestinians, including six unarmed adults and two children, over the weekend: 'The claim as to whether the army was trigger happy must be examined. If the army reaches the conclusion that this was the case, it will decide what to do but it would be hasty to draw conclusions now.' According to *Ha'aretz*, 30 of the 49 Palestinians killed by the army in August were civilians. Haim Ramon, a senior member of the Labour Party, a partner in Sharon's coalition, commented: 'The defense minister must examine whether the series of mishaps and apologies really stems from mistakes and not from a change in policy which makes it easier to press the trigger.'

Palestinian leaders dismissed the demands for an investigation as a propaganda ploy that would lead nowhere. Saeb Erekat, a senior Palestinian cabinet member, said: 'The calls for an investigation are meant for media consumption because we have never heard of any result of these panels created after killing of Palestinian civilians. We place full responsibility on the Israeli government for these crimes and this bloodletting.'

More Evictions

In early September 2002 nine judges in Israel's Supreme Court ruled that the relatives of a militant could be expelled from their homes in a transfer from the West Bank to Gaza – an action perceived by many observers as a war crime. This meant punishing some people for the crimes of someone else, an issue that Saeb Erekat was considering referring to the UN Security Council. It was pointed out that the Geneva Convention, Article 49, contained a prohibition not only against deportation but against forced transfer. Israel's violations of the Geneva Convention had already been condemned in Security Council resolutions (for example, SCRs 452, 465 and 478): there was no reason to assume that Israel would now begin to observe the demands of international law.

On 4 September the two deportees, having committed no crimes, were blindfolded, handcuffed and put in leg irons, before being transported in a tank to be dumped in a field near a Jewish settlement in the Gaza Strip. Ms Ajouri, one of the two (brother and sister) deportees, later said when she arrived in Gaza City:

> They drove us for about twenty minutes. Suddenly they took us out of the tank and freed our hands and we found ourselves in the middle of a farm ... We walked until we saw a farmer ... He told us we were in a very dangerous place where Palestinians were killed last week. The farmer told us, 'Hurry, hurry before the soldiers shoot you'.

It was at this place that five Palestinians, including a mother and three children, had been killed the previous week by a tank shell. Ms Ajouri, having been taken to the Palestinian Centre for Human Rights, protested that a war crime had been committed, saying that if the Israelis had any evidence against her she would have been jailed rather than deported. At the same time there was no doubt that the Israeli authorities would have impunity against any legal consequences following their actions. On 6

September an internal inquiry by the Israeli army into the killing of 12 Palestinian civilians the previous weeks had cleared the soldiers. The recent attack on the sleeping fruit pickers, using an air-burst shell packed with 3,000 flechettes, had been 'appropriate'. So too were the orders given to Israeli snipers to kill four Palestinian labourers in a West Bank quarry. And the order that had resulted in the killing by a helicopter-borne death squad of two Palestinian teenagers and two children, aged 6 and 10, was also judged to be 'appropriate'. Defense minister Binyamin Ben-Eliezer complimented the Israeli army on its 'thorough' enquiry.

Arafat at Bay

Arafat was again struggling to reassert his authority. He urged the holding of elections for the Palestinian parliament in January, and demanded that Israel lift the curfews imposed on the Palestinian towns. Arafat, who had given blood for the 11 September survivors, condemned Israeli efforts to link the Palestinian struggle to terrorism, and hoped that war would be avoided in Iraq: 'We hope the problem with the brothers in Iraq will be solved politically and without military violence so as to help in achieving peace in the Middle East.' At the same time Israeli tanks surrounded the Boureij refugee camp and two adjacent camps in Gaza, and Israeli troops moved in to blow up the house of a suspected militant.

Arafat's Fatah organisation was now urging an end to suicide bombings, while Israel was threatening war against Lebanon unless it abandoned a water-pumping plan that would affect the flow of water to Israel. Elections for the Palestinian parliament and the presidency were scheduled for 20 January 2003, but it seemed unlikely that Israeli restrictions would allow any meaningful elections to take place. On 17 September Israeli tanks and troops swept through Khan Yhounis in Gaza and destroyed metal workshops suspected of being arms factories. Thirty tanks and armoured vehicles were used and nine foundries were demolished. Ramez al-Fara, standing by his demolished tractor repair workshop, commented: 'They came in tanks and bulldozers, they called to us through megaphones to come out of the house, and then they threw explosives into it and destroyed it.'

On 18 September a Palestinian blew himself up at a bus stop in northern Israel – the first suicide bombing in more than six weeks – causing one Israeli fatality. Ziad Bashteti, a delivery van driver, described what had happened: 'The squad car pulled up beside a bus stop. There were two young people standing there ... A policeman got out of the car and called to the short man to step forward. I drove along then heard the explosion, and was forced to stop about 15 yards on. Flying body parts hit my van.' On the following day a suicide bomber killed at least five people on a bus in Tel Aviv, whereupon the Israeli cabinet decided to 'isolate' Arafat in his Ramallah compound. Tanks, troop carriers and other vehicles entered the Ramallah compound, sparking a brief exchange of fire that left two of Arafat's bodyguards wounded. Israeli tanks and helicopter gunships also attacked the outskirts of the Gaza City, firing into a densely populated residential district. Tanks and bulldozers then began demolishing the buildings surrounding Arafat's office, and his supporters began to fear for his life. Inside the devastated building an aide communicated by mobile phone: 'The president refuses to leave. He says, "I shall either be a martyr or a martyr or a martyr, period. I will not surrender" ... The siege is moving swiftly. I think they may be targeting the president himself.'[14]

Ignoring the UN

On 24 September 2002 the UN Security Council adopted a resolution *demanding* 'that Israel immediately cease measures in and around Ramallah including the destruction of Palestinian civilian and security infrastructure', and *demanding also* 'the expeditious withdrawal of the Israeli occupying forces from Palestinian cities towards ... the positions held prior to September 2000'. Arafat had achieved a measure of international support for an ending of the Ramallah siege, but it proved of little consequence. Sharon ignored the new Security Council resolution, SCR 1435 (24 September 2002), just as he had ignored the earlier resolutions (SCRs 1402, 1403 and 1405 – all adopted in 2002), demanding the withdrawal of Israeli forces from Palestinian cities and the setting-up by UN Secretary-General Kofi Annan of a fact-finding team to investigate the Israeli atrocities in Jenin. Israel was consistent in its contempt for international law.

In early October there were reports of the deteriorating conditions in Nablus, a West Bank City that, with others, had been under heavy control and confinement for more than three months. The city, with the neighbouring refugee camp of Balata, numbered about 200,000 people – who had been under a 24-hour curfew for 100 days. Once every 10 days the people were allowed out of their homes to buy food: shops were shut, streets were empty, and the municipal administration complex had been bombed three times by the Israelis. But then people began to leave their houses, unable to tolerate such conditions any longer. Colonel Tibon, an Israeli Officer, explained why Nablus had been subject to such treatment:

> The people in Nablus are responsible for more than 80 per cent of all the suicide bombs in Israel. This is the centre of terror networks: Hamas, Islamic Jihad, Tamzin are all tied together in Nablus. The biggest laboratories for making bombs are here, and many people who volunteer for suicide squads. The first step was to put pressure on families of the terrorists ... If there's something they care about it's not ideology, it's their families. People start to bring their kids to us because of the pressure.[15]

The policy of 'collective punishment' was obvious. 'They are living in shit', Tibon said. 'We put pressure on the population to show them that terror is taking them nowhere, to show them that if they continue to co-operate with the terror they will suffer.' But were the Israelis considering the depths of hatred that their policies were creating.

A distraught Nablus grandfather, Ali Hafi, 88 years old and in despair, had gone searching for his grandson, Rami al-Barbri. Then he learned that the 10-year-old Rami had joined a group of children throwing stones at a tank, whereupon a soldier had blown off the top of Rami's head: 'He was only 10-years-old. What sort of a threat could be he to a tank?' The boy's stepfather, Samir Imran, said at the memorial service: 'I think the Israelis want to send a message to the children that this is their future. They think of us as slaves. Before a child reaches the age of 13, it is time for him to die.' The real intention, declared Imran, was not for the Israelis to stop the 'terror' but to drive the Arabs out of the West Bank.

In October there were more tank shellings of Gaza, condemned by

Kofi Annan; more settler shootings at Palestinians trying to harvest their olives; more deaths from suicide bombers; and a growing deterioration of the Israeli economy. Then Israel was asking the United States for $10 billion to halt the recession, amid growing signs of domestic tensions over rising unemployment and inadequate social services. Palestinian villagers were fleeing armed settlers as they continued to target waterholes and the olive harvest, and with the exodus of a fresh batch of Palestinians the Israelis were able to steal more Arab land.[16] In late-October the 85-year-old Yusuf Sobeth, having refused to leave his home in 1967 under Israeli pressure, was fleeing his village, Yanoun, along with everyone else, after five years of harassment by Israeli settlers.

His son, Abdel Atif Sobeih, the mayor, said that he and other villagers had been repeatedly beaten up by the settlers, their amenities vandalised and their crops destroyed and stolen:

> It took five years of continuous attacks to force us to leave. They would shoot at us, at our sheep, our cattle. Then they started coming to the outskirts of the village and throwing rocks at the doors. After the beginning of the intifida in 2000, it got much worse. I have been beaten up in my house in front of my family, in the courtyard and out in the fields.

The strategy of the settlers, sometimes carrying M–16 assault rifles, seemed quite unambiguous. They all wore the kippah, a cap to remind them to act in a way that would benefit God, and most wore tzitzels under their shirts, with tassels to remind them to follow all the 613 commandments in the Torah. Here was a religious consciousness that would be highly sensitive to the message of Numbers, Chapter 33, declaring that God had given the land to the Jews. And so here they were, implementing God's word with the help of M–16 assault rifles, gradually but with unshakeable resolve, appropriating Arab land through terror and violence.

More War Crimes

Sharon had appointed Shaul Mofaz as defense minister, a singular choice since Mofaz was seemingly implicated in war crimes. On 31

October 2002 the British Home Office announced that the Director of Public Prosecutions had been asked to begin war crimes proceedings against the new Israeli defense minister for his involvement in the Jenin atrocities: for example, bulldozing houses and burying people alive, torture and the shooting of suspects. It was alleged that General Mofaz had personally supervised some of these activities, and could be prosecuted under the terms of the Fourth Geneva Convention. Amnesty International was making its own representations for the great arrest of soldiers 'responsible for war crimes' in Jenin and Nablus. According to Amnesty International the Israeli forces were guilty of:

- unlawful killings;

- torture;

- the use of civilians as human shields;

- the destruction of hundreds of homes;

- burying people alive;

- the blocking of medical help to the wounded.

If Israel refused to take no action over these accusations, then Amnesty said that those implicated in war crimes should be detained and tried when they went abroad: 'If you have an army commander ... who takes a holiday in a country that is a high contracting party to the Geneva Convention, like the UK, then the UK can launch an investigation and hold a trial if it chooses. *It has a legal obligation under international law to do so*' (my italics).

In November 2002 dozens of Israeli tanks were again moving into Palestinian cities; Palestinian gunmen ambushed and killed 12 Israelis in Hebron; and Sharon said that he would build more settlements – in defiance of international law – in the Occupied Territories. Iain Hook, a British relief worker with the United Nations, was shot dead by the Israelis in Jenin, along with another five Palestinians, including a 14-year-old-boy, killed in Ramallah. Kofi Annan condemned the Israeli demolition of a UN food warehouse, containing supplies for Palestinians, in the Gaza Strip. More than 500 tons of food were deliberately destroyed when Israeli forces entered Jaballia and used explosives to blast the World Food Programme (WFP) warehouse (see also Chapter 11, *Vetoing a Syrian Resolution*).

On 3 December 2002 the Israeli army killed a 95-year-old Palestinian woman near Ramallah, the oldest victim among nearly 2,000 Palestinians killed over the previous two years. Fatima Hassam was shot dead as she returned from a visit to the doctor; two other women were wounded. The killings continued: one when an 11-year-old girl appeared briefly at her bedroom window presenting an easy target for an Israeli sniper. One report told of tanks opening up with their machine-guns at the end of a street in Rafah in the Gaza Strip. Jihan Asful and his sister were sitting on the sofa when bullets flew over their heads and through the concrete wall into the next room. Jihan did not flinch, but continued drinking her tea and nibbling on a biscuit: 'It happens every night. This is our life.'[17]

In January 2003 Israel's election committee banned an Arab party from the imminent elections, there was further evidence of Palestinians being used as human shields,[18] and suicide bombers killed two dozen more Israelis. American troops were joining exercises with Israeli forces in preparation for the 2003 war, and the US began the task of reinforcing Israeli defenses. Sharon himself was being linked to kickbacks and pay-offs, just as Belgium was contemplating reviving the Sharon war crimes case – developments that some pundits thought would damage Sharon's chances in the election.[19]

On 25 January dozens of Israeli tanks tore into Gaza City in the bloodiest attack on the Palestinians for months. At least 12 Palestinians were killed and more than 40 wounded. Some 35 tanks had entered the city from three different directions and, supported by helicopter gunships, began demolishing metal workshops, foundries, offices and homes. Several storeys of flats were wrecked, the top-floor kitchen lying open as the apartment's façade was ripped off. In a nearby street a grocery shop between two metalwork shops was obliterated. Ahmed, an engineer, commented bitterly: 'Sharon thinks he can sell the Israelis an illusion that he will give them more security by destroying all these shops. This makes him look strong to them, but it is just an illusion.' Then Sharon ordered a total closure of the West Bank and Gaza, the entire Occupied Territories, until after the following day's Israeli election.

Sharon had made it plain that he was not about to follow any 'road map' to peace. As a prelude to the election he had killed and wounded hundreds of Palestinians, made no effort to negotiate any sort of agreement with the decimated Palestinian Authority, and reinforced the common perception that he felt no need to restrain his belligerent instincts in any way. On 28 January the Israeli people, in a low turn-out, were insufficiently impressed to give Sharon large gains in the parliamentary elections, but it was clear that he would begin a new parliamentary term with increased confidence in his policies on Palestine. The US war on Iraq would serve to encourage the Sharon philosophy of gun, tank, bomber and bulldozer.

Prelude to War

The anticipation of the US-led war on Iraq was certainly doing nothing to limit the Israeli depredations in the Occupied Territories. Food was running out in the Gaza Strip, where the Palestinians were trapped behind barbed wire controlled by Israeli guns.[20] Some 22 per cent of children were suffering malnutrition and the situation was set to worsen. Aqil Abu Shammala, head of the UN social services programme in Gaza, was noting an accelerating decline into poverty, and Peter Hansen, head of the UN Palestinian refugee agency (UNPRA), commented: 'We have asked the Israelis for a great many things, but apart from a consignment of rice they have given nothing. Instead, they have caused very great costs by destroying several of our installations and hindering us in doing our work.'[21]

In mid-February 2003, while the world's press was focusing on the UN Security Council and Baghdad, the violence was surging in Gaza. There were no suicide bombings in Israel but the Palestinian bodies were piling up in the Occupied Territories. Even the US State Department, happily shipping arms to Israel, was critical of Israeli military operations: 'We remain very concerned about civilian casualties ... especially among Palestinian children and young people. These casualties continue to result from Israeli military actions.' At the same time the Israeli government was evicting Bedouin families from the Negev desert in order to resettle the region – a further illegal displacement of Arab communities.[22]

By the end of February there was growing discussion about the allegedly US-approved 'road map' to achieve peace settlement between Israel and Palestine.[23] The plan demanded concessions from both sides, but Washington was indicating that it would not publish the details until after the Iraq war. Saeb Erekat was soon pointing out that Ariel Sharon would make no concessions: 'He is saying there is no road map, no peace process. It's a government for the settlers and by the settlers.' Sharon had made it clear 'that he wants the Palestinians to surrender to him.'[24] Sharon – using siege moats, physical damage to roads, concrete blockades, concrete walls – was systematically destroying the Palestinian economy and any hope for the future. One sewage-filled security ditch dug by Israeli bulldozers had cut off the Palestinian inhabitants of Salem from their olive groves and wheatfields. If they tried to reach them, they risked being shot from newly built Israeli watchtowers.[25]

On 6 March 2003, in response to a Palestinian suicide bomb detonated on a bus, Israeli forces swept through the Gaza Strip:

Israeli army kills 15 in 'revenge attacks' on Palestinians.[26]

Israelis 'shot fireman as he put out blaze.'[27]

Israeli forces seize land in north Gaza Strip.[28]

Israeli bulldozer kills US student.[29]

In the West Bank the Israelis killed at least ten Palestinians, while Ariel Sharon was telling his cabinet that he planned to extend the 'security fence' along the length of the West Bank so that it entirely encircled any future Palestinian state. Now the Occupied Territories were being turned in a vast prison defined by a 230-mile wall, six metres high and protected by barbed wire and guard towers. Already it was clear that the wall would extend deep into Palestinian territory for long stretches. Michael Tarazi, a Palestinian negotiator, said: 'This just confirms that the wall is not to separate the West Bank from Israelis. It's to separate Palestinians into their reservation. It means that the Israelis will take control of our border with Jordan and what remains of the best agricultural land we have.' The plan, commented Tarazi, would kill any chance of a negotiated settlement.[30]

The 'road map' to a settlement was mentioned at various times during the approach to war – but it was obvious that Washington had no enthusiasm for it, the Israelis were stalling, and the then unpublished scheme had only been advanced at all as a cynical attempt to minimise Arab opposition to the imminent war. Elements of the plan had been leaked and Israel was said to have more than one hundred objections to it (see Chapter 13). There was no sense of any scheme that was likely to bring equity and justice to the Israeli-Palestinian conflict.

War and Aftermath

The 2003 war was sure to occupy the world's attention. On 28 March President Bush allegedly threw his full weight behind the so-called 'road map', but there was a distinct American reluctance to provide details of the plan or a timescale for its implementation. Prime Minister Blair remained keen to obtain a commitment from the Bush administration but commentators were sceptical about America's good faith. It was now emerging that the Israelis had compiled their own version of the 'road map', a 'watered down' version that would be sure to prolong the conflict. What was particularly significant was that the Israeli scheme was initiated by the army.[31]

On 2 April Israeli troops rounded up around 2,000 Palestinians in Tulkaram, a West Bank city. Soldiers in tanks and armoured vehicles backed by helicopters searched homes and imposed curfews. Many of the Palestinians remained in custody without charge. On 4 April the Israelis used helicopters and tanks to kill seven Palestinians in Gaza and the West Bank. About 1,000 Palestinian men were expelled from their homes in a West Bank refugee camp and told not to return until the Israeli operations were over. The death of Iyad Alyan, 26, by tank fire brought to 3127 (2350 Palestinians and 719 Israelis) the number of people killed since the start of the Palestinian uprising against Israeli occupation in September 2000.

Since August 2002 the army had demolished around 200 houses in Gaza and the West Bank, in some areas creating an ever-widening no-man's land between the Occupied Territories and the surrounding terrain. The Israeli policies, consistent over the years, were then being reinforced by the American war on Iraq. In the context of a full-scale military invasion of a Muslim state the Israeli authorities felt emboldened to expand their penetration of the Occupied Territories and the suppression of the Palestinian people.

Prime Minister Blair, smarting at legitimate criticism of his double standards over Iraq and Palestine, was struggling to secure American commitment to action on the Palestine issue. On 4 April, interviewed by the BBC's Arabic service, Blair commented:

> We have got a situation now where the President of the United States of America ... has laid out a two-state vision – Israel, recognised by everyone, confident about its security; and a viable Palestinian state. I believe it is *every bit as important* that we make progress on that as we get rid of Saddam. (my italics).

Even this observation, scarcely original and lacking all practical detail, was too much for Israeli opinion. Dov Weissglass, Ariel Sharon's chief advisor, angrily responded on Israeli radio:

> We regret that Great Britain is pushing itself out of involvement in the peace process as a result of [the] extreme position it has adopted. A country that adopts such unbalanced positions cannot be expected to have its voice attended to seriously. We will not be able to bear Blair's statements and we will draw our conclusions.[32]

This meant that the so-called 'road map' to peace was dead before the details were even published. Two weeks before the Weissglass comments, Jack Straw had said in another BBC interview that the West had been guilty of double standards in insisting that Iraq implement United Nations resolutions while not making the same demands of Israel. Then the Israeli foreign ministry called in Sherard Cowper-Coles, British ambassador in Tel Aviv, to protest at such remarks.

Israel was delighted at the overthrow of the Saddam regime, but concerned that the post-war situation may involve fresh focus on the Middle East peace process. From the Israeli perspective a main threat to Jewish security had been removed, but Israel was not in the mood to make concessions to Palestinian 'terrorists'. Michael Soshan, 37, speaking in Jerusalem, expressed the widespread opinion: 'We shouldn't become indifferent because we are still under threat from the Muslim world. We should stay on alert because danger always awaits us.' The

Palestinians, confronted by a partisan Bush administration and the state terrorism of Israel, were not confident that political progress would be made.

Through April 2003 the Palestinians were being forced to acknowledge the total destruction of any meaningful resistance to the US-led forces in Iraq. Khaled Mohammed, 40, commented in Ramallah on the television coverage of Saddam's clear defeat: 'He's a cartoon tiger. We've been listening to how boastful he was about his Fedayin, his Republican Guard and his army. And look it's just a joke what happened. Saddam is empty. We Arabs have many leaders who are empty.'

In the aftermath of the 2003 war it seemed obvious that Israel would continue the policies that had been developed over the previous years. Ariel Sharon's statement (14 April) that he was prepared to make the painful decision to remove some settlements from the Occupied Territories was vacuous: no timescale or other details were offered, and it was plain that any such concession to international law (see Security Council resolutions 446, 465) would be linked to impossible demands on the Palestinians. Arab opinion (and suffering) would continue to count for nothing, the facile commentary of Blair and Straw could be ignored or abused, and President Bush could be relied upon not to upset the American Jewish lobby.

The United States would work to bolster Israel's role in a reshaped Middle East. The US-run administration in Baghdad would be indifferent to human rights abuses in the Occupied Territories, and would be concerned only with the obvious priorities of the Bush government – in particular, efforts to stabilise the regional client regimes that had been shaken by the war.

The Sharon instincts, and the policies they generated, were plain:

— to expand Israeli hegemony in the region;

— to acquire even more Arab land in Gaza and the West Bank;

— to build more settlements with linking roads and security zones;

— to expand Israeli control over regional water and other vital resources;

— to crowd the increasingly dispossessed Palestinians into smaller and smaller ghettoes and 'bantustans';

- to continue a *de facto* and *de jure* genocide (according to the terms of the 1948 UN Genocide Convention) – by increasing the degree of Palestinian impoverishment, disease, eviction and deportation;
- to sustain the vision of historical Zionism, requiring that the indigenous inhabitants of the land, the Arabs, be totally expelled for the sake of the Jews.

Such policies, outrageous in all natural justice, felt no constraints in a post-Saddam world increasingly subject to the whims and ambitions of US hegemony. The American president, a firm friend of Israel, was not about to desert Ariel Sharon – deeply implicated in the slaughter of 20,000 civilians in Lebanon (1982), the Sabra and Chatila massacres, and the daily abuses in Palestine – whom George Bush had publicly anointed as 'a man of peace'.

PART THREE

The Context

NINE

Iraq – the Background

The American pursuit of global hegemony takes particular account of the Middle East, not least because of the region's prodigious energy supplies. And in that region Iraq has been given much attention – as an oil supplier, as being central to the geography of the Arab world, and as – under Saddam – a robust opponent of the Israeli occupation of Arab land.

Saddam was a controversial figure, in large part because – like very few other national leaders in the world – he was not prepared to be intimidated by American abuse and military threat. In a long career he made many friends – favoured servants, Arabs 'on the street' in many countries, the Palestinian diaspora and the Palestinians under occupation, CIA agents and American businessmen. And he also made many enemies – political opponents, the tortured and the jailed, human rights activists, latter-day Washington strategists, and many of the bereaved in his land and in his neighbourhood. Saddam created *many* bereaved, though many fewer than did the United States, while at the same time he invested in education and health provisions, protected some religious freedoms, and outraged the Islamic fundamentalists by dramatically advancing the cause of women. And he was not the only regional leader to create many bereaved. All the states in the neighbourhood drank from a common culture. There have been many tears in the Middle East.

The CIA and Saddam

The world had long known the character of Saddam. The Americans knew it as early as 1963, at a time when he was helping to create the *Jihaz Haneen* (the so-called 'instrument of learning'), a special security body modelled on the Nazi SS and designed to protect the Iraqi Ba'athist Party by targeting the 'enemies of the people'. Hostile factions were harshly intimidated and power was sought through the systematic use of terror.

It was at this time that the Iraqi army staged a successful *coup d'état* against the first Iraqi republican president, General Abdul Karim Kassem, who had toppled the Hashemite monarchy in 1958. Kassem was briskly tried, tied to a chair and shot dead. The American CIA showed their appreciation by offering a large measure of co-operation, a fact that was widely acknowledged at the time. Thus Ali Saleh Saadi, minister of the interior in the new regime, declared: 'We came to power on a CIA train.'[1] The United States was happy to support a course of events that would set Saddam Hussein firmly on the road to power. One reason, as with many other American crimes against humanity, was the communist threat.

Washington had been gravely worried about the course of events. Kassem, seen as a growing threat to Western interests, had set about nationalising parts of the Iraq Petroleum Company (IPC), largely owned by Western companies, while resurrecting the historical and not unreasonable Iraqi territorial claim to Kuwait.[2] The British responded to the Kassem threat as the West would respond to the Saddam threat in 1990 – by sponsoring a Kurdish insurrection against the Iraqi government while at the same time the CIA and other US war planners developed their schemes for the overthrow of the Iraqi leadership. The American approach, frequently adopted throughout the world, included an extensive onslaught on all political groups judged to be hostile to Western interests This campaign included the physical extermination of members of the Iraqi Communist Party and various other factions.[3]

The CIA was quick to secure the terrain after the *coup* and the murder of Kassem. The civil insurrection, involving disaffected Ba'athists, had been successfully orchestrated and now it was essential to ensure that only the CIA-approved groups be allowed to fill the power vacuum. The answer, already well tried, was quite straightforward. The CIA prepared comprehensive lists of people to be murdered to guarantee that the old power factions could not regroup. CIA-orchestrated death squads were despatched on gruesome missions and the American planners contemplated the political developments with satisfaction. Said Aburish, once an advisor to several Arab governments, commented: 'The number of people eliminated remains confused and estimates range from seven hundred to thirty thousand. Putting various statements by Iraqi exiles together, in all likelihood the figure was nearer five thousand and, with some effort, I have managed to gather over six hundred names.'[4]

The murdered Iraqis included many ordinary men and women who continued to resist after the *coup*, and also a wide range of educated Iraqis (lawyers, teachers, senior army officers, professors, doctors and others) – anyone whom the CIA and the *coup* leaders judged to be a possible threat to the new regime and Western interests.

The death squads moved from house to house to carry out on-the-spot executions, often after hideous torture. The many victims included pregnant women and old men, tortured in view of their families, and seven out of the thirteen members of the Central Committee of the Iraqi Communist Party. The British Committee for Human Rights in Iraq likened the death squads to 'Hitlerian shock troops'. The CIA lists of people to be exterminated were drawn up in Cairo, Beirut and Damascus, with the help of Iraqi exiles and others. Saddam Hussein was one of several Iraqis who was keen to add names to the CIA death lists. The Kassem threat to Kuwait had achieved some success. An Iraq-Kuwait federation had been agreed, involving the creation of a single army and the ceding of Kuwaiti foreign policy and some Kuwaiti financial control to Baghdad. The *coup* had removed this threat to Western influence, and the subsequent phase of mass murder – to which

Saddam Hussein contributed – helped to consolidate the Western grip on the Gulf region.

Saddam Hussein then returned from exile in Cairo to Baghdad and, according to some accounts, became personally involved in the torture of political opponents in various prisons. Such behaviour was of no concern to Washington. Kassem had upset the Americans by withdrawing Iraq from the anti-Soviet Baghdad Pact, by taking over parts of the Iraq Petroleum Company and by pressing Kuwait into a federation with Iraq. It was natural in such circumstances that Saddam should be a darling of the CIA planners; he had successfully advertised his anti-communist credentials and endeared himself to the Washington strategists. When Saddam subsequently displayed reliable anti-Iranian attitudes after the collapse of the CIA-buttressed Shah and the emergence of the ayatollahs the United States was happy to support Iraq in the long war against Iran (1980–88). Kuwait and Saudi Arabia contributed around $50 billion, mostly in loans, to Saddam Hussein, content that Iraqi blood should be spilt in a war against non-Arab Muslims. Washington joined in the anti-Iran coalition and helped Saddam in many ways – providing intelligence information, offering economic support, providing the materials and expertise for the building of chemical and biological weapons ('weapons of mass destruction'), and becoming an active belligerent in the Gulf. Over a period of several years the US forces sank much of the Iranian navy, bombed oil platforms and achieved Iranian casualties that numbered in at least the hundreds. Today the United States is not keen to mention that less than twenty years ago American forces were fighting in firm alliance with Saddam Hussein against a country perceived as a common enemy.

Territory and Iran

Some of the Iraqi grievances against Iran, like much of the Iraq's case against Kuwait, were rooted in territorial disputes (see Chapter 6, *Iran-Iraq War*). In 1969 the shah of Iran decided to change the negotiated frontier agreement, a move that would have been unlikely without US approval (Washington was deeply involved in the shah's domestic security and foreign strategy, to the point of running a CIA-supervised terror apparatus to suppress political opposition). The shah was encouraged by a Kurdish rebellion in northern Iraq, which both diverted attention from Iran's own Kurdish problems and seemingly weakened the power of Baghdad to resist hostile frontier claims.

The situation rapidly deteriorated. Tehran was effectively abrogating the 1937 treaty regarding the Shatt al-Arab, and at the same time the shah was helping to supply arms, provided in part by America, to the Kurdish rebels in northern Iraq. Baghdad had a natural grievance about such Iranian activities and was registering other complaints. The region of Khurzistan/Arabistan was controlled by Iran but, according to Baghdad, had been stolen from Iraq under Turkish pressure in the time of the Ottoman Empire. On 30 November 1971 Iran occupied the Lesser Tunb Island, Iraqi territory, giving Baghdad further grounds for complaint. The United States, resolutely pro-shah, sanctioned all these events and guaranteed that Iraqi efforts to seek redress through the United Nations came to nothing. Baghdad, increasingly under the sway of Saddam Hussein, realised that no useful appeal could be made to the international community. If Iraq were to achieve what it perceived as a just settlement to its various grievances then it would be compelled to act alone.

Seizing Power

Saddam Hussein had achieved power in characteristic fashion. After a period of political turmoil the Ba'athists had regained power on 17 July in a *coup* staged by General Ahmad Hasan al-Bakr, supported by Michel Aflaq and Saddam Hussein. Now the Ba'athist Party was firmly ensconced in power and Saddam's path to ultimate control of Iraqi affairs was clear. He immediately made it plain that the Ba'athists, not the army, would have authority (though he would take steps to ensure army support): 'We should collaborate with them, the army officers, but see that they are liquidated immediately during or after the revolution.' And he added that he would volunteer 'to carry out this task'.[5] Saddam Hussein was now working assiduously to establish a regime in which he would become the dominant influence.

President Bakr seemed happy enough to have Saddam as his deputy, for he had enabled the Ba'athists to establish secure rule over what had always been turbulent and difficult country. But the days of Bakr's presidency were numbered. On 17 July 1979 Saddam Hussein, feeling secure in his control of the levers of power, declared himself president of Iraq. Ahmad Hasan al-Bakr, 'owing to poor health', resigned and was immediately put under house arrest.

Installing Terror

Five days later, Saddam carried out a terror purge of the Ba'athist Party in a closed session attended by nearly one thousand cadres. A videotape of these proceedings was later distributed among party members to signal the new political situation, the assumption by Saddam Hussein of ultimate power in Iraq. Extracts of the closed session have since been shown on several occasions on Western television and elsewhere. In the presence of a relaxed Saddam, perpetrating a supreme act of terror, prominent Ba'athists were forced to read out confessions of their parts in supposed plots against the nation and its leadership. Saddam, with a dreadful air of menace, slowly read out the names of the next men to confess. At times he hesitated, smiling and holding a cigar, moving over names and then returning to them, pausing for maximum dramatic effect. The great hall was quiet as the cadres, frozen in fear, wondered whether their names would be the next to be called.

At last, after proceedings that lasted days, a body of 'convicted' men was finalised, and the 'guilty' were forced to face the firing squad: it was reported that some of Saddam's chosen ministers were made to fire some of the bullets, to implicate them further in the creation of the new terror regime. No-one could doubt that Saddam had emerged victorious, without challenge to his new authority. He had complete power over the Ba'athist Party, the army, the security services, the courts – over all the organs of the Iraqi state. Saddam Hussein had resolved to consolidate and maintain his power through the ruthless exploitation of terror. But there would be inducements also.

Introducing Reform

The socialist elements in Ba'athist philosophy encouraged substantial investment in social infrastructure, which meant efforts to develop education and health provisions at all levels – until war and economic sanctions wrecked all the social gains. Saddam, a secularist, was prepared to show pragmatic support for Islam but not for fundamentalism, which meant that religious freedom would be tolerated provided the various religious groups – Sunni, Shi'ite, Christian, Jew, etc. – acknowledged a basic loyalty to the state. Saddam's hostility to the various fundamentalist aspirations made it possible to encourage departures from elements of traditional Arab culture – which meant that women were liberated as nowhere else in the Arab world.[6]

On 6 April 2003 Mani Shankar Aiyar, an Indian who had lived in Baghdad for two years as deputy chief of mission at the Indian Embassy (1976–1978), described the contribution made by Saddam Hussein to social reform:

> It was Saddam's revolution that ended Iraqi backwardness. Education, including higher and technological education, became the top priority. More important, centuries of vicious discrimination against girls and women was ended by one stroke of the modernising dictator's pen.
>
> I used to drive past the Mustansariya University on my way home from downtown Baghdad. It was miraculous ... to see hundreds of girl-students thronging the campus, none in 'burkhas' or 'chador' ... almost all in skirts and blouses that would grace a Western University.
>
> The liberation of women – that is, half the population of Iraq – has been the most dramatic achievement of Saddam's regime. To understand how dramatic just look across the Iraqi border at America's once-favoured satrap, Saudi Arabia.

This contribution, part of a 5-page 'portside' item on the internet, reveals an aspect of Saddam politics that is seldom publicised in the Western media.

Saddam Hussein also encouraged a fierce nationalism, a conscious pride in the glories of ancient Iraqi history – and proceeded to resurrect historical Babylon as a monument to his own egocentric rule. In such a climate it was inevitable that Saddam would see military action as a realistic option when other routes to a goal were blocked[7] – much in the way that the Bush administration behaves today. One of Saddam's first acts, after seizing the Iraqi presidency, was to launch a comprehensive military invasion of Iran. Washington approved.

More US Support for Saddam

On 22 September 1980 Iraq's armies invaded Iran along an 800-mile front, from Korramshahr in the south to Qasr-e Shirin in the north. Saddam had decided that Baghdad's residual territorial grievances could only be settled by the use of force, and that the United States would have no interest in defending the Muslim fundamentalist regime in Tehran that had toppled Washington's puppet shah. The US did not only abstain from any interference in the course of events at the start of the Iran-Iraq war but later became at first a practical supporter of Saddam's war effort and later an active belligerent in the military conflict.

America's military toleration of Saddam's military aggression was well illustrated in 1981, a few months after the start of the war. On 7 June Israeli aircraft carried out a 'pre-emptive' bombing strike against an Iraqi nuclear reactor being built with French assistance near Baghdad. The declared objective of the Israeli attack was to prevent the emergence of an Iraqi nuclear capacity that might have been used to produce nuclear weapons. But Israel found itself politically isolated on the issue. The bombing raid was immediately condemned by President Ronald Reagan and Prime Minister Margaret Thatcher, and at the same time the UN Security Council unanimously adopted Resolution 487, condemning Israeli action and calling upon Israel to refrain in the future from any such acts or threats. It is useful to note key elements of this UN resolution unhesitatingly supported by Washington and London (Figure 7).

Considered against the international political situation of 2003, Security Council Resolution 487 (1981) stands as a truly remarkable document. It specifically gave Saddam Hussein, after his invasion of Iran and his perpetration of terror, permission to develop nuclear power for peaceful purposes. Moreover, the 'international community' – in particular, the United States and Britain, were recorded condemning Israel for taking pre-emptive military action against Saddam's Iraq. It is clear also that the International Atomic Energy Agency (IAEA) was satisfied that Saddam Hussein was observing the specific safeguards

The Security Council

Taking note … of the resolution adopted by the Board of Governors of the [International Atomic Energy] Agency on 12 June 1981 on the 'military attack on Iraqi nuclear research centre and its implications for the Agency'

Fully aware of the fact that Iraq has been a party to the Treaty on the Non-Proliferation on Nuclear Weapons since it came into force in 1970, that in accordance with that Treaty Iraq has accepted Agency safeguards on all its nuclear activities, and that the Agency has testified that these safeguards have been satisfactorily applied to date.

Noting furthermore that Israel has not adhered to the Treaty …

Deeply concerned about the danger to international peace and security created by the premeditated Israeli air attack …

1. *Strongly condemns* the military attack by Israel in clear violation of the Charter of the United Nations and the norms of international conduct.

2. *Calls upon* Israel to refrain in the future from any such acts of threats thereof …

4. *Fully recognises* the inalienable sovereign right of Iraq … to establish programmes of technological and nuclear development … for peaceful purposes …

5. *Calls upon* Israel urgently to place its nuclear facilities under the safeguards of the International Atomic Energy Agency.

6. *Considers* that Iraq is entitled to appropriate redress for the destruction it has suffered, responsibility for which has been acknowledged by Israel …

Figure 7. *Security Council Resolution 487 condemns Israeli bombing of Iraq – extracts*

regarding the peaceful development of nuclear power. Washington and London were asserting publicly, and through the mechanism of Resolution 487, that Iraq was acting lawfully with regard to nuclear power whereas Israel had violated the UN Charter and was under obligation to bring its own nuclear development under the safeguards regime of the Agency. Such details may be judged highly relevant to the

2002–3 dispute over Iraq's alleged persistence with programmes designed to yield a nuclear-weapons capacity.

The war between Iran and Iraq dragged on inconclusively, with hundreds of thousands of casualties, for several years, but it became increasingly obvious that the United States was unwilling to tolerate an Iranian victory. On 17 May 1987 an Iraqi Super-Etendard aircraft fired two Exocet missiles at the US frigate *Stark*, apparently mistaking it for an Iranian ship. The vessel was badly damaged and 37 American sailors were killed – but US-Iraqi relations were such that the Reagan administration quickly accepted Iraqi expressions of regret. The United States, keen to see an Iraqi victory in the war, gradually moved towards a wholly active belligerent role, though on a limited basis.

In July 1988 the US frigate *Samuel B. Roberts* was badly damaged by a mine laid in the Gulf waters, and in September and October there were military confrontations between US and Iranian forces. The US Navy sank six Iranian warships and patrol boats, and attacked a number of Iranian oil platforms. When an Iranian Silkworm missile struck a US-flagged Kuwaiti supertanker the Reagan administration quickly threatened more reprisals. US forces had already killed several hundred Iranians and caused other casualties. On 29 May 1987 Richard Armitage, who was then US assistant defense secretary, publicly declared: 'We can't stand to see Iraq defeated.'[8] By now the American fleet was being supplemented by warships from Britain, France, Belgium, Italy and the Netherlands. It was plain that Iraq's supposed aggression against Iran – used today as a justification for US military action against Baghdad – was then being supported by a substantial coalition led by Iraq in allegiance with the United States and many other countries.

The Halabja Case

It is significant that the Iraqi use of chemical weapons in the Iran-Iraq war was directly facilitated by materials and technology supplied by the United States and other countries. Chemical weapons were used by both Iran and Iraq, but the most publicised use of such 'weapons of mass destruction' was the Iraqi attack on the Kurds of Halabja in March 1988 – another event that in 2002–3 was used to justify a new war against Saddam Hussein. It is interesting that the first US report on Halabja blamed the Iranians, not the Iraqis, for the deaths of 5000 Kurds: 'Iraq was blamed for the Halabja attack, even though it was subsequently brought out that Iran too had used chemicals in this operation ... it seemed likely that it was the Iranian bombardment that had actually killed for the Kurds.'[9] The authors of the report commented that congressmen who had rejected this conclusion were acting 'more on the basis of emotionalism than factual information'.[10]

The report should not be seen as showing that Saddam Hussein did not use chemical weapons at Halabja, but as clearly demonstrating how committed Washington was to protecting its Iraqi ally. In the two years after Halabja, when the effects of the chemical attack were widely known, the United States remained enthusiastic in its support for the Iraqi president. For example, the United States continued to ship strains of anthrax to Iraq.[11] But this was a minor matter in comparison with the vast quantities of weapons-linked material shipped by America to Iraq in previous years.[12]

Rumsfeld in Baghdad

By the end of the 1980s Washington had authorised the sale to Iraq of numerous items that had both civilian and military applications. These included poisonous chemicals and deadly biological viruses, including bubonic plague. In November 1983, a month before Donald Rumsfeld's first visit to Baghdad, the US Secretary of State George Shultz received intelligence reports showing that Iraqi troops were resorting to 'almost daily use' of chemical weapons against the Iranian forces. Rumsfeld visited Saddam Hussein on 19 December 1983, shook his hand and concluded – at a time when Saddam was using chemical weapons – that the Iraqi leader 'was not interested in making mischief in the world'. The invasion of Iran, in 2002–3 given as a reason for toppling the Saddam regime, was of no concern to Rumsfeld in 1983 – quite the reverse since Washington was aiding the aggression.

Jeane Kirkpatrick, then US ambassador to the United Nations, commented at the time that Iraq's use of chemical weapons was 'very serious', but on 29 March 1984 *The New York Times* reported from Baghdad that 'American diplomats pronounce themselves satisfied with relations between Iraq and the United States and suggest that normal diplomatic ties have been restored in all but name'. Two years later, reporting Rumsfeld's 1988 presidential ambitions, *The Chicago Tribune Magazine* recorded the Rumsfeld achievement of having reopened US relations with Iraq – at a time when Saddam Hussein was known to be using chemical weapons in Iran.

In this context the on-going US propaganda in 2002–3 regarding Iraq's development of weapons of mass destruction was scarcely telling the whole story. For example, a Senate Committee Report of 1994 talked of a 'veritable witch's brew of biological materials' exported from 1985 ('if not earlier') through 1989 by American companies.[13] These various materials were known to cause 'slow, agonising deaths', to attack 'lungs, brain, spinal cord and heart', to damage 'major organs' and to be 'highly toxic bacteria causing systemic illness'.[14] The biological agents were 'capable of reproduction' and identical to those the earlier (UNSCOM) inspectors found and removed from the Iraqi 'biological warfare programme'.[15]

Invading Kuwait

The illegal Iraqi invasion of Kuwait on 2 August 1990 was similarly attended by massive Western propaganda including lies, distortions and deliberate omissions of crucial information. On 30 May 1990 Saddam Hussein commented to participants at an Arab summit in Baghdad: 'War is fought with soldiers and harm is done by explosions, killing and coup attempts, but it is also done by economic means sometimes. I say to those who do not mean to wage war on Iraq, that this is in fact a kind of war against Iraq.'[16]

Here Saddam was complaining at how Kuwait and the United Arab Emirates (UAE), seemingly oblivious to the plight of the post-war Iraqi economy, continued to produce oil as they wished, exceeding the OPEC quotas and so drastically reducing Iraq's oil revenues. In addition Iraq charged that Kuwait was taking excessive amounts of oil from the Rumeila oilfield, which extends into Kuwait, and refused to transfer or lease the two islands of Warbar and Bubiyan, which dominate the estuary leading to Iraq's southern port of Umm Qasr. In the context of these and other grievances Saddam had little reason to believe that the United States, despite some unsympathetic words, would take action following an Iraqi move against Kuwait to forestall the ultimate collapse of the Iraqi economy.

On 12 April 1990 Saddam had met with five US senators: Robert Dole, Alan Simpson, Howard Metzenbaum, James McClure and Frank Murkowski. The US ambassador, April Glaspie, was also there. No-one reading the various transcripts of this meeting can doubt the general placatory tone. The senators, in their attempts to propitiate Saddam, even went so far as to criticise the US press, with Senator Dole pointing out that a commentator on Voice of America, who had not been given authority to speak on Iraq, had been fired from his job. Senator Simpson denounced the Western press, for presuming to criticise Saddam, as 'haughty and pampered', whereupon Senator Metzenbaum commented to Saddam: 'I have been sitting and listening to you for about an hour, and I am now aware that you are a strong and intelligent man and that you want peace.'

On 24 July 1990, as two Iraqi armoured divisions took up positions on the Kuwaiti border, US State Department spokeswoman Margaret Tutwiler emphasised that the United States did not have 'any defense treaties with Kuwait', and the next day April Glaspie said to Saddam: 'We have no opinion on Arab-Arab conflicts like your border disagreement with Kuwait ... when we see the Iraqi point of view that the measures taken by the UAE and Kuwait are, in the final analysis, tantamount to military aggression against Iraq, then it is reasonable to be concerned.' On 31 July, two days before the Iraqi invasion of Kuwait, John Kelly, US assistant secretary of state, stated before a House of Representatives subcommittee that the United States had no 'treaty commitment which would obligate us to engage US forces [to defend Kuwait]'.

Hence in late July 1990 various US officials were telling Saddam Hussein that they understood his grievances against Kuwait and that they were under no obligation to defend the emirate. On 2 August Iraqi forces rolled across Kuwait's border. This in turn led to the US-orchestrated Operations Desert Storm and Desert Sabre, the equivalent of seven Hiroshima bombs being dropped on Iraq, 200,000 Iraqi conscripts being variously dismembered and incinerated in the desert, a 13-year genocidal regime of bombing and economic sanctions and the escalating 2002–3 crisis. Throughout the 1990s and beyond the Iraqi civilian population was prevented by Washington and London from receiving food, clean water and medical care in adequate supply – with the result that by 2003 some 1,700,000 people, most of them children, had been killed through starvation and disease. None of this was sufficient for the Washington hawks, committed above all to the goal of 'regime change' whereby the stubborn figure of Saddam Hussein would be obliterated from the world stage.

Lobbying for War (1998)

On 26 January 1998 a group of influential Americans wrote an open letter to President Bill Clinton urging American action to overthrow the Saddam regime. The signatories included many who would become leading figures in the administration of George W. Bush: Donald Rumsfeld, Paul Wolfowitz, Robert Zoellick, Richard Armitage, John Bolton, Paula Dobriansky and Elliott Abrams. With the change of US administration these people were well placed to influence President Bush, if such influence were needed, into launching a fresh aggressive war against Iraq. And even then the priorities of American business were evident. When the present Vice President Richard Cheney, a noted hawk, was running Halliburton, it sold more equipment to Iraq than did any other company. Through 1998–9 Halliburton subsidiaries submitted $23.8 million worth of contracts with Iraq for approval by the UN sanctions committee. Cheney was happy to trade with the Iraqi government while plotting its collapse.

The impulse of Bush administration was to ignore the United Nations, to launch a new aggression without seeking a fresh Security Council resolution. But in August 2002, under mounting international pressure, the Bush administration at last hinted that it would be willing to seek United Nations authorisation for its intended war against Iraq. In October 2002 the Congress of the United States voted to give President Bush authorisation to make war on Iraq.[17] On 8 November the UN Security Council, after two months of American intimidation and bribery, unanimously adopted Resolution 1441, a highly intrusive weapons-inspection authorisation that extinguished any vestiges of Iraqi sovereignty. It soon became plain that the Bush administration regarded this resolution (see Chapter 11) as an enabling device for a massive new military onslaught on Iraq scheduled for 2003.

TEN

The Oil Factor

On 25 January 2003 Gore Vidal, interviewed by John Humphrys on BBC radio, said with characteristic acerbity that the United States had been taken over illegally by a junta of oil and gas people. He named them – Bush I, Bush II, Cheney, Rice, etc – and ridiculed the idea that Saddam Hussein was any sort of threat to the United States. What was happening was a strike for world supremacy comparable to the efforts of Hitler. And of course it was all about oil. In his bid for the American presidency a certain William Jefferson Clinton displayed on a wall of his campaign offices the slogan 'It's the economy, stupid!' In 2003, trying to glean any sense out of the US onslaught on Iraq, we need focus only on a sample variant of the Clinton banner – 'IT'S ABOUT OIL, STUPID!' Bush and Blair denied it, common sense suggested it, facts proved it and the people knew it.

The journalist Robert Fisk, writing from Amman, recorded certain impressions as he ate with a group of Muslim men:

Every man in the room believed President Bush wanted Iraqi oil. Indeed, every Arab I've met in the past six months believes that this – and this alone – explains his enthusiasm for invading Iraq. Many Israelis think the same. So do I.[1]

He noted the simple fact that when a pro-American regime is installed in Baghdad the US oil companies will have access to 112,000,000,000 barrels of oil and will have thereby secured control of a quarter of the entire world oil reserves. In this context the US Department of Energy announced at the beginning of January that by 2025, US oil imports will account for around 70 per cent of total US domestic demand. A few weeks later, Michael Runner of the Worldwatch Institute commented: 'US oil deposits are increasingly depleted, and many other non-OPEC fields are beginning to run dry. The bulk of the future supplies will have to come from the Gulf region.'[2] Of the eleven OPEC member states[3] Iraq holds the world's second-largest proven oil reserves, but more than a decade of war, bombing and sanctions has left much of the Iraqi oil industry in a dilapidated state. It is clearly not enough for the United States to take substantial quantities of oil under the UN-authorised 'oil for food' arrangements.[4] It is plain that the US has long wanted total control of the crucial Middle East oil reserves.

Oil History

Over the centuries there had been many clues to the presence of large oil deposits in the Arabian peninsula and beyond. Travellers' tales and Arabic literature made references to black oily substances, and bitumen had long been used for various purposes.[5] In 1869 oil was discovered in Egypt, thought it was not until 1908 that the massive Masjid-i-Suleiman (Temple of Solomon) well in Persia began to flow. Thirty years later the first highly productive well in Kuwait was discovered. These and the many other discoveries of oil resources in the region ensured that Kuwait, Persia (Iran), Saudi Arabia, Iraq and other regional states would become the focus of foreign imperial ambition over the decades. The oil bounty that should rightly have liberated the Arab peoples, the Iranians and others was destined to lead to their subjugation and humiliation. In 1990–1 and 2002–3 it was made plainly obvious, if not already, that the oil-rich nations of the Middle East were not about to escape the predatory designs of powerful Western nations in a shrinking and energy-hungry world – particularly in circumstances where the world's one megapower, in the illegal grip of a 'junta of oil and gas people', was massively expanding its energy consumption, polluting the planet to an unprecedented degree, and developing an unassailable military capacity to seize whatever it wanted from the other nations of the world.

In 1890 French geologist Jacques de Morgan, a member of an archaeological team in Persia, observed manifest oil seepages – and ten years later obtained financial backing to explore the matter further. A meeting with Sir Henry Drummond Wolff, former British ambassador to Persia, led to the acquisition of an exclusive concession for a British company to search for oil in Persia. On 28 May 1901 the concession assigning rights were signed, despite protests from the Russian government, though the actual company was not set up until 1903. Five years later, then in a syndicate with the Scotland-based Burmah Oil Company, the company found oil in commercial quantity at Maidan-i-Naftan. As a consequence, the Anglo-Persian Oil Company was founded in April 1909.

Stealing Kuwait

It was already becoming plain that an adequate access to oil was necessary to a country's war-making capabilities. One of Winston Churchill's first acts, when made First Lord of the Admiralty in 1911, was to resurrect an Admiralty committee on oil to ensure that British warships would not go short of fuel. Lord Fisher was made head of the Royal Commission on Oil for the Navy, and a group of of experts was sent to the Gulf to assess future oil prospects in the region. Britain had already perceived the strategic importance of Kuwait and had taken steps to guarantee a lasting British influence.

On 23 January 1899 Sheikh Mubarak, eager to consolidate a secession of Kuwait from the Ottoman province of Basra, had been induced to sign an agreement with Britain guaranteeing British protection in return for an assurance that neither he nor his heirs would 'cede, sell, lease or mortgage, or give for occupation or for any other purpose a portion of his territory to the government of any other power without the previous consent of Her Majesty's Government'.[6] Hence an agreement *in perpetuity* had been made between Britain and the successive rulers of Kuwait, despite the ambiguous relations between Kuwait – headed by a secessionist upstart – and the Ottoman state that continued to regard Kuwait as part of the Basra *vilayet*. Thus as early as the 19th century Britain had seen the strategic and commercial advantage of keeping Kuwait out of Iraqi control. This attitude was set to bear directly on the oil question and on many other matters in the years ahead.

Sheikh Mubarak, enjoying his new status as head of a nominally independent state, was quick to confirm the terms of the 1899 treaty. He welcomed British diplomats and oil experts to Kuwait, and in 1913 wrote to Sir Percy Cox, the British political representative in the Gulf: 'We are agreeable to everything that you regard as advantageous ... we will associate with the Admiral one of our sons to be in his service, to show the place of bitumen in Burgan and elsewhere and if in his view there seems hope of obtaining oil therefrom we shall never give a concession to anyone except a person appointed by the British government.'[7] The puppet status of Kuwait could not have been made clearer – and nor could the cynical *realpolitik* of British foreign policy.

Britain had encouraged Kuwait's secession and subsequently guaranteed its protection for all time, but later observers were happy to record the fragility of such a British commitment. In 1930 the British high commissioner in Baghdad proposed that 'Britain should encourage the gradual absorption of Kuwait into Iraq' and representatives of the British government observed that Kuwait was 'a small and expandable state which could be sacrificed without too much concern if the power struggles demanded it.'[8] Treaties had nothing to do with the matter; Kuwait would be protected by Britain only as long as it suited British foreign policy.

In 1918 the British government took a 51 per cent shareholding in the Anglo-Persian Oil Company via a parliamentary bill that received the Royal Assent six days before the start of the First World War. With a further investment of £3 million made in 1919, Kuwait was set to play a key role in the appreciation of British assets, 'and in affairs which would soon enmesh much of the Arabian peninsula, the USA, Britain and Europe, and many of the greatest commercial enterprises in the Western world, in a relationship that to say the least of it was delicately poised.'[9]

Subsequent events consolidated Western power in the Middle East, but initially to the relative exclusion of the United States.

Western Oil Hegemony

On 27 April 1919, at the San Remo Conference, Britain and France finalised their agreement to monopolise all Middle Eastern oil. When Washington subsequently protested Lord Curzon, British foreign secretary, observed that whereas Britain controlled only 4.5 per cent of the world oil production the United States controlled 80 per cent and that moreover the US excluded non-American interests from areas under its control. The UK-US confrontation reached the point at which Britain was accusing the United States of supporting the Arab revolt against British rule in the area. Thus a rebel leader arrested in Iraq by British security forces was said to have a letter in his possession proving that the American consul in Baghdad was funding Shi'ite rebels in Karbala. Subsequently the Americans were offered shares in the successor company to the Turkish Petroleum Company (TPC), founded by the Armenian entrepreneur Calouste Gulbenkian and later half owned by British Petroleum who managed to secure the Iranian concession.

The Iraqi oil industry was then monopolised by the Iraq Petroleum Company (IPC), jointly owned by the Anglo-Persian Oil Company (later BP), Royal Dutch Shell, an American group (eventually New Jersey Standard Oil and Socony-Vacuum, later Mobil), the Companies Française de Pétroles (CFP), and Calouste Gulbenkian. Hence the US companies were guaranteed secure pickings in IPS and 'the most remarkable carve-up in oil history' had been achieved. Gulbenkian adopted the simple expedient, very congenial to the partner companies, of using a red pencil to draw a line on the map and so created the so-called Red Line Agreement to preserve Middle East oil for its existing corporate owners (Figure 8).

The 'open door' policy espoused by the Americans – essentially to allow market penetration by US companies – had been abandoned but this was of no concern: US profits were assured. Gulbenkian commented that 'never was the open door so hermetically sealed', and rejoiced at how the 'carve-up'[10] had succeeded in parcelling out Arab oil resources among the Europeans and the Americans. The powers that had been

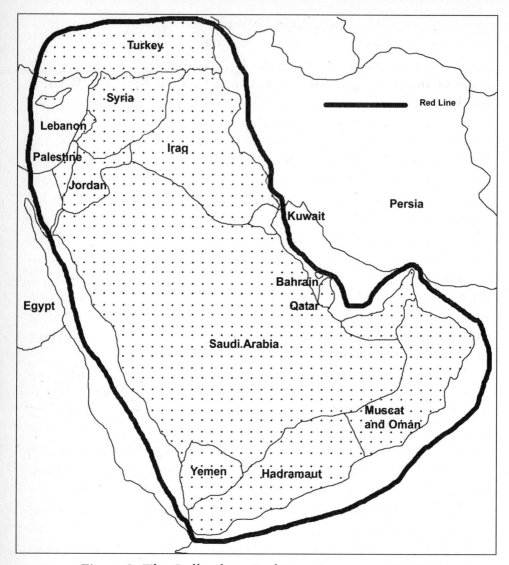

Figure 8. *The Gulbenkian Red Line Agreement (1928)*

victorious in the First World War had little interest in fact that 'the lands wrested from the Turks were, in fact, Arab lands'.[11] And it was also conveniently forgotten that the Arabs had fought on the side of the British and French on the understanding that Arab independence would be guaranteed after the war.

A New 'Red Line'?

It is interesting that the Gulbenkian 'Red Line' (Figure 8) accords with much of the strategic discussion that preceded the 2003 war. What, it had been wondered, were the real American plans? Assuming that the actual agenda focused on oil, what was the actual end-objective of the Washington strategists? It was obvious that command of Iraqi oil would be a colossal prize, but was that all? There was much discussion about the deteriorating US-Saudi relations. Did Washington also have its eye on a more comprehensive control of Saudi oil? It was obvious that a US military presence in Iraq, at the heart of the Arab world, would greatly bolster the constrained US presence in Saudi Arabia. It would then be relatively easy for American forces, securely entrenched in Iraq, to combine with other US forces in the region to take over the Saudi oil assets. Was there to be a new 'Red Line' – drawn by the Washington strategic planners – that would enable the United States to impose a fresh domination, more extensive than anything previously in place, of Iraq, Kuwait, Saudi Arabia and the other Gulf States?

There would be obvious advantages in such a strategy. Uncertainties about American access to Middle East oil would be removed, and the United States would attain a massively increased leverage over other states around the world that depend upon access to Gulf oil. For example, Washington would gain a stranglehold over the Japanese economy, wholly reliant on the vast oil tankers that ply from Gulf ports, and a principal commercial competitor of the United States. Moreover, Washington's increased leverage over the regional states would enable the strategic planners to derive maximum benefits from the Iraqi resource. It may be necessary, for instance, to force such states as Kuwait and Iran to waive their compensation claims against Iraq – in order to reduce the burdens on the dilapidated Iraqi oil industry that US companies would then be working to develop.

The US Oil Strategy

Iraq's current foreign debts had been estimated at around $130 billion, with the war compensation claims still topping $300 billion despite the many massive payouts that have already been made from Iraqi oil revenues. It was also estimated that the regeneration of the Iraqi oil industry – devastated by the 13 years of war, bombing and sanctions – would cost around $500 billion. In light of such economic factors it would be of obvious advantage to Washington to be able to manage the various economies of the region that impacted on Iraqi development. The more that Washington extended and strengthened its leverage the more it would be able to frame the debt and compensation burdens endured by the crippled Iraqi economy. The US would have no incentive to ease such burdens while Saddam Hussein remained in power, but in the post-Saddam world the US corporations would soon be demanding an international financial framework for Iraq that would maximise the profits from exploitation of the Iraqi oil resource.

In March 2002 it was plain that the United States was buying oil at a rate not seen since the 1991 Gulf War, encouraging speculation that substantial reserves were being readied for some future conflict or other crisis. It was seen as significant that the 7.4 million barrels of oil addressed in the new tenders were mostly intended for jet fighter fuel to be delivered to US bases in Afghanistan, Pakistan, the United Arab Emirates, Bahrain, Israel, Japan and the island of Diego Garcia later in the year. When it was realised that the US stocks had fallen sharply the international oil price rose to its highest level for six months. Thus in New York benchmark crude reached a six-month high of $25.89 before easing off.

US Dependence?

Such details may have encouraged the Iraqi regime to believe the United States was vulnerable to any interruption in its fuel supplies. On 2 April 2002 Iraq urged Iran to join it and use oil as a weapon against American and Israel as Arab anger grew at the ongoing Israeli military onslaught on the helpless Palestinian communities. By now the oil price had reached $27.63 a barrel. Hamum Abdul Khalek, Iraq's acting foreign minister, said that the Iraqi government was consulting the Iranian chargé d'affaires in Baghdad to discuss 'ways of drawing up a common action on the oil weapon to oblige the Zionist entity to leave Palestinian territories'. But Kamal Kharazi, Iran's foreign minister, commented that broad Muslim support was essential: 'If they decide to use oil as a weapon, certainly Iran will consider it. It will be effective if all Muslim countries would take such a decision.' The price for delivery of oil in May had now reached $28 a barrel, but only briefly. A boycott of oil in such circumstances, echoes of 1973 and 1978, would clearly have been damaging to Europe and America.

On 8 April, failing to achieve support from other Muslim states, Iraq suspended all exports for a month in protest at Israeli military outrages in the West Bank. Ali Rodriguez, OPEC secretary general, announced that he would consult with OPEC oil ministers: 'After the announcement of Iraq to suspend exports ... we could go directly to an oil crisis.'[12] Already the oil price surge was dashing hopes of an early global economic recovery. One observer, pointing out that 70 per cent of known oil reserves were in one of the world's most politically fragile regions, suggested that the Iraqi action might at least encourage energy conservation 'to wean off oil'.[13]

In August there were further signs that the United States was stocking up on oil supplies in preparation for war. Vast caverns under Texas and Louisiana were then being filled with crude oil in a move that was seen as vitally important to any military scenario. The vast sealed reservoirs, with a 700 million barrel capacity were intended to insulate the country, and the world economy, from the sort of oil price shocks experienced during the 1991 Gulf War. Since President Bush issued his enabling directive, crude oil was being poured into the caverns at the rate of 150,000 barrels a day, a process then set to continue for the rest of 2002. The United States was also discussing with Germany and Japan how they could co-ordinate their oil policies with those of the US strategic petroleum reserve (SPR) to help avert an international economic crisis in the months ahead. Observers were then speculating that in the event of a conflict Iraq might strike at other oilfields, terminals and tankers in the Gulf, and even block Saudi Arabia's exports of eight million barrels a day – with unpredictable consequences for the world economy.[14]

On 5 August the United States urged other countries to protect themselves against a sudden rise in petrol prices by stockpiling fuel, to follow the American strategy of achieving 'overall energy security'. Again it was a clear sign that Washington was set on a course that the Bush administration expected would lead to war, with Britain at the same time confirming that the carrier *Ark Royal* would soon be sailing for the Mediterranean to be available for action against Iraq if necessary.

It was again being made clear that the United States and the rest of the world were vulnerable to any substantial reduction in the oil supply, particularly in shipments from the Middle East. The United States was importing a third of its oil from the Persian Gulf, the European Organisation for Economic Co-operation and Development (OECD) somewhat more, and Japan more than three-quarters of all its oil imports.

At the same time many people were continuing to ask the question to which the answer seemed patently obvious: was it a lust for Iraqi oil that was driving US policy on Saddam Hussein? Thus Anthony Sampson, expert on oil matters, emphasised the simple fact that as the oil companies began to worry about the security of their Saudi supplies the more they would be interested in gaining access to Iraq. US Vice President Cheney, himself with significant oil interests, chose to prefix one of his many denunciations of Saddam with the observation that the Iraqi leader 'sits on 10 per cent of the world's oil reserves', a plainly attractive alternative to Saudi supplies threatened by Muslim fundamentalism. This was the ultimate Pentagon nightmare: an extremist Islamic regime in control of Saudi oil, hostile to the United States, prepared to defy the marketplace, and much less dependent on oil revenues than were corrupt Arab monarchies. But would Washington guarantee energy security by persisting with plans to develop a post-Saddam Iraq? The Bush administration had always been unwilling to consider negotiation as a realistic alternative to war:

> The belief that invading Iraq will produce a more stable Middle East and give the West easy access to its oil wealth, is dangerously simplistic. Westerners live in a world where most of their oil comes from Islam, and their only long-term security in energy depends on accommodating Muslims.[15]

There was by now an increasingly widespread view that the United States, worried by Saudi instabilities and ambiguities over terrorism (Osama bin Laden and most of the 9/11 bombers were Saudi), was keen to gain ultimate control over Iraqi oil as a hedge against insecurities in the Saudi supply:

'The secret partition' ('A plan to split Saudi Arabia gives the Saudis the holy sites and us the oil').[16]

Time to end our reliance on Saudi oil.[17]

'The real reason for attacking Saddam' ('the US simply wants Iraq to replace growingly hostile Saudi Arabia as its foothold in the oil-rich Middle East').[18]

The Economic Factor

But the impact of US policy was to add fresh insecurities to the world economy. The prospect of another oil crisis, caused by shortages and massive price rises, was then alarming many pundits. The US economy itself was stumbling along, American corporations were mired in corrupt practices, and there was fresh talk of the Bush administration having to preside over a 'a double-dip' recession. Were the Washington economic advisors gambling on a new war being good for the American economy? There was no doubt that public spending would be boosted: some pundits were rejoicing that Bush might be able to contrive a 'cut-price war' of only $50 billion, where formerly estimates of more than twice this amount had been gloomily discussed. In what passes as US socioeconomic thinking any suggestion that public spending might be boosted by investment in schools and hospitals is of course anathema, so Bush and his advisors might have calculated that war was a good investment – and a vast hike in oil prices might not be bad for such committed oilmen as Bush and Cheney.

The sensitivity of the oil markets was again demonstrated when Iraq's agreement to co-operate with UN weapons inspectors immediately caused a fall in the benchmark Brent blend of North Sea crude by 42 cents to $27.12 a barrel. A week before, when Cheney had uttered a characteristically soft-spoken bellicose speech, the price had soared to a five-month high. On 6 September 2002 further US and British bombing raids on Iraq, creating the impression of imminent war, caused the oil price to soar to the highest level for a year, to $28.75. Leo Drollas, at the London-based Global Energy Studies organisation, voiced a common perception: 'War drums are pushing the price higher.'

Oil After Saddam

There was also continuing debate about the possible fruits that could be harvested in the post-Saddam Iraq. Russia was looking for guarantees that it would not lose all the benefits of existing contracts, the US oil companies were contemplating their options, and the US government was funding schemes to train Iraqi exiles for the reconstruction of Iraq's economy on free-market lines – it seemed obvious that another carve-up of Iraqi assets was on the cards. Thus journalists writing in *The Washington Post*, citing Iraqi opposition sources, declared that the toppling of Saddam Hussein 'could open a bonanza for American oil companies long banished from Iraq, scuttling oil deals between Baghdad and Russia, France and other countries, and reshuffling world petroleum markets'.[19] James Woolsey, former CIA director, summarised the US position: 'It's pretty straightforward. France and Russia have oil companies and interests in Iraq. They should be told that if they are of assistance in moving Iraq towards decent government, we'll do the best we can to ensure that the new government and American companies work closely with them. If they throw in their lot with Saddam, it will be difficult to the point of impossible to persuade the new Iraqi government to work with them.'

Woolsey was right in saying the situation was straightforward: 'Co-operate in aggression and we'll reward you. Be difficult, and we'll punish you.' The INC's Chalabi had already demonstrated his pro-US credentials, saying that he favoured the creation of a US-led consortium to develop Iraq's oilfields: 'American companies will have a big shot at Iraqi oil.' But there were still many imponderables. Exactly how would the carve-up be managed? Would Iraq remain a member of OPEC? To what extent would existing contracts be honoured, if at all? And what was already on the covert agendas? What deals had already been struck between Washington and other countries? It was hard to imagine that the United States had not already planned its priorities for the post-war situation. And among these the policies on oil would be of primary importance.

On 19 September Saudi Arabia declared that, in the event of a US-led war on Iraq, OPEC would increase oil production to counter any shortages. Thus Ali al-Nuami, Saudi oil minister, said: 'In order to maintain stability in the market the conference decided that agreed production levels would be maintained. This is not a decision we took lightly. We had to take account of many uncertainties, including Iraq.' Jordan was now reportedly agreeing to the American use of its military bases in return for a guarantee of cheap oil, and Washington was making other deals to minimise foreign anxieties about the economic effects of the planned war. Donald Rumsfeld was heckled on the oil question ('Why are you obstructing the inspections? Is this not about oil?'), refused to answer the question and then applauded the 'precious gift of free speech'. He refused also to speak about the post-Saddam situation with regard to oil. It was already plain that any existing contracts would be in terminal jeopardy, and the Russians were reportedly talking to Iraqi exiles about the $7 billion already owed by Baghdad to Moscow from Soviet times. And Russia's President Putin was assumed to want financial and oil guarantees from the United States before he would be prepared to tolerate America's military enterprise.[20] On 3 October the Malaysian prime minister, Mahathir Mohammad, was urging the Muslim world to use its oil weapon, particularly relevant in the prevailing world circumstances:

> Oil is the only thing Muslim nations have which is needed by the rest of the world. If they can cut back on supply, people will not be oppressive to them. If we reduce oil output, prices will rise. It can be used as a weapon. When we are weak we will be exploited. We are now seeing worldwide Muslims being exploited. OPEC should control the price of oil, but there is no unity in OPEC. When the oil price goes up, there are other nations that increase output.

This was as much a gesture of importance as a plea for action.

Did the United States intend the overthrow of Saddam to be about oil? Was there anyone left who doubted it? The media, supposed opinion formers, had no doubts:

> 'Scramble to carve up Iraqi oil reserves lies behind US diplomacy.'

> 'Iraqi opposition to discuss oil at US meeting.'

'Wall Street/Washington insider spills the dirty secret of Iraq war' ('Getting control of that oil will make a vast difference.')

'The last oil rush.'

'BP Chief fears US will carve up Iraqi oil riches.'

'Crucial US allies on Iraq fall out over oil.'

'Carve-up of oil riches begins.'

'America' ('The US is making it clear that there will be rewards and punishments after a second Gulf War. Britain will replace France as the chief European dealer in Iraqi oil and equipment.')

Washington was already prepared to indicate that control of the oilfields would be a central objective of the US-led invasion. On 6 January 2003 *The New York Times* reported that Washington strategists were planning for military trials of the most senior Iraqi leaders and a quick takeover of the country's oilfields. (Later, Colin Powell was to declare that the war would not be about oil.) The companies close to the Bush administration expected to benefit, as did the most supportive states, such as Kuwait and Britain. The Turkish government, having to cope with a popular majority opposed to US troops on Turkish soil, was still prepared to claim its place at the carve-up table. Yasar Yakis, Turkey's foreign minister, claimed to be examining treaties from the early 20th century to ascertain whether Turkey had legitimate claims to Iraq's northern oilfields: 'If we do have such rights, we have to explain this to the international community and our partners in order to secure those rights.' Arab diplomats in Ankara responded with anger, suggesting that Turkey was playing a dangerous game.[21]

The oil consideration explained a lot, not only the US determination to wage war but the extent to which various countries around the world were prepared to support the various spasms of American aggression. Britain, enthusiastically bellicose for Bush, was running out of local energy. The Oil Depletion Analysis Centre had reported that the UK's North Sea production had been declining since 1999, leading to increased dependence on energy imports since the British government had shown little interest in energy conservation or renewable sources. This suggested that the Blair administration would not want to be left out when the time came for the carve-up of Iraq's oil resources.

The US-led war of aggression against Iraq in 2003 was not solely about oil but oil resources were a primary consideration. In the run-up to the 1991 Gulf War it was generally perceived that protection of access to oil was a primary reason for US involvement:

> '*If Kuwait grew carrots, we wouldn't give a damn*' – Lawrence Korb, former US assistant defense secretary, 1990

> '*I venture to say that if Kuwait produced bananas, instead of oil, we would not have 400,000 American troops there today*' – Congressman Stokes, Ohio, 12 January 1991

On 15 January 2003 Dennis Skinner, a Labour MP, asked Prime Minister Tony Blair in the House of Commons: 'Will you also tell him [President Bush] that a lot of British people are against the war because they can see that it's all about America getting their hands on the oil supplies in the Middle East?' Blair replied 'The very reason we're taking the action we are is nothing to do with oil.' On 6 January 2003 Jack Straw, foreign secretary, addressing 150 British ambassadors in London, had pinpointed security energy sources as a key priority of British foreign policy.

Preparing the Way

For months in the run-up to the 2003 war the US military had been drawing up detailed plans to secure and protect the Iraqi oilfields. In December 2002 the US State Department and Pentagon revealed something of these plans at a meeting in Washington with members of the Iraqi opposition parties when the Americans stressed that protection of the oilfields was 'issue number one'. Already American, British, Russian, French and other international oil companies were taking discreet soundings about the commercial opportunities offered by Iraq's massive oil resource. At the same time Washington and London refused to admit that such considerations had anything to do with planning for the coming war. On 22 January 2003 Mike O'Brien, British foreign office minister, declared: 'The charge that our motive is greed – to control Iraq's oil supply – is nonsense, pure and simple.'

At the same time Colin Powell was telling *The Boston Globe* newspaper: 'The oil of Iraq belongs to the Iraqi people. Whatever form of custodianship there is ... it will be held for and used for the people of Iraq. It will not be exploited for the United States' own purpose.' When asked whether US companies would operate the oilfields, Powell replied that he did not have an answer to that question. Some reports claimed that Dick Cheney and some Pentagon officials were advocating using Iraqi oil revenues to pay for the daily costs of the occupation force, while *The Wall Street Journal*, quoting oil industry officials, reported that Cheney staff had already held a meeting with Exxon Mobil, Chevron Texaco, Concoco Philips and Halliburton (see also Chapter 12). A foreign office source in London confirmed that the security of the Iraqi oil wells was a paramount consideration.

In 2001 Dick Cheney wrote a report for the US energy department predicting that America's imported oil would need to rise from 10.4 million barrels a day at that time to 16.7 million barrels a day by 2020. The Cheney report stressed the US dependency on a stable energy market and the need for a foreign policy that would protect energy supplies:

> In a global energy marketplace, US energy and economic security are directly linked not only to our domestic and international energy supplies, but to those of our traditional partners as well. A significant disruption in world oil supplies could adversely affect our economy and/or our ability to promote foreign and economic policy objectives, regardless of the level of US dependence on oil imports.

In the same vein Fadel Gheit, a former Mobil engineer and currently an investment specialist with a New York brokerage firm, told investors in December 2002 that the coming war 'was all about oil' and that the global fight against terrorism was just 'camouflage' to mask the real purpose. Later he told *The Guardian* (London):

> The Americans have nothing against the people of Iraq but our

way of life is dependent on 20m barrels a day and half of it has to be imported. We are like a patient on oil dialysis. It's a matter of life and death. The smart people all know this but it's not generally advertised on the kinds of shows that most people watch.[22]

This suggests that America's dependence on oil would force any White House administration to pursue similar foreign policies in this regard, particularly bearing in mind the weight of the corporate lobby, but the Bush administration has been stacked with a significant quota of former oil executives, all of whom may be assumed to be keeping in contact with their former energy interests. Here we need only mention:

- *George W. Bush*, failed Texas oilman. His prospecting company, Arbusto, was about to go bankrupt when it was bought out by Spectrum which in turn was bought out by Harken. Bush was kept on the board for his many contacts, primarily with his father (who had made James Baker, another oilman, his secretary of state);

- *Dick Cheney*, US vice-president and former head of Halliburton, the world's largest oilfield services company. The corporation also sells construction projects and other services to the US military;

- *Donald Rumsfeld*, defense secretary, former head of a pharmaceutical firm with links to the oil industry;

- *Condoleezza Rice*, national security advisor, formerly on the board of Chevron. For a time an oil tanker bore her name;

- *Don Evans*, commerce secretary, formerly chairman of Tom Brown Inc., a $1.2 billion oil and gas company based in Denver and formerly also a board member of TMBR/Sharp Drilling, an oil and gas drilling company;

- *Gale Norton*, interior secretary, a lawyer who represented Delta Petroleum and formerly ran the Coalition of Republican Environmental Advocates, co-funded by BP Amoco.

It seemed obvious that US foreign policy, shaped by a clique of oil interests, was being shaped by America's oil dependency, and that this in turn was presenting a unique challenge to the oil corporations and exacerbating international tensions. The prospects offered by Iraqi oil were particularly appealing since there were opportunities for a massive increase in production: Iraq's oil industry had been crippled by war and more than a decade of sanctions. The post-Saddam era promised rich pickings. This in turn implied an imminent battle between the oil corporations, with US and British companies in a favoured position and Washington likely to dominate the carve-up of Iraqi assets. As oilman John Paul Getty Jnr once said: 'The meek shall inherit the earth, but not the mineral rights.'

On 6 March 2003 Tony Blair, interviewed on the London MTV music channel to young people (16–25), dismissed as 'conspiracy theory' suggestions that the US and Britain were intending to take over the world's second largest oil reserves:

> A simple way out would be to make sure if there is a conflict that in any post-conflict Iraq there is a proper UN mandate for Iraq and the oil goes into a trust fund. We don't touch it and the Americans don't touch it without UN authority.

There was no suggestion that Washington would agree to any such idea, even if Blair believed it himself. President Bush had remarked that the oil belonged to the Iraqi people – which sounded good even if absurd from an American perspective. Surely Bush was not suggesting a publicly-owned Iraqi oil industry under a socialist regime. It was already clear that the most significant players in the game – the US oil corporations – would have no interest in UN trusts, nationalised oil or the proprietorial rights of the Iraqi people. In fact, according to Sheikh Ahmed Zaki Yamani, former Saudi oil minister, the United States was already drawing up detailed plans for the privatisation of the Iraqi oilfields: 'We know oil is very important and already the Americans have started to dispose of Iraqi oil ... they have even started studies of how to privatise the Iraqi oil industry. What does that tell you? The majority of people everywhere say this is a war which is about oil.'

Sheikh Yamani, head of the Centre for Global Energy Studies (CGES), also suggested that a privatisation of Iraqi oil could force OPEC to question its model of state control. Leo Drollas, Chief CGES economist, commented: 'OPEC is stuck in a rut of stagnant markets and static revenues, while the private companies have merged as far as cost-savings and synergies can possibly take them.' It seemed obvious that the United States would welcome the collapse of the OPEC cartel, representing as it did a constraint on American energy policy. How preferable, from a US perspective, for the United States to control as much oil as possible at source, giving the US a tightening stranglehold over America's energy-dependent rivals around the world:

> What an Anglo-American victory will mean is control of supply. The US plans for post-war Iraq include privatisation of the oil industry. Who doubts that when Iraq's assets are auctioned off, the man wielding the gavel will be an American general. Unlike Saddam Hussein, the winners in that auction won't sell their oil to just anyone.
>
> Sanctions and blockades are routine features of US foreign policy ... Washington happily uses economic coercion on a daily basis – and not just against pariahs like Iraq. With the bulk of the world's known oil reserves under its protection in a post-Saddam Middle East (backed up by the US role in central Asia, where China fears another US foot on its fuel pipeline), America will be able to switch off the Chinese economic boom.[23]

And where such economic coercion could be applied to China, it could also be applied to India, Japan and other states. Moreover, the United States itself will be immune to oil blockades and to the sorts of OPEC oil price rises that so angered Washington in 1973–74 and 1979–80. In early June 2003 Paul Wolfowitz, US deputy defense secretary, declared at an Asian security summit in Singapore: 'Economically we just had no choice in Iraq. The country swims on a sea of oil' (*The Guardian*, 4 June 2003).

The 2003 war was about oil, but not only about guaranteeing the future security of supplies to the United States. The Washington strategists also judged that it would be highly desirable to expand US control over the energy supplies to other countries. The crushing aggression against Iraq was a hegemonic war with global implications.

ELEVEN

The United Nations

The United Nations fulfilled its traditional role through the 2002–3 crisis, and after the 2003 war there were no grounds to suggest a different UN posture in the future. Secretary-General Kofi Annan had always been keen to stress that he was no more than the servant of the Security Council – an attitude that betrayed the moral authority of his office but satisfied the United States (which is why Annan, unlike Boutros-Ghali, was allowed a second term). The international organisation was variously abused, humiliated and exploited by Washington through the remorseless countdown to war – according to the familiar US principle that the United Nations would be instructed to serve American foreign policy where possible, and totally ignored where not. The United Nations did not have a good crisis and it did not have a good war. In the post-Saddam era Washington was determined to ensure that the humiliation of the UN would continue.

US Hostility to United Nations

There had always been a strong anti-UN element in American political opinion. With the creation of the United Nations in 1945 and the ceding, through the UN Act passed in the US Congress, of limited international rights over a small part of New York the scene was set for a degree of resentment over the years. Many Americans perceived the United Nations as a base for communist propaganda, with even the siting of the UN headquarters in New York seen as a triumph for Soviet subversion. One observer commented that the 'Communists in the United Nations' were able to reach directly to the American people, with Soviet 'spies and espionage agents posing as delegates and staff' able to gain entry to the United States under full diplomatic immunity.[1] By the mid–1950s, with colonial territories then beginning to achieve political independence and UN membership, the United States found it increasingly difficult to achieve voting majorities in the General Assembly, while in the Security Council many US designs were frustrated by the Soviet veto.[2] Such circumstances deeply affected American attitudes to the United Nations and much of this anti-UN antipathy remained obvious in the post-Cold War world.

The impulse of the Bush administration, typically hostile to the United Nations, had been to act unilaterally, in total disregard of world opinion. Through 2002–3 Washington spokespeople repeatedly asserted that the United States had no need of a new UN resolution authorising a fresh military attack on Iraq. It was asserted that existing Security Council resolutions were sufficient, and in any case Washington reserved the right to 'defend' the United States whatever other states said on the Iraq issue or any other matter.

Exploiting the UN

In the event the Bush strategists came to believe that it would be better to exploit the United Nations than to ignore it totally yet again.[3] There was plenty of time to develop such a strategy. The build-up of American forces around Iraq had continued through 2002–3 and it became obvious that Washington would not be ready to launch its new aggression until the early months of 2003. The countdown to war was under way, irrespective of world opinion and growing dissent within the United States.

The United States and Britain began their quest for a new Security Council resolution, designed to put Iraq under mounting pressure but intended also to prepare the ground for war. Diplomats suggested that Washington and London would 'co-promote' the text in an effort to gain the useful degree of international support, bearing in mind that both France and Russia were reluctant to provide a UN 'green light' for military action. President Putin, supposedly an Iraq ally on the Security Council, was declaring that no new UN resolution was necessary: 'We favour a rapid resolution of the situation by political and diplomatic means, on the basis of existing UN Security Council regulations and in line with the principles of international law.' France reported that it had won China's backing for an approach requiring the United States to work through the UN and not to take unilateral military action. Officials in Washington and London were said to be braced for a tough round of negotiations: 'It is going to be a long uphill struggle'.

There was now clear international hostility to the possibility of a new military conflict in the absence of UN authorisation. Chancellor Gerhard Schroeder had said that Germany would not join a purely US attack on Iraq, and senior British sources were suggesting that such an attack would probably be illegal in international law: 'Our position is that if we are asked to knock out Saddam's weapons of mass destruction, that's one thing. It could be covered by a United Nations resolution. But if we're going to have to invade and remove him, that's another thing altogether. For one thing it's very difficult, and for another it's totally illegal under international law.'

Iraq continued to object to the humanitarian impact of the economic sanctions, and tried to establish a linkage between this and the issue of the alleged weapons of mass destruction. Thus the official Iraqi News Agency (INA) reported a statement issued after a meeting of senior Iraqi officials chaired by Saddam Hussein:

> The real solution lies in the total, comprehensive and final lifting of sanctions. Within the framework of such a solution, agreement can be reached on a suitable transparency which exposes the lies of the Americans and their supporters who speak of Iraq's possession of chemical, nuclear and biological weapons of mass destruction.

At this time, June 2002, Iraq was also expressing a number of other grievances.

The Americans had introduced a new retroactive pricing mechanism for the sale of Iraqi crude oil which was at the heart of the 'food for oil' deal authorised by Security Council resolution 986 (1995). This meant that the pricing system would cause a '$4 billion drop in Iraqi revenue at the end of the current phase of the oil-for-food programme'. On 28 June Iraq protested to the UN over alleged Iranian breaches of the ceasefire agreement negotiated at the end of the Iran-Iraq War (1980–88). Thus a letter from Mohammed al-Douri, Iraq's UN ambassador, to Kofi Annan detailed some 41 breaches, including air flights over Iraqi sites, seizing Iraqi vehicles, and firing from Iranian forces that wounded a number of Iraqi civilians. Nothing could have been of less interest to the Bush administration.

Regime Change, Bush Doctrine

In early July 2002 Iraqi ministers sought UN protection from the declared American policy of 'regime change' in Iraq – an initiative that Washington tried to sabotage by delaying the provision of visas.[4] Already there was international discussion of the absurdity of the US position. Why should Baghdad agree to the UN weapons inspections if the United States was determined to topple the regime? And the discussion was expanding to consider the broader implications of the emerging 'Bush Doctrine'.

Thus the New York-based Committees of Correspondence for Democracy and Socialism, a radical group, was suggesting that the Bush policy intended to render the UN Charter itself inoperable:

> The White House now arrogantly asserts its right to declare any country, organisation or movement a 'threat' to either our own country, its interests abroad or the interests of any other country over whom we throw a blanket of protection – whether they ask for it or not. On that basis, says the 'Bush Doctrine', the US is justified in using offensive military force as part of the UN Charter's right to self-defense.

This bizarre Bush approach – citing the self-defense provisions of the UN Charter[5] to justify US military aggression anywhere in the world – was graphically illustrated by the Iraq issue:

> We can bomb them [the Iraqis] for ten years, embargo their country, kill their children with starvation and disease, and turn a whole nation into an international basket case, and then say we have to invade them to 'better serve' them [and to remove a threat to the security of the United States].[6]

It was in this context that Washington and London were working to secure a fresh UN mandate for war on Iraq.

A New Inspections Resolution?

On 6 September President Bush began to explore what kind of backing he could expect in the Security Council, in particular whether a new inspections resolution, authorising a US-led military response in the event of Iraq non-compliance, would be supported. At the same time the Western propaganda machine was gearing up to advertise Iraq's previous derelictions, ignoring the substantial degree of Iraqi co-operation with the weapons inspectors in the 1990s (Figure 9). It then seemed highly unlikely that the other permanent members of the Security Council, Britain apart, would agree a resolution that would lead to an American military aggression against the helpless Iraqi nation. But having decided to tackle the Security Council on the issue, the Bush administration then embarked on one of the most shocking bouts of diplomatic bullying in the history of the United Nations.

The basic theme in the global US plot was already plain: the United Nations, despite its supreme *de jure* authority, would do as it was told by Washington or it would be ignored. There was a bizarre surrealism in the implicit logic of the application of this principle on Iraq:

> *If you demonstrate your criminality by ignoring the United Nations we will demonstrate our virtue by doing the same.*

On 10 September 2002 Tony Blair, having signed up to the Bush

'The Iraqi authorities were keen to ensure that the inspection proceeded without incident. Iraq provided all the support requested by the inspection teams, access to all sites and areas to be inspected was guaranteed; no problems were encountered by the team in execution of its operational plan' – UN document S/1993/26910

'A marked improvement has occurred in the working relationship with the Iraqi side. An evident effort is now deployed by the Iraqi authorities to provide promptly the information needed to fulfil the requirements of the different resolutions to remove the remaining gaps or uncertainties' – UN document S/1994/490

'The Commission has received considerable assistance and support from Iraq in its efforts to install sensors and tags [to ensure that weapons-making equipment was not re-activated]' – UN document S/1994/1138

'The Iraqi attitude has enabled the inspectors' work to be conducted effectively and has contributed significantly to expediting the process of establishing ongoing monitoring and verification, as called for in the Security Council Resolutions' – UN document S/1994/1151

'Much has been achieved in the implementation of paragraphs 8–10 of Security Council Resolution 687 (1991) [the weapons-inspection resolution] – indeed the bulk of what was required' – UN document S/1995/494

'Iraq, at the Commission's request, has provided accurate information about the VX project and has fulfilled its promise as required by the Commission' – UN document S/1995/494

'The Commission is satisfied that Iraqi co-operation in carrying out the monitoring plan has been of a degree that satisfies the provisions of paragraph 5 of Security Council Resolution 715' – UN document S/1995/494

'The level of practical co-operation by Iraqi counterparts in facilitating and expediting IAEA field work continues to be high' – UN document S/1995/844

'Iraq has continued to provide the support requested by the Commission in the conduct of inspection and verification' – UN document S/1996/864

'The Iraqi side accepted all the comments and recommendations made by the Commission experts concerning the additional information to be included in the ... Full, Final and Complete Disclosures' – UN document S/1995/1038

Figure 9. *Iraqi co-operation with UN weapons inspectors (1993–6)*

Doctrine, announced at the TUC conference that he was ready to follow the UN route, but only if the United Nations was prepared to deliver the decision that Bush and Blair thought was appropriate: *we will observe the court's verdict if we agree with it.* Britain and the United States were declaring their willingness to work through the United Nations and against its decisions if necessary. Saddam Hussein could not have put it better.

Bullying the UN

On 11 September, addressing the nation from New York's Ellis Island, President Bush tried to set the tone for the coming war: 'Our generation has now heard history's call, and we will answer it. And we will not allow any terrorist or tyrant to threaten civilisation with weapons of mass murder. Now and in the future, Americans will live as free people, not in fear, and never at the mercy of a foreign plot or power ... We will not relent until justice is done and our nation is secure.'

On the following day Bush delivered his much-hyped speech to the UN General Assembly, surveying the past crimes of the Saddam regime and urging the world to join with the United States in confronting a grave threat:

> All the world now faces a test and the United Nations a difficult and defining moment. Are Security Council resolutions to be honoured and enforced or cast aside without consequence? Will the UN serve the purpose of its founding, or will it be irrelevant?
>
> The United States helped to found the UN. We want the UN to be effective and respected and successful ...
>
> The United States has no quarrel with the Iraqi people.

So the United Nations organisation would be 'irrelevant' if it refused to do America's bidding.

It was plain that the United Nations was facing a deep humiliation. If the Security Council responded by adopting the sort of resolution that the Bush administration wanted then it would be clear that the United States was being allowed to write international law to suit its own purposes. But if the Security Council declined, then Washington would take unilateral military action and demonstrate the legal and political irrelevance of the United Nations. In either case the United Nations was being bullied into acquiescence with the Bush policy. The Security Council, rather than Iraq, had for the moment become the target of American ambition:

> The UN challenged.

> Bush gives UN last chance.

> Bush bullies UN over Iraq.[7]

Kofi Annan had already remarked mildly that it would be 'unwise' to attack Iraq at the present time. Then, in a belated attempt to bolster UN authority, he stated that there was 'no substitute for the unique legitimacy provided by the United Nations' – a point grudgingly accepted by the Washington strategists.

Most of the members of the Security Council could be relied upon to follow any instructions issued by Washington. Such elected members as Mexico and Colombia were heavily dependent on US aid; Bulgaria and Cameroon were keen to secure Western aid, with the former seeking membership of the European Union (EU) and the North Atlantic Treaty Organisation (NATO); and countries such as Singapore, Guinea and Mauritius had no inclination to dispute American foreign policy. Britain, a veto-bearing permanent member, remained an absurdly supine US proxy – even to the point of echoing Washington statements verbatim – and so could be safely ignored. It seemed that Syria, without a veto, would be highly unlikely to vote for a war-enabling resolution against a brother Arab state, but it was possible that Americans threats against this US-declared 'terrorist state' might do the trick.

The main problems faced by the United States in the Security Council would be posed by the veto-bearing permanent members, Britain apart. It was obvious that Russia, France and China were not keen to approve a resolution that would probably lead to a massively increased US penetration of the oil-rich Middle East. The global political situation in late 2002 was very different to that of 1990–91: the anti-Iraq coalition had largely dissolved and it was likely that any fresh coalition would be smaller and less convincing.

Towards SCR 1441

The first draft of what would eventually emerge as Resolution 1441 was highly significant. The final operative paragraph of this draft (14 October 2002) ended with an authorisation for UN member states 'to use all necessary means to restore international peace and security in the area'. This wording – in particular, 'all necessary means', following the text of Resolution 678 (29 November 1990) – has been widely interpreted in propaganda as authorising a military response in the event of Iraqi non-compliance.[8] The flaws in SCR 678 do not detract from what was the clear intention of the Washington strategists: the first draft of 1441 was intended to emerge as a war-enabling resolution.

The other elements of the draft (see below) represented massively intrusive provisions for the UN inspectors. It seemed that such provisions had been deliberately designed to remove any vestiges of Iraqi sovereignty, and in consequence to be so provocative that the Iraqi regime would be driven inevitably into non-compliance, whereupon the United States would cite the new resolution as justification for fresh aggression. However, though these provisions were destined to survive through the various resolution drafts up to the actual Security Council resolution 1441, the phrase 'all necessary means' – a transparent trigger for war (following the SCR 678 precedent) – was doomed to extinction.

Over a period of two months (from early September to early November 2002) the United States, against all its instincts, was driven to moderate the war character of the resolution. The words 'all necessary means' were thrown out, largely as a result of Russian and French pressure, and France continued to press for a two-step approach: one resolution to authorise a tough new inspection regime, with a second needed to authorise a UN response in the event of Iraqi non-compliance. American dissatisfaction with what was evolving as a compromise resolution was evident in the words of a US official, speaking on 17 October: 'I suppose there will be some sort of resolution but it won't be a priceless piece of family silver.'[9]

The next draft of the resolution (25 October 2002) included an important provision that the Security Council would 'convene immediately' if the UN inspectors reported any Iraqi interference with their work. Hence the French succeeded in securing the continued involvement of the Security Council but failed to guarantee a second UN resolution in the event of Iraqi non-compliance.

Securing SCR 1441

The final draft of the resolution, which emerged as SCR 1441 (8 November 2002), included the provision for reference to the Security Council but included also a further toughening, at the instigation of the US negotiators. Thus operative paragraph 13 recalls, referring to paragraphs 11 and 12, that the Security Council:

> has repeatedly warned Iraq that it will face serious consequences as a result of its continued violations of its obligations.

The phrase 'serious consequences' was repeatedly cited during 2002–3 as justifying resort to military action. In fact, in isolation, it did no such thing. The phrase had already appeared in various Security Council resolutions and statements[10] – and in no case did it herald war. This means that 'serious consequences' did not legitimately serve as a synonym for 'all necessary means' (as in SCR 678) and could not be cited as a precedent for authorising war.

Resolution 1441 also stated, in operative paragraph 2, that this Security Council decision represents 'a final opportunity' for Iraq 'to comply with its disarmament obligations' – but it would be arbitrary to interpret paragraph 2 as any sort of authorisation for war. The words 'final opportunity' are ambiguous without further discussion and interpretation – which in any case should have involved an independent role for the Security Council without bullying from the United States. A 'final opportunity' for what? To get sanctions lifted? To obtain international finance for reconstruction of the economy? To re-enter the community of nations? Washington wanted the phrase to signal an imminent war – a partisan and unauthorised position.

The new resolution was remarkable in the extent of the new power ('revised or additional authorities') granted to the UN inspectors. For example, UNMOVIC and IAEA inspectors – if necessary, protected by armed personnel – were granted the power to establish 'exclusion zones, including surrounding areas and transit corridors, in which Iraq will suspend ground or aerial movement'. This provision, nominally intended to prevent the Iraqis from tampering with a site under inspection, in fact conferred massive powers on the foreigners intent on roaming over Iraq.

It meant that Iraqi officials and civilians could be barred from any part of their own country at the whim of UN staff. The resolution put no limits on the size of the exclusion zones, the surrounding areas, or the transit corridors; and no limit on how long Iraqi ground and aerial movements could be suspended. This was clearly a provision that would allow the effective occupation of Iraq by UN personnel protected by armed troops.

This provision was directly supported by other powers stipulated in SCR 1441. Thus there was to be 'free and unrestricted use and landing of fixed and rotary-winged aircraft, including manned and unmanned reconnaissance vehicles'. In short, fighter-bombers, spy planes, helicopters and unmanned drones (these latter capable of carrying missiles) were authorised to range over the whole of Iraq and to land anywhere. If a US plane were to bomb Iraqi territory and Iraqi forces tried to shoot it down, the Iraqi forces would be in 'material breach' of the resolution – a point made explicitly and with smug satisfaction by Richard Perle, a Bush advisor, a few hours after SCR 1441 had been adopted by the Security Council.

Hence the Security Council not only legalised the existing 'no fly' zones – long recognised in international commentary as illegal[11] – but gave UN staff the power to declare any part of Iraq a 'no fly', 'no drive' zone. This potentially denied Iraqi aircraft access to Iraqi air space.

The resolution also authorised UN personnel, accompanied by military personnel, to have an unrestricted right of access to any sites and buildings, including presidential sites. This may sound reasonable, if the aim were to detect weapons facilities, but the implications of such all-embracing authorisation were massive. It meant that foreign personnel could at any time demand access to Iraq's security apparatus, its military infrastructure, its research facilities, its government ministries, its schools and colleges, its clinics and hospitals, its factories – and all the homes of the Iraqi civilian population and government staff. Foreigners – many from countries hostile to Iraq – were to be allowed access to all Iraqi defense establishments, at a time when

Baghdad was expecting the United States to launch another war of aggression.

It is interesting to note that SCR 1441 reiterates the words that can be found in many UN resolutions on Iraq. The resolution 'reaffirms the commitment of all member states to the sovereignty of Iraq' – an obvious absurdity in view of the comprehensive powers granted to foreigners over every aspect of Iraqi life.

Moreover, the UN personnel were authorised to export or destroy anything – records, materials and equipment – that might have been judged relevant to their task, and to take Iraqi personnel and their families out of the country for interrogation. The resolution put no limit on how long such people should be held and made no gesture to the judicial rights of personnel held in such a fashion.

The Iraqi authorities were allowed no response to any action that the inspectors took. If the UN staff were to dismantle and export a factory, at Iraqi expense, Iraq would be allowed no appeal; if Iraqi scientists were taken out of the country and held incommunicado for lengthy periods, Iraq would be allowed no appeal; and if materials or equipment were exported and destroyed, Iraq would be entitled to no explanation or recompense.

It is obvious that in such circumstances all normal judicial rights would be ignored. A 'witness' or defector may make allegations against the Iraqi regime through malice or to win favour – and an income – from Washington. But Iraq was allowed no legal representation, no chance to hear the evidence and no appeal against the word of dissident Iraqis or the judgements of hostile foreigners with a political agenda.

It is hard to imagine that such a provocative UN was not designed to guarantee an Iraqi response that could be interpreted as a 'material breach' of Iraq's obligations. Significantly, unlike resolutions 687 (1991) and 1284 (1999),[12] SCR 1441 contained no reference to the ending of sanctions. The US and UK drafters of the resolution never expected that the sanctions issue would be relevant. They obviously worked on the assumption that Iraq would be found in 'material breach' and, on one pretext or another, the United States would launch its new aggression. In fact, shortly after the Security Council adoption of the resolution John Negroponte, US ambassador to the UN, President Bush and Prime Minister Blair were promising a military response if Iraq failed to comply with every UN demand in the new resolution. Negroponte revealingly declared that 'material breaches' of SCR 1441 could be reported by UNMOVIC, IAEA or *any member state* (my italics). Hence even before the UN inspectors had reached Iraq the United States was preparing to declare that Iraq was violating the resolution.

Not a War Resolution

The US-UK posture was dishonest and hypocritical. The unanimous vote for SCR 1441 had been secured only because the United States and Britain had given assurances that perceived 'material breaches' by Iraq would *not* act as 'hidden triggers' for war or to legitimise 'automaticity' in the resort to force. Instead, in accordance with operative paragraphs 11 and 12 of the resolution, any evidence of *material breach* would be referred to the Security Council for consideration. This is such an important point, in considering the origins of the 2003 war, that it should be emphasised.

Immediately after the adoption of the resolution, the members of the Security Council explained their votes in favour. Ambassador Negroponte, speaking for the United States, declared:

> As we have said on numerous occasions to Council members, this resolution contains no 'hidden triggers' and no 'automaticity' with respect to the use of force ... If there is a further Iraqi breach ... the matter will be referred to the Council for discussions ...

In the same vein Sir Jeremy Greenstock, speaking for Britain, echoed the American statement:

> We heard loud and clear during the negotiations the concerns about 'automaticity' and 'hidden triggers' – the concern that on a decision so crucial any Iraqi violations should be discussed by the Council ... There is no 'automaticity' in this resolution. If there is a further Iraqi breach ... the matter will return to the Council for discussion.

Other members of the Council – France, Mexico, Ireland, Russia, Bulgaria, Syria, Colombia, Cameroon, China – took pains to emphasise that this was also their own understanding of the resolution. Any perceived Iraqi breaches of the resolution could *not* be legitimately used as an excuse for a US military aggression.

On the same day, 8 November 2002, three permanent members of the Security Council – Russia, France and China – went further, strengthening their statements on the new resolution. They issued a joint statement confirming their understanding:

> Resolution 1441 (2002) adopted today by the Security Council excludes any automaticity in the use of force. In this regard, we register with satisfaction the declarations of the representatives of the United States and the United Kingdom confirming this understanding ... In case of failure by Iraq to comply with its obligations ... it will be then for the Council to take a position ...[13]

Hence in the period following the adoption of SCR 1441 the position was clear. Any threat by the United States or Britain to resort to military action, following a perceived Iraqi violation of SCR 1441, was a flagrant violation not only of the resolution itself but also of the explicit US and UK commentaries explaining their affirmative votes in the Security Council.

Syria, expected by many to have at least abstained, voted for the resolution. Mr Mekdad, speaking for Syria on 8 November 2002, explained why:

> Syria voted in favour of the resolution, having received reassurances from its sponsors, the United States of America and the United Kingdom, and through France and Russia through high-level contacts, that it would not be used as a pretext for striking against Iraq and does not constitute a basis for any automatic strikes against Iraq. The resolution should not be interpreted ... as authorising any State to use force. It reaffirms the central role of the Security Council in addressing all phases of the Iraqi issue.[14]

Syria, assured by the US and Britain that SCR 1441 did not authorise war, may have thought that its affirmative vote, against much Arab opinion, would have won it some favour with Washington. But Syria and others were soon reminded of the realities of global power.

Vetoing a Syrian Resolution

On 19 December Syria presented a draft resolution (Appendix II) to the Security Council expressing 'grave' and 'deep' concern, respectively, at the Israeli killing of several UN employees and at the deliberate destruction by the Israelis of a UN food warehouse intended to supply Palestinian families wholly dependent on UN support. The resolution condemned the killings and the destruction, and demanded that Israel, as the occupying power, comply with its obligations under the Fourth Geneva Convention relative to the Protection of Civilian Persons in Time of War.[15]

The resolution was so obviously just and reasonable that even Britain managed to vote in favour, as did eleven other members of the Security Council. Bulgaria and Cameroon, both with a nervous eye on Washington, abstained. The veto-bearing United States, ever keen to protect a criminally derelict Israel, voted against. Hence the Security Council voted 12 to one for a plainly just resolution – and for reasons of cynical US *realpolitik* the resolution fell.[16] Syria's effort to placate an aggressive superpower had bought it no favours, and there was worse to come (see also Chapter 7, *Syria*).

Preparing for War

Early in February 2003 US Secretary of State Colin Powell, formerly alleged 'dove', presented to the Security Council what he purported to be evidence of Iraqi 'lies' and 'evasions', ample reason – the Washington hawks believed – to justify another US-run orgy of mass murder in a foreign land. The Powell presentation was designed primarily to persuade the international community that the planned aggression against the Iraq was justified in ethics and law. At one level the Bush administration had already rendered the United Nations as irrelevance. The countdown to war continued.

The United States was also trying to bully Security Council members into support for the planned American aggression. President Bush had already told France and Germany that they would be 'held to account' if they did not back US policy, and few observers doubted that further diplomacy was pointless in a timetable clearly being dictated by military preparations. The smaller members of the Security Council were still being cajoled, bribed and intimidated into supporting the expected 'second' resolution designed to provide a spurious UN authorisation for war, but it seemed that such tactics were not achieving Washington's desired results. The required majority on the Council could not be guaranteed and there was a growing likelihood of veto by one or more of the Permanent Members.

A New Resolution?

On 21 February it was announced that the United States and Britain, with Spain as a co-sponsor, would introduce the new resolution (Appendix III) designed to justify the use of force against Iraq. American officials were acknowledging that it would be difficult to secure the required nine-vote majority on the 15-member Security Council, and to avoid a veto from France, Russia or China.

The draft resolution, dated 24 February 2003, was an unusual specimen containing a full page of preambular statements and only one significant operative paragraph. The Security Council variously recalled, noted, reaffirmed and recognised salient aspects of the matter, and declared itself 'mindful of its primary responsibility under the Charter of the United Nations for maintenance of international peace and security in the area'. The significant operative paragraph signalled that the Council 'decides that Iraq has failed to take the final opportunity afforded to it by resolution 1441 (2002)'. The resolution again absurdly reaffirmed Iraq's 'sovereignty and territorial integrity', at a time when Washington was plotting a massive military aggression against the country, and the absurdity was compounded by the emphasis on the Security Council's responsibility for 'the maintenance of peace'. Peace was applauded while the draft resolution, using cowardly euphemism, represented authorisation for war.

At the same time, France, Germany and Russia produced a joint memorandum emphasising the 'imperative objective' of 'full and effective [Iraqi] disarmament'. This document, also dated 24 February 2003, included the following words:

> The military option should only be a last resort. So far, the conditions for using force against Iraq are not fulfilled:
>
> – While suspicions remain, no evidence has been given that Iraq still possesses weapons of mass destruction or capabilities in this field;
>
> – Inspections have just reached their full pace; they are functioning without hindrance; they have already produced results;
>
> – While not yet fully satisfactory, Iraqi co-operation is improving, as mentioned by the chief inspectors in their last report.
>
> The Security Council must step up its efforts to give a real chance to the peaceful settlement of the crisis.

The United States totally ignored this significant contribution, not least because the American concerns had nothing to do with weapons of mass destruction. The real US agendas – control of the oil resource, expansion of regional hegemony, protection of Israel – were not being addressed in the Security Council or generating key memoranda from Council members.

Washington was now being accused of 'dirty tricks' in its increasingly desperate efforts to secure the necessary votes for the draft resolution. *The Observer* (London) obtained a document from a top official at the US National Security Agency (NSA) describing orders to staff to increase the Agency's surveillance operations 'particularly directed at ... UN Security Council Members [minus US and GBR of course], to provide up-to-the-minute intelligence for Bush officials on the voting intentions of Council members regarding Iraq.'[17] This meant that the NSA was bugging the e-mails and telephone calls of Security Council delegates to provide information on 'policies', 'negotiating positions', 'alliances' and 'dependencies' – the 'whole gamut of information that could give US policymakers an edge in obtaining results favourable to US goals or to head off surprises.[18]

It was not long before sources in Kofi Annan's office were confirming that the US spying operation – revealed by Frank Koza, NSA defense chief of staff (Regional Targets) – had been discussed by the UN's counter-terrorism committee.[19] Ari Fleischer, White House spokesman, asked about the surveillance operations, said he could not comment on security issues. Wayne Madsen, of the Electronic Privacy Information Centre and himself a former NSA officer, commented that the leak revealed the deep unhappiness in the intelligence world: 'My feeling is that this was an authorised leak. I've been hearing of people in the US and British intelligence community who are deeply concerned about their governments "cooking" intelligence to link Iraq to al-Qa'ida.'[20]

The bribes, the threats and the surveillance were not delivering the desired results. It seemed clear that Washington and the two co-sponsors would have to abandon the draft resolution. France and others, prepared in principle to support military action, had been suggesting that the UN inspectors be given a limited amount of extra time and that war might follow if Baghdad did not meet its obligations. It was the American rush to war, according to its own military timetable, that excluded the United Nations from any involvement in the military action against Iraq.

An Illegal Posture

President Bush and Prime Minister Blair were now asserting that war against Iraq would be justified, even if the United Nations failed to authorise such action. On 6 March 2003 Tony Blair, speaking in the MTV interview, declared that he would be prepared to override vetoes in the Security Council to go to war: 'if there was a veto applied by ... countries that I thought were applying the veto unreasonably, in these circumstances we would go ahead. But we are fighting very hard to get a second resolution through.'

It was plain that Bush and Blair were about to embark upon an illegal war, lacking the justification of either a Security Council resolution or Article 51 of the UN Charter (allowing 'individual or collective self-defense if an armed attack occurs'). On 10 March, Kofi Annan, in a rare appearance above the parapet, confirmed the widespread view that the planned war, lacking UN authority, would be illegal:

If the US and others were to go outside the Council and take military action, it would not be in conformity with the Charter ... If they [Security Council members] failed to agree on a common position, and action is taken without the authority of the Security Council, the legitimacy and support for any such action will be seriously impaired.

The planned Bush-Blair war would be a 'supreme international crime',[21] making the political initiators of the military action war criminals, and depriving the ordinary soldiers of legal protection in the war.

The United States was compounding its illegal behaviour in various ways – by moving towards using its own weapons of mass destruction, by beating prisoners to death at the Bagram airbase in Afghanistan (see also Chapter 12, *Practising Torture*), and by abusing its position in the Security Council through the use of bribery and intimidation. Donald Rumsfeld was arguing that America should be allowed to use allegedly 'non-lethal' chemical weapons in war, even though there was dispute about their effects and the extent to which their use would lead to the deployment of other chemical weapons.

In 1997 the United States declared to the Organisation for the Prohibition of Chemical Weapons (OPCW), that works to implement the UN Convention on chemical weapons, that it possessed:

15,637 tonnes of mustard gas

7,464 tonnes of sarin nerve gas

4,032 tonnes of VX nerve gas

1,698 tonnes of tabun nerve gas

By 2003, as required by international law, the United States was reportedly destroying this arsenal but the destruction programme was well behind schedule. At the same time the Pentagon was arguing for the use of 'small' nuclear weapons, for the use of certain chemical weapons, and for the continued development of other weapons of mass destruction with the explosive power of nuclear weapons.

War and Aftermath

The war created the predicted humanitarian catastrophe for the people of Iraq (see Chapter 1). The 'oil for food' programme, authorised by Security Council resolution 986 (1995), itself grossly inadequate and abused by Washington,[22] was suspended at the start of the war. The distribution of food and the supply of clean water were blocked, causing the inevitable rise in malnutrition and water- borne disease. On 20 March 2003 Kofi Annan noted that the Iraqi people were facing 'yet another ordeal' and he hoped that 'all parties will scrupulously observe the requirements of international law'.

Igor Ivanov, Russian foreign minister, declared what Kofi Annan should have said – that American and Britain were violating the UN Charter and that many resolutions on Iraq were specifically focused on disarming Iraq, not on removing its president and government (Iraq remained a fully accredited sovereign member of the United Nations): 'Not one of these decisions [UN decisions] authorises the right to use force against Iraq outside the UN Charter. Not one ... authorises the violent overthrow of the leadership of a sovereign state.'

Opponents of the war, knowing that it was impossible to win an anti-war resolution in the Security Council, then tried to move down another UN route. The UN Charter confers on the Security Council primary responsibility to keep the peace, but governments have recourse when the Council is unable to act. Thus General Assembly resolution 377 authorises the Assembly to adopt the Security Council role in certain circumstances. Either seven members of the Council or a majority of the members of the General Assembly can invoke the resolution, whereupon the Assembly can recommend collective measures to 'maintain or restore international peace and security'.

There was still no way that the General Assembly could discipline a recalcitrant United States or take steps to bring the war to an end, but it was obvious that a successful invocation of resolution 377 would have carried immense moral weight and seriously embarrassed Washington. The United States regarded the matter as sufficiently important to begin its own lobbying campaign. Jan Kavan, General Assembly president, commented: 'The United States is putting pressure on many countries to resist a General Assembly meeting on the issue', not least by issuing the following statement to the governments of various countries:

> Given the current highly charged atmosphere the United States would regard a General Assembly session on Iraq as unhelpful, and as directed against the United States. Please know that the question, as well as your position on it, is important for the United States.

The efforts came to nothing but world opinion was beginning to mobilise in efforts to exploit the existing UN options. *The New York Times* felt obliged to remark that world opinion was 'the new second superpower'.

The overwhelming majority of international lawyers had judged that the war was illegal under international law, initiated without UN Security Council authorisation and deriving legitimacy from no other source – inducing the Dalyell charge that Tony Blair was a 'war criminal'.[23] The inevitable corollary was that Blair's political team (Straw, Hoon, Brown, Short, etc), with shared cabinet responsibility, should also be indicted as war criminals, as should their American counterparts (Bush, Rumsfeld, Powell, Rice, etc.). The failure of law to take its appropriate course in such a matter demonstrated yet again how unassailable military power can abuse proper legal process.

On 28 March the Security Council voted unanimously to restart the 'oil for food programme', abandoned at the onset of war on 19 March 2003. The resolution, SCR 1472 (2003), again included the absurdity that all Member States were committed 'to the sovereignty and territorial integrity of Iraq' – at a time when it had been invaded and occupied by foreign powers. The resolution also contained abundant references to such considerations as 'essential civilian needs', 'humanitarian relief', 'emergency humanitarian supplies', etc. – pious aspirations that seemed far removed from events on the ground. There were problems too over the matter of sanctions. The US wanted them lifted, to maximise the opportunities for American contractors, but the existing sanctions regime gave France, Russia and China immense leverage over the disposal of Iraqi assets, including oil – another source of international dispute and division.[24]

The position of the United Nations in the post-Saddam Iraq at first seemed uncertain. President Bush declared that the UN would have a 'vital' role (see Appendix V) – a sentiment, including the identical adjective, echoed by Jack Straw 24 hours later. On 19 April representatives of the European Union decided in Athens that the United Nations would have a 'central' role, with British spokesmen later proclaiming that there may be several 'central' roles assigned to the various players in the situation. One thing was clear. The United Nations would only be allowed a 'vital' or 'central' role that was judged by Washington strategists to be consistent with American policy in the region (see Chapter 13).

TWELVE

US Hegemony

The scale of US power had been obvious long before the 2003 war. After the 1991 Gulf War the United States began creating a 'New World Order' in which the will and whim of Washington would be unassailable. At that time Noam Chomsky, academic and dissident, had accurately described the US attitude to war: the much weaker opponent 'must not merely be defeated but pulverised if the central lesson of World Order is to be learned: we are the masters and you shine our shoes'.[1] The 2003 war helped to carry the message around the world in terms so graphic and uncompromising that no-one could doubt or misunderstand.

The war was a massive escalation of a process that was already well under way. It had been made clear that the United States, with cynical contempt for the rule of law, manipulated the Security Council and the World Court in imposing punitive sanctions on Libya,[2] Iraq and other states; that it systematically betrayed UN resolutions on Indonesia, Israel, Turkey, South Africa and Bosnia; that it achieved an unjust UN 'tilt' in favour of US proxies in Angola and El Salvador; that it treated the World Court with contempt when it ruled against Washington on Nicaragua; that it manipulated the UN-linked financial institutions to advance the interests of American capital; that it delayed payment of obligatory UN dues, while bullying other states to observe the Charter; that it exploited UN-gathered intelligence for its own purposes – to the point that a UN Secretary-General was forced to issue a rebuke; and that Washington had often frustrated the best efforts of many UN agencies (UNICEF, WFP, FAO, WHO and others) by pushing policies designed to further a self-serving American agenda.

It is only American power that has enabled Washington to be so indifferent to ethics and international law over the years. Such power, like all substantial power, cannot be trusted. Today American economic and military power expands around the world, allowing further ethical and legal derelictions.

Nuclear Bully

A few years ago *Time* (4 August 1997) was asking whether the United States was 'in danger of becoming a global bully?' There was 'mounting umbrage at American "arrogance" abroad; with, for example, world leaders at the Denver economic summit being subjected to 'humiliation and braggadocio in equal measure'.[3] Today it is easy to see how the 1991 collapse of the Soviet Union, a seismic event in world affairs, encouraged the already-imperialist United States to develop an even greater ambition buttressed by vast and unchallengeable military power. Any states that tried to challenge the new political reality would be 'shunned, treated with suspicion, condemned, and punished accordingly'.[4]

As early as 1992 we learned that the Pentagon was drawing up plans to target selected Third World countries – 'pariah' or 'rogue' states, with nuclear weapons. The possible targets for nuclear strikes included Libya, Pakistan, China, India, Iran and Syria. Russia and Eastern Europe, formerly offering some 12,000 targets, were still considered to be a potentially threatening region but one that no longer warranted the focused attention of the US nuclear arsenal.

In May 2002 Richard Perle, then head of the Pentagon's Commission for Military Policies, was declaring that nuclear weapons might be used against Iraq, reiterating the policy considerations to which Washington and London were giving more and more attention. On 20 March 2002 Geoff Hoon, British defense secretary, told the House of Commons select committee on defense that states like Iraq 'can be absolutely confident that in the right conditions we would be willing to use our nuclear weapons'.

Four days later, Hoon appeared on ITV's Jonathan Dimbleby show and 'insisted that the government "reserved the right" to use nuclear weapons if Britain or British troops were threatened by chemical or biological weapons'. And in a Commons debate (29 April) Hoon declared that 'in certain specified conditions ... we would be prepared to use' nuclear weapons – a deliberate ambiguity favoured by the government as a useful form of deterrence.

The US policy document, *Nuclear Posture Review*, leaked in early March 2002, noted circumstances in which Washington would authorise the use of nuclear weapons: against targets able to withstand a non-nuclear attack; in retaliation for the use of nuclear, biological or chemical weapons; and 'in the event of surprising military developments' – this last being conveniently vague. The *Review* explicitly cited Iraq as a possible target for a nuclear attack.

It was now plain that a joint US-UK policy of nuclear intimidation was emerging as a way of demonstrating the global sway of the United States and its acolyte. In May 1997 President Bill Clinton had reaffirmed the American intention 'to lead the world'; the then Secretary of State Madeleine Albright declared on more than one occasion that the United States was the one 'indispensable' country; and the Bush administration – what Gore Vidal termed 'an unelected junta of gas and oil men' – was determined to advance the cause of US global hegemony. The 2003 war, having nothing to do with human rights or weapons of mass destruction, was part of this process – and contempt for the United Nations and international law was a necessary enabling attitude.

On 11 December 2002 the White House declared that it was prepared to launch nuclear missiles against Iraq if Saddam Hussein deployed chemical or biological weapons against American troops or allies. Ari Fleischer, White House spokesman, commented that the statement indicated 'how seriously the United States would take it if weapons of mass destruction were used'. In early March 2003 the Bush administration's 2004 budget proposals contained a single-line statement calling on the legislation to 'rescind the prohibition on research and development of low-yield nuclear weapons'. This indicated that the White House intended to develop a new range of nuclear weapons that would be more 'usable' in confrontation with 'rogue states'. In this context a Pentagon official said that the research ban had undercut America's ability 'to deter or respond to new or emerging threats'. Democrats in Congress were concerned that the new Bush policy was intended to end the US moratorium on nuclear testing and to foment a new international nuclear arms race.

It was significant that the Republicans had already approved $15 million for research on nuclear 'bunker buster' bombs, the B61 and B83 devices, modifications of high-yield bombs, but any attempt to expand America's nuclear arsenal with low-yield devices would require a series of tests. Daryl Kimball, executive director of the Washington-based arms control association, commented: 'The only reason why the administration might want to pursue low-yield nuclear weapons is to develop a weapon they believe is less damaging to the immediate environment. In the strange logic of these people, it would be more "usable" – the political costs, they believe, will be lower.' The White House was urging other countries not to develop nuclear weapons, while preparing to develop its own new range of nuclear devices.

Targeting UN Staff

There was a certain irony in the fact that while Washington was urging Iraq to observe its UN obligations the United States was showing its contempt for the international organisation. The US had already effectively sabotaged the UN Biological Weapons Convention by rejecting the 'verification protocol' essential for the banning of bioweapons. The United States had also violated the verification terms of the Chemical Weapons Convention, and managed to have the worthy Jose Bustani, head of the Organisation for the Prohibition of Chemical Weapons (OPCW), fired from his job because he refused to do America's bidding.

In the same way Dr Robert Watson lost his job as chairman of the UN-sponsored Intergovernmental Panel on Climate Change, because the White House supported Exxon Mobil's hostility to the 'aggressive agenda' – that is, pushing for climate-protection policies – espoused by Watson. Washington had also made it clear to Kofi Annan that the term of Mary Robinson, UN Human Rights Commissioner, should not be extended because she seemed to think that the US should observe human rights. And Washington had already vetoed the second term of UN Secretary-General Boutros Boutros-Ghali (vote in favour 14–1) because he insisted on publicising Israel's bombing of civilians and US derelictions elsewhere. Boutros-Ghali himself quoted Madeleine Albright, then US ambassador to the UN, as saying: 'I will make Boutros think I am his friend; then I will break his legs.'[5] The Kyoto Climate Change Protocol, missile conventions, the International Criminal Court – Washington was working hard to undermine any UN initiative that US strategists deemed unhelpful to American interests.

Practising Torture

On 24 July 2002 the United States refused to support a UN protocol against torture because of fears that it would allow international monitors to visit the prisoners in Guatanamo Bay, Cuba. Here terrorist suspects, denied access to relatives and lawyers, were being held in solitary confinement in cells 6ft by 12ft, and allowed out only 30 minutes a week – conditions that were causing many suicide attempts.

Human rights campaigners charged the United States with systematic attempts to sabotage the protocol, a necessary device to strengthen the UN torture Convention. The Americans objected to one specific protocol aim: 'To establish a system of regular visits undertaken by independent and international bodies to places where people are deprived of their liberty, in order to prevent torture and other cruel, inhuman or degrading treatment and punishment.'[6] There are many reports, not least from Amnesty International, describing the gross abuses of human rights in American penal institutions. One prisoner of many, requesting anonymity, testified in interview: 'Many are beaten and raped so badly, they're just left to die in the cell with no medical attention at all.'

After 11 September 2001 it soon emerged that the United States was prepared to use torture as an element in national policy in the alleged 'war against terrorism'. The journalist Alasdair Palmer spoke to CIA and FBI officers in New York and Washington and noted the prevailing attitude (*The Sunday Telegraph*, 15 December 2002): 'They were in no doubt what they would have to do: they would have to torture people.' Senior US lawyers were reportedly in agreement. One CIA officer commented to Palmer:

> In a sense, we already use torture anyway. When we arrest a foreign national who we think has important information, we hand them over to a foreign government such as the Egyptians. Its police will arrest the suspect's wife and children, put them at the other end of the same cell, and then produce a couple of pit bulls and say: 'Talk, or we let these dogs at your wife and child.' That usually works.

Some American lawyers were then advocating the introduction of 'torture warrants', with the FBI required to apply for them in the same way they obtain search warrants. Alan Dershowitz, a Harvard professor of law and a distinguished advocate of civil liberties, had concluded that judicial torture was not prohibited by the US Constitution. The Fifth Amendment, which prohibits self-incrimination, only meant that statements obtained by torture could not be introduced as evidence against the tortured defendant. Dershowitz argued that the Eighth Amendment, which prohibited 'cruel and unusual punishment' was not violated by torture since the Amendment only applied to punishment after an individual has been convicted. Here the American view was that the torture of unconvicted suspects was not unconstitutional.

On 26 December 2002 *The Washington Post* reported that torture was being used by CIA interrogators on captured men in Afghanistan. Former prisoners at the Bagram military base testified how they had been chained to the ceiling, shackled so tightly that the blood flow stopped, kept naked and hooded, and kicked to keep them awake for days. In early March it was revealed that two suspects, both Afghans, had been beaten to death by American interrogators (*The Guardian*, 7 March 2003). One of the dead prisoners, the 22-year-old Dilawar, a farmer and part-time taxi-driver, died as a result of 'blunt force injuries to lower extremities complicating coronary artery disease' – according to the death certificate signed by Major Elizabeth Rouse, a pathologist working under the auspices of the US Defense Department. Hakkim

Shah, a former prisoner at Bagram, said that he had been kept naked, hooded and shackled, and had been kicked to keep him awake. On one occasion he was kicked by a woman interrogator, while her male colleague held him in a kneeling position.

Another Bagram inmate, the 35-year-old Moazzam Begg, the only British prisoner, described how he was being held in a cluster of metal shipping containers at the American base (*The Observer*, 29 December 2002). Already US officials had admitted that suspects were being 'softened up' by brutal beatings from US military police and special forces soldiers. The prisoners were confined to tiny enclosures, often blindfolded, thrown into walls, tied up in painful positions, subjected to loud noises, deprived of sleep by bright lights, and made to stand for long periods. Often they were forced to wear hoods or spray-painted goggles to render them blind. Some of the suspects, with battle wounds, had been denied painkillers as a way of torturing them into providing information.

Jamie Feiner, US director of Human Rights Watch, commented: 'How can the US descend to the level of using terror in the war on terror? What sort of victory is that? This is illegal and it is appalling.' And the torture was compounded by many other violations of international law. Moazzam Begg, seized in Pakistan and smuggled to Bagram, was denied access to a lawyer, a Red Cross official and any member of his family.

Donald Rumsfeld had protested at the televising of American prisoners in Iraq, but was indifferent to his own abuses of human rights. In this context the Bagram horrors were only part of the picture. The prison camp at Guantanamo Bay, holding hundreds of uncharged suspects, breached no fewer than 15 articles of the Third Geneva Convention, and there were atrocities in the field – in both Iraq and Afghanistan – for which US troops were responsible.

In November 2002, at Qala-i-Zeini, near the town of Mazar-i-Sharif in Afghanistan, thousands of prisoners captured by the Americans and their allies were sealed in lorries that were left to stand in the sun for several days. When the prisoners, dying of thirst and asphyxiation, started to bang on the doors troops of General Abdul Rashid Dostum, a Northern Alliance ally of the United States, machine-gunned the containers. When the convoy reached Sheberghan most of the captives were dead.

American special forces soldiers watched the bodies being unloaded, and then told Dostum's men to 'get rid of them before satellite pictures can be taken'. One Northern Alliance soldier later testified: 'I was a witness when an American soldier broke one prisoner's neck. The Americans did whatever they wanted. We had no power to stop them.' Another soldier said that the Americans took prisoners outside and beat them up, and then returned them to prison: 'But sometimes they were never returned, and they disappeared' (*The Guardian*, 25 March 2003).

Many of the survivors were loaded back into the containers with the corpses and driven into the desert. About 40 US special forces watched the living and the dead being dumped into ditches before all the survivors were shot. The German newspaper *Die Zeit* concluded: 'No-one doubted that the Americans had taken part. Even at higher levels there are no doubts on this issue.' The activist George Monbiot, who helped to give publicity to events recorded in Jamie Doran's film *Afghan Massacre: Convoy of Death*, commented:

> It is not hard, therefore, to see why the US government fought first to prevent the establishment of the international criminal court, and then to ensure that its own citizens are not subject to its jurisdiction. The five [American] soldiers dragged in front of the cameras yesterday should thank their lucky stars that they are prisoners not of the American forces fighting for civilisation, but of the 'barbaric and inhuman' Iraqis.

In mid-May 2003 former Iraqi prisoners of war accused British and American troops of torturing them for long periods. Amnesty International, interviewing 20 former detainees, were told about men being kicked, beaten and subjected to electric shocks at Basra and Nasiriyah. One Amnesty International researcher reported a man who was beaten through the night, denied water, until he was bleeding and his teeth were broken (*The Guardian*, 17 May 2003).

It is useful to remember that the 2003 war was fought over – when all other pretexts collapsed – Iraqi abuses of human rights.

Abusing the UN

The United States has routinely vetoed inconvenient Security Council resolutions – as with the Syrian draft resolution (December 2002) condemning the Israeli murder of UN staff and the deliberate destruction of Palestinian food stocks (see Chapter 11) – and ignored overwhelming General Assembly votes against US policy. This latter is graphically illustrated by the annual Assembly vote opposing the American blockade of Cuba (Table 1), a US policy that the World Health Organisation (WHO) declares has taken 'a tragic human toll' among the Cuban people.[7] The White House also lobbied hard against international efforts to use GA resolution 377, the 'uniting for peace' resolution, to authorise a General Assembly debate on the 2003 was against Iraq.

GENERAL TOTALS											
UN General Assembly	1992	1993	1994	1995	1996	1997	1998	1999	2000	2001	2002
Against Blockade	59	88	101	117	137	143	157	155	167	167	173
For Blockade	3	4	2	3	3	3	2	2	3	3	3
Absent	46	35	33	27	20	22	14	23	15	16	11
Abstentions	71	57	48	38	25	17	12	8	4	3	4

Table 1. *UN opposition to US blockade of Cuba (1992–2002)*

Global Reach

The US arrogance that facilitates such indifference to world opinion fuels the prevailing policies on 'regime change', the cynical reshaping of political alliances, and the expanding American military presence around the world. Thus in September 1997, long before Bush's alleged 'war on terror', some 500 US paratroopers dropped onto the steppes of the former Soviet Republic of Kazakhstan in the heart of Central Asia as part of a multinational military exercise involving troops from

Kazakhstan, Uzbekistan, Kyrgyzstan and the United States. The US troops had flown for nineteen hours from North Carolina, an operation that required three in-flight refuellings. The US Marine Corps General John Sheehan explained a main purpose of the operation: '*I would like to leave the message that there is no nation on the face of the Earth that we cannot get to.*'[8]

In the same fashion the United States intimidated countries into acquiescence and support over the 2003 war. Turkish Cypriots were offered a degree of sovereignty in Cyprus to pressure Turkey into allowing use of its bases for an attack on Iraq; there were hints that Russia would be offered a share in the Iraqi oil resource if it would keep quiet in the Security Council; France and Germany were abused as 'old Europe' when they presumed to challenge Washington's Iraq policy; US strategists wondered whether to merge Jordan and Iraq after the 2003 war had been successfully concluded; staff were trained to convert the Iraq economy from state control to free market; and the world was told that it was either 'for Saddam Hussein or for the United States'. And already the plans were being laid for post-Saddam attacks on other countries. In the House of Commons (29 January 2003) Prime Minister Tony Blair implied that North Korea would be next, and when a heckler asked when it would all end, Blair replied: 'We stop when the threat to our security is properly and fully dealt with.' There were signs also that the United States, urged on by Israel, would target Iran when the Saddam regime had been toppled and a US military administration was firmly in control of Baghdad.[9] After Saddam, Syria was soon in US sights (see Chapter 7).

Halliburton and Others

It was being suggested that the US conquest and occupation of Iraq would cost the American taxpayer up to $200 billion, despite Bush's hope for a 'cheap' war – but such expenditure would clearly represent a welcome bonanza to many US companies. Perhaps it was no coincidence that President Bush and Vice President Cheney stood to make substantial financial gains. For example, the Halliburton Corporation, to which Dick Cheney would eventually return, was anticipating massive profits. When Cheney was running Halliburton, it sold more equipment to Iraq than any other company,[10] and there were expectations that Iraq revenues would again fill the corporate coffers:

> As the world's biggest oilfield construction contractor, Halliburton is positioned along the faults of global conflict, reaping billions and moving on to the next centre of petrol-fuelled intrigue. Halliburton employs 85,000 people in 100 countries, a presence often indistinguishable from that of the US government itself. Halliburton is the foreign legion of the military-industrial complex. Whether preparing for war or cleaning up afterwards, Halliburton is there.[11]

The scale of Halliburton's global reach is massive – Russia, the Philippines, Libya, Zaire, Haiti, Somalia, Afghanistan, Kosovo, Iraq, and the US army. The Brown & Root division of Halliburton has provided the bulk of the army's logistics services since 1992; building barracks, cooking the food, mopping the floors, transporting the goods, maintaining the water systems: Brown & Root provides the Pentagon with a private battalion of engineers, janitors and other support staff.[12] The company made enormous profits in the former Yugoslavia: 'From 1995 to 2000, Brown & Root billed the government for $2.2 billion for its logistic support in Kosovo, making the services contract the costliest in US history.'[13]

Halliburton and other US corporations stood to make enormous profits out of the 2003 war and its aftermath (see also Chapter 3). Cheney and his ilk knew where the best commercial advantage lay:

> Dick Cheney was Halliburton CEO and largest individual shareholder when he left to take charge of George Bush. His business is war and he will shape US policy to achieve it. Halliburton will get a large chunk of the $200 billion cost of maintaining the troops that invade and occupy Iraq and the lion's share of the rebuilding the infrastructure afterwards. Then they will move on to the next profit-centre of manufactured crisis. Most likely, they are already there ...
>
> Thus it is also logical that the Bush administration demands privatisation of every possible speciality in the US armed forces – both civilian and military. Hundreds of thousands, in and out of

uniform, will lose their positions so that Halliburton and other profiteers can claim more contracts. Put bluntly, Cheney and his crowd see war as a contractual arrangement.[14]

In the same vein, Donald Rumsfeld is particularly friendly with Frank Carlucci, a former defense secretary who now heads the Carlyle Group, an investment consortium with a large interest in the contracting firm United Defense. Carlyle's Board includes George Bush Sr and James Baker, the former secretary of state. One programme alone – the Crusader artillery system – has already earned Carlyle $2 billion in advance government contracts. John Major, former British prime minister, is Carlyle's European chairman. In late 2002 the British Ministry of Defence decided to declare Carlyle the 'preferred bidder' for a stake in its scientific research division. Dan Briody, in his book *The Iron Triangle*, describes how the Carlyle Group makes massive profits in the security and defense fields.

This all shows the symbiotic relationship between American politics and the corporate interest in the profits to be made from war. The corollary is that US governments are motivated to expand their military adventures, the covert *raison d'être* of a highly militarised society where leading politicians reap financial gain from every new aggression.

The Oil Imperative

It is inevitable in these circumstances that the international oil resource was always part of the picture; the modern military machine runs on oil. At one time the US government was negotiating with the Taliban to protect the oil corridors through Afghanistan. It is of interest that the Taliban, taking their discussions with the United States seriously, went so far as to appoint a public relations expert, Laila Helms, niece of former CIA director Richard Helms, to act on their behalf. At that time some in the US administration viewed the Taliban – known to be guilty of appalling human rights abuses – as a 'source of stability in central Asia', because of their capacity to control the great oil pipeline that might one day run from the rich fields of former Soviet central Asia through Afghanistan to the Indian Ocean.

In July 2002 the Asia Development Bank announced that it would finance a feasibility study for a gas pipeline running from Turkmenistan to Pakistan across Afghanistan. Already the United States had an eye on the possibilities. A US representative was present at the talks, and Washington was reportedly 'highly interested' in US development of the energy resources in the area.'

The United States was also backing the building of a 1075-mile pipeline by a BP-led consortium through Turkey, Georgia and Azerbaijan, that would allow Azeri crude oil to be carried to Western markets. At the same time the US was encouraging a massive increase in oil production in West Africa, and encouraging Nigeria to leave OPEC – to reduce the cartel's control of world oil prices and to broaden the American access to energy around the world. In 1998 John Maresca, vice-president for international relations at the giant energy corporation Unocal, had emphasised to a US House of Representatives committee the importance of the vast gas and oil reserves in the former Soviet republics of central Asia, and had urged US backing to ensure the development of 'appropriate investment climates' and 'economic reforms' in the region.

In June 2001 the United States was conducting a covert war in Macedonia with a keen eye on the strategic Bulgaria-Macedonia-Albania transport, communications and oil pipeline 'corridor' which links the Black Sea to the Adriatic coast. A principal Washington goal was to install a 'patchwork of protectorates' along strategic corridors in the Balkans to protect the pipeline routes. Here and in central Asia a main purpose of US military and economic penetration was to secure access to vast energy resources and – at that time – to reduce American dependence on oil supplies from the volatile Middle East.

The US was intent on controlling world energy resources wherever it could. On 17 May 2000 Kazakhstan went ahead with the controversial sale of a part of its stake in the giant Tengizchevroil (TOC) project to the US oil corporation Chevron, just as US officials were reporting the largest oil find in twenty years in the Caspian Sea off Kazakhstan. Political tensions in the region were rising as it became obvious that Washington was determined to block Iranian and Russian access to the growing oil supply. In July a political scandal erupted when it emerged that President Nazarbayev of Kazakhstan may have been given a substantial part of $35 million paid by three US oil giants for the May oil sale, money that was funnelled to numbered Swiss bank accounts:

The scandal casts light on methods by Western energy titans to carve up drilling rights in the Caspian and on the Kazakh steppe, where total oil and gas reserves may rival those of the Middle East.[15]

In March 2002 it was reported that American special forces troops were active in Kazakhstan, training young Kazakh men who would be expected to protect the growing American energy interests in the region. And it was also of interest that a Texas oil millionaire, Harold Stevens, was drilling for oil in Israel for what he believed could be one of the largest oil deposits in the world.

The Militarised Economy

The US corporate ambitions have been protected by enormous military spending, in 2003 running at a rate of about $400 billion a year. Billions were being spent, with British connivance, on the 'son of Star Wars' project, a technological nonsense supposed to protect the US from missile attacks but more realistically intended to feed cash to corporate America. Donald Rumsfeld decided that not enough attention was being given to US national security in space, linked to the 'Star Wars' caper and another useful trough for profiteers. In early 2001 the US air force was playing space computer games to give them ideas on where the next few billions should be spent.

In February 2002 some indication was given of the intended US expenditures on military equipment for 2003 (at a time when the war on Iraq had supposedly not been costed). Some of the planned items, not an exhaustive list, were given an airing in the public domain:

- Pilotless spyplanes: $1 billion;

- Boeing tail kits that convert unguided freefall bombs into laser-guided bombs: $1.1billion;

- 23 more Raptor combat fighters: $4.6 billion;

- LMC F–35 fighters: $3.5 billion;

- Osprey V22 tilt-rotor aircraft for US Marines: $2 billion;

- Converting Trident submarines, each to carry 150 tomahawk cruise missiles: $1 billion;

- Five ships: $8.6 billion;

- Development of satellite communication systems: $290 million.

This meant that, without specific war decisions, the US intended to spend around $70 billion on equipment alone, more than the entire military spending of any other major power. President Bush was announcing an increase in US military spending of 15 per cent, the biggest in 20 years, more than double the military spend in all of the European Union. The rise would be $36 billion in 2002, $48 billion in 2003 and $120 billion over the next five years, rising to a staggering two trillion dollars – $2,000,000,000,000 – in total. General Richard Myers, judging that this expenditure was insufficient, was urging in his capacity as chairman of the joint chiefs that the US defense budget should expand at an even greater rate.

The media response to these levels of expenditure indicated the sheer extravagance of the US military philosophy:

'Armed to the teeth' ('Is ... he [Bush] creating a force almost too powerful for its own good?');

'Bush to put Americans' money where his mouth is on defense' ('The plan is ... politically hazardous');

'Top gun – and the rest' (Nicholas Burns, US ambassador to NATO: 'Unfortunately our allies have not kept pace with us ... we may no longer have the ability to fight effectively together in the future');

'China claims the US wants world "military supremacy"';

'Pentagon to put general in charge of space.'[16]

On 16 July 2001 President Vladimir Putin and Jiang Zemin, the Chinese leader, signed an alliance to signal their hostility to US global dominance, a situation that was set to become more evident in the years ahead. They stressed that the treaty was 'not directed against any third country', but it obviously highlighted their growing unease at American primacy in international affairs. Putin suggested also that NATO should be abolished and replaced by a pan-European security body that would include Russia. The enlargement of NATO simply meant that the US-dominated organisation was moving ever closer to the Russian borders; 'The divisions will continue until there is a single security area in Europe'. The Sino-Russian agreement, the Good Neighbourly Treaty of Friendship and Co-operation, was bland and largely symbolic. It did nothing to constrain US military dominance or the power of the American economy: in 2000 Sino-Russian trade amounted to $8 billion, that between China and the United States around $115 billion.

The New Privatised Rome

In September 2002 Western pundits were speculating on the orchestrated movement towards a new war, where no state was capable of resisting the momentum of US ambition. Christopher Walker, writing in *The Independent* (15 September 2002), speculated on the United States walking alone – 'and all over us'. Jonathan Freedland (*The Guardian*, 18 September 2002) wondered whether America was 'the new Rome':

> The word of the hour is empire. As the United States marches to war, no other label quite seems to capture the scope of American power or the scale of its ambition ... One last factor scares Americans from making a parallel between themselves and Rome: that empire declined and fell. The historians say this happens to all empires ...
>
> Anti-Americans like to believe that an operation in Iraq might be proof that the US is succumbing to the temptation that ate away at Rome – overstretch. But it's just as possible that the US is merely moving into what was the second phase of Rome's imperial history, when it grew frustrated with indirect rule through allies and decided to do the job itself.

What was clear was that the United States was a 'playground bully',[17] a warmonger and an aggressor, impatient with negotiation and diplomacy, and content only with fulfilling its ambitions through the remorseless application of overwhelming military power. And underlying this essentially brutal posture was the untiring quest for global energy control and the related goal of worldwide corporate dominance.

The US Quadrennial Defense Review (QDR), produced soon after 11 September 2001, identified as one of its main priorities 'access to key markets and strategic resources' by 'precluding hostile domination of critical areas'. The message was plain then as it is plain in 2003. The United States would take what it wanted from whoever possessed it. Blair might plaintively appeal to Washington to listen to the world's fears,[18] scarcely aware that his role was becoming more and more irrelevant.[19] What *was* relevant was the importance of US corporations in White House philosophy, an importance that was leading inexorably to the privatisation of military enterprise.

By 2003 it had become plain that the Pentagon could not go to war without the help of private military contractors — a significant development from the time when private companies supplied military equipment and little else. Today the new military contractors, some even subsidiaries of Fortune 500 companies, have been depicted as 'the new business face of war', blurring 'the line between military and civilian' and providing 'stand-ins for active soldiers in everything from logistical support to battlefield training and military advice.'[20]

In Kuwait some contractors helped to conduct live-ammunition exercise for American troops, while another company was hired to guard President Hamid Karzai of Afghanistan. Some firms have been working under contract as military recruiters and instructors in reserve officers training corps (ROTC) classes, selecting and training the next generation of soldiers. Some private contractors, acting as effective mercenaries, have been asked to work in such places as Bosnia, Nigeria, Macedonia and Colombia. One of these companies, Military Professional Resources Inc. (MPRI), boasts of having 'more generals per square foot than in the Pentagon.'

The military contractors, operating in a market worth $100 billion, say little about their activities to the shareholders but are winning more and more business. Their role is sometimes controversial since their staff are not obligated to take orders from senior officers or to follow military codes of conduct. They are bound solely by their employment contract, with the result that they are empowered to exploit local conditions but are not constrained by traditional lines of command. Employees of US military contractors have been linked to a slave ring of young women in Bosnia, ethnic cleansing in Croatia and to the accidental shooting down of a US missionary in Peru.

MPRI, the most famous military contractor, working for the Pentagon and the State Department, has provided instructors for Fort Leavenworth and the Civil Air Patrol, and has designed courses at Fort Sill, Fort Knox, Fort Lee and other centres. It has even written military doctrine for the Pentagon, including the field manual *Contractors Support on the Battlefield*, detailing how the US Army should interact with private contractors like itself.[21]

In Britain the Ministry of Defence is going down the same route, entering a welter of partnerships with business in the most fundamental shake-up of the military for more than a century. Training, logistics and supply operations are being hived off to big business, now expected to operate in many areas that were formerly assumed to be the state's preserve. Even the management of the armed forces' secret files – covering Northern Ireland, Gulf operations and many sensitive and historic areas – are being handed over to a private contractor. And here it was inevitable that US contractors would become involved.

Halliburton was contracted to rebuild Devonport dockyard in Plymouth. The National Audit Office (NAO) stated in 2002 that the price had escalated from £505 million to £933 million and was expected to increase further. Another case concerned the purchase of US Apache helicopters and a contract given to a private firm to train the pilots. A British officer commented to *The Observer* (2 March 2003): 'The helicopters are ready but there are no pilots. They haven't been trained and I don't think they will be ready for at least three years. This is a shambles. And yet the indications are the ministry is proceeding with wholesale privatisation.'

A Democracy for Export?

A principal alleged aim of US foreign policy is to spread 'democracy' around the world: hence a 'democratic' Iraq would act as a beacon to other states in the Middle East (many observers noted that Washington was happier with dictators or feudal monarchs who could be relied upon than with undisciplined populations who might vote for the wrong people). It is important in such circumstances to glance at the character of American democracy.

George W. Bush himself seized the US presidency in what has widely been perceived as a *coup d'état* facilitated by the Supreme Court. The scene was well set. In the summer of 1999 Katherine Harris, Bush campaign co-chairwoman and secretary of state in charge of elections in the key 'swing state' of Florida, asked Database Technologies to remove anyone 'suspected' of being a former felon from Florida's voter rolls. Thousands of black former felons were quickly deleted from the voter lists – and so were many other people. Those with 'similar' names to known felons, the same birth dates or similar Social Security numbers were also removed from the voter rolls. Database, paid $4 million for its efforts, was told that an 80 per cent match of relevant information was sufficient to strike a voter's name from the rolls. This damaged Al Gore, expected to receive perhaps 90 per cent of these votes, more than George W. Bush – a fact that was well known to Katherine Harris and to Jeb Bush, George's brother and governor of Florida. Some 173,000 legitimate voters in Florida were deleted from the voter lists.

Harris, backed by Jeb Bush, was even more ambitious. Database was encouraged to use a false list supplied by another state. Felons who had been reinstated on the rolls were deleted, as were many people who had only committed misdemeanours – such as parking offences or dropping litter. The net was cast so widely that even Linda Howell, election supervisor of Madison County, received a notification that she would be barred from voting. The upshot was the Bush managed to win 537 more votes than Al Gore, but only after the deletion of likely Gore voters from the election rolls and after various other illegal practices had been tolerated by Katherine Harris. An investigation by *The New York Times* (July 2001) found that 680 flawed votes, most of which went to Bush, were counted, and that there were various other irregularities: undated ballots, overseas ballots postmarked in the US, ballots from unregistered voters, late ballots, and overseas ballots counted twice – amounting in total to more than 800 wrongly counted ballots, mostly for Bush.

When, despite all this, it seemed that Al Gore was gaining on George W. Bush in a mandated recount, the Supreme Court stopped the count and Bush was installed as president. Bush had come to power through illegal ballot-rigging, with Al Gore securing a substantial nationwide majority of the popular vote.[22]

American 'democracy' exhibits many other derelict features, apart from a Supreme Court prepared to underwrite an electoral *coup*. The plutocratic nature of the US system, where wealth shamelessly buys political power, has often been remarked by Americans themselves and by outside observers. It is of interest also that private companies, often declining to submit to software-security checks, are often used to manage computerised voting systems – which, in the typical absence of adequate controls, increases the chances of illegal voting and erroneous results. And then there is the matter of redrawing constituency boundaries.

The process of 'redistricting', the rejigging of district boundaries, is intended to take account of demographic changes to preserve a just distribution of voter numbers. In most countries, where this necessary process takes place, it is controlled by independent bureaucrats, but in every American state it is done by state politicians. In the United States the parties typically 'gerrymander' districts to cram supporters into districts to guarantee party advantage. This, according to one commentary, results in 'absurdly shaped districts: doughnuts, embryos, crabs, Rorschach tests.'[23]

This means that the ruling party generally cheats. For example, in Florida, an evenly divided state, the Republicans have managed to produce 17 Republican seats and eight Democratic ones. But often the two parties make clandestine deals to protect the incumbent politicians. The result is that some seats, like ten in Florida, are so safe that the candidates run unopposed (what was it that the US leaders said about unopposed elections in Iraq?). The law does nothing to stop this fraud; indeed the Voting Rights Act, encouraging majority-minority districts, provides a good excuse for cheating. Thus a bizarre sandwich-like fourth district in Illinois comprises two unconnected strips intended to gather up Democratic Latinos. Some party managers use computer software to determine exactly how the next phase of cheating should be conducted. In such circumstances democracy is reduced to farce.

The character of the American polity is also defined in part by its budgetary priorities. It is significant, though scarcely remarked, that at a time when the United States was spending an annual $400 billion on 'defense' and preparing to wage an illegal war that at conservative estimates would cost $50 billion, New York City was plunging towards bankruptcy.

Day-care centres for the elderly were being closed, inducing pensioners to parade with placards; eight fire stations were due for closure; and no other public services were secure:

> Every city service was on the chopping block: from transport to policing to tree pruning. There are plans to reduce public sector staff in every quarter, cut back on foster care, community education, library hours and family support, and to eliminate 2,500 infant day-care slots.[24]

Subway and bus fares were set to rise, along with zoo admission charges. The scale of unemployment was rising, and the number of homeless on the street was soaring, with countless more sleeping under piles of blankets and cardboard. More than 37,000 people, the highest number on record, were sleeping in New York shelters. The number of homeless families sleeping in shelters had more than doubled since 1998. James Inman, 54 was given a Thanksgiving dinner at a Manhattan mission: 'It's getting steadily worse out there. All the shelters are full.' Cuts to the police force were allowing certain types of violent crime to rise, and education leaders were invited to the mansion of Mayor Mike Bloomberg – known as 'Mike the Knife', elected to run New York like a corporation – to discuss cuts in school budgets at a time when schools were already overcrowded and teachers were struggling with reduced purchasing power.

The City deficit, $1.2 billion, was set to rise by $6.4 billion by 2003 – a trend that was caused in part by Bloomberg's tax policies: an income tax windfall was being introduced to benefit the rich. A person earning $24,000 a year was set to gain $74 on income tax, and to face rent increase of more than $300 after property tax rises had been passed on by the landlords. By contrast, a person earning $180,000 a year, the property-owning average, would see a gain of $1,200. The City Project Group, a budget watchdog, described the Bloomberg package as 'inadequate, irrational and unfair'. Bill de Blasio, a Democratic councillor, commented: 'People are really going to have to get used to doing without.'

One estimate suggested that some 300,000 mentally ill people were incarcerated in US prisons because there was nowhere else for them to go, while prison inmates were being forced – as virtual slave labour – to work for US corporations.[25] The condition of American jails also provided clues to the character of the prevailing culture. Reports from Amnesty International indicate that rape is practised as routine 'punishment', that inmates are tortured with stun-belts and stun-guns, and that suspects often do not have adequate legal representation. In 2003 more than 40 million Americans were without medical insurance, and those with policies were seeing massive increases in their premiums. Under Bush legislation, education was judged to be under-funded by around $6 billion.

One consequence of 11 September 2001 was to intensify these budgetary trends. The Bush administration had never given social services a priority status, but in 2002–3 resources were being diverted in increasing volume to 'homeland security' and preparation for war. A growing number of Muslims were being detained in the United States, to the point that a civil liberties law suit was launched against John Ashcroft, attorney-general.[26] The US policy, with manifest racist overtones, was designed in part to discourage immigration – an aim also of the British government.[27]

Not all US political figures were happy with the policies of the Bush administration. In March 2003 Robert Byrd, 85, the oldest and longest-serving man in the US Congress, denounced his nation's march to war:

> I believe in this beautiful country ... But, today, I weep for my country. I have watched recent events with a heavy, heavy heart ... Around the globe, our friends mistrust us, our word is disputed, our intentions questioned.
>
> Instead of reasoning with those with whom we disagree, we demand obedience or threaten recrimination ... We say the United States has the right to turn its firepower on any corner of the globe which might be suspect in the war on terrorism.
>
> We assert that right without the sanction of any international body. As a result, the world has become a much more dangerous place. We flaunt our superpower status with arrogance. We treat UN Security Council members like ingrates who offend our

princely dignity by lifting their heads from the carpet. Valuable alliances are split ...

What is happening to this country? When did we become a nation which ignores and berates our friends?...How can we abandon diplomacy when the turmoil in the world cries out for diplomacy?...

I pray we somehow recapture the vision which for now eludes us.[28]

Global Ambition

The American ambitions are global and multifaceted: the aim is to achieve 'full spectrum dominance' by whatever means are necessary. Here it is obvious that the sheer extravagance of the American agenda would not be possible without a military capacity that is unrivalled throughout the world and that has no historical precedent.

The scale of the US military capacity has often been described (see also *The Militarised Economy*, above), as has the controversy surrounding it. Observers have noted the illegality of many of America's chosen weapons, while US politicians gather to condemn the arsenals of other countries. We need only mention UN General Assembly resolution 32/84 (12 December 1977) which condemns 'radioactive material weapons ... and any weapons ... which might have characteristics comparable in destructive effect to those of the atomic bomb' – and set this United Nations statement against the American willingness to use depleted-uranium ordnance, which causes cancer and foetal deformity, and fuel-air explosives 'designed to produce nuclear-like levels of destruction without arousing public revulsion' (*The Guardian*, 21 June 1991).

The Americans have now generated a new generation of fuel-air explosives, to yield a 21,000lb high explosive device known as Moab (massive ordnance air blast). Reports suggested that the US air force was already working on a 30,000lb version with a cobalt-alloy body. It is known that fuel-air explosives were used in Afghanistan 'to alter the geography of the mountains', and it is likely they were used against Iraqi troop concentrations in the 2003 war. The Pentagon admitted that Moab had been moved into the Gulf area but would not discuss plans for its use. Some accounts suggested that Moab, equivalent to a tactical nuclear weapon, was destined for use over Tikrit to obliterate Saddam Hussein's home town. We do not yet know whether Moab, tested on 11 March 2003 in Florida, has been used in anger.

To depleted-uranium ordnance and atomic-scale high explosives must be added the American use of cluster bombs, widely judged to be illegal, the field use of toxic gases,[29] and the American preparedness to use nuclear weapons. There is also the 2,000lb Mark-84 Joint Direct Attack Munition (JDAM) bomb, depicted as the 'new workhorse of the US military'. David Wood, writing for the online Newhouse News Service (17 March 2003), describes the effects of this weapon: 'In nanoseconds it will release a crushing shock wave and shower jagged, white-hot metal fragments at supersonic speed, shredding flesh, crushing cells, rupturing lungs, bursting sinus cavities and ripping away limbs in a maelstrom of destruction.' These and other effects were carefully calculated and charted by US Defense Department war planners using a software program called 'Bug Splat', a nice indication of how the Washington strategists regard America's enemies.

The fearsome arsenal of weapons, many of them illegal, is complemented by a growing US military occupation around the world (Figure 10). Some 98,000 US military personnel remain in Europe: 56,000 in Germany; 12,400 in Italy; 9,200 in Britain; and 8,283 spread across Belgium, Greece, the Netherlands, Norway, Portugal, Spain and Turkey. The Mediterranean is patrolled by the US Sixth Fleet, reinforced with 2,000 marines. There are 2,000 US troops in Bosnia's Stabilisation Force; 5,000 in Kosovo; and nearly 1,000 in Hungary and Macedonia. Some 18,000 US personnel are camped in Japan, where the islands also host the Seventh Fleet and 20,000 marines. In South Korea 30,000 US troops guard the border with the North (and help to discourage southern revolts).

There are US naval and air bases on Guam and Diego Garcia, a US surveillance operation in Australia with 100 personnel, and various troop contingents in Thailand, the Philippines and East Timor. American military personnel are camped in Uzbekistan, Tajikistan and Kyrgyzstan, and there are still 7,500 active US troops in Afghanistan. Guantanamo Bay hosts more than 2,200 US troops, a permanent violation of Cuban sovereignty, and American military personnel remain in Qatar, Kuwait, Saudi Arabia, Egypt, Oman and Bahrain. Tens of thousands of US troops are active in Iraq. And there are also US military personnel in Colombia, Honduras, Bermuda, Iceland and the Azores.[30]

The American global ambitions are transparent, yet rarely acknowledged by Western politicians discussing aspects of US foreign policy. George Monbiot, activist and journalist, has drawn attention to the Project for the New American Century, a pressure group established by, among others, Cheney, Rumsfeld, Wolfowitz, Libby, Abrams and Khalilzad – all of them senior officials in the Bush administration (Jeb Bush is also a founder member). On 3 June 1997 these men signed the group's statement of principles, asserting that the key challenge for the United States is 'to shape a new century favourable to American principles and interests', which in turn requires:

> a military that is strong and ready to meet both present and future challenges; a foreign policy that boldly and purposefully promotes American principles abroad; and national leadership that accepts the United States' global responsibilities.[31]

A primary goal, involving a direct appeal to President Clinton, was the removal of Saddam Hussein – otherwise 'the safety of American troops in the region, of our friends and allies like Israel and the moderate Arab states, and a significant portion of the world's supply of oil will all be put at hazard'. The group further declared that the 'American policy cannot continue to be crippled by a misguided insistence on unamity in the UN Security Council'. The United Nations should be ignored and Iraq would not be the end of the matter. A subsequent confidential report produced by the Project in September 2000 declared that Saddam Hussein would offer an excuse for a US military expansion in the region: 'While the unresolved conflict with Iraq provides the immediate justification, the need for a substantial American force presence in the Gulf transcends the issue of the regime of Saddam Hussein'.[32]

The attitude was plain. Another document, written by Wolfowitz and Libby, called upon the United States to 'discourage advanced industrial nations from challenging our leadership or even aspiring to a larger regional or global role'. The Project had already asserted that the wider strategic aim was 'maintaining global US prominence'. From Bush's first week in office 'he began to engage not so much in nation-building as in planet-building'.[33] In the same vein Michael Ledeen, a former US

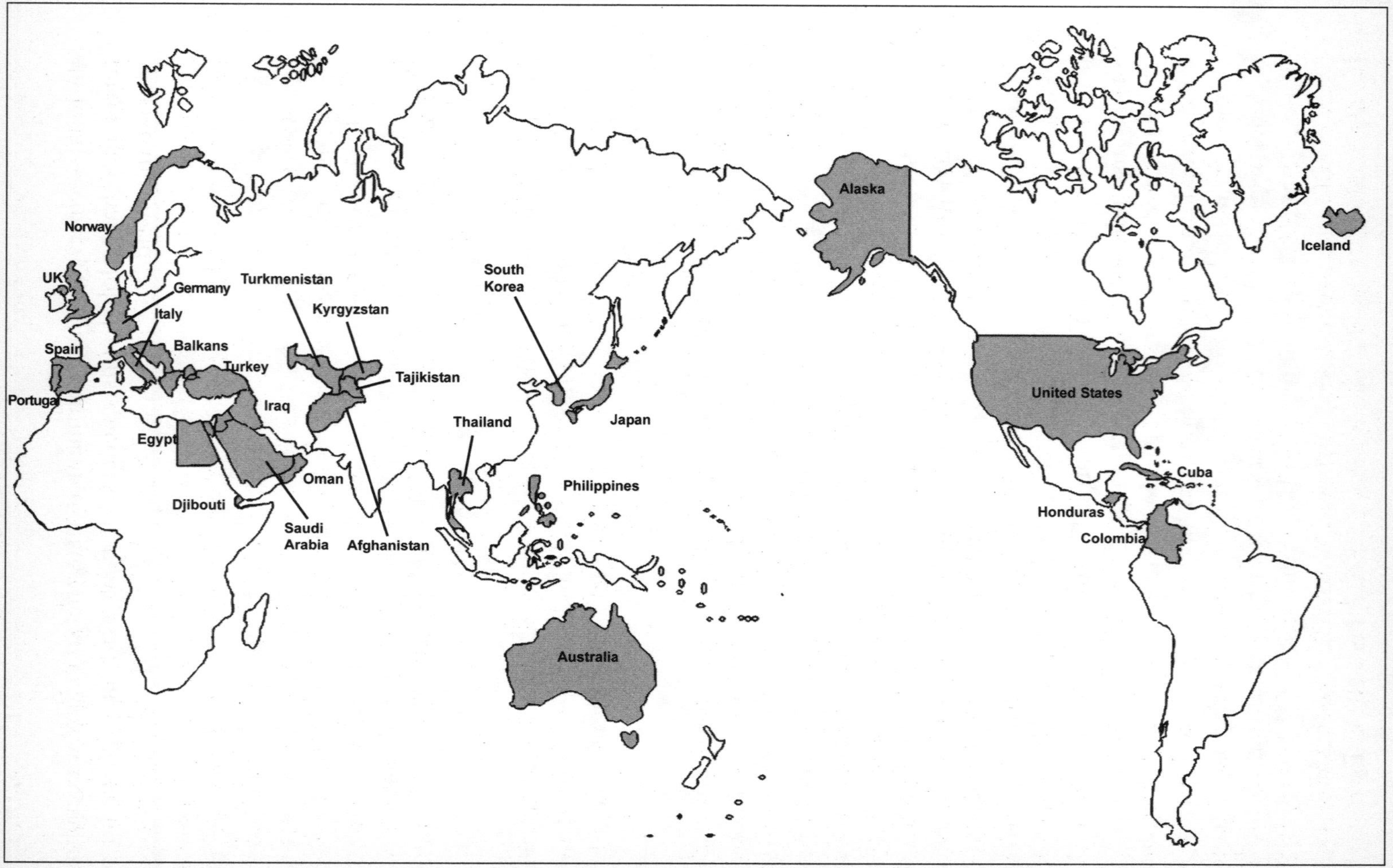

Figure 10. US Military Occupation Around the World

national security official, commented that the so-called war against terror may have global consequences: 'It may turn out to be a war to remake the world.'[34]

PART FOUR

The Future

THIRTEEN

Signposts

The aftershocks of the 2003 war reverberated around the world, with uncertain long-term consequences not only for Iraq but for the entire international community. Some pundits, commenting during the war, had already made important predictions – and been proved wrong by events. Thus Scott Ritter, a former UN weapons inspector and US intelligence officer, was interviewed on 25 March 2003 by Vincent Browne for Irish radio:

> *Ritter*: 'We now find we are being greeted with bullets and bombs ... It's the Shia in the south who are fighting us ... They're doing it because the American Crusader infidel has invaded and violated Holy Iraq ... no matter how many Iraqis we kill and slaughter, I predict that America will lose this war and ultimately the American military will leave Iraq with its tail between its legs ...'

> *Browne*: 'You think the Americans will lose this war?'

Ritter: '... we find ourselves with fewer than 120,000 boots on the ground, facing a nation of 23 million, with armed elements numbering around 7 million, who are concentrated at urban areas. We will not win this fight. America will lose this war ... I'm betting that we don't capture Baghdad. I'm betting that we stall outside Baghdad. I'm betting that this becomes an absolute quagmire ... Remember I'm a 12-year veteran of the Marine Corps. I fought in the first Gulf War. I know what war is about ...'[1]

In the same vein the journalist Simon Jenkins, normally a perceptive observer of events, predicted that Baghdad would be 'near impossible to conquer':

In Baghdad the coalition forces confront a city apparently determined on resistance. They should remember Napoleon in Moscow, Hitler in Stalingrad, the Americans in Mogadishu and the Russians at Grozny. Hostile cities have ways off making life ghastly for aggressors ... cities level the logistical playing field. Bombers are useless in house-to-house fighting. Helicopters become targets, not weapons. Every building is a fortress, every adult a suspect.[2]

However, we soon learned that Baghdad was effectively conquered ('liberated' in the parlance of US–UK propaganda), though by June 2003 not rendered completely secure or properly functional. The American commitment to war-making had not translated well into a determination to prevent looting, to police the streets of the Iraqi urban centres or to provide such essentials as water and electricity to the Iraqi people. And how and when would the Western military occupation yield to the promised democracy at the heart of the Arab world?

Towards Democracy

The war has devastated Iraq, not least its priceless cultural heritage. Baghdad museums unprotected by coalition forces had been looted, and in one estimate some 170,000 artefacts – a unique record of past civilisations – were missing. To some observers it seemed particularly significant that British and American troops were actually encouraging the looting.[3] One senior British officer, seemingly welcoming the social anarchy, commented that the looting 'sends a powerful message that the old guard is truly finished'. It was left to UN officials to rebuke the British commanders for encouraging local residents to loot official buildings – behaviour that was an abuse of the Hague Regulations and the Geneva Convention. But were the coalition forces encouraging the looting as a simple reprisal against the erstwhile Ba'athist regime, or was there also another agenda?

Perhaps the Washington strategists were intent on destroying Iraqi culture as a way of damaging the historical pride of a national people. The Israeli forces invading West Bank towns took pains to attack the Palestinian educational infrastructure, even to the point of destroying school records and children's paintings on classroom walls – as if to deny the Palestinians a national identity. There are clues that the American war planners had the same intention with regard to Iraq.

The US Air Force chief, General Michael Dugan, presented with a conventional list of Iraqi military targets for the 1991 war, declared: 'That's not enough'. It was important also to target 'what is unique about Iraqi culture that they put a very high value on'; it was important to know what it was 'that psychologically would make an impact on the population and regime'.[4] Throughout the 1991 war, as in April–May 2003, there was massive plunder of Iraq's archaeological treasures, not least by US troops. The archaeologist Dr Muayid Damirji, editor of the Iraqi journal *Akkad*, claimed that American soldiers had made their own bayonet excavations to obtain ancient artefacts.[5] According to Damirji, thousands of antiquities had been looted from Iraqi museums as a result of the war. In 1993 reports appeared in the Western press indicating that Iraqi artefacts were being acquired by private collections in the United States.[6] How long will it be before similar reports tell of the private acquisition of the Iraqi artefacts plundered in 2003?

On 5 May 2003 Major-General Tim Cross, a British collaborator with Jay Garner in the post-Saddam Iraq, admitted in a BBC radio interview that most Iraqis did not have electricity, drinkable water or hospitals with adequate resources (babies were still being delivered in the dark and without appropriate medical support).[7] The Iraqis were better off, explained Cross, because they could speak freely. Reports suggested that civilians had been targeted in the war and that the hospitals were not coping with the resulting flow of casualties. Thus human-rights worker Jo Wilding, after more than six weeks in Baghdad, decided on the basis of her investigations to come to the conclusion 'that the US and the UK have been deliberately targeting civilians, perhaps in the hope that they will take things into their own hands and remove Saddam themselves.'[8] In the same vein the Red Cross had reported 'horrific' conditions in the only Baghdad hospital to which they had managed to gain access.[9] Inadequate clean water, electricity failures and problems with sewage had created havoc in the city's hospitals. With the funding ambiguities and countless other practical difficulties it would obviously be many months before the civic infrastructure, punished by war and more than a decade of sanctions, would be brought up to acceptable modern standards.

On 12 April it had been revealed that Halliburton, whose former head was Dick Cheney, stood to make more than $7 billion rebuilding Iraq's oilfields.[10] The 'battle to rebuild' Iraq was already joined, with US and British companies – dubbed by some observers 'ambulance chasers' – determined to win whatever pickings were available.[11] But the doubts remained that the US–UK occupying forces could accomplish anything more than the creation of a puppet regime determined to allocate lucrative contracts to US-friendly corporations and to guarantee political plans approved in Washington. Thus Naomi Klein, writing in *The Guardian* (London, 14 April 2003), asked: 'When does reconstruction turn into privatisation?' The point is well made:

> Some argue that it's too simplistic to say this war is about oil. They're right. It's about oil, water, roads, trains, phones, ports and drugs. And if this process isn't halted, 'free Iraq' will be the most sold country on earth.
>
> It's no surprise that so many multinationals are lunging for Iraq's untapped market ... the reconstruction will be worth as much as $100 billion ...
>
> After all, negotiations with sovereign countries can be hard. Far easier to just tear up the country, occupy it, then rebuild it the way you want ... Pretty soon, the US may have bombed its way into a whole new trade zone.

The process will be aided by writing off much of Iraq's national debt (the 'odious debt' discussed earlier), by abolishing the residual elements of Ba'athist propaganda in schools and elsewhere and installing a new system of pro-West indoctrination. Teachers will be retrained, textbooks rewritten, and ideologues imported from US-friendly states to help the process along. Companies from states perceived as sympathetic to American ambitions – Britain, Spain, Italy, Australia – will be allowed opportunities in the new world order; firms from other countries – France, Russia, Germany – will be frozen out.

The United States will continue to talk about 'democracy' while its real ambitions are developed beneath the surface of public discourse. There was little in the war, its outcome or its aftermath to discourage Washington's ideological hawks, encouraged thereby to contemplate further manifestations of US power. They would certainly not be discouraged by the relatively light level of US casualties or the substantially higher levels of Iraqi deaths and maiming. In the second half of April 2003 reports confirmed that for Iraq's children the agony caused by war was continuing. In one week at least six children wounded by cluster bombs were taken to the Kadhimiya hospital in Baghdad, but the failure of the telephone system had made it impossible to compute the total number of child and other casualties in Baghdad or in Iraq as a whole.

On about 15 April the five-year-old Ali Mustafa picked up a cluster bomb, one of the thousands that remain lying around Baghdad. When it exploded he was blinded and his legs were scarred with shrapnel; his legs were expected to heal but young Ali would not see again. His mother, Ghaleb, commented: 'I have two wounded children, and two neighbours also have this tragedy.' In one hospital a doctor said of a child with a brain tumour:

> He needs chemotherapy. How can we provide it now? We still have the basics in the store ... we will run out in a few weeks. We need everything – gauze, cotton, gloves, silk for stitching, needles, X-ray film. We will not accept the United States or Britain as occupiers, because the conditions here are miserable.[12]

In the April–May period several of Baghdad's hospitals remained closed because of power shortages, the lack of clean water and the absence of staff because of transport problems and street crime. As Dr al-Sadoon commented on the death of a child in his hospital:

> The parents live 50km from Baghdad. Before the war they could have gone 5km to a local children's clinic, but it's closed because of the lack of electricity. So parents leave it to the final stage before they bring the child here, and often it's too late. This one could have been saved.[13]

The hospitals, much like the museums, had been looted and vandalised. On 18 April two cultural advisors to the Bush administration, Martin Sullivan and Gary Vikan, resigned in protest at the US military's failure, despite many warnings of looting, to protect Iraq's archaeological treasures. Vikan, noting how US forces had rushed to safeguard Iraqi oil, said: 'We certainly know the value of oil but we certainly don't know the value of historical artefacts.' Among the many priceless treasures missing were the 5000-year-old Vase of Uruk, the Harp of Ur and the bronze Statue of Basitki from the ancient Akkadian Kingdom (this latter hauled out of the museum despite its huge weight).

Now tens of thousands of protestors, led by the Sunni Muslim scholar Ahmed al-Kubaisi, were demonstrating against the US-led occupation of their country. On 18 April hundreds of thousands of Iraqi Shi'ites began their pilgrimage to the holy cities of Najaf and Karbala, heralding an Islamic resurgence and the prospect of schism in the largest religious group in the country.[14] It was now clear that substantial parts of the Sunni and Shi'ite communities were opposed to the presence of US–UK troops. Sunnis and Shi'ites, perhaps newly conscious of their shared Islamic roots, were even prepared to march together chanting: 'No to Bush, no to Saddam, yes to Islam. Leave our country, we want peace'. The American nightmare – mounting pressure for the creation of an Islamic state – was manifest on the streets of Baghdad and elsewhere.[15]

   The American occupation forces had little interest in restoring order or providing reliable electricity or drinkable water for the bulk of the Iraqi civilian population:

> General faces uphill task to restore water.[16]

This occupation is a disaster. The US must leave – and fast.[17]

Without the promised money, Iraq will become another Haiti.[18]

The US priorities were plain. Reports suggested that the oil was already flowing again, and the Washington strategists were planning a long-term military presence in Iraq. And there were hints that the United States would soon be ready to focus on the problem associates with other states in the region – Iran, Saudi Arabia and Syria. Plans for a 'democratic Iraq' were being developed, though it was widely assumed that these would exclude the long-banned Iraqi Communist Party, the emergence of an Islamic state, a reconstituted Ba'athist Party and adequate representation for women.[19]

Hans Blix, the UN chief weapons inspector, was now criticising the pre-war efforts of British and American propagandists to establish that the Iraq had weapons of mass destruction. If Washington continued to block the return of the mandated inspectors any weapons finds in post-war Iraq would lack credibility: 'We may not be the only ones in the world who have credibility, but I do think we have credibility for being objective and independent'. In a BBC radio interview Blix had already declared that the coalition forces had used 'shaky' evidence, including forged documents, as a pretext for making war on Iraq. It was, said Blix, 'very, very disturbing' that US intelligence had failed to identify forged documents as fake, while British officials were admitting that documents purporting to show that Iraq had tried to buy uranium from Niger were forgeries: 'Is it not disturbing that the intelligence agencies that should have all the technical means at their disposal did not discover this was falsified?'

There were fresh uncertainties about what role the United Nations would be allowed in the new Iraq. Washington was already violating the terms of Security Council resolution 1441 by refusing to permit the return of the weapons inspectors. What would happen to the mandated sanctions on Iraq and the 'oil for food' arrangements? How long would it be before an Iraqi administration would be able to run the Iraqi economy? On 5 May Jay Garner was asserting that a new Iraqi authority, including some former exiles, would soon be established, though how the actual individuals had emerged was a mystery. The Americans had vetted every candidate, and the new authority would be answerable to the occupation forces. It was obvious that the initial hesitant step in handing over power to the Iraqi people had nothing to do with democracy.

There were now further signs that resistance to the US occupation would grow. In the small town of Kut, where 10,000 British troops had been surrounded and killed in the First World War, people declared that only Iraqi traitors would collaborate with US forces in the post-Saddam Iraq. Then, on 25 April, the police station burned down while hundreds of Iraqis were guarding the gates of the governor's office, trying to ensure that no Americans entered the official buildings; they chanted 'NO, NO TO AMERICA! NO, NO TO ISRAEL! YES, YES TO UNITY! YES, YES TO ISLAM!' At the same time rival political parties were seizing former government buildings in Baghdad and declaring themselves open for business.

On 28 April about 250 leaders of Iraq's political and ethnic groupings assembled at a US-sponsored meeting in Baghdad and agreed to participate in a conference to choose an interim government. The meeting, protected by US troops and tanks, was long on symbolism and short on concrete results. Jay Garner was happy to display his grasp of Iraqi history: 'It is very humbling for me to be here before you, because the blood in your veins, in your land, gave force to civilisation. Society as we know it began in this land.' It was not clear how any of the delegates had been selected, or what support they enjoyed in Iraq. None of the participants seemed likely to emerge as a head of state, and the conference appeared to impress few ordinary Iraqis in Baghdad. One, Tariq Jalil, spoke of the exiles who had rushed back to Baghdad to fill the power vacuum: 'I would not vote for any of them. Exiles don't deserve to rule – they don't know the country, they have not suffered. Among our own people, the best ones are not interested in power.'

In Fallujah US troops fired on anti-American demonstrators, causing dozens of casualties.[20] To many observers such events did not resemble the much-heralded 'liberation' of the Iraqi people. In Moscow President Putin was reminding Prime Minister Tony Blair that the only alleged reason for the war was the danger posed by Saddam's weapons programme: 'Two weeks later they still have not been found ... Where are those weapons of mass destruction, if they were ever in existence? Is Saddam Hussein in a bunker sitting on cases containing weapons of mass destruction, preparing to blow the whole place up?'

In early May President Bush was reportedly preparing to appoint Paul Bremer, a career diplomat, as Iraq's senior civil administrator. Bremer was being appointed to report to the White House over the head of Jay Garner, who would remain in post as part of the rebuilding effort. What did this say about Garner's efforts to date? Why was a new appointment necessary? It was known that the Bremer was a hawkish State Department veteran, a *protégé* of Henry Kissinger and former managing director of Kissinger Associates. Kissinger himself commented that Bremer would help the US sort out 'the relationship between the need for order and the evolution that will take place toward pluralistic democracy ... relations with other departments of government become important, as well as a knowledge of how other countries react and an understanding of the various political currents in Iraq'. Did Jay Garner lack the subtleties needed to cope with the complexities of post-Saddam Iraq? Or did the new appointment merely signal the next phase in the turf war between the Pentagon and the State Department?

In a matter of days the US forces had dissipated much of the goodwill that might have been generated by the overthrow of the Saddam regime. The Washington strategists had focused on the needs of the military campaign and little else, seemingly unable to comprehend that an anarchic, lawless and lethal peace would be unlikely to stimulate enthusiasm for the US-led occupation. The thousands of civilian deaths caused by the collapsing health system – with overburdened hospitals deprived of clean water, electricity, drugs and staff; by the soaring disease levels caused by the desperate urban resort to polluted rivers; and by unexploded ordnance and landmines – none of this was being adequately addressed by the occupying powers. In one report the lethal residue of war – mines, shells, cluster bombs – had killed or maimed more people, many of them children, since the end of the war than during the fighting.[21] Thus Sean Sutton, of the UK-based Mines Advisory Group, commented: 'We are facing an emergency situation. Across Iraq, the detritus of war is killing, maiming and scarring for life adults and, most tragically, children.'

The occupation was widely perceived as a hated colonial presence, tolerated by the US-approved Iraqi appointees who coveted political power but despised by large sections of the Iraqi population:

The gaping hole in Iraq (No, this war is far from over. Indeed, when you consider the combustible elements now in play – a blundering, tactless foreign occupier confronting a nation surging with Islamic fervour – this battle may be just beginning.)[22]

Bloodshed and bullets fuel rising hatred of Americans.[23]

Iraqi cities seethe as trigger-happy troops blow away local goodwill.[24]

Such matters were helping to define the shape of things to come.

On 5 May 2003 the US named five Iraqis appointed to form the nucleus of a provisional government: Ahmad Chalabi (INC), Massoud Barzani, Jalal Talabani, Ayad Allawi (INA) and Abdul Aziz al-Hakim (whose brother headed the SCIRI, the Iran-based Shi'ite group). Jay Garner, soon to be replaced, commented: 'The five opposition leaders have begun having meetings and they are going to bring in leaders from inside Iraq, and see if we can't form the nucleus of leadership as we enter into June.' At the same time there was concern that the Americans were being forced to rely on the Ba'athist infrastructure, with Chalabi declaring that 30,000 senior party members should be blacklisted.

By mid-May UN observers were judging that much of the Iraqi population would face starvation in the summer months. A special study prepared by the Food and Agriculture Organisation had revealed a 'catastrophe in the making' (*The Observer*, 11 May 2003): government warehouses that would have provided seeds, fertilisers and pesticides had been bombed and looted; pumping stations that powered vital irrigation systems were no longer working; no seeds were being planted and in any case there was no longer any mechanism in place for purchasing the yield; animal vaccines, drugs and medicines had been destroyed or looted; thousands of poultry had starved to death because there was nobody to feed them. On 10 May American efforts to get Iraq's Health Ministry up and running descended into farce when it was revealed that the new Minister had been a key figure in the Saddam regime.

The food supplies had been disrupted, hospitals had been bombed and looted, and medical staff were struggling to cope in impossible circumstances. Dr Mofawa Gorea, working in Chuwada Hospital, Baghdad, reported that about 150 casualties a day were being taken in, 'the same as during the war'. Basia Zukheir, ripped open by an unexploded US cluster bomb, was typical of dozens of mutilated Iraqi civilians forced to endure surgery in hospitals without clean water or anaesthetics. The ayatollah Muhammad Baqr al-Hakim, having returned to Iraq from a 23-year exile, was touring the country demanding that the US-led forces leave Iraq. In Samawa some 60,000 people greed him with chants of –

YES! YES FOR ISLAM! NO AMERICANS! NO SADDAM!

It seemed obvious that American efforts to restore basic services, to impose order and to introduce 'representative' government were a dismal failure. Barbara Bodine, the 'mayor' of Baghdad, was being ordered home to America, and Jay Garner's three-month stint was being cut short. The neoconservative Paul Bremer, formerly the State Department's counter-terrorism chief, was taking over from Garner in a 'bloodless coup' (*The Times*, 13 May 2003). Such a panic move advertised the American post-Saddam failures for all to see, where even the treatment of mass graves south of Baghdad was seen as demonstrating the Americans' inability to impose order: vital forensic evidence had been inadvertently destroyed by desperate relatives, making possible future trials of responsible Ba'athist officials less likely to succeed. Baghdad and much of Iraq was in chaos, causing an unreckoned toll of the civilian population. All the government buildings – ministries, banks, museums, schools – had been looted, and homes were being targeted, forcing families to purchase weapons for defence. Abdul Hajid, a retired bank manager, was typical of many: 'I've never had a gun in my house in my whole life … but I have to protect myself and my family. What choice do I have?' Bremer, despite unconvincing denials, was reportedly introducing a policy of 'shoot to kill' in a desperate attempt to restore order. At the same time the Americans, in a dramatic volte-face, were said to be committed to the Chalabi insistence that 30,000 senior Ba'athists be banned from any future jobs.

On 17 May the US-UK plans to rebuild Iraq were descending into further chaos as officials admitted that they had scrapped plans for a transitional government and Spain revealed a massive hole in the available funding for reconstruction (*The Observer*, 18 May 2003). There seemed no prospect for an early transfer of power to an Iraqi administration, even of the puppet variety favoured by Washington. The US was seeking United Nations authorisation for a seemingly indefinite Western control of Iraq (see *Bellum Americanum*, below), and it appeared that there would be no end to the suffering of Iraqi people.

The Iranian Influence

Agitation among the Iraqi Shi'ites for an Islamic state was deeply worrying to the United States, not least because they constituted the largest sector of Iraqi society and because to the Washington planners the idea of an Islamic society necessarily evoked images of fundamentalist terrorism and 11 September. An initial US response was to suggest that the Iraqi Shi'ites were being influenced by infiltrators from Iran, itself a predominantly Shi'ite society and part of President Bush's famous 'axis of evil'. In fact, there had always been Iranians (Persians) in Iraq, a consequence of trade and war over centuries.

A British census of 1919, carried out on the eve of the formation of the Iraqi monarchy, suggested that there were then around 80,000 Persians in Iraq.[25] Arnold Wilson, the British acting civil commissioner, noted the large number of Persian consular officers present 'in every town and village of every size', and suggested that any unnecessary posts be allowed to lapse. With Persians comprising some 75 percent of Karbala's population, British policy was to reinforce the Arab features of the city's culture and to establish Arabic as the language of British administration. What was perceived as the problem of undue Persian influence was set to continue through the period of the Iraqi monarchy and beyond.[26] The issue encountered by the British occupiers during the ill-fated rule of the Hashemites was confronted anew by the US-led occupiers in 2003.

On 23 April 2003 the United States accused Iran of sending agents into southern Iraq to foster a like-minded Shi'ite regime. Thus Ari Fleischer, President Bush's spokesman, commented: 'We've made it clear to Iran that we would oppose any outside interference in Iraq's road to democracy. Infiltration of agents to destabilise the Shi'ite population would clearly fall into that category.' US officials said that they feared

Iranian agents were trying to foment an Islamic revolution: 'They are telling people that the Americans don't have staying power ... when they leave we'll still be here. We're your co-religionists. We hold the key to your future.' Thousands of Shi'ites had poured into Iraqi streets to welcome the end of Saddam's rule, but many had chanted 'DEATH TO AMERICA!' and demanded an end to the US occupation.

Jay Garner had admitted that the levels of anti-American protest were higher than he had anticipated, and blamed the Iranians: 'It concerns me the role I heard Iran is playing. I will be candid. I do not think the coalition will accept out-of-region influence.' By May, Shi'ite clerics had taken *de facto* control in districts, towns and cities all over Southern Iraq, as well as large parts of the capital. In all the Shi'ite demonstrations condemnation of the Ba'athist regime was accompanied by calls for the US forces to leave the country. The American response was to assert that Iraq would not be permitted to become a theocracy. Thus on 24 April Donald Rumsfeld, US Defense Secretary, declared: 'If you're asking how would we feel about an Iranian-type government with a few clerics running everything in the country, the answer is: That isn't going to happen.'[27] One Shi'ite merchant, the 41-year-old Kassem al-Sa'adi, responded: 'I thought the Americans said they wanted a democracy in Iraq. If it is a democracy, why are they allowed to make the rules?' It was obvious that Washington was alarmed by the Shi'ite displays of religious commitment and political ambition:

> For some, who watched from afar the processions, the blood [self-scourging] and the anti-American slogans, this eruption of religious feeling came as a shock. To the State Department it was hideously familiar. Iran was swept by a revolution [in 1979] in which religious extremism was harnessed to a burning resentment of Western, and especially American, influence. Already, nervous State Department officials speak about being 'unprepared' for such demonstrations, while more hawkish members of the Administration are giving warning that they will not tolerate any attempt to hijack Iraq's nascent democracy or set up a theocratic state.[28]

On 2 May 2003 hundreds of thousands of worshippers in the Shi'ite heart of Baghdad were exhorted by their spiritual leaders not to absorb the Western habits which were designed to 'harm Islam'. At the Friday prayers some leading Shi'ite clerics offered their vision of a future Iraq: alcohol would be banned, women would be covered from head to foot and Islamic scholars would run education at every level. Sheikh Mohammed Fartowzi, formerly detained by US forces, led prayers at the Mussehn mosque in a Baghdad suburb and declared that US troops should leave Iraq 'as soon as possible'. The main preacher, Sheikh Jaber al-Khafaji, denounced the Americans for presenting 'unacceptable gifts' to Muslim women and for encouraging the looting: 'Don't follow the law and regulations of the West. Follow the law and regulations of the Prophet, of Islam. Don't imitate Western people. Be pure Muslims.'

Here was another recipe for future turmoil – the mounting tensions between the upsurge in Islamic ambition and the determination of Washington to prevent the creation of a theocratic state. It seemed increasingly likely that Jay Garner's Iraqi appointees, none enjoying obvious public support, would soon be in serious confrontation with a Muslim majority unwilling to tolerate Western diktat.

The Arab Options

The Arab states were allowed few political options before the 2003 war and few in the post-Saddam era. Some – Kuwait, Qatar, Oman – abandoned any pretence at independent statehood and succumbed to US military occupation. Others – Egypt, Jordan, Saudi Arabia – chose to co-operate with the United States but to keep quiet about it. And some – Syria, Libya, Yemen – adopted an anti-war posture that would bode ill for the future. Syria was soon being warned of unspecified 'consequences' if it persisted in non-cooperation with US foreign policy, Saudi Arabia wondered if it would be next and Libya was trapped in a range of circumstances that made it a likely US target in the future.

Qatar, reluctant to antagonise the megapower, had agreed to become the permanent centre for American air operations in the Gulf – a development that was likely to reduce some of the domestic Islamic pressures in Saudi Arabia. Qatar was gambling that its future lay in modernising and courting the West, even if this meant a rift with the more conservative Arab states in the region. Thus General Tommy Franks declared that 'for the unforeseeable future', the US air operations in the Gulf would be based in Qatar. It was not long before Washington announced the end of its 12-year military presence in Saudi Arabia, heralding profound shift in US strategy for the region. According to Rumsfeld, the decision had been reached 'by very mutual agreement' and on military grounds. There was no question that the move would diminish US hegemony in the Gulf. The United States would still have military bases in Qatar, Bahrain and the United Arab Emirates, and a return to Saudi Arabia could always be demanded. Thus Paul Wolfowitz, Rumsfeld's deputy, commented:

> We maintain a close defence relationship with Saudi Arabia, whether or not we have forces there. I don't think either of us want to give up the capability to come back if and when we are needed.[29]

However, some Saudis, less than wholly convinced by Rumsfeld's 'very mutual agreement', were entertaining darker thoughts. Perhaps the Washington strategists were wondering about 'regime change' in the kingdom itself, as a route to achieving the control of Saudi oil at source. Perhaps Syria and Iran were more likely US targets for the immediate future, but after that? What if Israeli requirements pointed to 'reform' or 'regime change' in Saudi Arabia? How would the Bush administration respond to pressure from the Jewish lobby? It was certainly the case that Saudi Arabia was providing support for the Palestinians – anathema to Israel. The Saudi royals would need to assess the new Iraq scene with care. If the Iraqis began a war of liberation against the US-led occupation, whom should Riyadh support? To assist a Western colonial presence would stimulate domestic radicalism in the kingdom – precisely what the House of Saud was trying to avoid; but to back an Iraqi revolt would encourage a US-orchestrated regime change in Saudi Arabia.[30]

The Saudi regime believed that in the short term it would remain secure, then unaware of the imminent terrorist bombing raids set to shake the kingdom. Syria was in America's sights. Israel, always guaranteed US attention, was listing its demands on the Assad regime,[31] and Washington was soon amplifying this message to Damascus.[32] Syria was still calling for an end to the US-led occupation of Iraq, at the same time dismissing Rumsfeld's charges that Damascus was continuing to aid the Iraqi Ba'athists in various ways. Patrick Seale, a British expert on Syria, commented: 'The President of Syria had adopted a very tough line from the beginning and I think he will resist very strongly any form of intimidation. His aim is to remain in tune with domestic and Arab public opinion.' Such a posture seemed guaranteed to antagonise Washington: the long-term position of the Assad regime seemed less than secure.

On 12 May 2003 the expatriate housing complex in Riyadh, the Saudi capital, was rocked by bomb blasts which killed about 30 people and wounded nearly 200. There was early confirmation that the bombings, linked to the al-Qa'ida network, had killed seven Americans, seven Saudis, two Jordanians, two Filipinos, one Lebanese, one Swiss and the nine attackers. George Bush commented: 'These despicable acts were committed by killers whose only faith is hate. And the United States will find the killers and they will learn the meaning of American justice ... we will be on the hunt.'

Soon there were suggestions that the Bush administration, preoccupied with Iraq, had taken its eye off al-Qa'ida, and that the US campaign against the Saddam regime had stimulated further terrorist activity. Thus Sa'ad al-Fagih, a London-based Saudi dissident and director of the Movement for Islamic Reform in Arabia, declared that the American occupation of Iraq had 'invaded the brains and hearts of many Muslims and Arabs and replaced all the other reasons for hostility to America'. It seemed that the Saudi failure to guarantee the security of the expatriate communities had stimulated fresh anti-Saudi feeling in the United States. Was the House of Saud rapidly becoming a candidate for early regime change?

On 18 May various members of the American Enterprise Institute, interviewed for the BBC-televised *Panorama* programme, asserted the need for regime change throughout the Middle East. Various states were mentioned, including Libya. It is useful to glance at the case of the Qadhafi regime since it seems to mirror many of the features that the American Right cited in justification for the invasion and occupation of Iraq.

The United States has made many charges against Tripoli, and a number of the cited issues – Qadhafi's response to the Lockerbie outrage, Libya's alleged chemical weapons, Qadhafi's continued support for terrorism, UN–US sanctions against Libya – have remained unresolved. None of these are crucial matters to Washington but all could be used to frame a rationale for a US military initiative that would involve the toppling of the Qadhafi regime.

Qadhafi's attempts to appease the United States have only been partly successful, not least because Libya, at a comfortable geographical distance from Iraq and Palestine, has felt able to criticise American foreign policy. But the future of Libya, in particular the future of the Qadhafi regime, will not be set mainly by decisions taken in Tripoli. Libya has remained a thorn in the side of the megapower, and Washington will respond when it chooses.

There are several reasons why a US military attack on Libya seems likely over the next decade, since many of the factors that stimulated a US invasion of Iraq are present also in the case of Libya:

— Libya, like Iraq, contains abundant oil and gas resources – a tempting prize under the circumstances of an expanding, energy-hungry economy and diminishing yields from existing fields;

— Libya, like Iraq, is strategically well-sited – offering the benefits of an expanded US hegemony in the Mediterranean, already policed by the Sixth Fleet; proximity to an unstable Algeria riven by Islamic fundamentalism, and proximity to an unstable Egypt run by the Mubarak dictatorship.

— Libya is run by a recalcitrant regime, as was Iraq, manifestly hostile to crucial elements of American foreign policy – a bad example to the region;

— US control of Libyan oil would establish an enlarged American control over important elements of the European economy, allowing Washington a stranglehold over key sectors of European industry – just as US control over the oil tankers plying the Gulf could be used to strangle key sectors of the Japanese economy.

Hence the United States has a number of powerful reasons for wanting to take over the Libyan economy and to establish an expanded presence in North Africa.

The Arab world has limited options in confrontation with American ambition. Most regimes in the area have decided on appeasement: recalcitrant independence seems to guarantee a menacing criticism from Washington, to be followed in due course by military action.

The Israeli/Palestinian Tragedy

There was nothing in the 2003 war or its aftermath to constrain the Israeli oppression of the Palestinians in the Occupied Territories. The occasional suicide bomb, entirely counterproductive in political terms, was being used to justify the daily abuse of Palestinians as a route to expanding the local hegemony of a Zionist state. And Israel, like the United States, had its eye on the massive Iraqi oil resources. After the war discussions were held between Washington, Tel Aviv and potential future leaders of Baghdad on how Israel might benefit from Iraqi oil.[33]

The plan was to reconstruct an old pipeline, inactive since the end of the British mandate in Palestine in 1948, when oil from Iraq's northern fields was redirected to Syria. At a stroke, the US-dominated Iraq would win extra revenues, Syrian access to Iraqi oil would be blocked, and Israel's energy crisis would be solved. Until 1948 the pipeline ran from Mosul to Haifa on Israel's northern Mediterranean coast, and in 2003 a similar arrangement was an obvious possibility. The scheme was first openly discussed by Joseph Paritsky, Israeli minister for national infrastructures, according to the Israeli newspaper *Ha'aretz*, while one former senior CIA official admitted:

> It has long been a dream of a powerful section of the people now driving this [Bush] administration and the war in Iraq to safeguard Israel's energy supply as well as that of the United States. The Haifa pipeline was something that existed, was resurrected as a dream and is now a viable project – albeit with a lot of building to do.[34]

The implementation of the scheme would require good relations between Israel and the new puppet regime in Baghdad, and the US State Department had already declared that a peace treaty with Israel was 'top of the agenda' for the new Baghdad government. Ahmad Chalabi, INC head, was known to have discussed with American officials an Iraqi recognition of the state of Israel. In the mid–1980s a Kissinger plan was to run an oil pipeline from Iraq to Aqaba in Jordan, opposite the Israeli port of Eilat. The plan, promoted by Donald Rumsfeld at a time when Saddam Hussein was a US ally, was to be implemented by the Bechtel company, in 2003 awarded a multi-billion dollar contract for the reconstruction of Iraq. The memorandum, quietly renewed every five years, has special legislation attached whereby the United States stocks a strategic oil reserve for Israel even if this entails domestic US shortages – at a cost of $3 billion in 2002 to US taxpayers.

Such considerations did nothing to inhibit the usual Israeli onslaughts on the Palestinian towns of Gaza and the West Bank. Thus on 20 April six Palestinians, including a 14-year-old, were killed and 48 wounded when Israeli armoured vehicles attacked the Yibna district of Rafah in the south of the Gaza Strip. One Israeli soldier was killed and three were injured during the raid. On 25 April the British government criticised Israel over the building of a 'separation fence' – in fact a six-metre-high concrete wall – around the entire West Bank territory. The wall is topped with barbed wire and lined with guard towers, creating the impression of a concentration camp. In late April the publication of the 'road map' for peace – drawn up by the US, Russia, the UN and the EU – was imminent, with Bush saying that he intended to invite Mahmoud Abbas (known as Abu Mazen), Palestinian prime minister-designate, to the White House for talks.

Few independent observers thought that the new peace plan stood much chance of success. Israeli forces were continuing to invade Palestinian towns, the illegal Israeli settlements were being expanded, and further Palestinian land was being confiscated to build the 225-mile-long concrete wall and for other purposes. Mike O'Brien, British foreign minister, said that more than 100 Palestinian buildings had been destroyed to build the wall and that many Palestinians would be left on the 'wrong side' of the Israeli-imposed line separating Palestine from Israel: 'Approximately 10 per cent of the entire West Bank would lie to the west of the fence. Palestinian land is being seized for fence construction, cultivated farmland is being destroyed and some towns will be separated from surrounding farmland … the fence will leave 290,000 Palestinians on the Israeli side of the fence.'[35]

The 'road map' (Appendix IV) followed other schemes and peace negotiations (Figure 11), none of which was able to bring a comprehensive solution to the Israeli/Palestinian dispute. The new plan, introduced shortly after the defeat of the Palestinians' most stalwart Arab ally, cited the various contentious issues – terrorism, settlements, refugees, etc – but seemed less rather than more likely to provide a solution. Palestinian bargaining power had been gravely eroded over the

1978	Camp David Accords. In agreement with Egypt; Israel to withdraw from Sinai in return for peace.
1988	Israel enters dialogue with PLO after Yasser Arafat recognises the state of Israel and denounces terrorism.
1991	Madrid peace conference attended by Jordan, Syria, Israel and the Palestinians.
1993	Oslo principles. Signed by Yitzhak Rabin and Arafat. Self-government for Palestinians. Withdrawal of Israeli troops from Gaza and Jericho. Palestinian elections.
1995	Wye Plantation peace deal. Shimon Peres and Syria sign.
1997	Oslo stalls. Benjamin Netanyahu lifts freeze on building of new settlements and makes only partial withdrawal.
1998	Wye River memorandum. Netanyahu agrees withdrawal timetable but later abandons it.
1999	Wye River revision – not implemented.
2000	'Final status' talks. The terms satisfy neither side.

Figure 11. *Attempts to resolve Israeli/Palestinian differences*

years, and the United States and Israel were newly emboldened by the comprehensive US defeat of a leading Arab state. The most Palestinians could expect would be heavily patrolled bantustans, ghettos, concentration camps – with no hint of the independence that characterises a sovereign state in the modern world.

On 1 May 2003 Israeli troops killed 14 Palestinians, including a two-year-old boy. At 2am tanks and undercover troops in armoured cars entered the Shajaiyah neighbourhood of Gaza City and surrounded the apartment of Yusuf Abu Hein, a senior Hamas figure. Then the Israelis blew the building up, killing of the men inside, while Israeli tanks and helicopters fired shells, heavy machine guns and missiles into the district. Fadel Abu Hein, a child psychologist, commented: 'We are sitting in full darkness. Children are screaming. We are trying to calm them down, but bullets are coming from all directions. A reporter from Associated Press saw two boys, aged 12 and 14, hit by Israeli fire as they tried to run away. The 14-year-old, struck by a bullet in the throat, was later said by doctors to be paralysed from the neck down. The father of the dead two-year-old Amer Ayad asked: 'Is this the new peace President Bush promised? They wrote the answer using the blood of my son.'[36]

On 12 May Israel imposed sweeping closures on the Gaza Strip, just 24 hours after declaring the territory open in a gesture meant to bolster the latest peace plan. At the same time diplomats were confirming that Ariel Sharon would meet Mahmoud Abbas to discuss the proposals contained in the 'road map', though the killings were continuing. Israeli troops killed three more Palestinians in Gaza, one of them a farmer tilling his fields.

There were few signs that the 'road map' peace plan would be any more successful than the earlier schemes (Figure 11). The Palestinians, desperate for some hope for the future, had accepted its terms but the Israelis were refusing to issue a formal acceptance. Ariel Sharon had rebuffed American warnings that the continual expansions of settlements would jeopardise the peace deal, declaring that Israel would not surrender sovereignty of Jewish towns in the Occupied Territories. And Sharon was further aggravating the issue by declaring that the controversial 'security fence' being constructed around the West Bank would result in the annexation of yet more Palestinian land by Israel (*The Guardian*, 14 May 2003).

On 14 and 15 May a massive Israeli force surged into Gaza, killed five Palestinians, including a boy aged 12 and two aged 15. Some 70 tanks and armoured vehicles poured into various parts of Gaza, further outraging Palestinian public opinion and threatening the planned Sharon-Abbas talks. Thus Nabil Shaath, Palestinian foreign minister, commented: 'I have received calls from every part of Palestine asking me to prevail upon Abu Mazen [Mahmoud Abbas] not to meet with Prime Minister Sharon after the horror he has inflicted on Gaza.' Israel was already declaring that the 'road map' was unworkable and was insisting on 14 serious changes to the plan, fewer than the original one hundred objections but quite sufficient to sabotage any realistic prospect of agreement (*The Daily Telegraph*, 17 May 2003).

On 17 May seven Israelis were killing by a suicide bombing in Jerusalem, the first of a wave of attacks on Israeli targets that seemed designed to undermine any talks between Sharon and Mahmoud Abbas. Sharon cancelled a planned visit to Washington but continued his talks with the Palestinians. The suicide bombings received immense publicity in the Western media but no attention was given to the death of 12-year-old Mohammed al-Zaanin, left bleeding on a Gaza road after Israeli troops shot him in the head and refused to let an ambulance reach him.

The Palestinians were not only suffering in Gaza and the West Bank. The fall of the Ba'athists in Iraq had unleashed a torrent of rage against a minority seen as favoured collaborators with the Saddam regime. Ahmed Kadoura, a 55-year-old Palestinian refugee, was visited by a man and told to leave his home: 'He came and told us we had three days to get out.' As Ahmed struggled to pack he was attacked by a Shi'ite with a ceremonial knife, stabbing him three times in the chest. His family fled to a nearby football field where they continued their life in a makeshift tent. Another purge had begun.

The Oil Question

The primacy of oil as a reason for the 2003 war has already been considered (Chapter 10). Here it is enough to emphasise the resulting threat to OPEC, the sometimes US-unfriendly oil cartel; the speed with which Washington established control of the Iraqi oil resource; and the relevance of currency factors to the US-led war.

The resurgence of Iraqi oil, no longer crippled by sanctions, onto the international markets was expected to have a significant impact on OPEC. Since Iraqi oil would now be controlled by a US-dominated regime in Baghdad, many observers were wondering whether OPEC would even survive the trauma of the 2003 upheaval. Already Exxon Mobil, Texaco Chevron, BP and Shell had signalled their interest in the new energy possibilities, and Russia too was struggling to secure a share of the plunder.[37] The new contribution of Iraq, an OPEC member, to the energy markets would have seemed likely to strengthen the OPEC hand, but not if Iraq was in the pocket of the United States. However, some commentators were saying that Iraqi nationalism would constrain American ambition in the long term. It was obvious that OPEC would try to maintain oil prices at a particular level, but it seemed likely that there would be increased American influence over the world energy markets.

On 25 April *The Wall Street Journal Europe* reported: 'The US Government is setting up Iraq's oil industry to run much like an

American corporation, with a chief executive and management team vetted by US officials who would answer to a multi-national board of advisors.' The advisory board would be chaired by Philip J Carroll, a former chief executive of Shell Oil and chairman of Fluor Corporation, the engineering giant.[38] The appointment of a key figure in the American oil establishment was expected to cause resentment within the present management of the Iraqi National Oil Corporation (INOC), the state oil company largely staffed by technicians unconnected with the Saddam regime.[39]

It is significant that the United States was determined to control the Iraqi oil resource not only in order to guarantee adequate energy supplies and to gain a crucial strategic advantage *but also to support US currency*. It has been argued that the American economy would have run into serious difficulties if other oil-producing countries had followed the Iraqi decision of November 1992 and priced their oil in euros rather than dollars. The US economy, underpinned by the global pricing of oil in dollars, effectively requires all governments to hold US dollars as the principal element of their foreign currency reserves.[40] All of Bush's profligate expenditures – on war, 'son of Star Wars', etc – and the massive handouts to the American rich have been paid for by a doubling of US foreign debt. Countries buy all the dollars that the Bush administration decides to print – a strategy that would collapse if the OPEC countries decided to price their oil in euros. In such circumstances countries would sell back their dollar holdings, which in turn would force the Bush administration to raise revenue through taxation.

This means that the euro has the capacity to play a geopolitical role, one that would be totally unwelcome to Washington. Hence an American-backed junta in Iraq enables the United States to attack OPEC's hold over oil prices, to weaken the economies of the oil-producing nations, and to safeguard the relative stability of the US economy. Thus the activist George Monbiot, sensitive to these factors, commented on how well the United States does out of the present currency arrangements:

> In order to earn dollars, other nations must provide goods and services to the US. When commodities are valued in dollars, the US needs do no more than print pieces of green paper to obtain them; it acquires them, in effect, for free. Once earned, other

nations' dollar reserves must be invested back into the American economy. This inflow of money helps the US to finance its massive deficit.[41]

This system required that Iraqi oil be valued in dollars, a requirement that Iraq had flouted. Here was another important reason why it was essential for Washington to take control of the Iraqi oil resource and all the associated pricing details. And this is why Monbiot declared: 'There is only one way to check American power and that is to support the euro.'[42] Could this be why a fanatically pro-American Tony Blair is dragging his heels on British entry to the euro system?

Bellum Americanum

The end of the 2003 war saw speculation about fresh US wars to come. Attention was being given to making the American military more efficient,[43] and there was increasing discussion about the character of the expanding US empire.[44] Thus Niall Ferguson, Herzog professor of financial history at New York University, comments:

> In his new book, *American Empire*, Andrew J. Bacevich is quite explicit about the reality. As he puts it: 'the question is ... not whether the United States has become an imperial power. The question is what sort of empire [Americans] intend theirs to be'.
>
> So the possibility exists that Bush, Rumsfeld and Wolfowitz are faking it when they promise Iraqis democracy. Maybe, like the British back in 1917, they have every intention of installing a superficially popular puppet regime and staying in Iraq just as long as they please.
>
> ... the US today is in a position to create an empire even more powerful than Victorian Britain's.[45]

In May 2003 the US position in Iraq remained deeply ambiguous. There was constant talk of 'democracy' and 'Iraq being run by the Iraqis', but Iraqi officials were being *appointed* by the American authorities with no hint of democratic controls. And there was growing evidence that US troops had encouraged civil disorder in Baghdad and elsewhere. Thus on

16 April Professor Khaled Bayoumi, speaking to the Swedish newspaper *Dagens Nyheter*, said:

> I was there when the US troops invited people to start the looting … The rumour spread quickly and the building was emptied … the lack of rejoicing made the US troops need pictures of Iraqis who in different ways demonstrated some kind of protest against the Saddam regime.[46]

And it was not the residents of Baghdad who had pulled down the big Saddam statue: 'It was actually a US tank that did that, right next door from the hotel where all the journalists were staying.'[47]

On 22 May 2003 the journalist John Kampfner, writing in *The New Statesman* (London), revealed an important memorandum written by Lord Goldsmith, British attorney general, to Tony Blair.[48] This document, written six days into the war, declared that 'all US and British activity in Iraq from the end of the war, beyond essential maintenance of security, would be unlawful without specific authorisation from the UN'. This meant that there was no legal basis for the early US-UK efforts to form an interim Iraqi administration, to control the supply and sale of oil, and to award lucrative reconstruction contracts to US corporations.[49] The war of aggression had been illegal (see Chapter 11), though Goldsmith had tried to justify it, and the US–UK behaviour immediately after the war – according to the Geneva Conventions (1949) and the Hague Regulations (1907),[50] cited by Goldsmith – was also illegal.

Washington and London, aware that they were in violation of international law, were striving to secure a fresh UN Security Council resolution to 'legitimise' the US–UK occupation. An initial draft was issued on 8 May, followed by two weeks of negotiation in the Council and the adoption of Resolution 1483 on 22 May 2003. Washington, refusing to tolerate any fundamental dissent within the Security Council, had secured all its objectives. SCR 1483 recognised the United States and Britain as the 'Authority' in Iraq, notionally required to 'co-ordinate' its activities with a Special Representative to be appointed by the UN Secretary-General. The oil revenues would be held in a Development Fund 'disbursed at the direction of the Authority, in consultation with the Iraqi interim administration' (this latter in effect appointed by the United States and Britain). The use of Iraqi oil revenues to swell the profits of American corporations would continue, and the oil would be shipped in ever-increasing volume to the United States. SCR 1483 was adopted by a vote of 14–1, with Syria, the only Arab state on the Security Council, refusing to attend the handover of Iraq and its resources to the two principal Western imperialist powers.

The new resolution reiterated President Bush's original remark that the UN would be allowed 'a vital role' in the post-conflict situation, but it was obvious that the 'Authority' would have sole discretion about what the United Nations would be allowed to do. The United States had secured absolute control over the Iraqi nation, and in this context the abolition of the 13-year-old sanctions regime and talk of 'humanitarian relief' had no bearing on the welfare of the Iraqi people. By the end of May there were already many clues about what Iraq could expect.

On 22 May Richard Lugar, a senior US congressman, warned President Bush that the United States was on the brink of catastrophe in Iraq. Writing in *The Washington Post*, Lugar declared that Washington was in danger of creating 'an incubator for terrorist cells and activity, and charged that the government was not addressing the scale of the problem: 'I am concerned that the Bush Administration and Congress have not yet faced up to the true size of the task that lies ahead, or prepared the American people for it.[51] The evidence of chaos in Iraq was already accumulating.

On 18 May, from six o'clock in the morning, the elderly and infirm gathered in Baghdad to collect a promised relief payment ($40) – the first test of the capital's social support system under the American administration. The people then crowded forward in expectation: 'the old on crutches, the sick, the frail, widows with children to support and pensioners with grandchildren.'[52] The Americans responded by throwing a smoke grenade into the crowd, creating panic that forced elderly onto razor-wire barriers. One woman, flushed with anger, screamed at the troops wielding batons and shotguns: 'The soldiers hit us on our heads and they push us. The Americans are bad. I don't want them to stay in our country any longer.' One man had died on the street, overcome by the heat and the crush. A woman, struggling to protect her baby daughter, cried out: 'America is bad.'[53]

Elsewhere, Sabrir Hassan Ismael, a mother of six, had been forced to live with others in an abandoned prison: 'Look at me; look at my family

... We can't buy food because we don't have any money ... All night my daughters cry and they can't sleep. I live without any hope.'[54] In the north the Kurds were continuing their policy of ethnically cleansing thousands of Arab families. Yassim, Sabrir's husband, commented on the American intervention: 'None of the American promises has happened. It is unbelievable what has happened'; and his son added: 'We have discovered that Saddam is better than the Americans.'[55] The tribe's sheikh, Hadeb Hamed Hamed, said:

> The Americans promised us food and medicine and freedom. But we have lost our homes, our land, our crops. Now we live in prison with nothing, and they ignore us. It is the allied forces that have done this to us. When we run out of food I don't know what we will do. If we don't have a solution, we will fight the Americans even if they kill us. It is better than sitting here and just dying.[56]

In June 2003 the total number of Iraqi dead and dying was not known: as Colin Powell had famously declared, he had no interest in counting the number of enemy dead. *The Los Angeles Times* (19 May 2003), having surveyed some 27 hospitals in the area of Baghdad, estimated that the capital had suffered around 10,000 civilian casualties. A doctor, Mohammed Bashir, at the Kindi General Hospital, commented: 'The nature of injuries was so severe – one body without a head, someone else with their abdomen ripped open. Human beings are so frail in the face of these weapons of war.'

Commentators were observing that the United States was girding the globe 'with a ring of steel'[57] (see also Chapter 12). US forces were consolidating their power on all continents of the world, and planning to expand their presence wherever possible. In early May General James Jones, supreme commander of NATO, declared that the United States planned to boost its troop presence in Africa, where there were 'large ungoverned areas ... that are clearly the new routes of narco-trafficking, terrorists' training and hotbeds of instability'. Already there were around 2,000 US troops in Djibouti in the Horn of Africa, ordered to operate in a mission area that covered Somalia, Ethiopia, Eritrea, Djibouti, Sudan, Kenya and Yemen. At the same time Donald Rumsfeld, speaking in Baghdad, announced that the United States was 'systematically working with our friends and allies around the world to examine our footprint, to see where we are, how we want to be arranged for the future.'

The United States had deliberately undermined the UN weapons inspectors in Iraq,[58] and wages a systematic propaganda campaign of lies[59] – all in a calculated attempt to justify the recourse of war. At the same time the Bush administration was abusing former allies, preparing to develop a new range of nuclear weapons, ignoring international law and encouraging the erosion of evil liberties in the United States and throughout the world. In early May 2003 Jürgen Chrobog, Germany's state secretary, was reported as telling foreign ministry colleagues that America was turning into a 'police state' by 'restricting more and more its civil liberties at home.'

The US intentions were plain – to expand and consolidate a global military presence in order to crush competitive pressures, whether ideological, strategic or commercial. By May 2003 Pizza Hut and Burger King had arrived in Iraq; the port of Umm Kasr had been handed over to a private US contractor; Halliburton and Bechtel were winning massive reconstruction deals; and a Kissinger crony had been put in charge of the Iraqi oil industry. On 23 May Bechtel was awarded a $500 million contract for reconstructing work to British and other foreign firms. No one doubted that the vast bulk of primary contracts estimated to be worth around $100 billion would be awarded to Bechtel, Halliburton, Fluor and other American corporations, many of them with links to key members of the Bush administration.

The engine of American ambition is the dynamic corporate power backed by an unassailable military machine that straddles the globe. In this fact lie all the clues we need to comprehend the future of Iraq – a nation to be permanently condemned to inadequate social services, expanding financial inequalities and foreign exploitation. There are also clues here for the likely evolution of the Middle East and the wider world.

APPENDICES

Security Council Resolution 1441 (8 November 2002)

Resolution 1441 (2002) Adopted by the Security Council at its 4644th meeting, on 8 November 2002

The Security Council,

Recalling all its previous relevant resolutions, in particular its resolutions 661 (1990) of 6 August 1990, 678 (1990) of 29 November 1990, 686 (1991) of 2 March 1991, 687 (1991) of 3 April 1991, 688 (1991) of 5 April 1991, 707 (1991) of 15 August 1991, 715 (1991) of 11 October 1991, 986 (1995) of 14 April 1995, and 1284 (1999) of 17 December 1999, and all the relevant statements of its President,

Recalling also its resolution 1382 (2001) of 29 November 2001 and its intention to implement it fully,

Recognizing the threat Iraq's non-compliance with Council resolutions and proliferation of weapons of mass destruction and long-range missiles poses to international peace and security,

Recalling that its resolution 678 (1990) authorized Member States to use all necessary means to uphold and implement its resolution 660 (1990) of 2 August 1990 and all relevant resolutions subsequent to resolution 660 (1990) and to restore international peace and security in the area,

Further recalling that its resolution 687 (1991) imposed obligations on Iraq as a necessary step for achievement of its stated objective of restoring international peace and security in the area,

Deploring the fact that Iraq has not provided an accurate, full, final, and complete disclosure, as required by resolution 687 (1991), of all aspects of its programmes to develop weapons of mass destruction and ballistic missiles with a range greater than one hundred and fifty kilometres, and of all holdings of such weapons, their components and production facilities and locations, as well as all other nuclear programmes, including any which it claims are for purposes not related to nuclear-weapons-usable material,

Deploring further that Iraq repeatedly obstructed immediate, unconditional, and unrestricted access to sites designated by the United Nations Special Commission (UNSCOM) and the International Atomic Energy Agency (IAEA), failed to cooperate fully and unconditionally with UNSCOM and IAEA weapons inspectors, as required by resolution 687 (1991), and ultimately ceased all cooperation with UNSCOM and the IAEA in 1998,

Deploring the absence, since December 1998, in Iraq of international monitoring, inspection, and verification, as required by relevant resolutions, of weapons of mass destruction and ballistic missiles, in spite of the Council's repeated demands that Iraq provide immediate, unconditional, and unrestricted access to the United Nations Monitoring, Verification and Inspection Commission (UNMOVIC), established in resolution 1284 (1999) as the successor organization to UNSCOM, and the IAEA, and regretting the consequent prolonging of the crisis in the region and the suffering of the Iraqi people.

Deploring also that the Government of Iraq has failed to comply with its commitments pursuant to resolution 687 (1991) with regard to terrorism, pursuant to resolution 688 (1991) to end repression of its civilian population and to provide access by international humanitarian organizations to all those in need of assistance in Iraq, and pursuant to resolution 686 (1991), 687 (1991), and 1284 (1999) to return or cooperate in accounting for Kuwaiti and third country nationals wrongfully detained by Iraq, or to return Kuwaiti property wrongfully seized by Iraq,

Recalling that in its resolution 687 (1991) the Council declared that a ceasefire would be based on acceptance by Iraq of the provisions of that resolution, including the obligations on Iraq contained therein,

Determined to ensure full and immediate compliance by Iraq without conditions or restrictions with its obligations under resolution 687 (1991) and other relevant resolutions and recalling that the resolutions of the Council constitute the governing standard of Iraqi compliance,

Recalling that the effective operation of UNMOVIC, as the successor organization to the Special Commission, and the IAEA is essential for the implementation of resolution 687 (1991) and other relevant resolutions,

Noting that the letter dated 16 September 2002 from the Minister for Foreign Affairs of Iraq addressed to the Secretary-General is a necessary first step toward rectifying Iraq's continued failure to comply with relevant Council resolutions,

Noting further the letter dated 8 October 2002 from the Executive Chairman of UNMOVIC and the Director-General of the IAEA to General Al-Saadi of the Government of Iraq laying out the practical arrangements, as a follow-up to their meeting in Vienna, that are prerequisites for the resumption of inspections in Iraq by UNMOVIC and the IAEA, and expressing the gravest concern at the continued failure by the Government of Iraq to provide confirmation of the arrangements as laid out in that letter,

Reaffirming the commitment of all Member States to the sovereignty and territorial integrity of Iraq, Kuwait, and the neighbouring States,

Commending the Secretary-General and members of the League of Arab States and its Secretary-General for their efforts in this regard,

Determined to secure full compliance with its decisions,

Acting under Chapter VII of the Charter of the United Nations,

1. *Decides* that Iraq has been and remains in material breach of its obligations under relevant resolutions, including resolution 687 (1991), in particular through Iraq's failure to cooperate with United Nations inspectors and the IAEA, and to complete the actions required under paragraphs 8 to 13 of resolution 687 (1991);

2. *Decides*, while acknowledging paragraph 1 above, to afford Iraq, by this resolution, a final opportunity to comply with its disarmament obligations under relevant resolutions of the Council; and accordingly decides to set up an enhanced inspection regime with the aim of bringing to full and verified completion the disarmament process established by resolution 687 (1991) and subsequent resolutions of the Council;

3. *Decides* that, in order to begin to comply with its disarmament obligations, in addition to submitting the required biannual

declarations, the Government of Iraq shall provide to UNMOVIC, the IAEA, and the Council, not later than 30 days from the date of this resolution, a currently accurate, full, and complete declaration of all aspects of its programmes to develop chemical, biological, and nuclear weapons, ballistic missiles, and other delivery systems such as unmanned aerial vehicles and dispersal systems designed for use on aircraft, including any holdings and precise locations of such weapons, components, sub-components, stocks of agents, and related material and equipment, the locations and work of its research, development and production facilities, as well as all other chemical, biological, and nuclear programmes, including any which it claims are for purposes not related to weapon production or material;

4. *Decides* that false statements or omissions in the declarations submitted by Iraq pursuant to this resolution and failure by Iraq at any time to comply with, and cooperate fully in the implementation of, this resolution shall constitute a further material breach of Iraq's obligations and will be reported to the Council for assessment in accordance with paragraphs 11 and 12 below;

5. *Decides* that Iraq shall provide UNMOVIC and the IAEA immediate, unimpeded, unconditional, and unrestricted access to any and all, including underground, areas, facilities, buildings, equipment, records, and means of transport which they wish to inspect, as well as immediate, unimpeded, unrestricted, and private access to all officials and other persons whom UNMOVIC or the IAEA wish to interview in the mode or location of UNMOVIC's or the IAEA's choice pursuant to any aspect of their mandates; further decides that UNMOVIC and the IAEA may at their discretion conduct interviews inside or outside of Iraq, may facilitate the travel of those interviewed and family members outside of Iraq, and that, at the sole discretion of UNMOVIC and the IAEA, such interviews may occur without the presence of observers from the Iraqi Government; and instructs UNMOVIC and requests the IAEA to resume inspections no later than 45 days following adoption of this resolution and to update the Council 60 days thereafter;

6. *Endorses* the 8 October 2002 letter from the Executive Chairman of UNMOVIC and the Director- General of the IAEA to General Al-Saadi of the Government of Iraq, which is annexed hereto, and decides that the contents of the letter shall be binding upon Iraq;

7. *Decides* further that, in view of the prolonged interruption by Iraq of the presence of UNMOVIC and the IAEA and in order for them to accomplish the tasks set forth in this resolution and all previous relevant resolutions and notwithstanding prior understandings, the Council

hereby establishes the following revised or additional authorities, which shall be binding upon Iraq, to facilitate their work in Iraq:

- UNMOVIC and the IAEA shall determine the composition of their inspection teams and ensure that these teams are composed of the most qualified and experienced experts available;

- All UNMOVIC and IAEA personnel shall enjoy the privileges and immunities, corresponding to those of experts on mission, provided in the Convention on Privileges and Immunities of the United Nations and the Agreement on the Privileges and Immunities of the IAEA;

- UNMOVIC and the IAEA shall have unrestricted rights of entry into and out of Iraq, the right to free, unrestricted, and immediate movement to and from inspection sites, and the right to inspect any sites and buildings, including immediate, unimpeded, unconditional, and unrestricted access to Presidential Sites equal to that at other sites, notwithstanding the provisions of resolution 1154 (1998) of 2 March 1998;

- UNMOVIC and the IAEA shall have the right to be provided by Iraq the names of all personnel currently and formerly associated with Iraq's chemical, biological, nuclear, and ballistic missile programmes and the associated research, development, and production facilities;

- Security of UNMOVIC and the IAEA facilities shall be ensured by sufficient United Nations security guards;

- UNMOVIC and the IAEA shall have the right to declare, for the purposes of freezing a site to be inspected, exclusion zones, including surrounding areas and transit corridors, in which Iraq will suspend ground and aerial movement so that nothing is changed in or taken out of a site being inspected;

- UNMOVIC and the IAEA shall have the free and unrestricted use and landing of fixed- and rotary-winged aircraft, including manned and unmanned reconnaissance vehicles;

- UNMOVIC and the IAEA shall have the right at their sole discretion verifiably to remove, destroy, or render harmless all prohibited weapons, subsystems, components, records, materials, and other related items, and the right to impound or close any facilities or equipment for the production thereof, and

- UNMOVIC and the IAEA shall have the right to free import and use of equipment or materials for inspections and to seize and export equipment, materials or documents taken during the inspections, without search of UNMOVIC or IAEA personnel or official or personal baggage;

8. *Decides* further that Iraq shall not take or threaten hostile acts directed against any representative or personnel of the United Nations or the IAEA or of any Member State taking action to uphold any Council resolution;

9. *Requests* the Secretary-General immediately to notify Iraq of this resolution, which is binding on Iraq; demands that Iraq confirm within seven days of that notification its intention to comply fully with this resolution; and demands further that Iraq cooperate immediately, unconditionally, and actively with UNMOVIC and the IAEA;

10. *Requests* all Member States to give full support to UNMOVIC and the IAEA in the discharge of their mandates, including by providing any information related to prohibited programmes or other aspects of their mandates, including on Iraqi attempts since 1998 to acquire prohibited items, and by recommending sites to be inspected, persons to be interviewed, conditions of such interviews, and data to be collected, the results of which shall be reported to the Council by UNMOVIC and the IAEA;

11. *Directs* the Executive Chairman of UNMOVIC and the Director-General of the IAEA to report immediately to the Council any interference by Iraq with inspection activities, as well as any failure by Iraq to comply with its disarmament obligations, including its obligations regarding inspections under this resolution;

12. *Decides* to convene immediately upon receipt of a report in accordance with paragraphs 4 or 11 above, in order to consider the situation and the need for full compliance with all of the relevant Council resolutions in order to secure international peace and security;

13. *Recalls*, in that context, that the Council has repeatedly warned Iraq that it will face serious consequences as a result of its continued violations of its obligations;

14. *Decides* to remain seized of the matter.

Syrian Draft Resolution (19 December 2002) – Vetoed by US

The Security Council,

Reaffirming its resolution 242 (1967) of 22 November 1967, 338 (1973) of 22 October 1973, 1397 (2002) of 12 March 2002, 1402 (2002) of 30 March 2002, 1403 (2002) of 4 April 2002 and 1435 (2002) of 24 September 2002, as well as the statements of its President, of 10 April 2002 and 18 July 2002.

Reiterating its grave concern at the tragic and violent events that have taken place since September 2000 and the continuous deterioration of the situation,

Expressing grave concern at the killing by the Israeli occupying forces of several United Nations employees, including the recent killing of one international staff member in the Jenin refugee camp,

Expressing deep concern at the deliberate destruction by the Israeli occupying forces of a United Nations World Food Programme warehouse in Beit Lahiya in the Occupied Palestinian Territory, in which 537 metric tons of donated food supplies intended for distribution to needy Palestinians had been stored,

Recalling the protection accorded to such facilities under international humanitarian law,

> 1. *Condemns* the above-mentioned killings and destruction;

> 2. *Demands* that Israel, the occupying Power, comply fully with its obligations under the Fourth Geneva Convention relative to the Protection of Civilian Persons in Time of War, of 12 August 1949, and refrain from the excessive and disproportionate use of force in the Occupied Palestinian Territory;

> 3. *Requests* the Secretary-General to inform the Council on any developments in this regard.

Draft of 'Second Resolution' (24 February 2003) – Sponsors (US, UK and Spain) Declined to Put Draft to Security Council When Required Majority Seemed Unlikely and Veto Was Likely

The Security Council,

1. Recalling all of its previous relevant resolutions, in particular its resolutions 661 (1990) of August 1990, 678 (1990) of 29 November 1990, 686 (1991) of 2 March 1991, 687 (1991) of 3 April 1991, 688 (1991) of 5 April 1991, 707 (1991) of 15 August 1991, (715 (1991) of 11 October 1991, 986 (1995) of 14 April 1995, 1284 (1999) of 17 December 1999 and 1441 (2002) of 8 November 2002, and all the relevant statements of its President,

2. Recalling that in its resolution 687 (1991) the Council declared that a ceasefire would be based on acceptance of Iraq of the provisions of that resolution, including the obligations on Iraq continued therein,

3. Recalling that its resolution 1441 (2002), while acknowledging that Iraq has been and remains in material breach of its obligations, afforded Iraq a final opportunity to comply with its disarmament obligations under relevant resolutions,

4. Recalling that in its resolution 1441 (2002) the Council decided that false statements or omissions in the declaration submitted by Iraq pursuant to that resolution and failure by Iraq at any time to comply with, and cooperate with fully in the implementation of, that resolution, would constitute a further material breach.

5. Noting, in that context, that in its resolution 1441 (2002), the Council recalled that it has repeatedly warned Iraq that it will face serious consequences as a result of its continued violations and its obligations;

6. Noting that Iraq has submitted a declaration pursuant to its resolution 1441 (2002) containing false statements and omissions and has failed to comply with, and cooperate fully in the implementation of, that resolution,

7. Reaffirming the commitment of all Member States to the sovereignty and territorial integrity of Iraq, Kuwait, and the neighbouring states,

8. Mindful of its primary responsibility under the Charter of the United Nations for the maintenance of international peace and security,

9. Recognising the threat of Iraq's non-compliance with Council resolutions and proliferation of weapons of mass destruction and long-range missiles poses to international peace and security.

10. Determined to secure full compliance with its decisions and to restore international peace and security in the area,

11. Acting under Chapter VII of the Charter of the United Nations,

OP1.   Decides that Iraq has failed to take the final opportunity afforded to it resolution 1441 (2002),

OP2.   Decides to remain seized on the matter.

A Performance-Based Roadmap to a Permanent Two-State Solution to the Israeli-Palestinian Conflict – Extract

Phase I: Ending terror and violence, normalizing Palestinian life and building Palestinian Institutions – Present to May 2003

In Phase I, the Palestinians immediately undertake an unconditional cessation of violence according to the steps outlined below; such action should be accompanied by supportive measures undertaken by Israel. Palestinians and Israelis resume security cooperation based on the Tenet work plan to end violence, terrorism, and incitement through restructured and effective Palestinian security services. Palestinians undertake comprehensive political reform in preparation for statehood, including drafting a Palestinian constitution, and free, fair and open elections upon the basis of those measures. Israel takes all the necessary steps to help normalize Palestinian life. Israel withdraws from Palestinian areas occupied from September 28, 2000 and the two sides restore the status quo that existed at that time, as security performance and cooperation progress. Israel also freezes all settlement activity, consistent with the Mitchell report.

At the outset of Phase I:

- Palestinian leadership issues unequivocal statement reiterating Israel's right to exist in peace and security and calling for an immediate and unconditional ceasefire to end armed activity and all acts of violence against Israelis anywhere. All official Palestinian institutions end incitement against Israel.

- Israeli leadership issues unequivocal statement affirming its commitment to the two-state vision of an independent, viable, sovereign Palestinian state living in peace and security alongside Israel, as expressed by President Bush, and calling for an immediate end to violence against Palestinians everywhere. All official Israeli institutions end incitement against Palestinians.

Phase II: Transition – June 2003–December 2003

In the second phase, efforts are focused on the option of creating an independent Palestinian state with provisional borders and attributes of sovereignty, based on the new constitution, as a way station to a permanent status settlement. As has been noted, this goal can be achieved when the Palestinian people have a leadership acting decisively against terror, willing and able to build a practicing democracy based on tolerance and liberty. With such a leadership, reformed civil institutions and security structures, the Palestinians will have the active support of the Quartet and the broader international community in establishing an independent, viable, state.

Progress into Phase II will be based upon the consensus judgment of the Quartet of whether conditions are appropriate to proceed, taking into account performance of both parties. Furthering and sustaining efforts to normalize Palestinian lives and build Palestinian institutions, Phase II starts after Palestinian elections and ends with possible creation of an independent Palestinian state with provisional borders in 2003. Its primary goals are continued comprehensive security performance and effective security cooperation, continued normalization of Palestinian life and institution-building, further building on and sustaining of the goals outlined in Phase I, ratification of a democratic Palestinian constitution, formal establishment of office of prime minister, consolidation of political reform, and the creation of a Palestinian state with provisional borders.

Phase III: Permanent Status Agreement and end of the Israeli-Palestinian Conflict – 2004–2005

Progress into Phase III, based on consensus judgment of Quartet, and taking into account actions of both parties and Quartet monitoring. Phase III objectives are consolidation of reform and stabilization of Palestinian institutions, sustained, effective Palestinian security performance and Israeli-Palestinian negotiations aimed at a permanent status agreement in 2005.

Notes

Introduction

1. The compensation issue is discussed in Geoff Simons, *Targeting Iraq* (London: Saqi Books, 2002), Chapter 10, pp. 233–8.
2. Jason Nissé, 'Iraq conflict: $500 billion toll on world economy', *The Independent on Sunday*, London, 9 March 2003.
3. Henry Potter, 'War bill could feed the world', *The Observer*, London, 30 March 2003.
4. Ed Firmage, Samuel D. Turman Professor of Law, Emeritus, at the University of Utah College of Law, *The Salt Lake Tribune*, 17 March 2003.
5. Andrew Gumbel, 'Pentagon seeks freedom to pollute land, air and sea', *The Independent*, London, 13 March 2003.
6. John Simpson, 'When using a sat-phone puts you in the line of fire', *The Sunday Telegraph*, London, 2 February 2003.
7. 'Anglo-US forgery on Iraq exposed by UN', *Morning Star*, London, 26 March 2003.
8. James Buchan, 'And now, the battle for the mother of all contracts', *The Sunday Telegraph*, London, 6 April 2003.
9. Andrew Gumbel, 'US accused of hypocrisy on human rights', *The Independent on Sunday*, London, 6 April 2003.
10. Ambrose Evans-Pritchard, 'Britain accused of human rights abuses by EU parliament', *The Daily Telegraph*, London, 14 January 2003.

11. Julius Strauss, 'Tribes haggle to carve up defeated country', *The Daily Telegraph*, London, 2 April 2003.
12. Julian Borger, 'Air war weapon stockpile runs critically low', *The Guardian*, London, 1 April 2003.

Chapter 1

1. UN Food and Agriculture Organisation (FAO), December 1995.
2. Victoria Brittain, *The Independent*, London, 4 December 1995.
3. I have described in detail the impact of sanctions in *The Scourging of Iraq: Sanctions, Law and Natural Justice* (London: Macmillan, 1998, 2nd edition); and in *Targeting Iraq: Sanctions and bombing in US Policy* (London: Saqi Books, 2002), Chapter 2, pp. 63–83.
4. Kofi Annan, Press Release, SG/SM/8643, SC/7698, 19 March 2003.
5. *Ibid*.
6. *Likely Humanitarian Scenarios*, UN document, 'STRICTLY CONFIDENTIAL', 10 December 2002.
7. *Ibid*.
8. *Ibid*.
9. Data provided by the UN Children's Fund (UNICEF) and the World Health Organisation (WHO).
10. Data provided by the UN Health Sectorial Working Group in Iraq.
11. *Likely Humanitarian Scenarios*, op. cit.
12. Jonathan Glover, 'Can we justify killing the children of Iraq?', *The Guardian*, London, 5 February 2003.
13. *Ibid*.
14. *Our Common Responsibility: The Impact of a New War on Iraqi Children*, International Study Team, War Child Canada, Toronto, 30 January 2003.
15. *Ibid*.
16. *Ibid*.
17. Anthony Browne, 'Human disaster waits in wings as aid fund dries up', *The Times*, London, 21 February 2003.
18. Phil Reeves, 'Living in poverty and fear of abandonment, the barely functional state that trusted its saviours', *The Independent*, London, 24 February 2003.
19. See Geoff Simons, *Targeting Iraq, op. cit.*, Chapter 3, pp. 85–105.
20. Weekly Update (1–7), Office of the Iraq Programme, United Nations, 11 March 2003.
21. Robert Fisk, 'This is the reality of war. We bomb. They suffer', *The Independent on Sunday*, London, 23 March 2003.
22. *Ibid*.
23. Jon Swain, 'Surreal normality in Baghdad's ring of fire', *The Sunday Times*, London, 23 March 2003.
24. Oliver Burkeman, *The Guardian*, London, 24 March 2003.
25. Patrick Barkham, *The Times*, London, 31 March 203 (a case of friendly fire – 'There were all these civilians around. He had absolutely no regard for human life').
26. Robert Fisk, *The Independent*, London, 2 April 2003 ('babies cut in half and

children with amputation wounds … a father holding out pieces of his baby … two lorryloads of bodies').

27. Cahal Milmo, *The Independent*, London, 2 April 2003.

28. Samia Nakhoul, *The Independent*, London, 3 April 2003 (bombing of Red Crescent maternity hospital and other civilian buildings).

29. Christopher Ayad and Jean-Pierre Perrin, *The Independent*, London, 3 April 2003.

30. Robert Fisk, *The Independent*, London, 3 April 2003 ('Some victims died at once, mostly women and children, some of whose blackened, decomposing remains lay in the tiny charnel house mortuary at the back of the Hillal hospital. The teaching college received more than 200 wounded since Saturday night – the 61 dead are only those who were brought to the hospital or who died during or after surgery, and many others are believed to have been buried in their home villages – and, of these, doctors say that about 80 per cent were civilians').

31. Rupert Cornwell, *The Independent*, London, 1 April 2003.

32. 'The whole world is watching us die', Action Centre, New York, 2 April 2003.

33. Ewen MacAskill and Suzanne Goldenberg, 'Children killed in US assault', *The Guardian*, London, 2 April 2003.

34. *Ibid.*

35. Daniel McGrory, *The Times*, London, 5 April 2003.

36. Cahal Milmo, *The Independent*, London, 5 April 2003.

37. Tim Franks, *The Times*, London, 5 April 2003.

38. Anthony Browne, *The Times*, London, 7 April 2003.

39. Owen Bowcott, *The Guardian*, London, 8 April 2003.

40. Robert Fisk, *The Independent*, London, 8 April 2003.

41. Suzanne Goldenberg, *The Guardian*, London, 9 April 2003.

42. Bronwen Maddox, *The Times*, London, 9 April 2003.

43. Phillip Smucker and Michael Smith, *The Daily Telegraph*, London, 12 April 2003.

44. Robert Fisk, *The Independent on Sunday*, London, 13 April 2003.

45. Peter Beaumont, *The Observer*, London, 13 April 2003.

Chapter 2

1. Bill Spindle, 'An Exiled Engineer Tests The Waters With Proposal To Revive Iraqi Wetlands', *The Wall Street Journal Europe*, 15 January 2003.

2. *Ibid*. Here it is also pointed out that bombing of the upstream waterworks during a US-led attack on Iraq, leading to quick reflooding of the region could produce an even greater ecological disaster. The thick layer of salt, polluted by toxins, would contaminate any new water that rushed in. Alwash lobbied the US Defense Department to avoid bombing the upstream dams.

3. Stephen J. Glain, 'Stronghold Can Backfire: Iraqi Tribes Are Key Source of Loyalty, Rebellion', *The Wall Street Journal*, 23 May 2000.

4. *Ibid.*

5. *Ibid.*

6. *Ibid.*

7. Judith Yaphe, 'Tribalism in Iraq, the Old and the New', *Middle East Policy*, 1 June 2000.

8. There can be no guarantee that such Iraqi minorities will be protected by any post-Saddam regime run from Washington.

9. Jason Burke, 'US cash squads "buy" Iraqi tribes', *The Observer*, London, 15 December 2002.

10. The composition of Shi'ite society, the conversion of the Iraqi tribes to Shi'ism, the relations with the Baghdad regime, religious practices and other aspects are copiously described in Yitzhak Navash, *The Shi'is of Iraq* (Princeton University Press, New Jersey, USA, 1994).

11. Ian Cobain, 'Radical Shias are a worry for Bush as well as Saddam', *The Times*, London, 12 October 2002.

12. Richard Beeston, 'Saddam cultivates fickle tribes with bribes and bullets', *The Times*, London, 1 April 2003.

13. *Ibid.*

Chapter 3

1. William Rees-Mogg, 'A war in Iraq is easy: the problem will be the peace', *The Times*, London, 23 December 2002.

2. David Pryce-Jones, 'Muslim have nothing to lose but their chains', *The Spectator*, London, 28 September 2002.

3. Shyam Bhatia and Daniel McGrory, *Saddam's Bomb* (London: Time Warner, 2002), p.6, Stormtroopers were first employed by General Oskar von Hutier, nephew to Ludendorff, in the First World War. They later became notorious for the suppression of the Jewish Ghetto Uprising in Warsaw in April-May 1943.

4. Michael White, 'Searching for a hero: why America has turned to Winston Churchill', *The Guardian*, London, 29 August 2002.

5. John Keegan in *The Daily Telegraph*, London, 2 September 2002.

6. Alan Judd in *The Daily Telegraph*, London, 2 September 2002.

7. Roland Watson and Michael Evans, 'US plans military rule of Baghdad', *The Times*, London, 12 October 2002.

8. *The New York Times*, London, 11 October 2002.

9. Andrew Gumbell, 'US plans Baghdad military governor during occupation', *The Independent*, London, 19 October 2002.

10. Robert Fisk, 'Will Bush's carve-up of Iraq include getting hands on its oil', *The Independent*, London, 12 October 2002.

11. *Ibid.*

12. Richard Norton-Taylor, 'Allies "must prepare for long stay in Iraq"', *The Guardian*, London, 18 October 2002.

13. David Wastell, Robert Fox and Julian Coman, 'Alarm in Europe at US plan for general to govern Iraq', *The Sunday Telegraph*, London, 13 October 2002.

14. Stephen Farrell and Roger Matthews, 'Iran rejects scheme for US military rule in Iraq', *The Times*, London, 25 October 2002.

15. See, for example, W. G. Beasley, *The Modern History of Japan* (London: Weidenfeld and Nicholson, 1973), pp. 279–302; Meirion and Susie Harries, *Sheathing The Sword: The Demilitarisation of Japan* (London: Hamish Hamilton, 1987), pp. 33–93.

16. Oswald Garrison Villard, 'We must free Korea now', November 1945, p. 521,

quoted by Michael C Sandusky, *America's Parallel* (Alexandria, Va: Old Dominion Press, 1983), p. 26.

17. Geoff Simons, *Korea: the Search for Sovereignty* (London: Mcmillan, 2nd edition, 1995), pp. 218–30.

18. James Pinkerton, 'Iraq is no stage for MacArthur-Japan sequel', *Newsday*, 15 October 2002.

19. Editorial, 'Rebuilding Iraq: Japan is no model', *Los Angeles Times*, 17 October 2002.

20. *The New York Times*, 6 January 2002.

21. Seumas Milne, 'The recolonisation of Iraq cannot be sold as liberation', *The Guardian*, London, 30 January 2003.

22. *Ibid.*

23. Neil Tweedie, 'Our troops will stay in Iraq for three years', *The Daily Telegraph*, London, 5 February 2003; Adrian Roberts, 'Troops will occupy Iraq for 3 years', *Morning Star*, London, 5 February 2003.

24. Christopher Simpson, *Blowback: America's Recruitment of Nazis and its Effects on the Cold War* (London: Weidenfeld & Nicolson, 1988).

25. Philip Webster, James Bone, Rosemary Bennett and Greg Hurst, 'Coalition to stay in charge for task of rebuilding', *The Times*, London, 27 March 2003.

26. Oliver Morgan, 'Man who would be "king" of Iraq', *The Observer*, London, 30 March 2003; Iain Cobain and Elain Monaghan, 'Retired general waits in the wings for Saddam's fall', *The Times*, London, 31 March 2003; 'The US general waiting to replace Saddam', *The Independent*, London, 5 April 2003.

27. Rupert Cornwell, 'Pentagon vetoes new task force to take control of Baghdad', *The Independent*, London, 2 April 2003; Rupert Cornwell, 'Turf war rages in Washington over who will rule Iraq', *The Independent*, London 5 April 2003.

28. *Ibid.*

29. Robert Bryce and Julian Borger, 'Cheney is still paid by Pentagon contractor', *The Guardian*, London, 12 March 2003.

30. Kellogg, Brown & Root was awarded $33 million to build the detention camp at Guantanamo Bay, Cuba, for Taliban and al-Qa'ida suspects. Plainly, Cheney and Halliburton were happy to profit from the illegal detention of men, denied legal representation, against whom no charges had been brought.

31. Dominic O'Connell, Andrew Porter and Dennis Rushe, 'Scramble for the spoils of war', *The Sunday Times*, London, 30 March 2003.

32. James Fallows, 'A "liberated" Iraq could end up like Weimar Germany', *The Guardian*, London, 24 February 2002.

33. Toby Harnden, 'Plotter of Saddam's fall pleads case in US', *The Daily Telegraph*, London, 27 April 2002.

34. *Ibid.*

35. Richard Beeston, 'Exiled generals prepare for march on Baghdad', *The Times*, London, 11 July 2002; Brian Whitaker, 'Magnificent Seventy gun for Saddam', *The Guardian*, London, 12 July 2002.

36. Anton La Guardia and Adel Darwish, 'Iraqi exiles split on post-Saddam plan', *The Daily Telegraph*, London, 27 July 2002.

37. Richard Beeston, 'US meets leaders vying to rule Iraq', *The Times*, London, 10 August 2002.

38. *Ibid.*
39. Roula Khalaf and Stephen Fidler, 'Opposition groups mull post-Saddam structures', *Financial Times,* London, 6 September 2002.
40. David Pratt, 'Unveiled: the thugs Bush wants in place of Saddam', *Sunday Herald*, Scotland, 22 September 2002.
41. Hamid Karzai, former war-lord and ally of the Taliban, was established as the pro-US leader of a post-Taliban government, pending the return of the king, Zahir Shah. In the event Washington decided that the former monarch would serve their interests less satisfactorily than would Karzai. Under heavy pressure from the United States and the pro-US Afghan leadership Zahir Shah was forced to renounce all political ambitions whereupon Hamid Karzai, seen by many as a puppet of the Americans, became the permanent leader of Afghanistan. Washington, seeing this development as highly congenial to American interests, desperately sought an Iraqi national who could serve the same purpose in a post-war Iraq. Their search was unsuccessful and other expedients had to be adopted.
42. Martin Wollacott, 'The US will soon have to choose Saddam's successor', *The Guardian*, London, 15 November 2002; Marie Colvin and Tony Allen-Mills, 'US divided on Saddam successor, *The Sunday Times*, London, 17 November 2002.
43. Hala Jaber, 'Iraqi exiles split on post-Saddam plans', *The Sunday Times*, London, 15 December 2002; Christina Lamb, 'Iraqi opposition strives to unite for post-Saddam rule', *The Sunday Telegraph*, London, 15 December 2002.
44. Ahmad Chalabi, 'Iraqis can govern themselves without American supervision', *The Daily Telegraph*, London, 20 February 2003; Anton La Guardia, 'Let us rule our nation, exile tells Americans', *The Daily Telegraph*, London, 20 February 2003.
45. *Ibid.*
46. Julian Borger, Michael Howard, Luke Harding and Dan De Luce, 'US falls out with the Iraqi opposition', *The Guardian*, London, 21 February 2003.
47. Patrick Cockburn, 'Armed US guards lay down law for Iraqi exiles', *The Independent*, London, 27 February 2003; Richard Beeston, 'Opposition factions hit out at America's plans for Iraq after Saddam', *The Times*, London, 30 February 2003.
48. Anton Mohr, *The Oil War* (New York: Harcourt Brace, 1926).
49. Samir al-Khalil, *Republic of Fear* (London: Hutchinson-Radius, 1990), p. 150; cites also A. Shakira, 'Faisal's ambitions of leadership in the Fertile Crescent: aspirations and constraints', in *The Integration of Modern Iraq*, A Kelidar (ed), (London: Croom Helm, 1979).
50. Arthur Goldschmidt, *A Concise History of the Middle East* (Boulder, Col.: Westview Press, 1979), p. 271.
51. For example, it is useful to explore the powers of 'royal assent' and 'royal consent', the latter authorising royal scrutiny of and comment on certain intended legislation before it ever reaches the House of Commons.
52. Mario Farouk-Sluglett and Peter Sluglett, 'The Transformation of Land Tenure and Rural Social Structure in Central and Southern Iraq c. 1870–1958', *International Journal of Middle East Studies*, 15, 1983, p. 491.
53. Mario Farouk-Sluglett, 'Contemporary Iraq: Some Recent Writing Reconsidered', *Review of Middle East Studies*, 3, 1978, p. 92.

54. Doreen Warriner, *Land Reform and Development in the Middle East: A Study of Egypt, Syria and Iraq*, London, 1987, pp. 181–2.

55. Alan Cowell, 'London Journal: If Iraq Ever Needs a King, Here's a Dapper Hopeful', *The New York Times*, 2 April 2001.

56. Fahed Fanek, 'Jury out on anti-Saddam move by Prince Hassan', *The Daily Star* (on line), 24 July 2002.

57. 'A King for Iraq', *The Economist*, London, 18 July 2002.

58. Brian Whitaker, 'Jordan Prince touted to succeed Saddam', *The Guardian*, London, 19 July 2002.

59. Michael Rubin, 'If Iraqis want a king, Hassan of Jordan could be their man', *The Daily Telegraph*, London, 19 July 2002.

60. Leonard Doyle, 'Subtle performance from the pretender to Saddam's throne', *The Independent*, London, 26 October 2002.

61. John Casey, 'If Saddam goes bring back the king', *The Guardian*, London, 24 October 2002.

62. *Ibid.*

63. Peter Preston, 'Democracy in the new Iraq is a myth', *The Guardian*, London, 10 February 2003.

64. Neal Ascherson, 'Only Iraqis can decide', *The Guardian*, London, 24 March 2003.

65. Simon Carr, 'Commons unleashes the reptiles of war', *The Independent*, London, 1 April 2003.

66. David Usborne, 'US and allies at odds over secret plans to rule Iraq', *The Independent*, London, 7 April 2003.

67. Elain Monaghan, Richard Beeston and Philip Webster, 'US delays naming team to form a new government', *The Times*, London, 7 April 2003.

68. Richard Lloyd Parry and David Charter, 'Fear grips Iraqis as rivals vie for power', *The Times*, London, 14 April 2003.

69. Tim Reid, 'US plans Iraq bases to keep region in its grip', *The Times*, London, 21 April 2003.

70. Stephen Farrell, 'Christians fear future more than Saddam', *The Times*, London, 21 April 2003.

71. *Ibid.*

Chapter 4

1. Hugh Pope and John Carlin, 'Missiles fail to save the Kurds', *The Independent on Sunday*, London, 8 September 1996.

2. Peter Sluglett, *'The Kurds' in Saddam's Iraq: Revolution or Reaction*, CARDRI (Committee against Repression and for Democratic Rights in Iraq) (London: Zed Books, 1989), p. 177.

3. Cited by Patrick Brogan, *World Conflicts* (London: Bloomsbury, 1989), p. 296: many states, UN members, have smaller populations than the Kurdish nation.

4. The Twelfth Point declares that: ' ... the nationalities now under Turkish rule should ... be assured ... an absolutely unmolested opportunity of autonomous development'. Was this aspiration expected to apply to the Kurds or only to larger ethnic political groupings then under colonialism or other forms of oppression?

5. Televised interviews were broadcast on Channel 4 (London) in the 'Secret History' programme 'The RAF and the British Empire' on 6 July 1992. The quotations in this section are from that programme.

6. *Ibid*.

7. *Ibid*.

8. From the Tenchard Papers, quote in Philip Knightley and Colin Simpson, *The Secret Lives of Lawrence of Arabia*, London, 1969, p. 139.

9. C Townshend, 'Civilisation and Frightfulness', 148, Wg/Cdr to CAS, 19 February 1920, Trenchard Papers MFC 7/1/36: Martin Gilbert, *Winston S Churchill*, IV, Heinemann, London, 1975, pp. 494, 810; Companion IV ii, pp. 1066–7, 1083, 1170; quoted in David E. Omissi, *Air Powers and Colonial Control, The Royal Air Force 1919–1939* (Manchester: Manchester University Press, 1990), p. 160.

10. In the chaos that followed the 1991 Gulf War the United States urged Iraqi dissident groups, including the Kurds, to rebel against the Saddam regime. The subsequent nationwide revolt, that clearly shook the Baghdad authorities, was given no practical support from the United States, and the rebels were duly crushed by Saddam's forces. This American dereliction – where it has even been argued that US help was given to the Iraqi armed forces – is remembered as a gross American betrayal of courageous Iraqis who had every reason to expect decisive Western support.

11. Majid Abd al-Ridha, al-Masal Kuridya fi'l Iraq (The Kurdish Question in Iraq), al-Tariq al-Jadid, Baghdad 1975, p.83; quoted by Peter Sluglett, 'The Kurds', *op. cit.*, p. 182.

12. Sluglett, *op. cit.*, p.182.

13. *The Washington Post*, 22 June 1973.

14. Saddam Hussein, *Khadaq Walind am Khandaqan* (Baghdad: Dar al-Thawra, 1977), p. 31, quoted by Efraim J Karsh and Inari Rautski, *Saddam Hussein, A Political Biography* (London: Futura, 1991), p.80.

15. *Iraq's Crime of Genocide: The Anfal Campaign against the Kurds*, Human Rights Watch/Middle East (New Haven: Yale University Press, 1995).

16. Jon Swain and Marie Colvin, 'Iraqi army hammers Kurds', *The Sunday Times*, London, 1 September 1996.

17. Hugh Pope, 'West Flounders as Saddam goes to war again', *The Independent on Sunday*, London, 1 September 1996.

18. Jon Snow, 'Iraqis and Kurds fear ethnic bloodletting when bombing stops', *The Sunday Telegraph*, London, 2 February 2003.

19. Wendell Stevenson, 'Don't send Turks, warning to US', *The Daily Telegraph*, London, 24 February 2003; Patrick Cockburn, 'Iraqi Kurds "terrified", by prospect of Turkish invasion', *The Independent*, London, 24 February 2003.

Chapter 5

1. 'Turkish jets hit Kurds in Iraq', *The Independent*, London, 8 August 1991; Jonathan Rugman, 'Ataturk vision blinded by hatred of Kurds', *The Observer*, London, 11 August 1991.

2. Jonathan Rugman, 'Kurds bombed by Turkey in "safe haven"', *The Guardian*, London, 12 October 1991.

3. David Sharrock, 'A weekend of brutality in Turkey's Kurdish war', *The Guardian*, London, 21 April 1992.

4. Hugh Pope, 'Ankara hardens line as Kurdish rebellion grows bloodier', *The Independent*, London, 10 September 2002.

5. Hugh Pope, 'Turks plan to set up "security zone" in Iraq', *The Independent*, London, 30 November 1991.

6. Jonathan Rugman, 'Turks round up Kurd villagers in Iraq', *The Guardian*, London, 23 March 1995.

7. Amberin Zaman, 'Turks "used Kurds as mine detectors"', *The Daily Telegraph*, London, 6 March 1997.

8. Chris Morris, 'Turks pursue Kurds inside northern Iraq', *The Guardian*, London, 8 April 2000.

9. *Ibid*.

10. Justin Huggler, 'Behind Turkey's smiling face is a masked torturer', *The Independent*, London, 15 July 2000.

11. James Dorsey, 'Turkey puts rape victims in the dock', *The Observer*, London, 25 March 2001.

12. Amberin Zaman, 'Turks wary of joining US-led war on Iraq', *The Daily Telegraph*, London, 12 December 2002; Suna Erdem, 'Allied brass pay court to anxious Turkey', *The Times*, London, 24 January 2003.

13. Suna Erdem, 'Turkey will accept up to 80,000 US troops', *The Times*, London, 1 February 2003.

14. Patrick Cockburn, 'Turkey close to agreeing deal with American military', *The Independent*, London, 28 February 2003.

15. Amberin Zaman, 'Kurds fear repression as Turkey bans main party', *The Daily Telegraph*, London, 14 March 2003; Richard Lloyd Parry, 'Ankara set to quash Kurdish ambitions', *The Times*, London, 20 March 2003.

Chapter 6

1. Herodotus, *The Histories*, translated by Aubrey de Sélincourt (Harmondsworth, England: Penguin, 1954), pp. 89–91.

2. Ann Lambton, *State and Government in Medieval Islam* (Oxford, 1981), pp. 213–3; Yitzhak Nakash, *The Shi'is of Iraq* (New Jersey: Princeton University Press, 1994), pp. 14–15, 17–18, 22–23.

3. The Persian Sassanian state crumbled into a chaos of petty administrations, helpless against the Arab conquest. The Persian commander Rustam was killed at Qadisiya in Iraq. The last of the Sassanian kings, the child Zazdgard, raised a fresh army but was crushed by the Arabs on the plain of Nihawand. The Sassanian empire had been forced to yield to the fanatical onslaught of the Bedouin.

4. Cited by Daniel Pipes, 'A Border Adrift: Origin of the Iran-Iraq War', on-line 1983; Pipes thinks this interpretation to be nonsense.

5. Daniel Pipes catalogues many grievances between Iraq and Iran.

6. *Jumhouri-ye Islami*, 2 January 1980; quoted by Dilip Hiro, *The Longest War* (London: Paladin, 1990), p. 24.

7. *The Middle East*, 26 July 1982, p. 25; cited by Hiro, *ibid*, pp. 34, 274.

8. Nicola Byrne, 'My journey into macho madness', *The Observer*, London, 18 November 2001.
9. In January 2003 one American television satirist complained that Iran, witnessing significant political changes, was not playing its proper part in the 'axis of evil', but Iraq and North Korea could be relied on – more a 'duet' than an 'axis'.
10. David Hirst, 'Israel thrusts Iran in the line of US fire', *The Guardian*, London, 2 February 2002.
11. 'Comfort to the enemy', ('US hostility towards Iran boosts Saddam'), leader, *The Guardian*, London, 22 July 2002; Toby Harnden, 'Bush drops Iran reformists and backs dissidents', *The Daily Telegraph*, London, 24 July 2002.
12. Erick Rockwell 'Smuggled pictures reveal mass hangings in Iran', *The Daily Telegraph*, London, 13 October 2002; Miranda Eeles, 'Iran death sentence kindles revolt, *The Times*, London, 14 November 2002.
13. Wendell Steavenson, 'Pollsters who produced the wrong results on US stand trial in Iran', *The Daily Telegraph*, London, 5 December 2002.
14. Simon Tisdall, Michael White, Ewen MacAskill and Giles Tremlett, 'Iran to use talks with Blair to signal support', *The Guardian*, London, 29 January 2003.
15. Richard Beeston and Stephen Farrell, 'Tehran protesters stone embassy in anti-British riot', *The Times*, London, 29 March 2003.
16. 'Rocket, "probably" from Iraq war, kills Iranian – official', Tehran (AFP), The Jordan Times, 9 April 2003.

Chapter 7

1. Richard Beeston and Rana Sabbagh-Gargour, 'Middle East plans for aftermath of "inevitable" war', *The Times*, London, 11 October 2002.
2. Comparing the Mongols to the US forces may be judged an unfortunate analogy, from the Iraqi perspective. In 1258 the Mongols shattered Baghdad's defensive walls, ravaged the city, and instructed the civilian population to assemble on the plain beyond the walls where they were hacked to death. Some 800,000 men, women and children were killed over a period of days.
3. The Saudi government was reported to be canvassing a plan whereby Saddam Hussein would be granted exile (Jonathan Steele and Ewen MacAskill, 'Arab nations tell Saddam: go now and we avoid war', *The Guardian*, London, 18 January 2003.
4. 'Women not admitted: Kuwait perpetuates the indefensible' – 'Is this what we fought the [1991] war for? To watch while Sunni fundamentalists and tribal conservatives combine to thwart women's legitimate aspirations to participate fully at every level of society?', leader, *The Guardian*, London, 3 December 1999.
5. George Galloway, interviewed by Paul Moorcraft, 'The Secret Partition', *The New Statesman*, London, 5 August 2002.
6. The Sykes-Picot Agreement, approved by the British and French cabinets in February 1916, contrived the post-WWI carve-up of the Middle East between Britain and France.
7. Galloway, *op. cit.*
8. Mo Mowlam, 'The real goal is the seizure of Saudi oil', *The Guardian*, London, 5 September 2002.

9. Rana Sabbah-Gargour, 'Jordan faces unrest and hardship if war breaks out', *The Times*, London, 18 January 2003.

10. According to Globalsecurity.org, which posted satellite pictures on its website.

11. Owen Bowcott, 'Egypt pressed over "torture" of Britons', *The Guardian*, London, 21 September 2002; Sandra Laville, 'Briton "was tortured for joining Islamic group"', *The Daily Telegraph*, London, 19 October 2002; Owen Bowcott, '"The worst thing was the screaming of victims"', *The Guardian*, London, 21 October 2002; Alexis Akwagyiram, 'Egyptian judges dismisses Britons' torture claims', *The Guardian*, London, 30 October 2002.

12. Stephen Farrell and Issandr El Amrani, 'Farewell in sea of arms to father of militants', *The Times*, London, 16 November 2002.

13. Richard Beeston, '"Badly behaved Syria" is now firmly in US sights', *The Independent*, London, 12 April 2003.

14. 'What chance things will get better?', *The Independent*, London, 12 April 2003.

15. Andrew Stephen, 'And now, the next American war', *The New Statesman*, London, 14 April 2003.

Chapter 8

1. Old Testament, Numbers, Chapter 33, Verses 50–55, part of the Talmudic Pentateuch comprising Genesis, Exodus, Leviticus, Numbers and Deuteronomy.

2. Chaim Weizmann, speech to French Zionist Federation, Paris, 28 March 1914, in B Litvinoff (ed.), *The Letters and Papers of Chaim Weizmann*, Volume 1, Series B (Jerusalem: Israel Universities Press, 1983), paper 24, pp. 115–6.

3. All citations for this paragraph are given in Naseer Aruri (ed.), *Palestinian Refugees: The Right to Return* (London: Pluto, 2001), Chapter 2.

4. *Ibid.*

5. The historical dimension of this charge is amply documented but cannot be developed in the present book.

6. Uri Davis, *Israel: An Apartheid State* (London: Zed Books, 1987), Chapter 1.

7. Israel has violated, or is in violation of, about 80 UN Security Council resolutions from 1948 to the present.

8. Anton La Guardia, 'Israel divided by policy of "target killing"', *The Daily Telegraph*, London, 26 July 2002.

9. Anton La Guardia, 'Israeli court may help to created Palestinians' future leader', *The Daily Telegraph*, London, 15 August 2002; Jonathan Steele, 'Terror trial may put Israel in the dock', *The Guardian*, London, 15 August 2002.

10. Security Council resolution 242 (1967) required Israel to withdraw from the conquered territories. Resolution 338 (1973) subsequently reiterated the 242 demands, and 338 was restated many times over the years (for example in 1974, 1976, 1979, 1998, 2000, 2001 and 2002).

11. *Israel and the Occupied Territories and the Palestinian Authority, Killing the Future: Children in the Line of Fire*, Amnesty International, MDE 02/005–2002, 30 August 2002.

12. *Ibid.*

13. *Ibid.*

14. Jonathan Steele, 'Arafat helpless as Israel tears down his people's flag', *The Observer*, London, 22 September 2002; Inigo Gilmore, 'Defiant Arafat refuses to

capitulate as Israeli soldiers pin him down', *The Sunday Telegraph*, London, 22 September 2002; Ross Dunn and Richard Beeston, 'Arafat appeals for intervention by West to end siege', *The Daily Telegraph*, London, 23 September 2002.

15. Justin Huggler, 'Children of Nablus defy deadly curfew', *The Independent*, London, 5 October 2002; Chris McGreal, 'City under curfew reaches boiling point', *The Guardian*, London, 5 October 2002.

16. Conal Urquhart, 'Armed settlers force out villagers', *The Observer*, London, 27 October 2002.

17. Justin Huggler, 'In Rafah, the children have grown up so used to the sound of gunfire they cannot sleep without it', *The Independent*, London, 23 December 2002.

18. Chris McGreal, 'Israel's human shields draw fire', *The Guardian*, London, 2 January 2003.

19. The Israeli Kahan Commission (1982) found Ariel Sharon personally responsible for the Sabra and Chatila massacres. It was this case that Belgium wanted to address.

20. Chris McGreal, 'Food running out in Gaza as aid appeal fails', *The Guardian*, London, 11 February 2003.

21. *Ibid*.

22. Chris McGreal, 'Bedouin feel the squeeze as Israel resettles the Negev desert', *The Guardian*, London, 27 February 2003.

23. Roland Watson, '"Road map for peace" with Palestine at its heart', *The Independent*, London, 1 March 2003.

24. Chris McGreal, 'Sharon in Palestine state U-turn, PM drops road map to peace in favour of settlers', *The Guardian*, London, 28 February 2003.

25. Stephen Farrell, 'Sharon's policy is strangling Palestinian life, UN say', *The Times*, London, 6 March 2003.

26. Alan Philps, *The Daily Telegraph*, London, 7 March 2003.

27. Stephen Farrell, *The Times*, London, 7 March 2003.

28. *Morning Star*, London, 8 March 2003.

29. Robert Tait, *The Times*, London, 17 March 2003.

30. Chris McGreal, 'Israeli wall to encircle Palestine', *The Guardian*, London, 18 March 2003.

31. Patrick Wintour and Chris McGreal, 'Bush will stand firm on Middle East road map', *The Guardian*, London, 29 March 2003.

32. Robert Tait, 'Blair's peace efforts too extreme, says Israel', *The Independent*, London, 7 April 2003.

Chapter 9

1. Ghassan Attiyah, *Al Quds Al Arabi*, London, 14 February 1996; quoted by Said K Aburish, *A Brutal Friendship: The West and the Arab Elite* (London: Victor Gollancz, 1997), p. 46.

2. Saddam's 1990 claim represented a persistent theme in Iraqi nationalism.

3. Aburish, *op. cit.*, p. 137.

4. *Ibid*, p. 139.

5. Amir Iskander, *Saddam Hussein: The Fighter, the Thinker and the Man* (Paris: Hachette, 1980), p. 110.

6. Nicholas Kristof, *The New York Times*, 1 October 2002 ('Iraq offers an example of how an Arab country can adhere to Islam and yet provide women with opportunities').

7. This is a common political posture, not confined to rules like Saddam Hussein. In twenty years, Saddam attacked two countries (once as an American ally, once with American encouragement). The United States, over the same period, has attacked dozens.

8. Richard Armitage, *MERIP Middle East Report*, September-October 1987, p. 4.

9. Stephen C. Pelletiere, Douglas V Johnson II and Lief R Rosenberger, *Iraqi Power and US Security in the Middle East*, Strategic Studies Institute, US Army War College, Carlisle Barracks, Pennsylvania 17013–5050, 1990, p.52.

10. *Ibid.*, p.53.

11. *The New York Times*, 11 October 2002.

12. See, for example, Kenneth R Timmerman, *The Death Lobby: How the West Armed Iraq* (London: Fourth Estate, 1992).

13. 'US Chemical and Biological Warfare-Related Dual Use Exports to Iraq and their Possible Impact on the Health Consequences of the Persian Gulf War', Senate Committee on Banking, Housing and Urban Affairs with Respect to Export Administration, reports of 25 May and 7 October 1994.

14. *Ibid.*

15. *Ibid.*

16. Baghdad Radio, 18 June 1990.

17. Joint Resolution, H. R. RES. 114 (war powers), October 2002.

Chapter 10

1. Robert Fisk, 'This looming war isn't about chemical warheads or human rights: it's about oil', *The Independent*, London, 18 January 2003.

2. Quoted in *ibid*.

3. Algeria, Libya, Venezuela, Nigeria, Iraq, Kuwait, Saudi Arabia, Indonesia, Qatar/United Arab Emirates.

4. According to the terms of Security Council resolution 986 (14 April 1995).

5. The 'Greek fire' used by the Turks against Arab ships a thousand years ago probably had a petroleum base.

6. H. V. F. Winstone and Zabra Freeth, *Kuwait: Prospect and Reality* (London: George Allen and Unwin, 1972), p.125

7. *Ibid.*

8. *Ibid.*, p. 111.

9. William Stivers, *Supremacy and Oil: Iraq, Turkey and the Anglo-American World Order 1918–1930* (Ithaca NY and London: Cornell University Press, 1982), p. 111.

10. Anthony Sampson, *The Seven Sisters: The Great Oil Companies and the World they Made* (London: Hodder and Stoughton, 1975), p. 67.

11. Thomas Kiernan, *The Arabs* (London: Sphere, 1978), p. 302.

12. The situation was compounded by the sacking of senior oil executives in

Venezuela, another OPEC member, amid accusations that they had brought Venezuela's oil production to a halt.

13. Hamish McRae, 'Iraq may be doing us a favour by raising oil prices', *The Independent*, London, 10 April 2002.

14. None of such speculations even hinted at how Saddam Hussein would be able to find the resources to mount such an ambitious military campaign. This was consistent with the general propaganda about Iraq, the aim being to create an impression of a mighty demon about to ravage all and sundry.

15. Anthony Sampson, 'West's greed for oil fuels Saddam fever', *The Observer*, London, 11 August 2002.

16. Paul Moorcroft in *The New Statesman*, London, 5 August 2002.

17. Irwin Stelzer in *The Sunday Times*, London, 11 August 2002.

18. Peter Hitchins in *The Mail on Sunday*, London, 11 August 2002.

19. Dan Morgan and David B Ottaway, 'In Iraqi War Scenario, Oil is Key Issue', *The Washington Post*, 15 September 2002.

20. Carola Hoyos, 'Putin drives hard bargain with US over Iraq's oil', *The Financial Times*, London, 4 October 2002.

21. One element in the Turkish claim was that Kirkuk and Mosul are dominated not by the Kurds but by the Turkomen, an ethnic Turkish group.

22. Terry Macallister, Ewen MacAskill, Rory McCarthy and Nick Paton-Walsh, 'A matter of life, death – and oil', *The Guardian*, London, 23 January 2003.

23. Mark Almond, 'It's all about control, not the rise of petrol', *The New Statesman*, London, 7 April 2003.

Chapter 11

1. G Edward Griffin, *The Fearful Master: A Second Look at the United Nations*, (Belmont, Mass: Western Islands, 1964), p. 72.

2. The United States also used its veto extensively to protect its proxy states and to pursue its own foreign policy interests.

3. Washington had ignored the UN over many issues, not least over the 1999 bombing campaign against Yugoslavia, when no Security Council resolution was sought, the UN Charter was abused and the purely defensive treaty of the NATO states was comprehensively violated.

4. In consequence the meeting between Iraqi officials and Kofi Annan was held in Vienna instead of New York.

5. The main self-defence provision in the UN Charter is Article 51: 'Nothing in the present Charter shall impair the inherent right of individual or collective self-defense if an armed attack occurs against a Member of the United Nations, until the Security Council has taken measures necessary to maintain international peace and security.' The Bush Doctrine could exclude the Security Council from any influence over US policy – potentially allowing comprehensive violations of the UN Charter.

6. 'Bush's dangerous doctrine on Iraq', Committee of Correspondence for Democracy and Socialism', New York, 6 July 2002.

7. Headlines from London-based *The Daily Telegraph*, *The Guardian* and *The Morning Star*, respectively.

8. See discussion of Resolution 678 in Geoff Simons, *Targeting Iraq: Sanctions and Bombing in US Policy* (London: Saqi Books, 2002), Chapter 4.

9. Toby Harnden, 'Bush gives way on Iraq resolution', *The Daily Telegraph*, London, 18 October 2002; Anton La Guardia, 'US waters down Iraq demands at Security Council', *The Daily Telegraph*, London, 22 October 2002.

10. See, for example, Security Council Resolutions and presidential statements S/RES/949, S/RES/1137, S/PRST/1995/51, S/PRST/1997/49, S/PRST/1994/23 and S/PRST/1994/19. In none of these cases did the phrase 'serious consequences' serve as an authorisation of war.

11. Boutros Boutros-Ghali, former UN Secretary General, was one of the many observers, who noted the illegality of the 'no fly' zones (see Boutros-Ghali, *Unvanquished*, New york: Random House, 1999, pp. 295–6).

12. See discussion of these resolutions in Simons, *op. cit.*, Chapter 4.

13. Letter plus Annex dated 8 November 2002 from the representatives of China, France and Russian Federation to President of the Security Council, S/2002/1236, 8 November 2002.

14. The Syrian statement and the statements of all the other members who voted for SCR 1441 are contained in UN document S/PV.4644, 8 November 2002.

15. UN document, S/2002/1385, 19 December 2002.

16. The various member-state commentaries on Syria's draft resolution are given in UN document S/PV.4681, 20 December 2002.

17. 'Revealed: US dirty tricks to win vote on Iraq War: secret document details American plan to bug phones and emails of key Security Council members', *The Observer*, London, 2 March 2003.

18. *Ibid.*

19. Martin Bright and Ed Vulliamy, 'Bugging row prompts UN investigation', *The Observer*, London, 9 March 2003.

20. *Ibid.*

21. Mark Littman QC, 'A supreme international crime', *The Guardian*, London, 10 March 2003.

22. See discussion of SCR 986 in Geoff Simons, *Targeting Iraq*, *op. cit.*, pp. 112–114, 234–235.

23. Tam Dalyell, 'Blair, the war criminal', *The Guardian*, London, 27 March 2003.

24. James Bone, 'Allies face veto threat over UN sanctions', *The Independent*, London, 16 April 2003.

Chapter 12

1. Noam Chomsky, 'The weak shall inherit nothing', *The Guardian*, London, 25 March 1991.

2. Geoff Simons, 'Lockerbie: Lessons for International Law, *The Journal of Libyan Studies*, Oxford, England, Volume 1, Number 1, Summer 2000, pp. 33–47.

3. James Walsh, 'America the Brazen', *Time*, 4 August 1997, pp. 23–7.

4. Abdel Rahman Manif, 'The war against a civilisation', *The Guardian*, London, 1 April 1991.

5. Boutros Boutros-Ghali, *Unvanquished: a US-UN Saga* (London: I.B. Tauris, 1999), p. 304.

6. The protocol had been passed by the UN economic and social council

(ECOSOC) by a majority of 35 to 8, with 10 abstentions, and – against US wishes – was then set to move to the UN General Assembly.

7. *Denial of Food and Medicine: The Impact of the US Embargo on Health and Nutrition in Cuba*. A report from the American Association for World Health, serving the US Committee for the World Health Organisation (WHO), Executive Summary, March 1997, p.6.

8. Allan Philps, 'Pentagon shows its teeth', *The Daily Telegraph*, London, 16 September 2002.

9. Eric Margolis, 'After Iraq, Bush will attack his real target', *Toronto Sun*, 10 November 2002; Stephen Farrell, Robert Thomson and Danielle Haas, 'Attack Iran the day Iraq war ends, demands Israel', *The Times*, London, 5 November 2002.

10. In 1998–9 Halliburton subsidiaries submitted $23.8 million worth of contracts with Iraq for approval by the UN sanctions committee (*Financial Times*, 3 November 2000).

11. Glen Ford and Peter Gamble, 'Rule of the Pirates', *Morning Star*, London, 20 December 2002.

12. Cited in *ibid*.

13. Quoted in *ibid*.

14. *Ibid*. Simon English, 'Investigators move in on Halliburton', *The Daily Telegraph*, London, 21 December 2002.

15. Giles Whitell, 'President "was paid in £25m oil deal scandal"', *The Times*, London, 10 July 2000.

16. Headlines in London-based *The Observer*, *The Guardian*, *The Morning Star* and *The Times* respectively.

17. David Marquand, 'The playground bully', *The New Statesman*, London, 21 October 2002.

18. Michael White and Ewen MacAskill, 'Listen to the world's fears, Blair tells US', *The Guardian*, London, 8 January 2003.

19. Edward Luttwak, 'Britain's role in the coming war is diminishing by the day', *The Sunday Telegraph*, London, 12 January 2003.

20. Leslie Wayne, 'Uncle Sam calls up soldiers Inc.', *The New York Times*, 13 October 2002.

21. *Ibid*.

22. There is much commentary on how George W Bush and his supporter subverted the US constitution to facilitate a Republican victory. See, for example, Vincent Bugliosi, *The Betrayal of America: How the Supreme Court Undermined the Constitution and Chose our President* (New York: Thunders Mouth Press, 2001). ('In the 12 December 2000 ruling by the US Supreme Court handing the election to George W Bush, the court committed the unpardonable sin of being a knowing surrogate for the Republican Party instead of being impartial arbiter of the law'). See also Jake Tapper, *Down and Dirty: the Plot to Steal the Presidency* (Boston: Little, Brown & Co., 2001).

23. *The Economist*, London, 19 October 2002.

24. Ed Vullliamy, 'Poor foot the bill as New York goes bankrupt', *The Observer*, London, 1 December 2002.

25. Eve Goldberg and Linda Evans, 'The prison industrial complex and the global

economy', *Nexus*, Australia, June-July 1999, pp. 17–22; Duncan Campbell, 'Anger grows as the US jails its two millionth inmate – 25% of world's prison population', *The Guardian*, London, 15 February 2000.

26. Andrew Gumbel, 'California orders mass arrests of Muslim foreigners', *The Independent*, London, 20 December 2002; Elaine Monaghan, 'Muslims sue US over mass arrests', *The Times*, London, 26 December 2002.

27. The British policy of discouraging immigration reached the absurd pitch of Jack Straw, when home secretary, praising Saddam Hussein's judicial system. In January 2001 an Iraqi refugee seeking asylum was sent a Home Office letter: 'The Secretary of State [then Jack Straw] has at his disposal a wide range of information on Iraq which he has used to consider your claims. He is aware that Iraq, in particular the Iraqi security forces, would only convict and sentence a person in the courts with the provision of proper jurisdiction. He is satisfied, however, that if there are any charges outstanding against you and if they were to be proceeded with on your return, you could expect to receive a fair trial under an independent and properly constituted judiciary.'

28. Robert Byrd, 'I weep for my country', *The Observer*, London, 23 March 2003.

29. Michael Evens and Michelle Henery, 'Charities demand cluster bomb ban', *The Independent*, London, 1 March 2003; Severin Carrell, 'Use of CS gas in Gulf is illegal, says Red Cross', *The Independent*, London, 9 March 2003; George Monbiot, 'Chemical hypocrites' ('As it struggles to justify its invasion, the US is getting ready to use banned weapons in Iraq'), *The Guardian*, London, 9 April 2003.

30. Thomas Withington, 'How US forces patrol the world', *The Observer*, London, 6 April 2003.

31. Quoted in George Monbiot, 'A wilful blindness', *The Guardian*, London, 11 March 2003.

32. Quoted in *ibid*.

33. *Ibid*.

34. Quoted in Robert Dreyfuss, *'The American Prospect'*, Volume 14, Number 4, 1 April 2003.

Chapter 13

1. Scott Ritter, interviewed by Vincent Browne, Irish RTE1 radio, 'Tonight Show', 25 March 2003.

2. Simon Jenkins, 'Baghdad will be near impossible to conquer', *The Times*, London, 28 March 2003.

3. Daniel McGrory, 'UN and Army at odds as troops encourage looting', *The Times*, London, 5 April 2003.

4. Quote in Bob Woodward, *The Commanders* (New York: Simon and Schuster, 1991), p. 291.

5. Muayid S Damirji, editorial, *Akkad*, Department of Antiquities and Heritage, Baghdad, Number 2, December 1994.

6. *Chicago Herald Tribune*, 15 January 1993.

7. Major-General Tim Cross, interview with John Humphrys, 'Today', BBC Radio 4, 5 May 2003.
8. Jo Wilding, letter, 'I saw the injuries to Iraqi civilians', *The Guardian*, London, 8 April 2003.
9. 'Red Cross reveals "horrific" conditions in Iraqi hospitals', *The Morning Star*, London, 8 April 2003.
10. Malcolm Moore, 'Pentagon admits Halliburton could make $7 billion in Iraq', *The Daily Telegraph*, London, 12 April 2003.
11. Dominic O'Connell, 'After the war: the battle to rebuild', *The Sunday Times*, London, 13 April 2003.
12. Jonathan Steele, 'Bombs no longer falling, but still the children are suffering', *The Guardian*, London, 18 April 2003.
13. *Ibid*.
14. Philip Smucker, 'Threat of schism overshadows the pilgrimage of joy', *The Daily Telegraph*, London, 19 April 2003.
15. Julian Coman and Sean Rayment, 'America nervous as militant cleric's rallies attract mass support', *The Daily Telegraph*, London, 20 April 2003; Peter Beaumont, 'Revolution City', *The Observer*, London, 20 April 2003.
16. Robin Gedye, *The Daily Telegraph*, London, 22 April 2003. In the same issue David Rennie reported senior Bush officials urging an early US withdrawal in the face of political and financial constraints on a lengthy occupation.
17. Jonathan Steele, *The Guardian*, London, 21 April 2003.
18. Nial Ferguson, *The Daily Telegraph*, London, 23 April 2003.
19. The Iraqi Communist Party won the race to publish the first Baghdad newspaper in the post-Saddam era. On 19 April 2003 the eight-page *People's Path* was distributed free and quickly snapped up. Iraqis were amazed to see criticism of Saddam Hussein in writing. The occupation forces were already broadcasting propaganda on Alliance Television, on frequencies once used by Iraq's state television, but few in Baghdad had the electrical power to tune in. Regarding the issue of female representation se Natasha Walter 'Where are the women?', *The Guardian*, London, 25 April 2003; Lesley Abdel, 'No place for a woman', *The Times*, London, 29 April 2003.
20. Catherine Philp, 'US forces kill 14 as protesting crowd fire guns', *The Times*, London, 30 April 2003; Ian Fisher, 'US troops fire on Iraqi protestors again: 2 reported killed, *The New York Times*, 30 April 2003 ('United States soldiers opened fire here today on marchers protesting a clash late Monday night in which 15 anti-American demonstrators were reported killed by American troops').
21. Michael Howard, 'Fighting is over but the deaths go on', *The Guardian*, London, 28 April 2003.
22. Jonathan Freedland, *The Guardian*, London, 30 April 2003.
23. Ed Vulliamy, *The Observer*, London, 4 May 2003.
24. Matthew Campbell, *The Sunday Times*, London, 4 May 2003.
25. Yitzhak Nakash, *The Shi'is of Iraq* (Princeton: Princeton University Press, 1994), p. 100.
26. *Ibid*, pp. 100–105.
27. Ewen MacAskill, 'US accuses Iran of stirring up protests', *The Guardian*, London, 25 April 2003.

28. 'Shia power: religious zeal is driving Iraq's majority', editorial, *The Times*, London, 26 April 2003.

29. Oliver Burkeman, 'America signals withdrawal of troops from Saudi Arabia', *The Guardian*, London, 30 April 2003.

30. David Hurst, 'Saudis wonder, will they be next?', *The Guardian*, London, 1 May 2003.

31. 'Israel joins in with US attacks on Syria', *The Morning Star*, London, 15 April 2003.

32. Bronwen Maddox, 'Powell heads to Syria with a mixed message', *The Independent*, London, 2 May 2003; Tony Allen-Mills, 'Powell warns Syria as hawks push for attack', *The Sunday Times*, London, 4 May 2003; Elaine Monaghan and Nicholas Blanford, 'Powell tells Syria, play ball or pay the price', *The Times*, London, 5 May 2003.

33. Ed Vulliamy, 'Israel seeks pipeline for Iraqi oil', *The Observer*, London, 20 April 2003.

34. *Ibid*.

35. Kamal Ahmed and Conal Urquhart, 'UK censures Sharon over fence around West Bank', *The Observer*, London, 27 April 2003.

36. Conal Urquhart, 'Boy, 2, among 14 killed by Israeli troops', *The Guardian*, London, 2 May 2003.

37. Abigail Townsend, 'After the three decades of dominance, are Opec's sheikhs staring down a barrel?', *Independent on Sunday*, London, 13 April 2003; Mary Fagan, 'The battle begins for 112bn barrels', *The Sunday Telegraph*, London, 13 April 2003.

38. For background to Fluor Corporation see p. 19.

39. David Teacher, 'American to oversee oil industry,' *The Guardian*, London, 26 April 2003.

40. Alan Simpson, 'Bursting the bubble', *The Morning Star*, London, 12 April 2003.

41. George Monbiot, 'The bottom dollar', *The Guardian*, London, 22 April 2003.

42. *Ibid*.

43. Wesley Clark, 'Strategists win their spurs with overhaul of military', *The Times*, London, 12 April 2003.

44. Niall Ferguson, 'The empire that dare not speak its name', *The Sunday Times*, London, 13 April 2003.

45. *Ibid*.

46. Khaled Bayoumi, *Dagens Nyheter*, 16 April 2003, quote in *Morning Star*, London, 17 April 2003.

47. *Ibid*.

48. John Kampfner, 'Blair was told it would be illegal to occupy Iraq', *The New Statesman*, London, 23 May 2003.

49. *Ibid*.

50. These instruments of international law list the 'limitations placed on the authority of an Occupying Power'. These include attempts at 'wide-ranging reforms of governmental and administrative structures'; 'any alteration in the status of public officials or judges'; changes to the penal laws; and 'the imposition of major structural economic reforms'.

51. Roland Watson, 'Ally warns Bush of catastrophe, *The Times*, London, 23 May 2003.
52. Anthony Browne, 'Anguish of the pensioners of Baghdad', *The Times*, London, 19 May 2003.
53. *Ibid.*
54. Anthony Browne, 'Victims of the peace decide Americans are worse than Saddam', *The Times*, London, 23 May 2003.
55. *Ibid.*
56. *Ibid.*
57. Ian Traynor, 'How American power girds the globe with a ring of steel', *The Guardian*, London, 21 April 2003.
58. David Usborne, 'Hans Blix vs the US: "I was undermined"', *The Independent*, London, 23 April 2003.
59. Raymond Whitaker, 'Revealed: How the road to war was paved with lies', *The Independent*, London, 27 April 2003.

Select Bibliography

Aburish, Said K., *A Brutal Friendship: The West and the Arab Elite*. London: Gollancz, 1997.

Aburish, Said K., *Saddam Hussein: The Politics of Revenge*. London: Bloomsbury, 2000.

Ali, Tariq, *The Clash of the Fundamentalisms: Crusades, Jihads and Modernity*. London: Verso, 2002.

Al-Radi, Nuha, *Baghdad Diaries*. London: Saqi Books, 1998.

Arnove, Anthony (ed.), *Iraq Under Siege: The Deadly Impact of Sanctions and War*. London: Pluto Press, 2000.

Aruri, Naseer (ed.), *Palestinian Refugees: The Right of Return*. London: Pluto Press, 2001.

Bennis, Phyllis, *Calling the Shots: How Washington Dominates Today's UN*. New York: Olive Branch Press, Interlink Publishing, 1996.

Bhatia, Shyam and McGrory, Daniel, *Saddam's Bomb*. London: Little Brown and Company, 1999.

Butler, Richard, *Saddam Defiant: The Threat of Weapons of Mass Destruction and the Crisis of Global Security*. London: Weidenfeld and Nicholson, 2000.

CARDRI. (Committee Against Repression and for Democratic Rights in Iraq), *Saddam's Iraq: Revolution or Reaction?*. London: Zed Books, 1989.

Carey, Roane (ed.), *The New Intifada: Resisting Israel's Apartheid*. London: Verso, 2001.

Cockburn, Andrew and Cockburn, Leslie, *Dangerous Liaison: The Inside Story of the US-Israeli Covert Relationship*. London: The Bodley Head, 1992.

Cockburn, Andrew and Cockburn, Patrick, *Out of the Ashes: The Resurrection of Saddam Hussein*. New York: Verso, 2000.

Couchlin, Con, *Saddam: The Secret Life*. London: Macmillan, 2002.

Graham-Brown, Sarah, *Sanctioning Saddam: The Politics of Intervention in Iraq*. London: I.B. Tauris, 1999.

Halliday, Fred, *Two Hours that Shook the World – September 11, 2001: Causes and Consequences*. London: Saqi Books, 2002.

Hazleton, Fan (ed.), CARDRI, *Iraq since the Gulf War: Prospects for Democracy*. London: Zed Books, 1994.

Heikal, Mohamed, *Illusions of Triumph: An Arab View of the Gulf War*. London: Harper Collins, 1992.

Hiro, Dilip, *War Without End: Rise of Islamic Terrorism and Global Response*. London: Routledge, 2002.

Human Rights Watch, *Iraq's Crime of Genocide: The Anfal Campaign Against the Kurds*. New Haven and London: Yale University Press, 1995.

Israel in Lebanon. The report of the International Commission to inquire into reported violations of international law by Israel during its invasion of the Lebanon. London: Ithaca Press, 1983.

Leonard, Mark (ed), *Re-ordering the World: The Long-term Implications of 11 September*. London: The Foreign Policy Centre, 2002.

Rai, Milan, *War Plan Iraq: Ten Reasons Against War on Iraq*. London: Verso, 2002.

Ritter, Scott, *Endgame: Solving the Iraq Problem – Once and for All*. New York: Simon and Schuster, 1999.

Ritter, Scott and Rivers Pitt, William, *War on Iraq*. London: Profile Books, 2002.

Salinger, Pierre and Laurent, Eric, *Secret Dossier: The Hidden Agenda Behind the Gulf War*. London: Penguin Books, 1991.

Simons, Geoff, *Targeting Iraq: Sanctions and Bombing in US Policy*. London: Saqi Books, 2002.

Simons, Geoff, *The Scourging of Iraq: Sanctions, Law and Natural Justice*, 2nd edn. London: Macmillan, 1998.

Simons, Geoff, *Iraq – Primus Inter Pariahs: A Crisis Chronology, 1997–98*. London: Macmillan, 1999.

Timmerman, Kenneth R., *The Death Lobby: How the West Armed Iraq*. London: Fourth Estate, 1992.

Trevan, Tim, *Saddam's Secrets: The Hunt for Iraq's Hidden Weapons*. London: Harper Collins, 1999.

Wasserstein, Bernard, *Israel and Palestine: Why They Fight and Can They Stop?* London: Profile Books, 2003.

Woodward, Bob, *The Commanders*. New York: Simon and Schuster, 1991.

Index